# Smarter Decisions – The Intersection of Internet of Things and Decision Science

Enter the world of Internet of Things with the power of data science with this highly practical, engaging book

Jojo Moolayil

BIRMINGHAM - MUMBAI

# Smarter Decisions – The Intersection of Internet of Things and Decision Science

First published: July 2016

Production reference: 1220716

Published by Packt Publishing Ltd.
Livery Place
35 Livery Street
Birmingham
B3 2PB, UK.
ISBN 978-1-78588-419-1

www.packtpub.com

# Credits

**Author**

Jojo Moolayil

**Reviewer**

Anindita Basak

**Commissioning Editor**

Veena Pagare

**Acquisition Editor**

Sonali Vernekar

**Content Development Editor**

Sumeet Sawant

**Technical Editor**

Danish Shaikh

**Copy Editor**

Tasneem Fatehi

**Project Coordinator**

Shweta H Birwatkar

**Proofreader**

Safis Editing

**Indexer**

Mariammal Chettiyar

**Graphics**

Disha Haria

**Production Coordinator**

Nilesh Mohite

# About the Author

**Jojo Moolayil** is a data scientist, living in Bengaluru—the silicon valley of India. With over 4 years of industrial experience in Decision Science and IoT, he has worked with industry leaders on high impact and critical projects across multiple verticals. He is currently associated with GE, the pioneer and leader in data science for Industrial IoT.

Jojo was born and raised in Pune, India and graduated from University of Pune with a major in information technology engineering. With a vision to solve problems at scale, Jojo found solace in decision science and learnt to solve a variety of problems across multiple industry verticals early in his career. He started his career with Mu Sigma Inc., the world's largest pure play analytics provider where he worked with the leaders of many fortune 50 clients. With the passion to solve increasingly complex problems, Jojo touch based with Internet of Things and found deep interest in the very promising area of consumer and industrial IoT. One of the early enthusiasts to venture into IoT analytics, Jojo converged his learnings from decision science to bring the problem solving frameworks and his learnings from data and decision science to IoT.

To cement his foundations in industrial IoT and scale the impact of the problem solving experiments, he joined a fast growing IoT Analytics startup called Flutura based in Bangalore and headquartered in the valley. Flutura focuses exclusively on Industrial IoT and specializes in analytics for M2M data. It is with Flutura, where Jojo reinforced his problem solving skills for M2M and Industrial IoT while working for the world's leading manufacturing giant and lighting solutions providers. His quest for solving problems at scale brought the 'product' dimension in him naturally and soon he also ventured into developing data science products and platforms.

After a short stint with Flutura, Jojo moved on to work with the leaders of Industrial IoT, that is, G.E. in Bangalore, where he focused on solving decision science problems for Industrial IoT use cases. As a part of his role in GE, Jojo also focuses on developing data science and decision science products and platforms for Industrial IoT.

*I would like to sincerely thank my employers Mu Sigma, Flutura and GE for all the opportunities and learnings I got to explore in decision science and IoT. I would also like give deep thanks and gratitude to my mentors Mr. Samir Madhavan and Mr. Derick Jose, without their efforts this book quite possibly would not have happened.*

# About the Reviewer

**Anindita Basak** works as Azure and big data consultant for one of the global software giant and helps partners/customers to enablement of Azure SaaS solution architecture development, data platform & analytics guidance implementation. She is an active blogger, Microsoft Azure forum contributor and consultant as well as speaker. In her 8+ years of experience lifecycle majorly worked in Microsoft .Net, Azure, Big Data and Analytics. Earlier in her career, she worked with Microsoft as FTE as well as v-employee for various internal Azure teams. She recently worked as technical reviewer for the following books from Packt Publishing: HDInsight Essentials First Edition, HDInsight Essentials Second Edition, Hadoop Essentials, and Microsoft Tabular Modeling Cookbook.

*I would like to thank my mom and dad—Anjana and Ajit Basak—and my loving brother Aditya. Without your help and encouragement I can't reach the goal of my life.*

# eBooks, discount offers, and more

Did you know that Packt offers eBook versions of every book published, with PDF and ePub files available? You can upgrade to the eBook version at www.PacktPub.com and as a print book customer, you are entitled to a discount on the eBook copy. Get in touch with us at customercare@packtpub.com for more details.

At www.PacktPub.com, you can also read a collection of free technical articles, sign up for a range of free newsletters and receive exclusive discounts and offers on Packt books and eBooks.

https://www2.packtpub.com/books/subscription/packtlib

Do you need instant solutions to your IT questions? PacktLib is Packt's online digital book library. Here, you can search, access, and read Packt's entire library of books.

# Why subscribe?

- Fully searchable across every book published by Packt
- Copy and paste, print, and bookmark content
- On demand and accessible via a web browser

# Table of Contents

# Chapter 3: The What and Why - Using Exploratory Decision Science for IoT

# Preface

The Internet of Things and decision science are among the most trending topics in the industry right now. The problems we solve today have become increasingly ambiguous, uncertain and volatile, and therefore the means to solve them. Moreover, problem solving has evolved from solving one specific problem using data science to the art of problem solving using decision science. The Internet of Things provides a massive opportunity for business to make human life easier which can only be leveraged using decision science. Smarter Decisions – The Intersection of Internet of Things and Decision Science, will help you learn the nuances of IoT and Decision and practically aid you in smarter decision making by solving real-life Industrial & Consumer IoT use cases. The book gives paramount focus on solving a fundamental problem. Therefore, the entire journey of addressing the problem by defining, designing and executing it using industry standard frameworks for decision science is articulated through engaging and easy-to-understand business use cases. While solving the business use cases, we will touch base with the entire data science stack that is descriptive + inquisitive + predictive + prescriptive analytics by leveraging the most popular and open source software 'R'. By the end of this book, you'll have complete understanding of the complex aspects of decision making in IoT and will be able to take that knowledge with you onto whatever project calls for it.

## What this book covers

Chapter 1, *IoT and Decision Science*, briefly introduces the two most important topics for the book in the most lucid way using intuitive real-life examples. The chapter briefs about IoT, its evolution and the key differences between IoT, IIoT, Industrial Internet, Internet of Everything. Decision science is narrated by providing paramount focus on the problem and its evolution in the universe. Finally we explore the problem solving framework to study the decision science approach for problem solving.

Chapter 2, *Studying the IoT Problem Universe and Designing a Use Case*, introduces a real life IoT business problem and aids the reader to practically design the solution for the problem by using a structured and mature problem solving framework learnt in the preceding chapter. The chapter also introduces the two main domains in IoT that is connected assets and connected operations and various artefacts and thought leadership frameworks that will be leveraged to define and design a solution for the business problem.

Chapter 3, *The What and the Why – Using Exploratory Decision Science for IoT*, focuses on practically solving the IoT business use case designed in the preceding chapter using the R software for exploratory data analysis. Leveraging an anonymized and masked dataset for the business use case along with the hands on exercises aids the reader to practically traverse through the descriptive and inquisitive phases of decision science. The problem's solution is addressed by answering the two fundamental questions What and Why by performing univariate, bivariate analyses along with various statistical tests to validate the results and thereby render the story.

Chapter 4, *Experimenting Predictive Analytics for IoT*, enhances the solution of the business use case by leveraging predictive analytics. In this chapter, we answer the question "when" to solve the problem with more clarity. Various statistical models like linear regression, logistic regression and decision trees are explored to solve the different predictive problems that were surfaced during the inquisitive phase of the business use case in the preceding chapter. Intuitive examples to understand the mathematical functioning of the algorithms and easy means to interpret the results are articulated to cement the foundations of predictive analytics for IoT.

Chapter 5, *Enhancing Predictive Analytics with Machine Learning for IoT*, takes an attempt to improve the results of predictive modelling exercises in the preceding chapter by leveraging cutting edge machine learning algorithms like Random Forest, XgBoost and deep learning algorithms like multilayer perceptrons. With improved results from improved algorithms, the solution for the use case is finally completed by leveraging the 3 different layers of decision science: descriptive + inquisitive + predictive analytics.

Chapter 6, *Fast track Decision Science with IoT*, reinforces the problem solving skills learnt so far by attempting to solve another fresh IoT use case from start to end within the same chapter. The entire journey of defining, designing and solving the IoT problem is articulated in a fast track mode.

Chapter 7, *Prescriptive Science and Decision Making*, introduces the last layer of the decision science stack i.e. prescriptive analytics by leveraging a hypothetical use case. The entire journey of evolution of a problem from descriptive to inquisitive to predictive and finally to prescriptive and back is illustrated with simple and easy to learn examples. After traversing the problem through prescriptive analytics, the art of decision making and storyboarding to convey the results in the most lucid format is explored in detail.

Chapter 8, *Disruptions in IoT*, explores the current disruptions in IoT by studying a few like fog computing, cognitive computing, Next generation robotics and genomics and autonomous cars. Finally the privacy and security aspects in IoT is also explored in brief.

Chapter 9, *A Promising Future with IoT*, discusses about how the near future will radically change human life with the unprecedented growth of IoT. The chapter explores the visionary topics of the new IoT business models such as, AssetDevice as a service and the evolution of connected cars to smart cars & connected humans to smart humans.

# What you need for this book

In order to make your learning efficient, you need to have a computer with either Windows, Mac, or Ubuntu.

You need to download and install R to execute the codes mentioned in this book. You can download and install R using the CRAN website available at `http://cran.r-project.org/`. All the codes are written using RStudio. RStudio is an integrated development environment for R and can be downloaded from `http://www.rstudio.com/products/rstudio/`.

The different R packages used in the book are freely available to download and install for all operating systems mentioned above.

# Who this book is for

*Smarter Decisions – The intersection of Internet of Things and Decision Science* is intended for data science and IoT enthusiasts or project managers anchoring IoT Analytics projects. Basic knowledge of R in terms of its libraries is an added advantage, however the verbiage for interpretation of the results will be independent of the codes. Any non-technical data science and IoT enthusiast can skip the codes and read through the output and still be able to consume the results.

# Sections

In this book, you will find several headings that appear frequently (Getting ready, How to do it, How it works, There's more, and See also).

To give clear instructions on how to complete a recipe, we use these sections as follows:

# Getting ready

This section tells you what to expect in the recipe, and describes how to set up any software or any preliminary settings required for the recipe.

# How to do it...

This section contains the steps required to follow the recipe.

# How it works...

This section usually consists of a detailed explanation of what happened in the previous section.

# There's more...

This section consists of additional information about the recipe in order to make the reader more knowledgeable about the recipe.

# See also

This section provides helpful links to other useful information for the recipe.

# Conventions

In this book, you will find a number of text styles that distinguish between different kinds of information. Here are some examples of these styles and an explanation of their meaning.

Code words in text, database table names, folder names, filenames, file extensions, pathnames, dummy URLs, user input, and Twitter handles are shown as follows: "We can include other contexts through the use of the include directive."

A block of code is set as follows:

```
<Contextpath="/jira"docBase="${catalina.home}
/atlassian- jira" reloadable="false" useHttpOnly="true">
```

Any command-line input or output is written as follows:

```
mysql -u root -p
```

New terms and important words are shown in bold. Words that you see on the screen, for example, in menus or dialog boxes, appear in the text like this: "Select **System info** from the **Administration** panel."

 Warnings or important notes appear in a box like this.

 Tips and tricks appear like this.

# Reader feedback

Feedback from our readers is always welcome. Let us know what you think about this book-what you liked or disliked. Reader feedback is important for us as it helps us develop titles that you will really get the most out of.

To send us general feedback, simply e-mail feedback@packtpub.com, and mention the book's title in the subject of your message.

If there is a topic that you have expertise in and you are interested in either writing or contributing to a book, see our author guide at www.packtpub.com/authors .

# Customer support

Now that you are the proud owner of a Packt book, we have a number of things to help you to get the most from your purchase.

## Downloading the example code

You can download the example code files for this book from your account at http://www.packtpub.com. If you purchased this book elsewhere, you can visit http://www.packtpub.com/support and register to have the files e-mailed directly to you.

You can download the code files by following these steps:

1. Log in or register to our website using your e-mail address and password.
2. Hover the mouse pointer on the **SUPPORT** tab at the top.

3. Click on **Code Downloads & Errata**.
4. Enter the name of the book in the **Search** box.
5. Select the book for which you're looking to download the code files.
6. Choose from the drop-down menu where you purchased this book from.
7. Click on **Code Download**.

You can also download the code files by clicking on the **Code Files** button on the book's webpage at the Packt Publishing website. This page can be accessed by entering the book's name in the **Search** box. Please note that you need to be logged in to your Packt account.

Once the file is downloaded, please make sure that you unzip or extract the folder using the latest version of:

- WinRAR / 7-Zip for Windows
- Zipeg / iZip / UnRarX for Mac
- 7-Zip / PeaZip for Linux

The code bundle for the book is also hosted on GitHub at `https://github.com/PacktPublishing/repository-name`. We also have other code bundles from our rich catalog of books and videos available at `https://github.com/PacktPublishing/`. Check them out!

# Errata

Although we have taken every care to ensure the accuracy of our content, mistakes do happen. If you find a mistake in one of our books-maybe a mistake in the text or the code-we would be grateful if you could report this to us. By doing so, you can save other readers from frustration and help us improve subsequent versions of this book. If you find any errata, please report them by visiting `http://www.packtpub.com/submit-errata`, selecting your book, clicking on the **Errata Submission Form** link, and entering the details of your errata. Once your errata are verified, your submission will be accepted and the errata will be uploaded to our website or added to any list of existing errata under the Errata section of that title.

To view the previously submitted errata, go to `https://www.packtpub.com/books/content/support` and enter the name of the book in the search field. The required information will appear under the **Errata** section.

# Piracy

Piracy of copyrighted material on the Internet is an ongoing problem across all media. At Packt, we take the protection of our copyright and licenses very seriously. If you come across any illegal copies of our works in any form on the Internet, please provide us with the location address or website name immediately so that we can pursue a remedy.

Please contact us at `copyright@packtpub.com` with a link to the suspected pirated material.

We appreciate your help in protecting our authors and our ability to bring you valuable content.

# Questions

If you have a problem with any aspect of this book, you can contact us at `questions@packtpub.com`, and we will do our best to address the problem.

# 1
# IoT and Decision Science

The **Internet of Things** (**IoT**) and Decision Science have been among the hottest topics in the industry for a while now. You would have heard about IoT and wanted to learn more about it, but unfortunately you would have come across multiple names and definitions over the Internet with hazy differences between them. Also, Decision Science has grown from a nascent domain to become one of the fastest and most widespread horizontal in the industry in the recent years. With the ever-increasing volume, variety, and veracity of data, decision science has become more and more valuable for the industry. Using data to uncover latent patterns and insights to solve business problems has made it easier for businesses to take actions with better impact and accuracy.

Data is the new oil for the industry, and with the boom of IoT, we are in a world where more and more devices are getting connected to the Internet with sensors capturing more and more vital granular dimensions that had never been touched earlier. The IoT is a game changer with a plethora of devices connected to each other; the industry is eagerly attempting to untap the huge potential that it can deliver. The true value and impact of IoT is delivered with the help of Decision Science. IoT has inherently generated an ocean of data where you can swim to gather insights and take smarter decisions with the intersection of Decision Science and IoT. In this book, you will learn about IoT and Decision Science in detail by solving real-life IoT business problems using a structured approach.

In this chapter, we will begin by understanding the fundamental basics of IoT and Decision Science problem solving. You will learn the following concepts:

- Understanding IoT and demystifying **Machine to Machine (M2M)**, IoT, **Internet of Everything (IoE)**, and **Industrial IoT (IIoT)**
- Digging deeper into the logical stack of IoT
- Studying the problem life cycle
- Exploring the problem landscape
- The art of problem solving
- The problem solving framework

It is highly recommended that you explore this chapter in depth. It focuses on the basics and concepts required to build problems and use cases. As hands-on exercises are not added, I am sure most software engineers would be tempted to skip this and move to the later chapters. The later chapters will frequently refer to concepts and points elucidated here for more realistic context. Hence, it's very important to go through this chapter in detail before moving on.

# Understanding the IoT

To get started with the IoT, lets first try to understand it using the easiest constructs. Internet and Things; we have two simple words here that help us understand the entire concept. So what is the Internet? It is basically a network of computing devices. Similarly, what is a Thing? It could be any real-life entity featuring Internet connectivity. So now, what do we decipher from IoT? It is a network of connected Things that can transmit and receive data from other things once connected to the network. This is how we describe the Internet of Things in a nutshell.

Now, let's take a glance at the definition. IoT can be defined as the ever-growing network of Things (entities) that feature Internet connectivity and the communication that occurs between them and other Internet-enabled devices and systems. The Things in IoT are enabled with sensors that capture vital information from the device during its operations, and the device features Internet connectivity that helps it transfer and communicate to other devices and the network. Today, when we discuss about IoT, there are so many other similar terms that come into the picture, such as Industrial Internet, M2M, IoE, and a few more, and we find it difficult to understand the differences between them. Before we begin delineating the differences between these hazy terms and understand how IoT evolved in the industry, lets first take a simple real-life scenario to understand how exactly IoT looks like.

# IoT in a real-life scenario

Let's take a simple example to understand how IoT works. Consider a scenario where you are a father in a family with a working mother and 10-year old son studying in school. You and your wife work in different offices. Your house is equipped with quite a few smart devices, say, a smart microwave, smart refrigerator, and smart TV. You are currently in office and you get notified on your smartphone that your son, Josh, has reached home from school. (He used his personal smart key to open the door.) You then use your smartphone to turn on the microwave at home to heat the sandwiches kept in it. Your son gets notified on the smart home controller that you have hot sandwiches ready for him. He quickly finishes them and starts preparing for a math test at school and you resume your work. After a while, you get notified again that your wife has also reached home (She also uses a similar smart key.) and you suddenly realize that you need to reach home to help your son with his math test. You again use your smartphone and change the air conditioner settings for three people and set the refrigerator to defrost using the app. In another 15 minutes, you are home and the air conditioning temperature is well set for three people. You then grab a can of juice from the refrigerator and discuss some math problems with your son on the couch. Intuitive, isnt it?

How did it his happen and how did you access and control everything right from your phone? Well, this is how IoT works! Devices can talk to each other and also take actions based on the signals received:

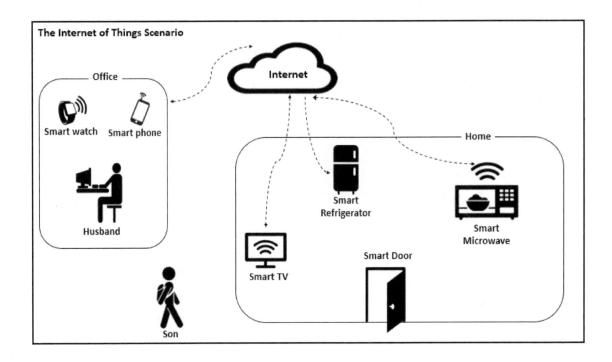

The IoT scenario

Lets take a closer look at the same scenario. You are sitting in office and you could access the air conditioner, microwave, refrigerator, and home controller through your smartphone. Yes, the devices feature Internet connectivity and once connected to the network, they can send and receive data from other devices and take actions based on signals. A simple protocol helps these devices understand and send data and signals to a plethora of heterogeneous devices connected to the network. We will get into the details of the protocol and how these devices talk to each other soon. However, before that, we will get into some details of how this technology started and why we have so many different names today for IoT.

# Demystifying M2M, IoT, IIoT, and IoE

So now that we have a general understanding about what is IoT, lets try to understand how it all started. A few questions that we will try to understand are: Is IoT very new in the market?, When did this start?, How did this start?, Whats the difference between M2M, IoT, IoE, and all those different names?, and so on. If we try to understand the fundamentals of IoT, that is, machines or devices connected to each other in a network, which isn't something really new and radically challenging, then what is this buzz all about?

The buzz about machines talking to each other started long before most of us thought of it, and back then it was called Machine to Machine Data. In early 1950, a lot of machinery deployed for aerospace and military operations required automated communication and remote access for service and maintenance. Telemetry was where it all started. It is a process in which a highly automated communication was established from which data is collected by making measurements at remote or inaccessible geographical areas and then sent to a receiver through a cellular or wired network where it was monitored for further actions. To understand this better, lets take an example of a manned space shuttle sent for space exploration. A huge number of sensors are installed in such a space shuttle to monitor the physical condition of astronauts, the environment, and also the condition of the space shuttle. The data collected through these sensors is then sent back to the substation located on Earth, where a team would use this data to analyze and take further actions. During the same time, industrial revolution peaked and a huge number of machines were deployed in various industries. Some of these industries where failures could be catastrophic also saw the rise in machine-to-machine communication and remote monitoring:

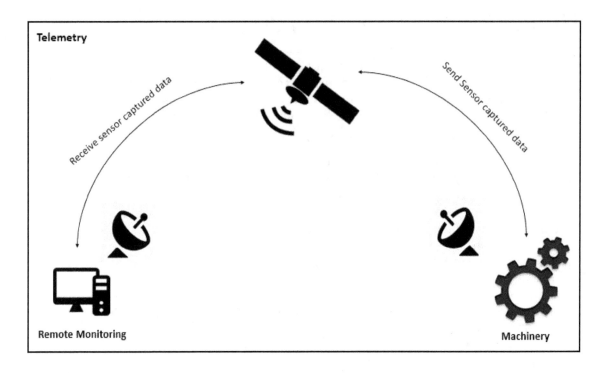

Telemetry

Thus, machine-to-machine data a.k.a. M2M was born and mainly through telemetry. Unfortunately, it didnt scale to the extent that it was supposed to and this was largely because of the time it was developed in. Back then, cellular connectivity was not widespread and affordable, and installing sensors and developing the infrastructure to gather data from them was a very expensive deal. Therefore, only a small chunk of business and military use cases leveraged this.

As time passed, a lot of changes happened. The Internet was born and flourished exponentially. The number of devices that got connected to the Internet was colossal. Computing power, storage capacities, and communication and technology infrastructure scaled massively. Additionally, the need to connect devices to other devices evolved, and the cost of setting up infrastructure for this became very affordable and agile. Thus came the IoT. The major difference between M2M and IoT initially was that the latter used the Internet (IPV4/6) as the medium whereas the former used cellular or wired connection for communication. However, this was mainly because of the time they evolved in. Today, heavy engineering industries have machinery deployed that communicate over the IPV4/6 network and is called Industrial IoT or sometimes M2M. The difference between the two is bare minimum and there are enough cases where both are used interchangeably. Therefore, even though M2M was actually the ancestor of IoT, today both are pretty much the same. M2M or IIoT are nowadays aggressively used to market IoT disruptions in the industrial sector.

IoE or Internet of Everything was a term that surfaced on the media and Internet very recently. The term was coined by Cisco with a very intuitive definition. It emphasizes Humans as one dimension in the ecosystem. It is a more organized way of defining IoT. The IoE has logically broken down the IoT ecosystem into smaller components and simplified the ecosystem in an innovative way that was very much essential. IoE divides its ecosystem into four logical units as follows:

- People
- Processes
- Data
- Things

Built on the foundation of IoT, IoE is defined as *The networked connection of People, Data, Processes, and Things*. Overall, all these different terms in the IoT fraternity have more similarities than differences and, at the core, they are the same, that is, devices connecting to each other over a network. The names are then stylized to give a more intrinsic connotation of the business they refer to, such as Industrial IoT and Machine to Machine for (B2B) heavy engineering, manufacturing and energy verticals, Consumer IoT for the B2C industries, and so on.

# Digging deeper into the logical stack of IoT

Now that we have a clear understanding of what is IoT and the similar terms around it, lets understand the ecosystem better. For convenience, IoE will be referred as IoT while exploring the four logical components of the stack in brief.

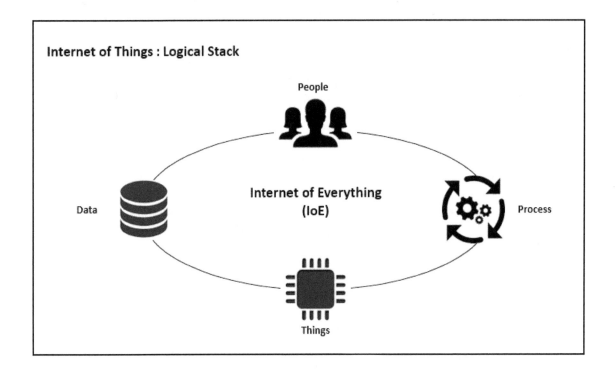

IoTs logical stack

When we deconstruct the IoT ecosystem into logical units, we have People, Processes, Data, and Things. Lets explore each of these components in brief.

# People

People or we interact with devices and other people on a daily basis. The communication could be either People to People, People to Device, or Device to People. Considering People as a separate dimension in the IoT ecosystem is an essential move as the complexity in understanding this is really challenging. When any form of communication occurs where People play a role on either end of the interaction, it embeds a unique pattern that is intrinsic to the People dimension. Lets understand this better with an example. Most of us use social networking sites such as Facebook, Twitter, LinkedIn, and so on, where we are connected to multiple people/friends. Here, the communication paths are mainly People to People. Considering the previous example, we had people to device and device to people communication paths (communication between the smartphone and microwave). Considering People as a dimension, everyone would differ in the way they interact with the system. I might find the new interface of Facebook very difficult to use but a friend may find it extremely easy. The real problem here is everyone is skilled, but the skillsets differ from person to person. The characteristics of the interaction identified by a person may be a representative for a very small community.

We have a population of six billion plus, and over 1/6th of them have already been connected. With such a huge population consisting of a plethora of communities representing people of different geographical areas, culture, thinking, and behavior, defining one generic set of rules or characteristics to define people interaction is very challenging. Instead, if we understand the People dimension in a more constructive way, we can tap the opportunity to capture the behavior more accurately and help them benefit from the ecosystem in the best way.

With the advent of IoT, we have sensors capturing information and characteristics at more granular levels than ever before. Here, if we can accurately define People as a complete dimension, personalized experience will be a complete game changer. The smart watch industry is investing humongous efforts to get its offering more personalized; if it succeeds, it will be a pivotal player in the coming revolution.

# Processes

The most lucid definition for Processes would be *everything required to deliver the right information to the right person/system at the right time*. A wide variety of things fall in the Processes dimension that includes technology, protocols, business logic, communication infrastructure, and so on. Broadly, they can be classified into two components-*Technology* and *Business Processes*. Lets explore these two components in brief in order to understand the Processes dimension in more detail.

# Technology

The technology required in the **Processes** dimension of IoT comprises of the *software, protocol, and infrastructure*. We will explore Technology by understanding its three broad divisions for **Processes**.

## Software

Software consists mainly of the **operating system**. Devices in IoT require a special kind of an operating device. Smart devices such as the smart refrigerator, smart microwave, and many others require an operating system running on them that can then enable it to be an active component in the network. Tasks executed can vary from sending, processing, and receiving data or executing instructions and sending signals to respective controllers within the device for action. Now, the question is, why do these devices require a special operating system? Why cant the existing rich flavors of Unix/Linux, Windows, Mac, or even Android be used? The answer is the same as the reason that we used Android for smartphones and not the existing OS back then. The devices that connect to the network in IoT are small or sometimes tiny. Ideally, these devices would be equipped with less powerful computing capabilities, lower memory, and lower battery life. It is almost impossible to run a fully-fledged operating system on them. We need a specially designed OS that can take care of the limited memory, processing power and battery life of the device and yet provide maximum functionality to tag the device as a smart device. Google recently launched an operating system for IoT devices called **Brillo**. Brillo is an Android-based embedded operating system specifically designed for low power and memory-constrained IoT devices. It provides the core platform services required for IoT devices along with a developer kit freely available for developers/hardware vendors to get the OS running and build additional services on their devices. Some similar examples would be Apple's Watch OS for Apple Watch, Android Wear from Google for smartwatches, and others. Soon, we can expect a vast community of devices running Brillo and a plethora of apps that can be installed additionally for even better functionality (*something very similar to the Google Play store*).

## Protocol

Once the devices are software-enabled, we need to get a protocol in place that can help them communicate with other heterogeneous devices in the network. To understand this better, recollect the first example where we could defrost the refrigerator using our smartphone. The smartphone needs to talk to the refrigerator that also needs to understand what exactly is being communicated. With a huge variety of heterogonous devices, this communication path just gets more and more complicated. Hence, we need to have a simplified protocol in place where complicated process can be abstracted and the devices can communicate with each other effectively. Google recently launched an open source protocol called **Weave**. Weave is basically an IoT protocol that is a communications platform for IoT devices that enables device setup, phone-to-device-to-cloud communication, and user interaction from mobile devices and the web. It has ushered productivity in the developers efforts by easing up device interoperability regardless of the brand or manufacturer.

## Infrastructure

Infrastructure can simply be defined as the integration of the operating system, communication protocol, and all other necessary components to harmonize the environment for an IoT use case. All major cloud infrastructure providers are now focusing on providing an IoT-specialized environment. Google launched **IoT Cloud Solutions**, Amazon launched **AWS IoT**, Microsoft launched **Azure IoT Suite**, and so on. All of these solutions integrate the disparate systems together to make the ecosystem scalable and agile. Digging deeper into these suites will be beyond the scope of this book.

# Business processes

The second part of the **Processes** dimension is Business Processes. It basically covers the set of rules and processes to govern the communication and operation of the devices connected in the IoT ecosystem. There isn't a concrete definition till now that can be used here and the discussion of the topic will be beyond the scope of this book. However, we will take a look at this closely while solving an IoT use case in Chapter 3, *The What And Why – Using Exploratory Decision Science for IoT* and Chapter 4, *Experimenting Predictive Analytics for IoT*.

# Things

Things form the crux of the IoT ecosystem. They include any form of sensors, actuators, or other type of devices that can be integrated into machines and devices to help them connect to the Internet and communicate with other devices and machines. These things will be always active during their lifetime and will sense events, capture important information, and communicate them with other devices.

A typical example would be the refrigerator, TV, or microwave that we considered in the previous use case. The sensors installed in these devices capture data and send information/signals to other devices that can then be used to take action.

# Data

Data is by all means the most value-adding dimension in the IoT ecosystem. Today, the devices that are connected to the Internet are capturing tons and tons of data that can represent the most granular-level details for the devices they are connected to. The magnitude of this data is colossal. Storing and processing such vast and varied amounts of data questions the fact whether the data is really valuable. In a true sense, most of the data is transient in nature and loses its value within minutes of generation. With ever-improving technology and computing capabilities, the amount of data processing and storage that the devices are capable of today is great, but we can leverage this power to deliver better value than just delivering raw data. Tons of algorithms can be executed and business rules can be applied where a lot of value can be extracted from the data before sending it over to the server. This requires the combination of multiple disciplines together to solve the problem and deliver value.

To understand this better, consider the example of a pedometer installed in our smart watch. Rather than just reporting the number of steps that we have walked, it can calculate the amount of calories we have burned, average time taken for the activity, metrics like deviation from the previous days activity, deviation from milestones, and other social information such as how do we compare with our friends, and so on. To capture and process all of this information locally and send the final results to the server that can be directly stored for future actions requires the combination of multiple disciplines to make the task efficient. Math, business, technology, design thinking, behavioral science, and a few others would need to be used together to solve the problem. In reality, it would be futile to send across all the raw data captured from devices to the servers assuming that it can be leveraged for future use. A variety of new algorithms have been designed to ingest this data locally and deliver only rich, condensed, and actionable insights in real time. We will explore this in more detail with fog computing in `Chapter 8`, *Disruptions in IoT*. Smart watches such as the Microsoft Band and self-driving cars such as Tesla Model S are the best examples to understand the true scenarios where we can study the challenges of processing data in real time for insights and actions. In all true sense, data is what essentially helps in delivering the last mile value in the IoT fraternity. Hence, we need talent to deal with the data as a separate dimension in the IoT stack.

# The problem life cycle

You learned about IoT and explored its logical stack to understand more about People, Processes, Data, and Things. The core agenda of this book is to solve IoT business problems using Decision Science. Problem solving has been an art and has its origin ever since mankind evolved. I would like to introduce **The Problem Life Cycle** to learn how the problem keeps evolving. Understanding this topic is very essential to solve better problems in IoT.

Every industry has been trying to solve a problem. E-retail solved the problem of inconvenience in physical shopping for busy and working consumers, the printing press solved the problem of mass producing documents for the consumers, and so on. A few visionaries such as Apple Inc. have tried to solve a problem by first creating it. The iPod and iPad were devices that were a part of this revolution. The biggest challenge in solving a problem is that the problem **evolves**. If we take a deeper look at the problem life cycle, we can understand that the problem evolves from a **Muddy** to **Fuzzy** and finally to a **Clear** state and keeps repeating the cycle:

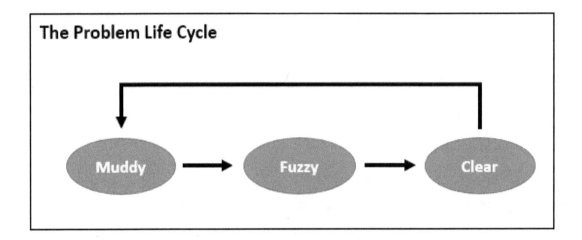

The problem life cycle

Lets take a simple example to understand this better. Consider the **Marketing** problem. Every organization wants to promote their products and services better by marketing them. Marketing has been a problem since ages. Lets assume that the inception of marketing happened with the invention of the printing press. Initially, the problem for marketing would be in the *muddy* phase, where a team of analysts would try to get the best strategy to market a product or service in place. Back then, newspapers and print media were the only medium, and the strategies and nature of the problem was very much limited to them. When the problem is new, it is in the **muddy** stage; we have **no clear idea about how to solve it**. We would try to understand the problem by experimenting and researching. Gradually, we gain some knowledge about the system and problem and then define a couple of best strategies and guidelines to solve the problem. This is when the problem evolves to the **fuzzy** stage. Here, the solution for the problem is still not clear, but we **have a fair understanding of how to go about it**. Finally, after a lot of research and experiments from a large pool of people sharing their results and understandings, we might finally have a concrete methodology in place that can be used as a complete guide to solve the problem. This is when the problem reaches the **clear** stage. It is the pinnacle of the problem solving methodology where we have a **clear understanding about how to tackle the problem** and solve it. However, one fine day, a big disruption happens and the problem that was finally in the clear state collapses and returns to the muddy stage. In the case of marketing, when people aced the best strategies to advertise using print media and newspapers, it collapsed with the invention of the radio. All of a sudden, the nature of the problem changed and it required a radically different approach to solve it. The experts, who had concrete approaches and strategies for the problem solving back then, had to revisit and start from the beginning as the problem went back to the muddy stage. The problem life cycle kept evolving, and this was repeated when television was introduced and again when social media was introduced. Today, with the social media booming and expanding to newer areas, we have the marketing problem currently stable at the fuzzy state. Soon, with the advent of virtual reality and augmented reality, it is expected to roll back to the muddy phase.

To get more real, lets relate the scenario with a more recent version of the problem. Consider a social media analyst trying to solve a problem: optimizing targets for sponsored ads that need to be placed in the Facebook newsfeed for a user based on his behavior. If we find the user to be a football enthusiast, we would insert an ad into his newsfeed for a sportswear brand. To keep things simple, assume that we are the first ones to do this and no one has ever attempted this in history. The problem will currently be in the **muddy** state. So logically, there would be no references or material available over the Internet for our help and research. Our problem solving task begins by identifying the users interest. Once he has been identified as a potential user with an interest in football, we need to place a sponsored ad in his newsfeed. How do we discover the users interest? There are a variety of metrics that can help us discover his interests, but for simplicity, lets assume that the users interests will be identified purely by the Status Updates he posts on his wall.

We can then simply try to analyze the statuses updated by the person and define his interests. If the word Football or names of any popular football players or football teams appear more than a desired threshold, we can possibly say that he would be following football and hence would be a potential target. Based on this simple rule, we create better strategies and algorithms where our accuracy of finding the potential users can be reached with the minimum amount of time and effort. Gradually, the problem moves from the muddy stage to the fuzzy stage. We now have a good amount of understanding regarding the problem. We may not have the best and most effective solution for the problem, but we definitely have a fair idea to get started and find a solution without too much research. Over a period of time, we, and many other similar folks, conduct various experiments, publish various blogs and research papers of the results, and help others learn from our methods and experiment more. Eventually, there would be a time when we will have attempted the exhaustive solution paradigms and have the knowledge for the best and most effective solution for any sort of analysis in that domain. Finally, it reaches its pinnacle point-the **clear** stage.

One day, all of a sudden, Facebook and other social media giants launch a new feature. Users can now share photos along with their status updates. A radical change will be seen in the way the user will now use the social network. People tend to post more photos than text updates. All the thought-leadership frameworks and research papers and blogs that proved to be highly successful earlier now seem to be ineffective. We are not sure how to analyze photos updated by the user in order to understand his interests. Unfortunately, the problem goes back to the **muddy** stage. These big changes keep happening again and again. After photos, it will be videos, then audios, and so on, and the cycle keeps repeating as usual. Recently, the user behavior on social networks has dramatically changed. People post more pictures than type any comment or status updates. These photos may or may not be symbolic of the message that the user wants to convey. Sarcasm or satire may be the objective. The memes that get viral over the Internet have no clear message embedded in them. It may be sarcasm or simple smileys that the user wants to comment on. Analyzing the meaning of these images (memes) to understand the actual message that the user wants to convey with algorithms and computers to find out his interests is a challenging deal.

Hence, understanding the problem life cycle helps prepare us better for the evolution of the problem and adapt the problem solving strategies better and faster.

# The problem landscape

Two questions that will have definitely surfaced in our thoughts are as follows:

- Why is understanding the problem life cycle really important?
- How does this add any value to the IoT problem solving?

Lets see how this will be helpful. While solving a problem, understanding the current state of the problem is essential for the analyst. Whenever we solve a problem, we would always prepare for the next state of the problem life cycle knowing that change in the problems current state is inevitable. If the problem is currently in the clear state, then the amount of time and effort we would invest as a data scientist would be considerably less than if the problem would have been in the muddy or fuzzy stage. However, the problem remains for the least amount of time in the *clear stage*. The jump from clear to muddy is shorter compared to any other transition in the problem life cycle. Being aware about the problem life cycle, an organization/data scientist would then prepare better for radical changes that are bound to happen in a short while. We would need to design our solution to be agile and prepare for the next change. Similarly, if the problem is in the fuzzy stage, a lot of our solutions will be designed in such a way that they can be productized for a particular use case or industry. Finally, when the solution is in the muddy state, our solutions in problem solving will be more of a service-based offering than a product. The amount of experiments and research that we would need for the problem to be solved is highest in the muddy state and least in the clear state:

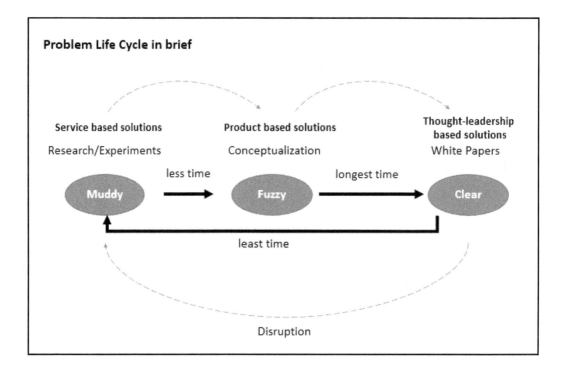

The problem life cycle in brief

So how does this relate to IoT and Decision Science and the intersection of the two? Decision Science has been a bit more widespread and prevalent in the industry than IoT. There have been tons of experiments and research conducted on data to find insights and add value that make Decision Science currently in the **fuzzy stage**. IoT, on the other hand, is fairly new and requires loads of research and experiments to get tangible results, which makes it in the **muddy stage.** However, when we talk about the intersection of the two, we are dealing with a set of interesting problems. On one side, we have a fairly mature ecosystem of Decision Science that has given tangible value to the industry through its experiments whereas IoT is still nascent. The intersection of the two is a very promising and lucrative area for business. It is in a position where it is steadily moving from the muddy to fuzzy stage. Very soon, we will see tangible results from large-scale IoT use cases in the industry that will immediately trigger the revolution for productization on Decision Science for IoT. Decision Science for IoT is rapidly being experimented and the initial results seem to be very promising. The era, where Decision Science for IoT will be in the fuzzy state, is very near.

With this in mind, we can now get to the basics of problem solving while being prepared for the use case to evolve into a fuzzy state. With the understanding of the problem life cycle concrete, lets now explore the problem landscape in detail.

What is the problem landscape? Why do we need to bother about it?

A simple answer would be, understanding the current state of the problem is just one dimension, but understanding the type of problem is a more essential part of problem solving. Lets make this simple. To understand the problem landscape, refer to the following image and try to visualize the problems on two dimensions-frequency and impact. Just like any other scatterplot, this one can also be divided into four major areas:

- Low impact: Low frequency
- Low impact: High frequency
- High impact: Low frequency
- High impact: High frequency

Apart from these four components, we can identify one large spot/circle that has a flavor of all these areas. Here, the problems can be with a high or low frequency and also a high and low impact. So we name it the **Region of Uncertainty**:

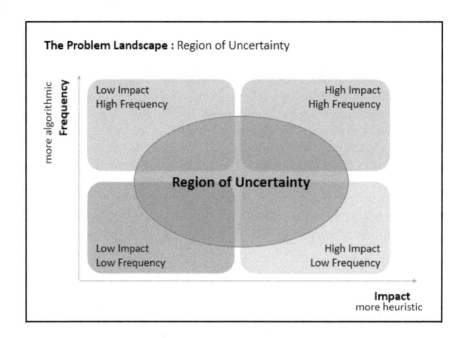

The Region of Uncertainty

Lets understand what kind of problems appear in each of these boxes. Every organization will have a plethora of problems; some of them occur very frequently and some of them very rarely. Some may have a huge impact whereas some may have a small impact. Consider a large organization with hundreds to thousands of employees. There are a couple of problems where the frequency might be low and impact might also be very low. We would generally tend to avoid solving these problems as they are not worth the effort. Some problems, even though they may have a low impact, might have a huge frequency. They would mostly happen on a daily basis. These problems are solved with the typical IT solution approaches such as Support for Technology Infrastructure, CRM, attendance management, employee leave application portal, and so on. There are some problems where the impact will be extremely huge, but the frequency will be extremely low. Events such as making the company public, acquiring a new company, or changing the business model would happen probably once in a lifetime or once in a few years. These problems can be solved from a consulting approach. Then there is one class of problems that has an extremely huge impact and occurs very frequently, for example, a pricing model for Amazon, Google's page rank algorithm, Search Engine Optimization, and others. These problems again require a completely different approach to solve. Here, we would need an approach that would be a combination of heuristics as well as algorithms blended with products.

Apart from these four obvious types of problems, we will have a special set of problems that has a flavor of all these types: **moderate problems**. Here, we might have a moderately good impact and frequency. Solving these problems requires a special approach. These are neither completely heuristic-based nor completely algorithmic. These are sweet spots for businesses where the tangible results can be experimented and validated very early and many companies can target for conceptualizations to deal with specific areas of the problem landscape:

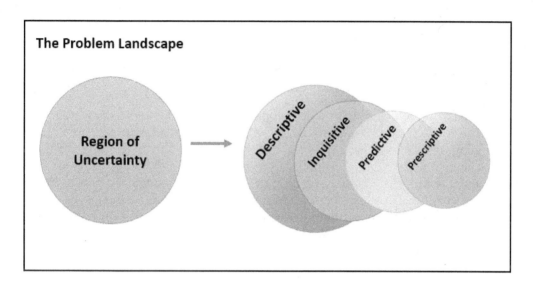

The problem landscape

When we explore the sweet spot, that is, the Circle of Uncertainty, we find that the problems again are of a different nature. They could be any one of the following:

- Descriptive: What happened?
- Inquisitive: How and why it happened?
- Predictive: When will it happen?
- Prescriptive: So what/now what?

To understand the nature of the problem, we basically try to ask what question is the solution answering. It could be what, how, when, why, and so on. Lets understand this better with a simple example.

Consider a Loyalty Program launched by a retail giant such as Walmart, where customers can use a Loyalty Membership Card to earn and burn cash points on each transaction. For simplicity, lets assume that the campaign ran for around three months and the *Director of the Loyalty Program* would like to know the answers to a few questions.

He would first like to know **what happened?**

This means how many people enrolled, how many transactions were recorded, how many products were sold, how many points were earned or burned, how much profit was earned during this season, how much revenue was generated, and so on. We basically get into the details of what happened during the period.

The nature of the problem that we are trying to solve here is **Descriptive**. The entire solution can be captured by asking one question-**What happened?**

Once he has a fair understanding of what happened, he would want to know about-Why it happened in a few scenarios. For example, he will have observed that sales from one particular geographical location, say Texas, have not increased in spite of the Loyalty Program, so he would like to understand specifically, why did that happen? Here, the problem solving will focus on understanding the reasons for no increase in sales in the Texas area when other areas have performed much better. We would then try to understand the Why question by digging deeper into the problem. We may study the offers that were rolled out to Texas compared to other regions or analyze how targeting customers and marketing campaigns differ between them and so on.

Here, the nature of the problem would be **Inquisitive**. The entire solution can be captured by asking one question-**Why did it happen?**

After understanding the reasons for why the event happen, we would probably want to take precautions to avoid failure due to the reasons found. Say, we found out that due to bad services, a lot of customers churned out to other competitors. We would then try to understand more about customer churn propensity where we would like to predict when the customer might churn out, so that we can take preventive measures to keep the customers happy.

Here, the nature of the problem would be Predictive. The entire solution can be captured by asking the question-**When** will the event happen?

Finally, once we have a complete picture of the series of events that happened and why and how it happened, we would like to take corrective measures to mitigate the perils of the event. So we would then ask Now what/So what, where we would try to seek guidelines for corrective actions. For example, we might have observed that due to bad service, a large number of customers churned out to other competitors and we would like to run customer retention programs and campaigns that could win back the churned customers.

Here, the nature of the problem would be Prescriptive. We can understand the entire solution with the question, Now what/So what?

To understand the nature of the problem better from an IoT perspective, consider the following example of an Oil and Gas Industry. Lets say that Shell, a leading oil company, has subsea operations set up in one of its prime locations. It would then deploy tons of machinery for the operations in order to extract oil from the reserves. In the IoT ecosystem, all the machinery or assets here would form a connected network where machines are equipped with a variety of sensors that can capture information about various real-time parameters and communicate to other machines and a central server. Assume that you are now the Operations Head for the plant and you are entitled with the responsibilities of executing the operations smoothly and effectively. As the head of Operations, at the end of the day, we would like to know what happened during the day in course of the oil extraction process. This would be answering the question, *What happened?* We would basically explore how much amount of oil was extracted, how many hours the machinery was under operation, and how many man hours and machine hours were utilized. This would be the basic set of analyses where the nature of the problem would be **Descriptive**. During the analysis, we discovered that the total amount of oil extracted today was extremely low compared to the threshold benchmarks and targets. We would then want to know what exactly happened, why the production decreased, and what were the causes. We would try to dig deeper into the problem and understand whether there was any issue with the workforce, did any device/equipment have a downtime, or whether any machine was underperforming. Here, the nature of problem would be **Inquisitive,** where we try to answer, Why did the event happen? Similarly, when we identify that the root cause for the problem was the downtime due to the failure of the drill machine deployed on the site, we would then try to understand when the assets would fail in future so that we could prepare in advance with maintenance and logistics to reduce downtime. A statistical model can be built that predicts the failure of an asset based on the real-time dimensions captured from the sensors to implement predictive maintenance for the assets to reduce downtime. This would be a classic Predictive problem. Finally, when the failure was catastrophic, we understood that we need to get a corrective action plan in place to reduce the effects to the best extent. We would get logistics ready for periodic maintenance of assets and condition-based maintenance for the machinery deployed on the site. Here, the nature of the problem is **Prescriptive**.

In a nutshell, we have explored the problem landscape and studied various dimensions of the problem. We studied how problems can be in different stages of the life cycle, how problems can be defined based on their type as low and high impact and frequency, and we also synthesized the nature of the problem, which can be Descriptive, Inquisitive, Predictive, or Prescriptive. Now that we have understood how the problem can be defined, lets move on to another important topic: understanding what it takes to solve a problem.

# The art of problem solving

Now that we have a concrete understanding of how we can define the problem, lets try to understand what it takes to solve a problem. There could be a problem that could possibly be in any stage of its life, say **fuzzy**, the **impact** that it could create could be high with a moderately high **frequency**, and the nature of the problem could be **predictive**. Such a problem is really complicated if we try to understand it from its initial vibes. To make the example sound more concrete, lets assume that a renewable energy (solar) provider has one of its plants set up in a completely off-grid location to supply electric energy to a large college campus for its daily operations. The problem to solve would be predicting the amount of solar energy that would be generated based on weather and historic operational parameters. As the operations are completely off-grid, the admin of the campus would be keen to know the amount of energy that would be generated in the coming days so as to take necessary precautionary measures in cases of low production and high consumption. This would be a classic case of a predictive problem with a high impact and moderately high frequency and still in the fuzzy state. We know a few things about how to go about but no clear roadmap has been identified.

How do we solve this problem? What does it take in terms of skillsets or disciplines to get started with solving the problem? Decision Science, on a high level, takes multiple disciplines together to solve the problem. It generally takes the combination of math, business, and technology to design and execute the initial version of the solution, and then design thinking, behavioral science, and other disciplines to improvise the solution. Lets understand how and why this is required.

# The interdisciplinary approach

Solving the problem of predicting solar energy generation will initially require **math** skills where we would apply a variety of statistical and machine learning algorithms to get the predictions more and more accurate. Similarly, we would need **technology** skills to program in one or more computer languages based on the infrastructure where the data would be stored. The technology skills will help us extract data from various internal and external sources and clean, transform, and massage the data to render in the format where we can perform analysis. Finally, we will require **business** skills where we would have an understanding on how the college operates during the day, which operations are the most energy-consuming, how does the forecasted result add value for the college operations, and how do they plan to take precautionary actions for survival. The business skills required will make more sense if we would try to imagine a classic retail industry problem where we are trying to forecast the sales at a store level. We would need to take into account a variety of features and dimensions that are crucial from the business perspective but may be statistically insignificant. For example, the customer value bucket (high / medium / low) may appear insignificant mathematically during the analysis, but it would probably be one of the most crucial variables for business that may persuade us to consider the problem rather than ignore it.

Additionally, to get more and more granular in the problem solving phase, we would need skillsets on **engineering** and **other disciplines**. In our example, where we try to predict energy that would be generated in the future, a sound background of physics and engineering that would aid us in understanding the functioning of the photovoltaic cells and solar panel architecture and its engineering will be of great value when improving the solution becomes the core objective.

Similarly, in some other use cases, we would need disciplines of **behavioral science** and **design thinking** in more depth to study user behavior in specific scenarios and its implications in the business context. Thus, to solve any problem, we would need a **curious mindset** where our approach would be very **interdisciplinary**. With the use cases in IoT, the level of granularity of data that gets captured using sensors is altogether different. This mammoth and rich dataset now brings us the opportunity to deal with use cases at more and more granular levels than before. We can talk about use cases as abstract as increasing the product/asset life for an oil and gas refinery equipment or something as granular as reducing the vibrations in the gears of a diesel engine.

# The problem universe

Now that we have a fair understanding about what skillsets are required to solve the business problem, lets try to understand how we go about solving the problem. Generally, the initial vibes that we get from a problem is the complexity. Not every problem is complicated; the simplicity of the problem is represented when it is broken down into smaller problems and we study how these smaller problems are connected to each other. Solution design gets easier when we think about one small problem at a time than the entire big problem.

Lets say that we are trying to solve the problem of increasing sales for a retailing customer. Here, increasing sales is the bigger problem that can be broken down into smaller and more focused problems where we deal with one small problem at a time. Increasing sales for a customer can be composed of smaller problems such as improving marketing campaigns, optimizing marketing channels, improving customer experience, designing customer retention programs, optimizing the supply chain model, and so on. The bigger problem can always be broken down into smaller and more focused problems. Similarly, when we solve one problem, it is also important to understand how these problems connect with other problems in the universe. The solution of the current problem may have a direct impact on another problem or solving this problem also requires solving the other connected problem. Here, we are talking about the art of problem solving rather than solving specific problems. Every problem is a part of a universe, where it may be connected to one or many other problems and may have a direct or indirect impact with other problems. Understanding the network of the problem is crucial before finalizing the design for our solution to the problem.

When we map the smaller problems connecting with each other to create the bigger problem, we have a universe of problems where each small problem can be identified with its life stage, nature, and type. Then we can solve each of these problems using a different approach meticulously drafted for its type and nature rather than using one generic approach. An incremental step-by-step approach to problem solving is not only time-saving but also impactful. The following diagram showcases the example discussed here visually. We can see how large problems are essentially smaller problems interconnected to each other:

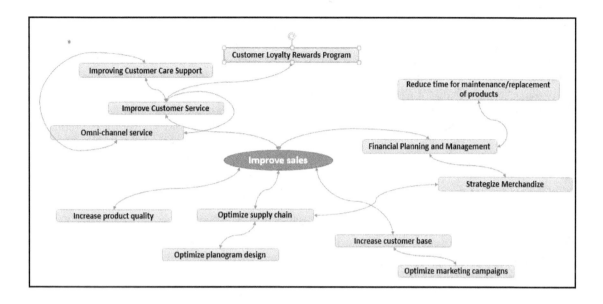

The problem universe

# The problem solving framework

You have learned about how the problem evolves through its life stages and how it can be represented using its type and nature. We also studied how Decision Science and problem solving require a curious mindset with an interdisciplinary approach for the solution. We also explored how problems are actually interconnected in nature and internally composed of smaller problems that can again be of a different type, nature, and life stage. Lets now go ahead and study the *problem solving framework*.

The problem solving framework basically represents a blueprint for the entire solution designed for the problem. Lets say that we are building a software or house; we would basically have an entire list of items that we need to acquire as resources and steps to be executed as per the plan for the end product to look as we have envisioned. Problem solving is also a similar story. Here, the first step is to break down the problem into smaller problems (in case the problem is a big one) and then gather an exhaustive list of hypotheses. To solve a problem, we basically collect a plethora of hypotheses and then test them to get results. Finally, we combine all the results together in such a way that we create a story where we have an answer to the question that we are trying to answer in the problems context. The hypotheses can be **data-driven** or **heuristics-driven.**

Lets take an example to understand how the problem solving framework looks. Consider the case of a hydroelectric power plant, where we have a small setup of devices necessary for the hydroelectric power generation: a turbine, generator, transformer, dam, penstock with an intake control gate, and other essential ones. These devices have their regular roles, such as the dam takes care of storing water for the hydroelectric plant, and there would be a penstock that is basically a long intake pipe that carries the water from the reservoir through controlled gates into a powerhouse that hosts the turbine. The turbine is a device equipped with large blades that rotate when water falls on them, and finally the generator generates AC electric energy from the rotation of these blades in the turbine. (Lets ignore the physics behind this to an extent.) The transformer then converts the electric energy to a higher voltage energy. In the entire flow, the gates of the penstock can be controlled to change the rate of the flow of water into the powerhouse:

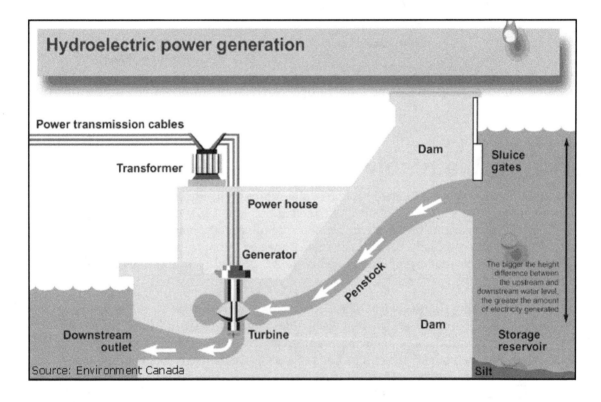

The hydro power plant diagram

**So, what would be the problem?**

You are the site engineer who has been asked the question: **Why has the generation of hydroelectric energy been low for the past one month?** Assume that you have no physical access to the location currently, but still you would first like to gather the maximum amount of information before you begin working on the site when you have access. This would be a scenario where you only have time at the site to fix the problem and not go there and then find out the root cause by testing and inspecting a couple of things. This is a use case that you can solve using data, data, and data. So, as a high-level approach, you would now use every dimension of data and find out the root cause that is possibly dipping the energy generation from the power plant.

Now that the context of the problem is clear, lets take a step back and try to understand more about the problem and then enter the problem solving framework. In this problem, we are trying to find out the root cause of an event-in a nutshell, we are trying to answer the question, Why did the event happen? This indicates that it is **inquisitive** in nature. Secondly, the problem is not radically new and neither has it been completely solved and tested to have an exhaustive solution guideline for all problems. Therefore, the problem is in the **Fuzzy** stage. Finally, the problem definitely has a high impact and is not a once-in-a-lifetime or once-in-a-couple-of-years event. We can probably conclude that the problem has **moderate to high impact and moderate to high frequency**. With the current landscape of the problem, we should probably build a product for this problem with a permanent automated solution. For now, lets explore the problem solving framework.

The framework is a very simple deal. If we are new to the business domain, we would first gather knowledge around the business domain before starting with the problem. In this scenario, we would explore the working of the hydroelectric workstation and how each component in the plant contributes to the overall process. Then we start collecting the list of hypotheses that can be a factor to the problems solution. So here, we lay down all the factors that could possibly be a reason for the root cause of the problem we are trying to solve:

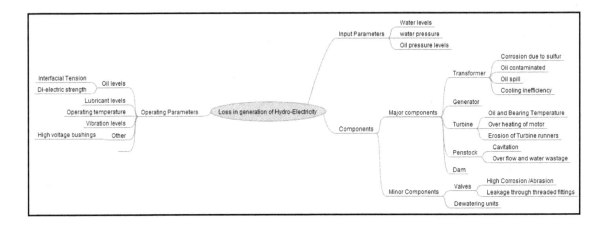

Hydroelectric

In this scenario, we can think of a few factors that can be valid hypotheses for the root cause. For example, there would contamination in the oil of the transformer or there could be an oil spill. The rotors of the turbine could have overheated or the runners could have eroded. The amount of water flowing into the penstock and the water levels set in the gate control could be different, that is, water pressure in the penstock may be lower than usual, the RPM of the turbine blades is lower, or the critical parameters for the turbine have been operating at a lower value for a longer duration. Similarly, the critical parameters for the transformer or generator could have been performing beyond the normal operating range for a longer duration. Oil levels in the gears of the devices may be below the ideal point or the devices may be operating at a temperature beyond the normal range. For these devices, we would have multiple parameters in place that define the status of operation for the devices and deviance from normal operations. A closer look at these parameters will help us define the entire picture of the power plant. All of these factors that build our initial layer of root cause analyses forms the collection of heuristic-driven hypotheses.

Once we have the **heuristics-driven hypotheses** defined, we have action items in place to test what went wrong. We can individually test these hypotheses, evaluate the results from them, and gather insights. Secondly, our collection of hypotheses is still not exhaustive. We might have missed out on tons of important correlated factors that are probably latent in nature and might only be visible when we explore the data in more detail. Lets keep the data-driven hypotheses aside now. (This will be more realistic as we move to `Chapter 3`, *The What And Why – Using Exploratory Decision Science for IoT*). Consider a usual problem solving approach where we have collected a couple of heuristic-driven hypotheses, performed exploratory data analysis for the data, and tested the hypotheses collected. We would find that a few of the hypotheses that we designed earlier are not accurate as the results were not intuitive. We may discard a few hypotheses and prioritize a few others. We would also find a lot of new relationships between data dimensions that we had not accounted for initially. Now, if we revisit the previous list of hypotheses, we would probably have a version with better and more accurate hypotheses and also new hypotheses that we uncovered during our data exploration exercises. The new hypotheses may not be our final version. It may go through a series of iterations before it gets finalized. The refined final list of hypotheses can be called the problem solving framework. This is where the **convergence of data-driven hypotheses and heuristic-driven hypotheses** takes place. This can be represented as a matrix or prioritized list of hypotheses, which needs to be validated to solve the problem:

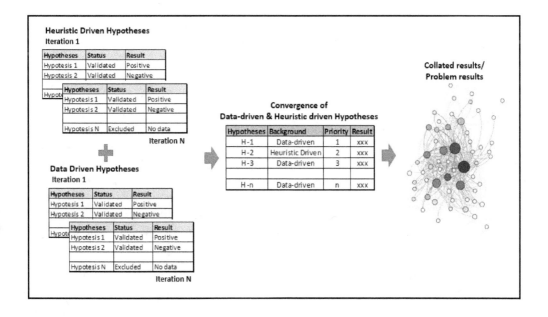

The problem solving framework

The initial list may have a few hypotheses that may not make sense to test as there may be data limitations or they may be counter intuitive with a few latent data relationships that we explored during our analysis. Once all the hypotheses have been tested, we will have results gathered from various tests from them under a single roof. The next step is to assimilate the results so that we can make sense of the story from the results. Synthesizing the results assimilated, we may find the root cause for the event as a result of a few other events. Lets say that while gathering results from our data, we might conclude that the malfunctioning of the controlled gates in the penstock was the root cause. This might be inferred from the critical parameters of the turbine and generator operating at lower thresholds continuously for a prolonged stint. A few data tests on the water pressure and its correlation with the value from the controlled gates differing over a period of time can be an indicative value for the same.

In a nutshell, we have glanced through a very high-level problem with a structured approach using the problem solving framework. The problem solving framework is a simplified approach to design and draft the exhaustive hypotheses generated as a result of the convergence of heuristics and data exploration. With the exhaustive list of hypotheses, we conduct various data tests and assimilate results from them to synthesize and solve the problem by gathering insights and creating a story. In the coming chapters, we will solve real business problems using the problem solving framework and also understand each incremental phase in more detail.

# Summary

This chapter was an introduction to Decision Science and IoT. You learned about the basics of IoT and how it evolved and understood the differences between ambiguous names such as M2M, IIoT, IoE, and others. We studied the logical architecture of the IoT ecosystem by considering IoE and learned how People, Processes, Data, and Things together form the IoT ecosystem. We also discussed decision science and understood more about defining a problem based on the current life stage as **Muddy**, **Fuzzy**, or **Clear**, based on its type as **Impactful and Frequent**, and finally based on its nature as **Descriptive**, **Inquisitive**, **Predictive**, or **Prescriptive**. We also studied that problem solving in decision science requires an interdisciplinary approach using a combination of **math, business, technology**, and so on. Finally, we also studied about the problem solving framework using a generic example of a hydroelectric power plant.

In the next chapter, you will learn in depth about the IoT problem universe and use a concrete example to understand the problem and design the blueprint for the problem using the problem solving framework.

# 2
# Studying the IoT Problem Universe and Designing a Use Case

IoT is spread across the length and breadth of the industry. It has touched every possible industry vertical and horizontal. From consumer electronics, automobiles, aviation, energy, oil and gas, manufacturing, banking, and so on, almost every industry is benefiting from IoT. Problems arise in each of these individual business areas that need to be solved connoting the industry it is addressing, and therefore people often segregate the wide spectrum of IoT into smaller and similar groups. Thus, we see names such as Industrial IoT, Consumer IoT, and so on being referenced quite often these days. Keeping aside these broad divisions, we can simply divide the problems to solve in IoT into two simple categories, that is, 'Connected Operations' and 'Connected Assets'.

In this chapter, we will study about the IoT problem universe and learn to design a business use case by building a **blueprint** for the problem using the problem solving framework that we studied in Chapter 1, *IoT and Decision Science*. We will do this by first understanding **Connected Assets and Connected Operations** in detail with examples. We will then build the foundation to solve an IoT business problem-designing a use case by first studying the problem's context, identifying the associated latent problems, and finally designing it using the problem solving framework.

We will cover the following topics in this chapter:

- Connected Assets and Connected Operations
- Defining the business use case
- Sensing the associated latent problems
- Designing the heuristic-driven hypotheses matrix

By the end of the chapter, we will have complete context about the business problem that we will solve and the areas where we need to dig deeper along with the roadmap we will take to solve it step by step.

# Connected assets & connected operations

With the swift progress of IoT in every dimension in the industry, the associated problems also diversified into the respective domains. To simplify problems, industry leaders took the most intuitive step by defining logical segregations in the IoT domain. Today, there is a plethora of articles and papers published over the Internet, which cite different names and classifications for IoT. As of now, we don't have any universally accepted classification for IoT, but we do see different names such as **Consumer IoT**, **Industrial IoT**, **Healthcare IoT**, and so on. All the IoT-related problems and solutions in the industrial domain were termed as Industrial IoT and so on.

Before studying Connected Assets and Connected Operations, let's explore a simplified classification for the IoT domain. This is definitely not the most exhaustive and widely recognized one, but it will definitely help us understand the nature of the problem better:

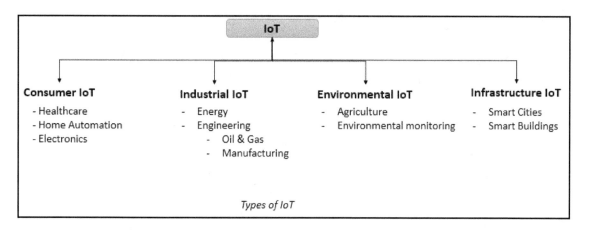

*Types of IoT*

When we look at the entire IoT landscape, we can think about four broad areas where we can help IoT evolve. These are groups of problems associated with consumers, industry, environment, or infrastructure. As the name suggests, everything that can be tagged directly to a consumer, namely, electronics, home appliances, healthcare, retail, automobiles, and so on, where each of them can also individually represent a cluster of problems can be classified as **Consumer IoT**. The problems in this domain would need to be addressed in a different way as it interacts directly with the consumers. Similarly, the industry vertical can also be visualized as the domain where the results can be directly tagged to machines like the ones in the manufacturing and engineering industry. Heavy engineering, smart factory, oil and gas, and energy domains now have machines talking to each other and power IoT. The names go on and we have a never-ending list of industry verticals, each showcasing a shared problem set for the domain.

When we look at the IoT problem landscape from a holistic perspective, it all boils down to two simple areas:

- Connected assets
- Connected operations

Even though using a classification to represent a smaller domain while solving the problem is always beneficial, at the broader level, any problem that exists in IoT can be directly represented by one of these two categories. Let's now begin exploring the crux of the IoT problem space-Connected Assets and Connected Operations

# The journey of connected things to smart things

The IoT revolution began by just connecting things to a network. There is an old saying that says, Networking is the key to success in any business. The IoT fraternity is also loosely based on this principle. Let's consider a simple analogy to understand this. Consider, you are a software engineer and you are now eager to enter the analytics industry, but you are completely new in this field and have barely any friends who can help you get started. So you start researching over the Internet and assimilate a whole bunch of books and videos to study about analytics. Then, after working diligently for three months, you apply for jobs for analytics positions in multiple companies. You attend a couple of interviews and figure out that you need more specialized preparations in some topics. You then keep learning and attending interviews and then finally after a lot of attempts, you nail it. Let's say that the whole process took you around six months; what could have been an easier alternative? If you knew people in the analytics industry, one of them could guide you to learn the required skillsets for the position open in their organization. The entire effort could have been reduced to two months! That is a whole lot of saving in time. Networking helps you receive the required information faster and easier, which in turn helps you take better decisions and evolve faster.

The same holds true for machines and devices. The following diagram is a visual to understand how legacy devices eventually evolved to become smart devices:

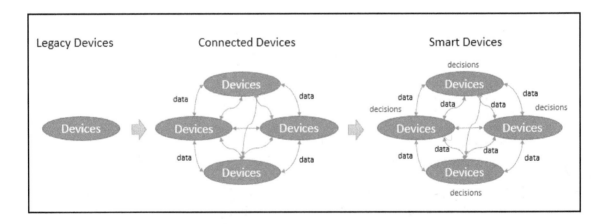

Connected assets

Let's take the analogy to the field of IoT. What IoT essentially does as a first step in the ecosystem is it connects the devices/things. Once they are connected, they can talk to each other; once they talk to each other, they get smarter. To make it even simpler, consider the air conditioner in your house. Earlier, it used to be a standalone device that needed to be switched on/off whenever required. In course of time, they got connected to a network, and now they can be controlled using a remote/smartphone or tablet connected to the Internet. They have now become 'Connected Devices' and offer services to you at more convenience. Let's say that you forgot to switch off the AC before leaving for work and you suddenly realize it on the way. You could quickly turn it off using your smartphone while you are still on the way to work. Finally, when devices are connected, they are provided with huge amount of data that was initially unavailable. This data can be leveraged to take decisions that make life even more comfortable. The connected AC, which could connect to your smartphone through the Internet, can also connect to a sensor that detects the number of people in the room and then change the settings automatically based on the data. So we have a smart AC that automatically powers on when someone enters the room and changes the settings when more and more people enter the room. Once devices are connected, making them smart is the next agenda.

The same thumb rule applies for every other use case.

In today's world, we have smart connected devices booming up. Almost every other business model has started realizing the potential value that can be reaped from smart connected devices. It could just be your home automation or a mammoth factory machine; there is definitely a gold mine that can be extracted if we have things connected to each other.

# Connected assets – A real life scenario

Let's take a real-life example to understand how *Connected Assets* will work for a large organization. We will study the use case of a **Coffee Making Machine** to understand this better. Consider any coffee making machine in the market, say, **Sage Appliances** is planning to launch a new coffee machine called *Caffeine Express* that will be a part of the connected assets experiment for the manufacturer. So how does the traditional business work? Well, the company would sell the appliance to customers all over the world and set up service centers at strategic points. For simplicity, let's assume that they sell their appliances in just one country, hence they would preferably set up service care centers in the capital or prominent cities. Let's say that it has set up service centers in a total of five cities in a country.

In the **traditional business model**, once the appliance is sold, the company has only limited information about the sales or how the appliance is performing. It would probably know about the total volume of sales that has happened till date and how much of these sales happened online or through stores. They would also know which store/area sold how many units and a few other simple details. Also, the company would understand how the appliance is being used and its performance from user opinions over social media or the customer service centers. However, from a holistic viewpoint, this information is still far less than what is required:

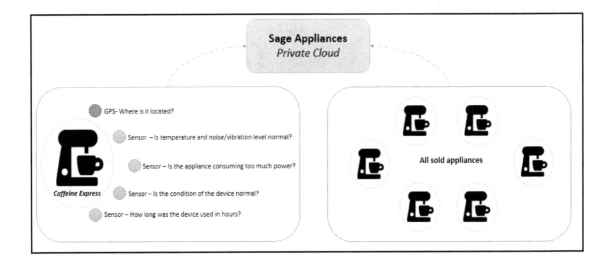

Connected assets: the coffee machine use case

Now consider the **IoT business model**; assume that each of the appliances sold-*Caffeine Express – Coffee machine*-is equipped with a GPS, Internet connectivity through Wi-Fi, and a couple of sensors that can monitor the internal parameters. The GPS locates the device geographically and the sensors collect periodic data from the appliance about how many cups of coffee were brewed in a day and when they were brewed. It would also capture the operational parameters of the machine such as the health index of the motor, temperature of the device, amount of energy used, noise and vibration levels, and so on. All of this information is then sent to the company's private cloud with the customer's consent. Now, with IoT in the ecosystem, we have a whole new level of connectivity with the appliance even after it is sold to the customers. An extremely rich source of data is now available to the company that they can use to help the customer as well as the business. This is technically a simple example for 'Connected Assets'. Here, each coffee machine is equipped with Internet connectivity, sensors, and a GPS that can connect to the central server on the private cloud of the company.

So what exactly will happen if the devices are now connected; how does this help?

This is where **Connected Assets** bring in the difference. The earlier decisions taken by the company were all driven by judgements, heuristics, and market research. The company would have researched and experimented before finalizing where to set up the service centers, which medium to target for marketing, which state/city to focus more on sales, and so on. With IoT's connected assets, all these decisions can be made more accurate and data-driven.

The company can now understand exactly how many units are sold in each geographical area, how often they are used, how they are performing, and so on. The decisions taken earlier might not be really accurate but all of that can now be validated with the data. Let's say that the maximum sales of the appliance were observed in London and the company set up a customer service center in North London. However, what if, from all the sales that were observed in London, 90% of them were in South London? Assume that the customers who are located in South London purchased them from North London to avail some offer. The convenience of the end customer would have been dramatically improved had the company set up the center in South London.

Similarly, the sensors installed in the appliance send periodic information to the company's cloud about the usage and state of the device. This data could help the company understand how the coffee machines are performing and if they are on the verge of breaking down. Are they showing unusual usage? Are they heating up too much or are they consuming too much power? An answer to all of these questions will help the company take better data-driven decisions about how to fix them. They can be proactive in calling up the customer and sending a technician before the device breaks down or educate the customer about the malfunctioning appliance that consumes too much power proactively and fix it. It could also help them serve the customer service center better with a planned inventory based on the issues studied from the performance data.

With such a connected ecosystem, the customer and business both benefit in the long run. The customers get world-class service at the least cost and business can be more lucrative with reduced operational costs and planned activities.

# Connected operations – The next revolution

The second part of the IoT problem landscape is 'Connected Operations'. Generally, organizations first begin with getting the ecosystem ready for connected assets. Once the system is mature enough, the next level of connectivity is brought by connecting the operations in the company. These operations could be everything associated with the company-manufacturing, inventory, supply chain, marketing, transportation, distribution, customer service, and so on. Imagine an organization that has all of these operations connected to each other and streamline processes. The entire bottleneck areas can be eliminated and the overall process can be very smooth, efficient, and cost-effective. The industry is currently moving slowly toward this revolution; it's called **Industry 4.0** and sometimes also referred to as **Smart Factory**.

# What is Industry 4.0?

The current era is the fourth Industrial Revolution and has been specifically triggered by IoT. Looking back in history, the first form of revolution came when mechanization was brought into the industry. Long back when the entire industrial work was done by laborers, the early 18th century saw the first breakthrough when the factory was mechanized in the textile industry. Tasks previously done laboriously by hand in hundreds of weavers' cottages were brought together in a single cotton mill, and the factory was born. The second industrial revolution (Industry 2.0) was born in the early 20th century, when Henry Ford revolutionized the moving assembly line and steered mass production. These revolutions brought humongous benefits to mankind with urbanization and money. Recently, we witnessed the third Industrial Revolution (Industry 3.0) when information technology was born. A plethora of things were made digital and IT played a pivotal role in transforming the industry. The major organizations that we see worldwide are still a part of the third Industrial Revolution.

Industry 4.0, that is, the fourth industrial revolution, started blooming with the boom of Internet of Things. Connected Assets was the beginning that eventually led to the idea of Connected Operations and conceptualized the idea of a smart factory. A smart factory would be one where all operations could talk to each other and coordinate to take decisions automatically in order to reduce operational overheads-a truly revolutionary industry.

Let's take a simple example to understand how Industry 4.0–**Smart Factory**-will work. We will consider the same example of the coffee machine used in the previous section. Consider the scenario in the factory; we will be having multiple operations or processes. Assume that the following processes are a part of the entire operations list, say, we have supply chain, manufacturing, transportation, distribution, and customer service.

The life cycle of the operations can be visualized in the following diagram:

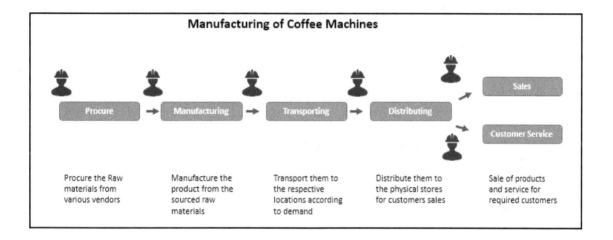

Legacy operations

Let's assume a simplified process.

The raw materials are sourced from multiple vendors, and once the required amount is stocked for the manufacturing process, the system initiates the manufacturing of products. Once the products are manufactured and packed, they are transported to warehouses in various cities/states within the country. From these warehouses, the goods need to be distributed to the various stores from where customers can purchase them. After using the appliance for a while, some customers revert to the service care center for the issues they come across. These products might need repair or replacement, which can then be sourced back to the distribution chain. This is how a general model of a factory with various operations looks like. A person would be in charge of each of the intermediate processes to take a call on the immediate next step.

Let's now understand how the connected operations will look in the smart factory:

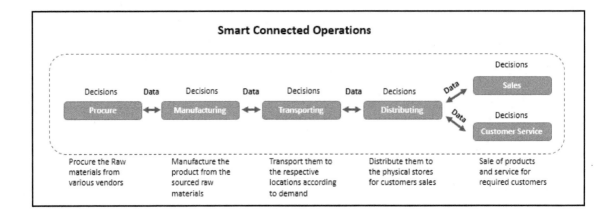

Connected operations

What if all of these operations could actually talk to each other? With the communication between these operations, they could also take decisions on their own to get the best and most optimized results. Consider a scenario where once the raw material supplies are ready in the factory's storehouse, the manufacturing process automatically initiates a process to ingest the required raw materials from the source in the required amount for production. The manufacturing operation can talk to the transportation operation; hence, based on the products manufactured, the manufacturing operation automatically decides the type and number of products to be transported to different locations. The transportation operation receives the information from the manufacturing operation and automatically assigns the load to respective trucks (vehicles for the transportation) and the associated driver gets notified about the load that he needs to transport to the destination (warehouse) along with the desired timeframe. The drivers quickly transport the loads to the respective destinations. After the load arrives at the warehouse, the system automatically updates the database about the stock arrival. The distribution operation would then receive the information from the stores about which store requires how many and what kind of products; the system automatically assigns smaller loads to each store and notifies the same to each distributor. The products finally reach the store and are up for sale. Once the stock is about to expire, the store/sales operations automatically notify the need for a fresh load and the message eventually reaches the other operations.

This was a glimpse into the smart factory, that is, Industry 4.0, where every operation can talk to other operations and take decisions to transform the legacy factory into a smart connected factory.

# Defining the business use case

So far, we have explored what kind of problems arise in a typical IoT scenario and how they can be classified into Connected Operations and Connected Assets. Let's now focus on designing and solving a practical business use case for IoT. We will explore how we can solve problems using the interdisciplinary approach of decision science in IoT.

We'll start with a simple problem in the manufacturing industry. Assume that there is a large multinational consumer goods company, say, Procter & Gamble, who owns a plethora of products. Consider their detergent product, Tide, to study our example. Tide is a detergent powder that comes in liquid form as well, has a variety of scents, different cleanliness levels, and so on. Assume that the company owns a plant in which one production line (the assembly line in which the goods are manufactured end to end) manufactures detergent powder. It manufactures 500 Kgs of detergent powder in a single go. The operations head of the plant, John, has a problem and has now reached out to us to help him. John feels that the quality of the detergent produced in the manufacturing process is quite often not in sync with the required levels. Whenever the quality of the manufactured detergent powder goes below the standard level, they have to discard it and manufacture it all over again. This results in a huge loss of time and money. He is not sure about the exact reasons for the issue; he feels it could be because of faulty machinery or errors made by the laborers, but he's not really sure about the actual reason. John has therefore reached out to us to check whether we can help him.

This is where decision science comes in action. A problem is identified and the solution to the problem can help John take better decisions. We assure John that we would definitely help in solving the problem. John heaves a sigh of relief and gets back to work. As he leaves, he mentions that we can have a meeting with him the next day to discuss the problem.

Doesn't this sound great? Let's quickly understand what it would take to solve the problem. First of all, what we heard from John is just the problem statement (which is still raw and needs a lot of improvement before we can term it as a problem statement). He mentioned that the quality of the detergent manufactured many times is below the acceptable range and hence needs to be discarded, which results in financial losses. Can we help him, what are the different analytical operations that we can perform, how do we find out the reason for bad quality, do we need to reduce financial losses or increase the quality of the produce. Too many questions start bothering us. This is indeed a common scenario for everyone who tries to solve a problem. Let's take a pause and understand how we can structure the problem and understand it better.

As a golden rule in problem solving, there are five simple and essential steps that we need to plan and execute for any use case:

1. Defining the problem.
2. Researching and gathering context.
3. Prioritizing and structuring hypotheses based on the availability of data.
4. Validating and improving the hypotheses (iterate over steps 2 and 3).
5. Assimilating results and rendering the story.

Let's go step by step for our use case.

# Defining the problem

The first step in any problem is to clearly define the problem. Let's define the problem by framing the problem statement in the most succinct way we can. To accomplish this, we will use a very famous framework, which is used by industry leaders such as McKinsey, Mu Sigma, and others, to represent the problem in a structured way, called –**SCQ- Situation, Complication, Question.**

To define the problem, we ask three simple questions:

- What is the **Situation**, that is, the problem you are facing?
- What is the **Complication** you face while solving it?
- What **Questions** need answers to solve the problem?

When we gather answers to these three simple questions, we can frame the most lucid representation of the problem statement. Let's go ahead and build an SCQ for this.

The following image is a simplified **Situation – Complication – Questions** representation for our business use case:

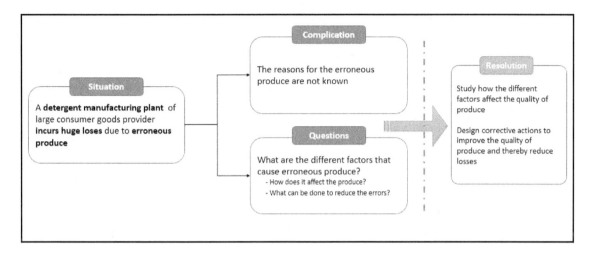

SCQ

We capture the situation in simple words and highlight the key complications that we face while solving the problem. In this use case, we are not sure about what factors contribute to the erroneous or low quality produce while manufacturing the detergent, and therefore we highlight it as the key **complication**. To solve the problem, we need answers to a couple of questions. Following up directly from the *complication*, we can understand the key questions that need answers are: what factors contribute to the dip in quality and how do they affect it? Once we have an understanding about how each factor affects the quality of the detergent produced, we also need to understand what can be done to improve the detergent quality. Finally, once the SCQ is clearly defined, we can take an easy shot at the resolution required to solve the problem (which is represented in the box on the extreme right in the preceding diagram).

The SCQ can be used to represent any problem with the least verbiage. Once the business problem is clearly defined, we can proceed to the next logical step for problem solving, that is, gather more context and generate an exhaustive list of hypotheses for the problem.

# Researching and gathering context

Researching about the problem and gathering more and more context is a lengthy step. It requires way more effort than we could imagine. Moreover, this is an iterative step as you keep discovering newer things in the course of your analysis.

For our use case, we are trying to solve a small problem for a detergent manufacturing company. The company owns a manufacturing plant that has been bearing huge losses in time and money due to the bad quality of produce. To understand what factors impact the quality and how and solve the problem better, we need to understand the problem's context in more depth. We will need the acumen about what is happening and, to a certain extent, also why it is happening in the manufacturing process. To begin with, we can probably start by understanding the operations of the manufacturing plant with the engineer's mindset, trying to understand more about the operations and raw materials, and so on. Our research can include learning about the detergent manufacturing process, what kind of raw materials are used, how long it takes, and what machinery does the company use. However, before we go into research mode, let's take a pause and analyze the kind of problem we are solving.

As discussed in the first chapter, we'll analyze the type of the problem in three simple dimensions-the life stage of the problem, frequency and impact of the problem, and nature of the problem.

# Gathering context – examining the type of problem

The problem is definitely not new; almost every other manufacturer would have come across a similar issue and definitely tried experimenting to solve it. Additionally, it has not been completely solved; there is humongous scope for the problem's solution to improve. Hence, it is in the **fuzzy** state. The frequency of the problem is quite high, though not extremely high. The frequency would vary from once a week to probably even once a day. Similarly, the impact will definitely be moderately high as it delays the production process resulting in loss of valuable time, energy, and resources. Therefore, the problem can be defined as **moderate frequency and moderate impact**. To understand the nature of the problem, we can analyze the questions that we are trying to answer. If we glance back to the previous paragraph, we can notice that the question we are trying to answer is why/how-this shows that the nature of the problem initially would be **Inquisitive**.

Therefore, we can conclude that the problem will require a bit of experimentation to explore and understand as it is in the fuzzy state. Also, it is a very valuable problem to solve as the impact and frequency both are moderately high. Finally, the nature of the problem as of now is inquisitive; hence, we would need a forensic mindset to solve and find the root cause. As the problem progresses, the findings in the solution may change the nature of the problem-it could evolve from inquisitive to predictive or even prescriptive based on the insights we capture from the analysis. This said, let's move on to understand the business context about the use case.

# Gathering context – research and gather context

To solve problems better, it is crucial for us to do good ground research and accumulate robust context about the problem. Understanding more about the company, manufacturing environment, the manufacturing process and so on will add great value to our approach and solution. Our research will include reading articles over the Internet, watching videos to understand the high-level process, interacting with people/laborers to understand the operations and more about the problem, and so on. Walking you practically through the entire research is out of the scope for this book, but we will go through the high-level flow for the research approach.

We start our research by studying the **obvious gap** in our problem-the **Complication** defined in the SCQ. The complication then gives rise to a few questions that need answers and there we are! We have our easy start ready.

Refer to the following diagram to visualize the flow of the research and context gathering for our detergent manufacturing quality use case:

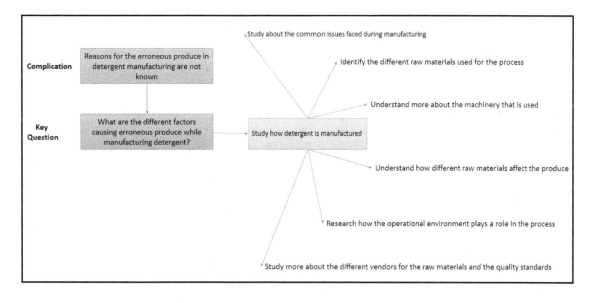

Research

We will start simply with the key question: What are the different factors that cause erroneous produce during manufacturing the detergent?

To answer the question, we can start our research on understanding the first area that comes to your mind, that is, to study how detergent is manufactured in the industry. Once we have a fair understanding about the process, we can spontaneously come up with immediate areas that need research. Understanding how different raw materials affect the end produce, studying the common issues faced during manufacturing, exploring more about the machinery used in the process, digging deeper to understand the effects of the raw materials, the role of operational environment and operational parameters in the entire process, and understanding whether same raw materials from different vendors can cause an issue. When we explore and research more on different topics, we get a deeper and concrete understanding about the problem we are trying to solve. Let's assume the following research outcome.

# Research outcome

The following excerpts have been kept very short; an actual research for a problem will render a huge download of context and answers to all your questions.

## How is detergent manufactured?

(The following context details a generic detergent `<ie>manufacturing</ie>` process. The way detergent is manufactured in a large industry will be quite different that cannot be elaborated here for obvious reasons.)

Detergent is manufactured in four simple steps: saponification, removing glycerin, purification, and finishing. The saponification basically involves heating animal fat and oil with sodium hydroxide. Glycerin is then removed from the resultant solution, and then the solution is purified by adding weak acids. Finally, detergent powder is prepared through agglomeration, spray drying, and dry mixing, and preservatives, color, and perfume are added to the power.

(Understanding the complex process of manufacturing can be abstracted at a high level for now.)

## What are the common issues that arise in the detergent manufacturing process?

During the manufacturing phase, there is a variety of issues that can arise. These issues could be related to the raw materials used or machinery used. It could also be issues related to the operating conditions of the factory/place or the manufacturing process (recipe).

In the case of detergent manufacturing, we observe common issues such as overheating, incorrect proportion of raw materials, bad quality of raw materials, inappropriate operating conditions of the factory, delay in processing, or machinery problems such as vibrations, unclean containers, operational inaccuracy, and so on. All of these issues along with a few latent ones contribute to the low quality of the end produce.

## What kind of machinery is used for the detergent manufacturing process?

The concerned production line in the manufacturing plant consists of multiple machines such as mixers, blenders, and so on connected to each other with conveyor belts. The machine processes the raw materials and then moves it to another in containers using the conveyor belts. The detergent manufacturing process consists of 4-5 phases, of which each phase can contain multiple machines. In the current scenario, we can assume that each phase in the manufacturing process contains exactly one machine. Refer to the following diagram to get a high-level overview of the system:

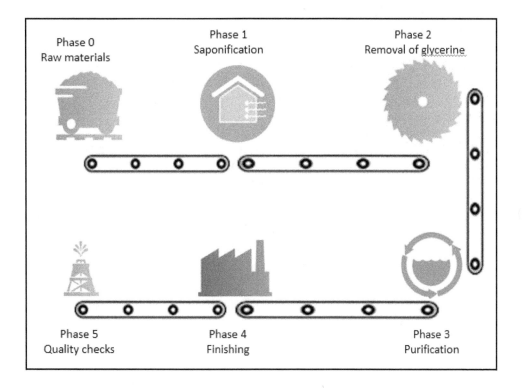

The manufacturing process

Different raw materials such as animal fat, sodium hydroxide, coconut oil, and so on are fed into the process using different containers. The system automatically consumes the required amount of materials for the production. In the first phase, these materials are processed, heated, and mixed to form a unified mixture. The mixture is then passed in containers to the next phase through conveyors. In the second phase, the machine processes the mixture solution to remove glycerin. Salt and a few other raw materials are added to the solution to separate glycerin from it. In the third phase, the remaining impurities and water are removed by adding weak acids. In the fourth phase, the machine adds preservative, fragrance, and other required materials to the detergent produced. Finally, in the fifth phase, the detergent is tested for various quality parameters. If the quality of the produce is maintained in the desired levels, the product is sent for packaging, otherwise, it is discarded and needs to be manufactured all over again.

## What do we need to know more about the company, its production environment, and operations?

The customer has multiple manufacturing plants spread across the globe and each plant has multiple production lines. A production line in the manufacturing plant is the assembly line that conveys the raw material through different machines and finally delivers the manufactured product. Multiple consumer products are manufactured in the same plant as there are close to 10 different production lines. Let's say one of these plants is in India located in the city of Pune, where John heads the operations for the detergent product, *Tide*. John's role is to head the manufacturing operations of multiple products for the company. He is responsible for timely manufacturing and delivery of high-quality products for the company with reduced operational cost and lower rejection rates. However, recently John observed that the quality of the detergent manufactured is often below the acceptable level and hence the plant has been incurring huge losses.

# Prioritize and structure hypotheses based on the availability of data

Once we have gathered enough context about the problem, our next step is to get started with hypotheses generation. We need to ideate and brainstorm as a team to capture what all factors could possibly play a role in helping us find out the reasons for low-quality produce. Such brainstorming sessions can be held in a group of three or more members. We begin by penning down all the ideas on a paper or whiteboard, which we feel could be a potential reason for the problem. After a small session, we take a pause and try to assimilate the hypotheses that can be framed around the ideas we have listed on the whiteboard and then try to contemplate how this will be useful. With a few good iterations, we can boil down our hypotheses to the most important and effective ones. The ideal hypotheses list should be mutually exclusive and collectively exhaustive, but there is a very high chance that we might not get it, and this is absolutely fine. If we have a relatively exhaustive list of hypotheses, our next step is to analyze the importance of each of the hypotheses that we have listed and then assign a weight/priority to it based on its importance. Once all the hypotheses are assessed and prioritized, we need to find out which of these hypotheses can be validated with the data we have. This is a very important step as the solution for many problems can halt here endlessly if the most important hypotheses for the problem cannot be validated with data. It may so happen that we define the problem and frame an exhaustive list of hypotheses by researching the context necessary for the solution and fail to validate the most important ones due to lack of data. In such cases, it will not make any sense to move ahead and solve the problem by validating the remaining less important hypotheses as we will still miss out on the bigger picture.

In case we have data to validate a good chunk of important hypotheses, we can organize them and start validating them one by one. The results may be counterintuitive in some cases but we still need to consider them in framing the final story. For the current use case, we are limiting the exploration of data from Chapter 3, *The What and Why – Using Exploratory Decision Science for IoT* onward. Hence, in this chapter, we will only draft an initial version of the hypotheses and refine it. Structuring and prioritizing of the hypotheses based on availability will be explored in detail in the next chapter:

Hypotheses list

The preceding image showcases a high-level list of hypotheses generated from the team's brainstorming sessions for the problem statement. Around 12-13 hypotheses have been listed for the problem. They come from simple ideas such as issues related to operational parameters, raw materials, process-level issues, laborer issues, machinery issues, and so on On each of these broad ideas, we can have a list of hypotheses that may sometimes be very obvious or just an intuition. It is a good practice to collect all such possible hypotheses combinations and later filter them as a team with solid reasoning.

In general, for an average problem, a brainstorming session can gather approximately 15-20 broad ideas or reasons for the issue, which will then result in around 50-60 odd hypotheses. After a more detailed discussion and narrowed-down research, we may land up filtering around 20-30 good constructive hypotheses. Finally, after prioritizing and checking for data availability, we would have a handful of 15-20 hypotheses that can be validated with the data. From this final prioritized list of 15, there would be around 5-6 very important and critical hypotheses that we have identified and will form the major part of the story for your solution.

# Validating and Improving the hypotheses (iterate over #2 and #3)

The next logical step in the problem solving process is to start validating the hypotheses one by one from the final assimilated list. This would involve diving deep into the data to perform a variety of analytical tests and checks. We would start initially with univariates, then move on to bivariate, and even multivariate, analysis. Based on the hypotheses, we may perform few statistical checks/hypotheses testing to validate our research and heuristics. (In case, any of these terms-bivariate, univariates, or statistical tests-are new to you, nothing to worry about. We will get into these topics in detail in the next chapter.) In the course of the analysis, we may find numerous counterintuitive results and also there would be cases where our initial understanding from our research needs to be updated. This will result in tweaking the existing hypotheses and, in some cases, even adding or removing a few hypotheses.

Too much abstraction through text would be making things a bit difficult to fathom. Let's take a small example to understand this step better. Assume that we are in a scenario where we have our problem statement clearly defined, the research to solve the problem is exhaustive, and we have drafted a final and prioritized version of the hypotheses. We now dive deep into the data and start validating them using a variety of methods. Let's say that we are in the process of validating the hypothesis: Bad quality of the raw material results in bad quality of the end produce. This is a hypothesis that may seem very obvious. We would expect that whenever detergent was manufactured in the plant and the quality of the raw materials were not in sync with the expected quality, the quality of the end produce would always be bad. However, what if we find the results completely counterintuitive? It may happen because our research was incomplete; maybe the quality of the end produce gets affected only if the quality of the raw material goes beyond an abnormal range. It could also be the case that the quality parameters we have considered might not be exhaustive or may not be the valid one to test our hypothesis. It could be any reason and we may or may not have an answer to it. This is a very common scenario in the analysis. In such situations, we take a pause in our analysis to explore data/hypotheses validation and get back to basics. We refresh our heuristics by researching more focused and specific areas of interest. After some research, we may find that the quality of the raw materials becomes critical if the operating temperature is below a specific temperature. We would then tweak our hypothesis so as to validate a more accurate one. In some cases, we might find something even more interesting that we may add as a new hypothesis and sometimes also drop an existing one.

Overall, this step in the problem solving process is an iterative one. It may take multiple iterations to get a more improved and refined version of hypotheses results.

# Assimilate results and render the story

This would ideally be the final step in our problem solving process. In many cases, a new problem gets identified here and the course of analytics heads to a new direction. By the time we reach this step, we would have all our refined and tweaked hypotheses tested. Our heuristics and judgements based on our research and context gathering process will now be having a more concrete answer. However, we have still not solved the problem! We need to synthesize the results to complete the story and find reasons for the bad-quality detergent manufactured. This is when we start storyboarding the results. We would have around 15-20 or sometimes fewer hypotheses validated with results. The results may be counterintuitive or incomplete, but still it is important to gather all of them together to understand how one result complements another and what is the root cause for all the problems. A simplistic form of the story will be like the following section.

(The following is just an example for our understanding and doesn't necessarily hold true for any detergent manufacturing company or even our use case).

The major reason for the bad quality of the end produce while manufacturing detergent is due to the inappropriate operational parameters and environmental factors of the manufacturing plant. The machinery, when overloaded, doesn't produce the required temperature to heat the raw materials, and the RPM of the mixer reduces by 20% resulting in a semi-processed mixture solution from Phase 1. The quality gets further affected if the input quantity of the two most important raw materials varies even by a fraction. Furthermore, if the same raw material from different vendors have variations in input quality parameters, it may uptick the bad quality of the end produce. Also, when the machinery is overloaded, the processing delays by around 5% and also causes inappropriate intermediate solutions.

Therefore, we can conclude that the losses in the detergent manufacturing plant are mainly due to improper operational parameters that mainly resulted from overloaded machinery. Similarly, quality variations within the raw material due to different vendors and deviations in the input proportion of important raw materials also contribute to the bad quality of the detergent manufactured. Also, we can positively say that the laborers' roles in the bad quality produce is very minimalistic.

The storyboarding process is often tedious and, in most cases, requires inputs from the business team who have more in-depth domain knowledge. There would be many cases where a few results may be statistically significant but may not make any business sense. There would be teams who would have extensive domain knowledge and can also help in drafting the conclusion into a story more effectively. The final story will be best if framed in a lucid way, which answers the question we drafted in the SCQ in the previous section. The SCQ with the solution will be a complete summary of the problem we are trying to solve with the end results/answer.

# Sensing the associated latent problems

Problems in real life are often never solo; they are mostly interconnected with multiple other problems. Decision science is also no exception to this feature. While solving a decision science problem, we would often reach a point where we understand that solving the associated problem is more important than the current problem. In some cases, solving associated problems becomes inevitable in order to move ahead. In such cases, we would not be able to practically solve the current problem until and unless we solve the associated problems.

Let's take an example to understand this better. Consider that while solving the problem to **identify the reasons for bad-quality detergent manufactured**, we inferred that the vital cause for the problem is the difference in raw materials from different vendors or because of insufficient labor in the manufacturing plant (assume). In some cases, the machinery downtime or inefficiency can also be vital reasons for the problem. In such cases, we are often solving multiple problems, though we started with solving just one simple problem. Problems are often interconnected in nature, and to solve the whole problem, we might need to solve multiple problems creating a problem universe. In this scenario, we would need to work on Vendor Management as a separate problem and **Workforce Optimization** as another. In real-life scenarios also, we face a similar situation. In many cases, solving the current problem might be less important as the bigger problem would be identified as another problem.

In core IoT problems, sensing the associated problems in the big picture gets really difficult as they are mostly latent. Sensing them to identify the problem universe becomes a bigger challenge. While solving an IoT or any other problem, we would move ahead in steps by breaking down the bigger problem into multiple smaller problems and then approaching them individually. Sensing latent problems is one of the most challenging step in problem solving. There is no predefined rule to identify associated latent problems in any problem solving exercise. For a simplified start, it would be relatively beneficial to revisit the final consolidated hypotheses list. We would need to go through the nuances of the hypotheses that we framed based on our heuristics and research, especially in cases where the results were counterintuitive while validating the hypotheses.

These areas can be used as a starting point for easy identification of associated latent problems. We would then need to perform extensive deep dives into the data with cross-dimensional analysis across every other dimension that we have in order to find any relevant and interesting signals. Identifying these signals from noise will require in-depth business and domain knowledge.

We'll consider revisiting this topic in more depth in Chapter 7, *Prescriptive Science & Decision Making*. By that time, we will have solved enough use cases and experiments to actually try and find latent signals from the problem to create the big picture.

# Designing the heuristic driven hypotheses matrix (HDH)

Designing the framework for heuristics-driven and data-driven hypotheses forms the foundation of the problem solving framework. The entire blueprint of the problem and problem universe can be captured in this single framework. This isn't a fancy document or any complicated tool. It's just a simple and straightforward way to structure and represent the problem solving approach.

There are three parts to it:

- **Heuristics-driven Hypotheses Matrix (HDH)**
- **Data-driven Hypotheses Matrix (DDH)**
- The convergence of HDH and DDH

The heuristics-driven hypotheses is the final and refined version of the hypotheses list that we discussed earlier. The matrix captures every minute detail we need from the hypotheses. It helps us prioritize and filter the hypotheses based on data availability and other results. It also helps us gather all our results in one single place and assimilate in order to render a perfect story. Once the entire HDH is populated, the initial part of the story rendering becomes smooth and straightforward.

The HDH matrix captures the entire blueprint of the initial part of the problem. However, as the problem evolves in scope and nature, we have different problems getting added to the current problem. The hypotheses also evolves as we discover counterintuitive results from our analysis. The evolved hypotheses and results are all captured in the DDH matrix. The HDH and DDH together create one unified structure to represent and solve the problem. The next steps and identification of associated problems and latent signals become extremely clear to interpret and solve.

We will explore the DDH matrix and the convergence of DDH and HDH in more detail in the next chapter when we will have the data, hypotheses, and results all in one place.

The following is a sample snapshot for the HDH:

| Idea | Hypotheses | Importance | Priority | Data Availability | Result | Research context | Needs Revisit |
|---|---|---|---|---|---|---|---|
| Category X | xxx | High | 1 | Yes | Postive | yyyy | No |
| Category X | x1 | Medium | 2 | Yes | Negative | yyyy | No |
| | | | | | | | |
| | | | | | | | |
| Category M | m | Medium | 8 | Yes | Negative | x-x-x-x-x | Yes |

The heuristics-driven hypotheses matrix

# Summary

In this chapter, you learned about the IoT problem universe by exploring Connected Operations and Connected Assets in detail. You also learned how to design a business use case for IoT using a concrete example to understand the detergent manufacturing problem in detail and design a blueprint for the problem using the problem solving framework.

This was accomplished by designing the SCQ and understanding how to get started with defining the problem holistically. We also studied about identifying the associated and latent problems and finally explored how to design HDH for the problem.

In the next chapter, we will solve a business use case with a dataset using R. All the context and research gathered in this chapter while defining the problem and designing it will be used to solve the use case step by step.

# 3
# The What and Why - Using Exploratory Decision Science for IoT

Problems in any given scenario always keep evolving and so does the solution. The hypotheses that we define while solving the problem will refine with new findings, which will then change the approach partially or completely. Hence, we need to keep our problem solving approach very agile. The problems we solve are often interconnected in nature; a big problem is often composed as a network of multiple smaller problems. These smaller problems can germinate from completely disparate domains, so we would need to accommodate diversity in our approach. Also, the solution can have different approaches based on the problem's scenario. The approach could be top-down, bottom-up, or hybrid; therefore, our solutions need to be flexible. Lastly, the problem can inflate to a mammoth size, thus our solutions need to be scalable.

In this chapter, we will solve the business problem that we defined in Chapter 2, *Studying the IoT Problem Universe and Designing a Use Case* using the problem solving framework. We will use a masked and encrypted data set from a detergent manufacturing firm to solve the problem. We will start with understanding the data and then try to answer the 'What and Why' questions, that is, descriptive and inquisitive analytics. In the course of the analysis, we might find counter intuitive results and latent patterns that we would not have considered before. We will keep our approach agile by accounting the new insights and dynamically adding the learnings to our solution. We will touch on the *When* question, that is, predictive analytics, in the next chapter.

In this chapter, we will cover the following topics:

- Identifying gold mines in data for decision making (*descriptive statistics*)
- Exploring each dimension of the IoT ecosystem through data (*univariates*)
- Studying relationships (*bivariate, correlations, and other statistical approaches*)
- Exploratory data analysis
- Root cause analysis

By the end of the chapter, we will have explored and studied the data in depth, have answers to the questions 'What and Why', and therefore surface the waves of descriptive and inquisitive analytics. We will also draft the first version of the **Data-driven Hypotheses (DDH)** Matrix and refine the previously designed **Heuristics-driven Hypotheses (HDH)**.

# Identifying gold mines in data for decision making

As a first step, before we dig deeper into the data exploration and analysis phase, we need to identify the gold mines in data. In the previous chapter, we designed the **heuristic-driven hypotheses (HDH)** while defining the problem. We now need to revisit the list and explore it to understand whether we are in a position to solve the problem using the data. We will be able to do this by examining and validating the data sources for the identified hypotheses. In case we do not have data to prove/disprove majority of our important hypotheses, it would not add any value by proceeding any further with the current approach. With data being available, we can get our hands dirty with codes for the solution.

## Examining data sources for the hypotheses

If we take a look at the *Prioritize and structure hypotheses based on the availability of data* section in the previous chapter, we can see that we have listed a couple of hypotheses that could be potential areas to mine insights. The following image showcases the list:

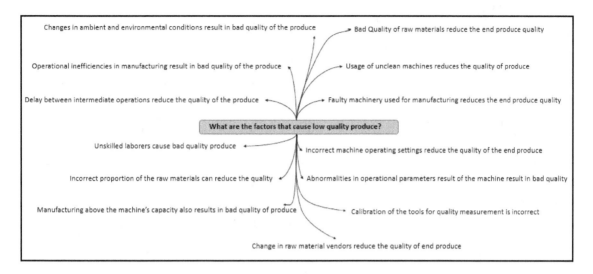

We have hypotheses surfacing incorrect proportions of raw materials being used, operational inefficiency, delay between intermediate operations, labor skills, ambient conditions, machine capacity, raw material quality, faulty machinery, machine cleanliness, machine operations configuration, raw material vendor details, operational parameters, and tool calibration-related topics. Let's quickly explore the data at a high level to understand whether we have good data points to analyze and validate our hypotheses.

Data can be downloaded from the repository for this chapter from your Packt account. A spreadsheet with the metadata for each column in the dataset is provided for reference. Before we get there, let's try to understand what different types of data would be required for our analysis. The answer would always be 'more the merrier', but based on our solution design, we should at least identify a few important areas for the problem.

As we can observe from the hypotheses, we will require data providing information in the following areas:

- **Raw material proportion / quantity / quality data**: Data regarding what are the different raw materials used, how much they were used, and were they used in excess. Also, the quality of the raw material measured across the important parameters.
- **Operational data**: Manufacturing process-related data that captures delays during processing, time exceeded or lost during processing, and so on.
- **Technician skillset data**: Data capturing skillsets of workers/technicians who handle the manufacturing process.

- **Machine configuration and calibration data**: Data capturing machine configuration and calibration settings during the manufacturing process.
- **Vendor data**: Data regarding information on the vendors for respective raw materials.
- **Other data sources**: Information regarding ambient conditions; external data that could add value for the current exercise.

You can glance through the csv file containing metadata for the use case.

Now, let's take a look at the data to explore what sources are available and also examine to what level they can be useful. The data provides a collection of 1,000 records representing 1,000 manufacturing processes. One row captures data that is corresponding to one manufacturing order, which is a complete batch. In the detergent manufacturing industry, the end product is manufactured in bulk and later catered to smaller packets. One manufacturing order/batch could be for 1,000 Kgs of detergent or even more. This entire batch is represented using a single row of data, which captures all the dimensions of the manufacturing process.

So what dimensions does the data capture?

- **End product-related information**: The product ID, product's name, required and produced quantity, and product output quality parameters (four different parameters)
- **Manufacturing environment information**: Details regarding the site and location, assembly line, and resources used
- **Raw material data**: Details of the raw material and its quality parameters at each stage of the manufacturing process
- **Operational data**: Data for the manufacturing process regarding the processing time, processing stages, indicators for delay at different stages, quantity of the raw material consumed, stage-/phase-level quality parameter data, stage-/phase-level processing time, and so on

The list seems pretty neat! What have we missed out?

# Data surfacing for problem solving

Though we have quite a good number of data points to move ahead, we do miss out data related to vendor information for raw materials, skillsets of technicians, and machine configuration data. However, our existing list is relatively rich enough to get started. With the existing data, we can attempt to prove > 60% of our ideated hypotheses and majority of them are very influential (high-priority). External data regarding ambient conditions and other events can be captured from the Internet for specific cases. We will keep this for later and now start with the data in more depth.

What dimensions do we have in each of the previously mentioned data sources?

# End product related information

The end product for our use case is a detergent powder, that is, Tide (assume). Information regarding how many Kgs of the detergent powder were supposed to be manufactured and were manufactured along with four different end quality parameters (namely, Quality Parameter 1, 2, 3, and 4) for the product are captured. These quality parameters decide how good or bad the end product is, and therefore decide whether the produce can be accepted or rejected.

# Manufacturing environment information

A variety of machinery is used for the manufacturing process and often different products are manufactured using the same resources/assembly lines at different times. A flag indicating whether the previous product manufactured in the resource or machine was similar or different. Similarly, processing time at each stage of manufacturing (usually 5-6 stages or phases are involved in the manufacturing of the product).

# Raw material data

Details regarding the raw materials used, its quality parameters before the manufacturing process, and intermediate quality parameters are captured. Let's say that in phase one, two raw materials are mixed and processed to form one output, which is then sent to phase two along with one or two other new raw materials, then quality parameters are measured and captured before the manufacturing process for individual raw materials and also after each stage for the combined mixture. Additionally, the required quantity/proportion of individual raw materials and the actual consumed quantity of the raw materials in each phase of the process are captured.

# Operational data

Operational data captures information regarding the time required for the processing in each phase/stage. Details regarding the different processing stages and indicators for delays at each individual stage are captured. In each stage, a stipulated amount of the raw material is supposed to be consumed in accordance with the predefined recipe. Sometimes these quantities are overridden by the operator/technician. Details regarding how much quantity was supposed to be consumed and how much was consumed along with the tolerance level for each individual raw material is captured.

Now that we have a detailed understanding of the data dimensions, let's get one step closer to actually solving the problem.

To study what factors affect the output quality of the detergent, let's try to explore the entire data dimension landscape. We will be using the **R programing language** to process and visualize the data along with the IDE **RStudio**-both of which are free and available for a wide variety of UNIX platforms, Windows, and Mac OS. The interpretation of results shared will be independent of the codes. In case you are not technically sound with programming, you can simply read through the codes or skip and read the results to understand the steps; you won't miss out any details of the problem solving and result interpretation steps.

We'll first import the data and explore the length and breadth of the dataset.

The data can be downloaded directly from my public repository (created for this book) or we can use the csv file by downloading it from the Packt repository. For convenience, we'll use the direct public repository link to get the data:

```
#Read data
url<-
"https://github.com/jojo62000/Smarter_Decisions/raw/master/Chapter%203/Data
/BO5341_IoTData.csv"

data<-read.csv(url)
#Check the dimensions of the dataset

 #Result

> dim(data)
[1] 1000   122

> colnames(data)[1:20]
 [1] "X"                          "Product_Qty_Unit"
 [3] "Product_ID"                 "Production_Start_Time"
 [5] "Output_QualityParameter1"   "Material_ID"
```

```
 [7]  "Product_Name"                "Output_QualityParameter2"
 [9]  "Output_QualityParameter3"    "Output_QualityParameter4"
[11]  "ManufacturingOrder_ID"       "AssemblyLine_ID"
[13]  "Order_Quantity"              "Produced_Quantity"
[15]  "Site_location"               "Manufacturing_StartDate"
[17]  "Manufacturing_EndDate"       "Manufacturing_StartTS"
[19]  "Manufacturing_EndTS"         "Total_Manufacturing_Time_mins"
```

Once the data is imported to the software, we check the size or dimension of the dataset. It shows us `1000 x 122`, which indicates that we have 1,000 rows of data and 122 columns. Additionally, by exploring the names of the first 20 columns in the data, we can see Product ID and Product Name, Output Quality Parameters, and a few other manufacturing process-related columns. To understand how the data is organized, we need to explore the content for each column:

As the number of columns is very high (>100), we will explore the data in small chunks (20 columns at a time). We will be using a couple of packages in R that are freely available over the Internet. To install a new package in R, use the following command:

```
> e.g. install.packages("package-name")
```

Once installed, you can load the package in memory using the 'library' command:

```
>library(package-name)
```

```
> library(dplyr)
> glimpse(data[1:20])
```

```
Observations: 1,000 Variables: 20 $ X (int) 1, 2, 3, 4, 5, 6, 7, 8, 9,... $
Product_Qty_Unit (fctr) KG, KG, KG, KG, KG, KG, KG... $ Product_ID (fctr)
Product_0407, Product_040... $ Production_Start_Time (int) 40656, 201026,
81616, 202857,.. $ Output_QualityParameter1 (dbl) 380.0000, 391.0821,
386.162,... $ Material_ID (int) 1234, 1234, 1234, 1234, 1234... $
Product_Name (fctr) Tide Plus Oxi, Tide Plus Ox... $
Output_QualityParameter2 (dbl) 15625.00, 14202.98, 16356.87,.. $
Output_QualityParameter3 (dbl) 39000.00, 36257.61, 39566.61,. $
Output_QualityParameter4 (dbl) 7550.000, 7151.502, 8368.513,. $
ManufacturingOrder_ID (int) 1, 2, 3, 4, 5, 6, 7, 8, 9, 10,. $
AssemblyLine_ID (fctr) Line 2, Line 2, Line 2, Line.. $ Order_Quantity
(int) 3800, 3800, 3800, 3800, 3800,. $ Produced_Quantity (dbl) 0, 3140, 0,
```

```
3800, 0, 4142,... $ Site_location (fctr) Pune, Pune, Pune, Pune, P... $
Manufacturing_StartDate (fctr) 20-02-2014 00:00, 24-02-201... $
Manufacturing_EndDate (fctr) 20-02-2014 00:00, 25-02-20... $
Manufacturing_StartTS (fctr) 20-02-2014 04:06, 24-02-20... $
Manufacturing_EndTS (fctr) 20-02-2014 10:06, 25-02-201.. $
Total_Manufacturing_Time_mins (int) 360, 1080, 180, 360, 240,...
```

We will be using a special package in R called dplyr for easy data engineering steps. The glimpse command from the dplyr package gives us a close view into the dataset. Here, we explore the contents of the first 20 columns and try to get a better sense of the data.

The first column X is an integer variable and a serial number. Let's validate this:

```
> length(unique(data$X)) #counting the number of unique values
[1] 1000
```

True, there are exactly 1,000 rows of data and the count of unique data points in the column is also 1,000.

Product_Qty_Unit indicates the unit of measurement for the quantity of the product, that is, detergent produced. Let's see what different units are used to measure the quantity of the product:

```
> unique(data$Product_Qty_Unit)
[1] KG
Levels: KG
```

There is exactly one value for the column, hence we can conclude that all records have the same unit of measurement for the product's produced quantity.

Product_ID & Material_ID uniquely identifies each product manufactured in the plant and we can check for the distinct number of products in the dataset. However, in our dataset, we have data for exactly one material and one product. Let's say that the product is Apple iPhone 6S and material is iPhone 6S 64 GB. In our case, we have the material *Tide Plus Oxi*, which is a detergent powder variant for the product *Tide*. The following code explores the distinct count of Product_ID and Material_ID in the data and views the value:

```
> length(unique(data$Product_ID))
[1] 1
> length(unique(data$Material_ID))
[1] 1
> length(unique(data$Product_Name))
[1] 1
> unique(data$Product_Name)
[1] Tide Plus Oxi
```

```
Levels: Tide Plus Oxi
```

The Output_QualityParameter 1 to 4 columns capture the final output quality of the product. These parameters together decide whether the end product can be accepted or rejected. Let's explore the output parameters for our problem.

The following code gives a summary (quantile distribution) of the four columns:

```
> summary(data$Output_QualityParameter1)
   Min. 1st Qu.  Median    Mean 3rd Qu.    Max.
  368.6   390.5   421.1   414.3   437.5   478.4
> summary(data$Output_QualityParameter2)
   Min. 1st Qu.  Median    Mean 3rd Qu.    Max.
  12130   14330   15220   15280   16110   20800
> summary(data$Output_QualityParameter3)
   Min. 1st Qu.  Median    Mean 3rd Qu.    Max.
  29220   35020   37150   37320   39650   48000
> summary(data$Output_QualityParameter4)
   Min. 1st Qu.  Median    Mean 3rd Qu.    Max.
   5725    7550    8012    8029    8485   10600
```

As we can see, all four parameters are completely different in terms of range, values, and distribution. Output Quality Parameter 1 mostly ranges from 350 to 500, whereas Parameter 2 ranges between 12000 and 25000 and so on.

ManufacturingOrder_ID indicates a unique key for each manufacturing order. Our data represents one row of data for each manufacturing order.

AssemblyLine_ID indicates on which line (the production line) was the product manufactured. Generally, in any manufacturing unit, there would be multiple lines manufacturing multiple products. Here, as we can see in the following code, we have two distinct lines used for the manufacturing, that is, Line 1 and Line 2:

```
> unique(data$AssemblyLine_ID)
[1] Line 2 Line 1
Levels: Line 1 Line 2
```

**Order_Quantity** and **Produced_Quantity** indicate the required quantity for the order and the actual produced quantity. Let's see if they are always the same or different:

```
> summary(data$Order_Quantity)
   Min. 1st Qu.  Median    Mean 3rd Qu.    Max.
      0    5000    5000    4983    5600    5600
> summary(data$Produced_Quantity)
   Min. 1st Qu.  Median    Mean 3rd Qu.    Max.
      0    4980    5280    5171    5757    8064
>#Let's summarize the absolute difference between the two
```

```
> summary(abs(data$Produced_Quantity - data$Order_Quantity))
   Min. 1st Qu.  Median    Mean 3rd Qu.    Max.
    0.0    89.6   201.6   344.8   336.0  5600.0
```

The preceding code gives the summary (that is, quantile distribution) of `Order_Quantity`, `Produced_Quantity`, and the absolute difference between the two. In most cases, the required order_quantity is around 5,000 Kgs (refer median in summary of order_quantity), but the produced quantity differs by a small fraction here and there. The summary of the absolute difference between the produced and required quantity shows an average, that is, mean of ~345 and median-50th percentile-at ~200, which indicates that there is definitely a difference in most cases between the required and produced quantity.

`Site_location` gives us the location of the manufacturing plant where the product was manufactured. In our use case, we have data for only one site (as our operations head is responsible for only one location):

```
> unique(data$Site_location)
[1] Pune
Levels: Pune
```

`Manufacturing_StartDate`, `Manufacturing_EndDate`, `Manufacturing_StartTS`, and `Manufacturing_EndTS` capture the start date, end date, start timestamp, and end timestamp for each manufacturing order. `Total_Manufacturing_Time_mins` captures the total processing time in minutes:

```
> summary(data$Total_Manufacturing_Time_mins)
   Min. 1st Qu.  Median    Mean   3rd Qu. Max.
    0.0   180.0   240.0   257.8   240.0  2880.0
```

From the distribution of processing time, we can easily identify that there are outliers (the huge difference between the 3rd quartile and maximum value), which we need to deal with separately. There are possibly some anomalous data points that have a processing time as 0.

This was a quick glimpse at the first 20 columns of the dataset. Let's move ahead with the next 20:

```
> colnames(data)[21:45]

 [1] "Stage1_PrevProduct"          "Stage1_DelayFlag"
 [3] "Stage1_ProcessingTime_mins"  "Stage1_RM1_QParameter2"
 [5] "Stage1_RM1_QParameter1"      "Stage1_RM2_QParameter2"
 [7] "Stage1_RM2_QParameter1"      "Stage1_RM2_RequiredQty"
 [9] "Stage1_RM2_ConsumedQty"      "Stage1_RM2_ToleranceQty"
[11] "Stage1_ProductChange_Flag"   "Stage1_QP1_Low"
[13] "Stage1_QP1_Actual"           "Stage1_QP1_High"
[15] "Stage1_QP2_Low"              "Stage1_QP2_Actual"
```

```
[17] "Stage1_QP2_High"          "Stage1_QP3_Low"
[19] "Stage1_QP3_Actual"        "Stage1_QP3_High"
[21] "Stage1_QP4_Low"           "Stage1_QP4_Actual"
[23] "Stage1_QP4_High"          "Stage1_ResourceName"
[25] "Stage2_DelayFlag"
```

As we explore the next 25 columns, we see columns giving us more information about stage-level details. All the attributes of stage one are suffixed with the word 'Stage1'. If we explore all the columns ahead, we can understand that there are exactly five stages in the manufacturing process for the current product of interest:

```
> #Identify the distinct Stages present in the data
> unique(substring(colnames(data)[grep("Stage",colnames(data))],1,6))
[1] "Stage1" "Stage2" "Stage3" "Stage4" "Stage5"
```

The preceding code first extracts the indices of column names that start with "Stage" and the first six characters from the names and finally checks the unique ones.

For Stage 1, we have `Stage1_DelayFlag` indicating whether there was a delay in processing Stage 1 during manufacturing; similarly, `Stage1_ProductChange_Flag` indicates whether there was a product change while manufacturing, that is, whether the previous product manufactured on the same machine was different or same:

```
> unique(data$Stage1_DelayFlag)
[1] No  Yes
Levels: No Yes
> unique(data$Stage1_ProductChange_Flag)
[1] No  Yes
Levels: No Yes
```

`Stage1_RM1_QParameter1` captures values for the first quality parameter for the first raw material used in Stage 1.

Decoding the naming convention is fairly straightforward-**Stage-x**. Here, x indicates the stage of processing, which could be any value from 1-5. RM stands for Raw Material and hence RM1 for Raw Material 1 and so on. QParameter1 indicates the quality parameter and 1 indicates the first one. Therefore, **Stage1_RM1_QParameter1** indicates the first quality parameter for the first raw material used in Stage 1. Similarly, **Stage1_RM1_QParameter2** indicates the second quality parameter for the first raw material used in Stage 1.At a particular stage, there could be multiple raw materials used and each of them could individually have multiple quality parameters.

Moving on, **Stage1_QP2_Low** indicates the second quality parameter for the resultant combined mixture in Stage 1. The 'Low', 'High', and 'Actual' indicate the respective values for each parameter. 'Low' indicates the upper control limit, 'High' indicates the upper control limit, and 'Actual' indicates the actual value of the quality test for the resultant mixture.

Similarly, **Stage1_RM2_ConsumedQty** indicates the quantity of Raw Material 2 consumed in stage 1 and **Stage1_RM2_RequiredQty** indicates the required quantity for the respective material. At each stage, each raw material will have a different quantity level for consumption and tolerance level for variation. The required, consumed, and tolerance for each individual raw material may or may not be available.

**'Stage1_PrevProduct'** captures the previous product that was manufactured on the machine during the previous manufacturing order and **Stage1_ResourceName** indicates which resource/machine was used for the process in Stage 1.

The same convention follows for the next stages, that is, Stage 2 to Stage 5.

Let's explore the details of Stage 1 in more detail:

```
> summary(data$Stage1_RM1_QParameter1)
   Min. 1st Qu.  Median    Mean 3rd Qu.    Max.
   3765    4267    4275    4275    4319    4932
> summary(data$Stage1_RM1_QParameter2)
   Min. 1st Qu.  Median    Mean 3rd Qu.    Max.
  2.400   3.361   3.394   3.394   3.454   4.230
> summary(data$Stage1_RM2_QParameter1)
   Min. 1st Qu.  Median    Mean 3rd Qu.    Max.
  132.0   138.8   146.8   146.8   155.0   162.7
> summary(data$Stage1_RM2_QParameter2)
   Min. 1st Qu.  Median    Mean 3rd Qu.    Max.
  41.29   46.53   50.22   50.22   52.76   68.82
```

For stage 1, we have two raw materials used, and for each of the raw materials, we have two quality parameters measured. The values of each quality parameter are in a different range.

Similarly, if we look at the required and consumed quantity for each raw material in Stage 1, we can see that there are minute differences, and in quite a few cases we can affirmatively say that these are above the tolerance quantity:

```
> summary(data$Stage1_RM2_RequiredQty)
   Min. 1st Qu.  Median    Mean 3rd Qu.    Max.
  300.0   450.0   450.0   443.7   504.0   504.0
> summary(data$Stage1_RM2_ConsumedQty)
   Min. 1st Qu.  Median    Mean 3rd Qu.    Max.
```

```
   291.0    448.5    451.5    442.9    505.7    505.7
> summary(data$Stage1_RM2_ToleranceQty)
   Min. 1st Qu.  Median    Mean 3rd Qu.    Max.
  1.000   1.500   1.500   1.478   1.680   1.680


> Studying the summary of absolute difference between Required and Consumed
Quantity

> summary(abs(data$Stage1_RM2_RequiredQty- data$Stage1_RM2_ConsumedQty))
   Min. 1st Qu.  Median    Mean 3rd Qu.    Max.
  0.000   1.500   1.500   2.522   1.680  10.080
```

On a similar note, after the processing in stage 1 is complete, we have a final mixture created from Raw Material 1 and Raw Material 2. The Stage1_QP1_Low column has values for the lower threshold of the quality parameter of the final mixture. Around four different quality parameters are measured at each stage after the processing is complete:

```
> summary(data$Stage1_QP1_Low)
   Min. 1st Qu.  Median    Mean 3rd Qu.    Max.
  180.0   188.3   195.5   203.1   217.4   254.8
> summary(data$Stage1_QP1_Actual)
   Min. 1st Qu.  Median    Mean 3rd Qu.    Max.
  194.4   246.5   270.0   277.8   298.7  2760.0
> summary(data$Stage1_QP1_High)
   Min. 1st Qu.  Median    Mean 3rd Qu.    Max.
  280.0   292.9   304.2   315.4   337.9   396.4
```

Lastly, we have the resource name that indicates the machine that was used for the manufacturing process and information regarding the previous product manufactured. In all, we have five distinct machines used in Stage 1 and around 26 distinct products that were previously manufactured before manufacturing the current product:

```
> length(unique(data$Stage1_PrevProduct))
[1] 26
> length(unique(data$Stage1_ResourceName))
[1] 5
```

In a similar way, data dimensions for Stages 2, 3, 4, and 5 can be studied. The naming conventions of the column names for each stage are in sync with Stage 1. A detailed self-exploration of all columns before we move on to the exploratory data analysis step is recommended.

Finally, we can find a column named **Detergent_Quality,** which defines whether the product manufactured was finally accepted as `Good Quality` or `Bad Quality`. This dimension will be of great interest for our upcoming analyses. The following code showcases the summary of the column. We can see that approximately 20% of the produce is rejected due to bad quality:

```
> summary(data$Detergent_Quality)
 Bad  Good
 225   775
```

## Summarizing the data surfacing activity

Our data exploratory exercises to surface the data are still naïve. We just have a basic understanding about what the hypotheses we could prove, what the data looks like, and what information the data provides, and so on All these exercises give us a glimpse only from a bird's-eye perspective. We explored the data dimensions of the manufacturing process such as the location, product manufactured, produced and required quantity, and other high-level details. For Stage 1, we explored the quality parameters of individual raw materials used and the resultant mixture in stage 1. We studied the required and consumed quantity for each raw material along with the respective tolerance level. We also peeped into the various categorical factors such as stage delays, product change flags, and processing time for the stage. Further self-exploration of all the data dimensions for Stages 2, 3, 4, and 5 is highly recommended.

## Feature exploration

In our data surfacing activities, we glanced at the data at a broad level. With this understanding, we can feasibly identify the promising areas in the data where we can dig deeper. A thorough drill-down into the specifically identified sweet spots or pocket areas is a very lucrative deal for every decision scientist. In this section, we won't be going into the length and breadth of the deep dive; this would be explored more in the coming sections. The current scope is to identify the sweet spots in data surfaced during our initial exercise.

We'll first start by understanding the features for the drill-down, that is, 'Feature Engineering', which is a process to create features/variables using domain knowledge. While we explored the data at a high level, we saw some variables/columns in the dataset that could add much value from a direct usage perspective. For example, the manufacturing start date or end date is something that won't really add value from the initial vibes. However, if we take a closer look, it could very much be possible that the day of the week or the month of manufacturing can have an impact. Reasons could be various, and in many cases the variation could be bare minimum in the end comparison; however, if one such rare case blossoms in our use case, the benefits could be huge. To understand this better, let's take the analogy of cooking. The time required to sauté food would have minute variations based on seasons. In some specific manufacturing cases, such minute variations can lead to erroneous produce; hence, studying the seasonality and taking preventive measures accordingly for the process is an activity that becomes indispensable.

Similarly, there are a couple of variables that indicate the quantity of raw material consumed, required, and tolerance level for each of the raw materials at different stages. These are three different variables in the datasets, but we can render a new feature indicating what percentage of deviance was observed in the raw material consumption process. Try to think from a layman's perspective: one feature giving more powerful and easily understandable results is far better than multiple variables together inferring the same result. The process keeps evolving; in many cases, the features we create may not be only domain knowledge-driven, but instead a combination of statistics and business together. There might be scenarios where we need more powerful statistical techniques to uncover latent features from the data that could help us understand the problem better. Similarly, there are also completely statistical-driven features that can be created using sophisticated algorithms such as PCA. These features may not be really intuitive from a layman's perspective, but aid dramatically when we are trying to get deeper into the problem (inquisitive and predictive).

In the coming sections and the next chapter, we will delve deeper into each of these scenarios to solve our problem better.

# Understanding the data landscape

### Adding context to the data

As of now, we have approached the data in the data way, that is, we have limited domain knowledge for the data and problem. In this scenario, we understand the data from 1,000 feet above the ground. We need to come closer and understand the data from a more domain- and process-oriented way so that we could solve the problem better. After receiving the data, the normal approach in any decision science use case would be to explore the data end to end. This covers diving deep into every dimension of the data and then trying to uncover latent signals and patterns to understand how the problem can be related using data-driven insights. What we miss out over here is the domain context! This is the most important context. With more detailed domain context and process-level information, we would be in a much better position to make sense out of the data.

The next step in identifying the gold mines in the data is to understand the domain and process-level information associated with the data. The usual approach would have been to perform initial data surfacing exercises and then approach the **subject matter expert (SME)** or domain expert with the questions and clarifications in the data. Here, for convenience, the required initial context and a few domain-related aspects are provided upfront. In a general problem solving scenario, it is highly recommended to approach an SME with all the consolidated questions required to get the complete data landscape.

# Domain context for the data

The following excerpts provide domain knowledge about the data and problem in more depth. In a real-life scenario, this task can be achieved with the help of a few domain experts, data experts, and operation experts with a few verbal conversations and domain research.

The company-P & G in our use case-is a leading consumer goods manufacturer and manufactures a plethora of products across the globe. One of the many manufacturing units of the company is located in Pune, India. Pune's manufacturing unit has around 10 assembly lines. (One assembly line is responsible for the manufacturing of one product end to end.) Each of these assembly lines are equipped with multiple machines, that is, resources, where each machine takes care of a phase/stage in the manufacturing process. One assembly line can manufacture multiple products, such as detergents of different brands can be classified as different products and can be manufactured on the same assembly line.

Our use case deals with the manufacturing of a detergent powder, that is, a variant of **Tide** (assume). In a single process, around 5,000 Kgs of detergent powder is produced that can then be packaged into packets of 1 kg/0.5 kg and so on. The manufacturing process is partially automated; the technician responsible for the process can sometimes override a few settings to overcome erroneous produce. To understand this better, let's understand an analogy of cooking curry as an example. Consider that you are cooking tomato curry and you are well aware of the recipe. Midway into your cooking exercise, you find out that you have added too much water. You then heat and sauté the mixture for a little longer to get the desired curry in your recipe. Sometimes you may add extra salt or spices when you find out the same product from a different vendor has difference in taste. The same is applicable to the detergent manufacturing process. Even though a major part of the process is automated, it is possible that the same product can be manufactured in multiple ways and still lead to the same result (properties).

The detergent manufacturing process in our use case is separated into five different stages/phases. Each stage has a specific process to be completed. (While cooking noodles, we can classify boiling noodles as Stage 1, then cooking veggies with spices as Stage 2, and then finally sautéing boiled noodles with veggies as Stage 3.) Raw materials can be added at different stages in the process. In our use case, Stage 1 has two raw materials getting mixed together to form a mixture. This mixture is processed by heating for several minutes in a machine. Once processed, the mixture is then passed on to stage 2, where the mixture is then processed under different settings without adding any new raw materials (ingredients) and then passed on to the next stage. In Stage 3, two new raw materials are added and then the resultant mixture is processed for several minutes to create a new mixture. The output of Stage 3 is then passed on to Stage 4 and Stage 5, where it is further processed under different settings such as pressure/temperature and so on Finally, the output of Stage 5 is the detergent produced in the manufacturing process.

The following diagram captures the entire process at a high level:

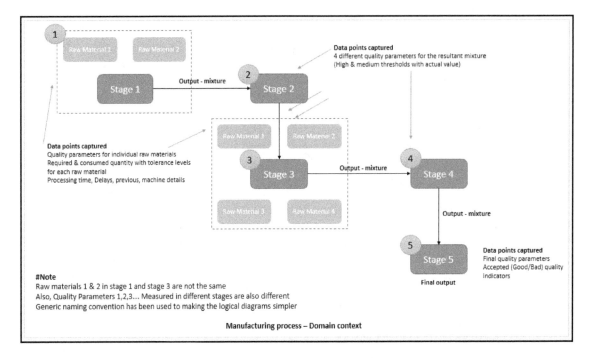

Manufacturing process – Domain context

The entire manufacturing process is monitored and controlled using the **supervisory control and data acquisition** (**SCADA**) system. The outputs and properties of interest at each stage during and after the process are available to the technician responsible for the process. The data is collected through SCADA systems and then stored to other sources where it can be used for investigation and analysis. In our use case, we are considering data for only one product manufactured in one site located in Pune (India).

For security reasons, names of the raw materials and quality parameter names have been masked. Similarly, values of the quality parameter have been scaled algorithmically to change the visual representation but to keep the relationships intact. In case the values of a few quality parameters seem to make no scientific sense, assume that the values are masked.

The entire process for data acquisition, processing, and analyzing in the manufacturing plant can be studied from the following figure:

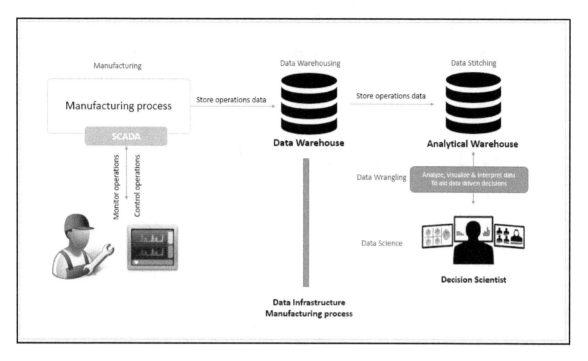

The manufacturing process is carried on in the factory where a technician is supervising the overall process. The supervisor has access to a sophisticated software and system-controlling infrastructure, which helps in monitoring the quality parameters and process-related parameters in real time. Based on existing conditions, the technician may take a call to heat or process for a longer duration in a particular stage. The data monitored during the manufacturing process is then stored in a data warehouse, which can later be used for investigation and analysis. The decision scientist then accesses the analytical warehouse (analytically-ready data warehouse) for his analyses. The scientist extracts, processes, and gleans through vast volumes of data to analyze and find patterns that aid in the decision making process.

The process of creating analytical tables specifically tailored for use cases is called **Data Stitching** (collating data from different sources together for a specific use case). Similarly, the process of using these datasets to explore data, derive new data, and uncover latent patterns is called **Data Wrangling.** Finally, the art and science of using the newly created, derived, and existing datasets to find patterns, solve problems, and answer business questions is called **Decision Science**.

# Exploring each dimension of the IoT Ecosystem through data (Univariates)

Let's dig deeper into each dimension in the IoT use case to understand more realistically what the data showcases. We will perform extensive univariate analysis to study and visualize the entire data landscape.

## What does the data say?

We visited the data dimensions while exploring the gold mines in data (in the previous section) and understood that Product_Qty_Unit, Product_ID, Material_ID, and Product_Name indicate that the columns contain a single value. Therefore, we conclude that the data in the use case is provided for a specific product and its output is measured in Kgs. Let's start exploring **Order Quantity** and **Produced Quantity** in depth. We initially studied the data dimensions using summary commands that gave us the percentile distribution. Let's take this one step further.

Order Quantity and Produced Quantity are both continuous variables, that is, a variable that can have infinite number of values possible (say, any number between 0 and a million). To study continuous variables, we can use a histogram or frequency polygon and study how well the data is distributed:

```
#We will use the library 'ggplot2' to visualize the data
> library(ggplot2)

#Plot a Histogram for Order Quantity

> #setting Bin width to 500, as we have a range of 0 to 5000+
> ggplot(data = data, aes(data$Order_Quantity))
+geom_histogram(binwidth=500)

#Plot a Histogram for Produced Quantity
> ggplot(data = data, aes(data$Produced_Quantity))
+geom_histogram(binwidth=500)
```

The preceding code plots two separate histograms for the Order Quantity and Produced Quantity variables. With just a simple glance, we can clearly identify that there are differences between the two variables, but a bit difficult to do an apple-to-apple comparison. The width of each bin in the plot is 500, and we can see that the values in Produced Quantity are more spread across 2,500 to 7,500 than Order Quantity:

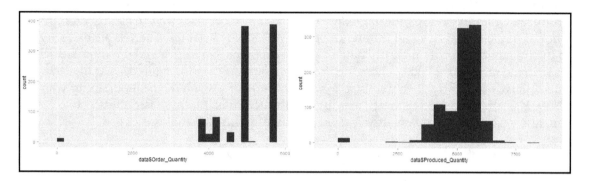

To make the comparison easier, let's use a frequency polygon. A frequency polygon can be used instead of a histogram in cases where we have to compare two data dimensions together:

```
ggplot(data = data) +
geom_freqpoly(binwidth=500,aes(data$Order_Quantity),color="red",size=1) +
geom_freqpoly(binwidth
=500,aes(data$Produced_Quantity),color="blue",size=1)
```

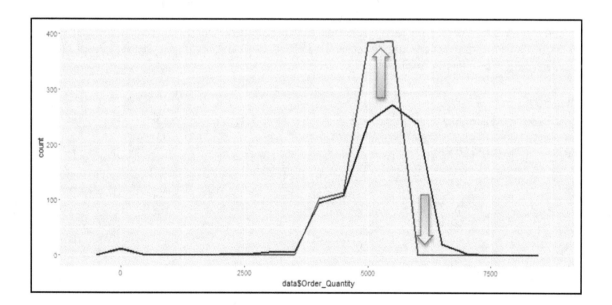

The preceding plot represents a frequency polygon showcasing the distribution of Produced Quantity and Required Quantity on the same chart. As we can clearly identify from the data, there is a small difference between the two variables. There is a small surge in the frequency of order quantity between 5000-6000; the same surge is compensated with a sag in the range 6000-7000, where the Produced Quantity leads Ordered Quantity. In a nutshell, we can clearly conclude that, for many resources, when the order quantity was ~5,000 Kgs, the produced quantity was higher. Instead of using these variables as two separate variables, we can create a feature and use it in further analyses:

```
>ggplot(data = data) +
    geom_freqpoly(binwidth=10,aes(abs(data$Order_Quantity -
data$Produced_Quantity)))
```

Observing the following plot, we can affirmatively say that there are quite a few records with a 0-500 unit deviation from the actual order. Rather than using the two variables separately, we can use the deviation in each manufacturing order. The new variable conveys more information than the other two together. Similarly, we can also consider creating a new category for the deviation, that is, high, medium, and low. We can look at the distribution of the deviation; consider the first 30-40 percentile as Low, the next segment as Medium, and the last segment as High approximately. There is a very high chance that all the deviations in a similar range will be a result of similar behavior, that is, similar errors or patterns in the manufacturing process. Therefore, defining a category to represent them together will aid in easier analyses:

```
#Creating a new feature/segments for Quantity deviations

>temp<-(abs(data$Order_Quantity - data$Produced_Quantity))
>data$Quantity_Deviation<-ifelse(temp<= 150,"Low",ifelse(temp<=
300,"Medium","High"))

>ggplot(data, aes(x=Quantity_Deviation)) + geom_bar()
```

The plot is placed on the left-hand side of the following diagram:

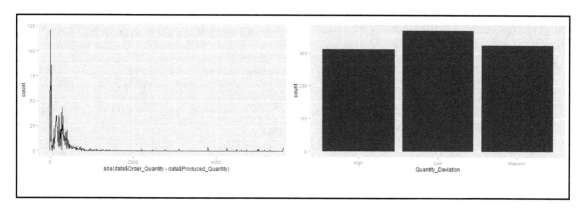

The figure on the left showcases the distribution of absolute deviation between the produced and required order quantity, whereas the image on the right shows the histogram for the derived feature, that is, **Quality Deviation** segments.

Next, let's explore the date- and time-related dimensions. We can see three variables in the data, namely, `Manufacturing_StartTS`, `Manufacturing_EndTS`, and `Total_Manufacturing_Time_mins`, which give details about the date and time for the manufacturing. Even though we can use the processing time taken as an important variable, the start and end timestamp won't really add value as the variable would probably be having 1,000 distinct timestamps. Instead, if we try to create a feature where we can gather information from less data, interpreting patterns will become phenomenally easier. We can create features such as the hour of the day, day of the week, and month to understand whether the variation in time will have any impact on the end problem. Also, if we create a feature where we can overlay the processing time taken along with the seasonal feature, the new resultant feature will be a very powerful dimension in our problem:

```
>
quantile(data$Total_Manufacturing_Time_mins,c(0.1,0.5,0.7,0.9,0.95,0.98,0.9
9,1.0))
    10%    50%    70%    90%    95%    98%    99%   100%
  180.0  240.0  240.0  300.0  360.0  600.0  842.4 2880.0
```

Exploring the percentile distribution of processing time, we can clearly see that there is an outlier (a huge jump from the 98th percentile to 100th percentile). As a thumb rule, to remove outliers, we replace all values higher than the 98th percentile with the 98th percentile. Without outlier treatment, there is a high chance that you might misinterpret the data:

```
#Treating outliers, by replacing the values above 98th percentile with the
98th percentile

> threshold<-quantile(data$Total_Manufacturing_Time_mins,0.98)
> temp<-data$Total_Manufacturing_Time_mins
> temp<-ifelse(temp>threshold,threshold,temp)
> data$Total_Manufacturing_Time_mins<-temp
> quantile(data$Total_Manufacturing_Time_mins)

  0%   25%   50%   75%  100%
   0   180   240   240   600
```

The other variables that capture information at the manufacturing process level-Product ID, Product Name, Manufacturing Order ID, Assembly Line ID, and Site Location-are variables that were explored in the previous sections (Identifying gold mines). All other dimensions provide us with context on the data such as the product being manufactured, the location of the manufacturing plant, and so on As these dimensions have only one degree of representation, that is, only one value, except for **Assembly Line ID**, it will not be of much value to consider them in the onward journey. Assembly Line ID will be of use in further analysis as it identifies the assembly line that was used to manufacture the product.

Moving on, let's explore the dimensions with an added level of granularity-stage-wise processing. The following are the dimensions that represent the Stage 1 process:

```
> colnames(data[21:44])

 [1] "Stage1_PrevProduct"           "Stage1_DelayFlag"
 [3] "Stage1_ProcessingTime_mins"   "Stage1_RM1_QParameter2"
 [5] "Stage1_RM1_QParameter1"       "Stage1_RM2_QParameter2"
 [7] "Stage1_RM2_QParameter1"       "Stage1_RM2_RequiredQty"
 [9] "Stage1_RM2_ConsumedQty"       "Stage1_RM2_ToleranceQty"
[11] "Stage1_ProductChange_Flag"    "Stage1_QP1_Low"
[13] "Stage1_QP1_Actual"            "Stage1_QP1_High"
[15] "Stage1_QP2_Low"               "Stage1_QP2_Actual"
[17] "Stage1_QP2_High"              "Stage1_QP3_Low"
[19] "Stage1_QP3_Actual"            "Stage1_QP3_High"
[21] "Stage1_QP4_Low"               "Stage1_QP4_Actual"
[23] "Stage1_QP4_High"              "Stage1_ResourceName"
```

We'll start with `Stage1_PrevProduct` and `Stage1_ProductChange_Flag` that represent the previous product manufactured on the same assembly line and a flag indicating whether the product manufactured was different. The product change flag is straightforward and can be used directly for our analysis. It explains that around 35% cases exist where the previous product manufactured on the same line was a different one. We can hypothesize that the cases where we have a product change while manufacturing in the same assembly line might have more errors due to the slight chemical effects of other raw materials used earlier.

# Exploring Previous Product...

To make our representation easier, let's find out the percentage of occurrences of each individual Previous Product dimension (stage1):

```
>library(dplyr)
#Applying a group by operation using 'tapply' for aggregated count
> temp<-
as.data.frame(tapply(data$Product_ID,data$Stage1_PrevProduct,length))

> colnames(temp)<-"prev_product_count"
> temp$Product<-rownames(temp)

> temp$product_perc<-temp$prev_product_count/sum(temp$prev_product_count)

> temp<-arrange(temp,desc(product_perc))
> temp<-mutate(temp,cum_perc=cumsum(product_perc))

> nrow(temp)
[1] 26

> head(temp)
```

|   | prev_product_count | Product | product_perc | cum_perc |
|---|---|---|---|---|
| 1 | 469 | Product_545 | 0.469 | 0.469 |
| 2 | 352 | Product_543 | 0.352 | 0.821 |
| 3 | 30 | Product_547 | 0.030 | 0.851 |
| 4 | 26 | Product_546 | 0.026 | 0.877 |
| 5 | 18 | Product_555 | 0.018 | 0.895 |
| 6 | 16 | Product_563 | 0.016 | 0.911 |

We can see that there are around 26 unique products that were previously manufactured on the same line before manufacturing the product Tide. 26 is quite a big number-not sure whether we will be able to find any pattern here. Let's look at how they are distributed in the data. The preceding code aggregates the frequency count of the previous products and calculates the percentage of the overall frequency. The product_perc column displays the percentage of records each product caters in the data. Taking a cumulative sum of the percentage and displaying the first six ordered rows, we see that there is a huge gap in the percentage distribution of the previous products. Product_545 was manufactured ~50% times before "Tide" on the same line. The top five products from the total of 26 contribute to ~90% of the data. We can consider either the top five and the rest 21 as 'Others' or only two categories-Product_545 and All others-as the first one is phenomenally higher in percentage than all others. Creating a new feature either with six categories, that is, top five and all others or two categories, Product_545 and All others can be useful to understand the causes of bad products. Clubbing together multiple categories and reducing the levels not only reduces the noise in the data, but also makes pattern finding easier and more intuitive for people as well as algorithms. For now, let's create both of these features; later we will figure out which one would be better to use:

- Creating the first feature:

```
>temp<-ifelse(data$Stage1_PrevProduct== "Product_545",
"Product_545","Others")
>data$Stage1_PrevProduct_1<-as.factor(temp)

>temp<-ifelse(data$Stage1_PrevProduct %in%
 c("Product_545","Product_543",
"Product_547","Product_546","Product_555"),as.character(data$Stage1_PrevPro
duct),"Others")
```

- Creating the second alternative feature:

```
>data$Stage1_PrevProduct_2<-as.factor(temp)

>summary(data$Stage1_PrevProduct_1)
    Others      Product_545
      531          469

> summary(data$Stage1_PrevProduct_2)
 Others Product_543 Product_545 Product_546 Product_547 Product_555
   105         352         469          26          30          18
```

Similar to the overall processing time, we have outliers in the Stage 1 processing time; we can treat the outliers in the same way that we did earlier using the 98th percentile cutoff:

```
> quantile(data$Stage1_ProcessingTime_mins,c(0.1,0.5,0.9,0.98,1))
      10%        50%        90%        98%       100%
   35.0380    50.1500    79.0500   136.1852  2578.4800


> threshold<-quantile(data$Stage1_ProcessingTime_mins,0.98)


> temp<-data$Stage1_ProcessingTime_mins
> temp<-ifelse(temp>threshold,threshold,temp)


> summary(temp)
   Min. 1st Qu.  Median    Mean 3rd Qu.    Max.
   0.92   40.77   50.15   52.28   57.57  136.20
> data$Stage1_ProcessingTime_mins<-temp
```

Moving on, let's study the **Raw Material Quality** raw materials. In stage 1, there are two raw materials used, and each of them have two individual quality parameters measured. As explored in the previous section (identifying gold mines), all the quality parameters measured for the raw materials are continuous in nature and the standard deviation is much lower than the mean. Therefore, we will not require any major transformations to the variable. At the most, we may need to standardize them during our predictive analysis journey (more context in the next chapter).

The following codes aid in studying the mean, standard deviation, minimum, and maximum of all the quality parameters for each raw material in Stage 1:

```
#creating a temporary dataframe
> sample<-data[,c("Stage1_RM1_QParameter1","Stage1_RM1_QParameter2",
+                "Stage1_RM2_QParameter1","Stage1_RM2_QParameter2")]
> t(apply(sample,2,function(x) c(min=min(x),max=max(x),sd=sd(x))))
```

|  | min | max | mean | sd |
|---|---|---|---|---|
| Stage1_RM1_QParameter1 | 3765.00000 | 4932.332160 | 4274.782808 | 210.39327 |
| Stage1_RM1_QParameter2 | 2.40000 | 4.229568 | 3.394041 | 0.2802995 |
| Stage1_RM2_QParameter1 | 132.00000 | 162.657600 | 146.784481 | 8.62362 |
| Stage1_RM2_QParameter2 | 41.28572 | 68.820011 | 50.222232 | 4.38986 |

Moving on to the next dimension, we have Stage1_RM2_RequiredQty, Stage1_RM2_ConsumedQty, and Stage1_RM2_ToleranceQty. The names are intuitive enough for us to understand how they help. Let's take a look at the first six rows of data to get some more details:

```
> head(data[,c("Stage1_RM2_RequiredQty",
"Stage1_RM2_ConsumedQty","Stage1_RM2_ToleranceQty")])
```

```
Stage1_RM2_RequiredQty Stage1_RM2_ConsumedQty Stage1_RM2_ToleranceQty
1                  300                    292
2                  300                    292
3                  300                    292
4                  300                    292
5                  300                    292
6                  300                    292
```

As we can see, it shows us the quantity of respective raw materials required and how much was consumed along with the deviation that is allowed. The first six rows all seem to be outside the normal consumption range. Let's create a feature called `Stage1_RM2_ConsumptionFlag` that will indicate whether the consumption was normal or abnormal based on the difference between the Required and Consumed Qty along with the tolerance. We can notice that we have abnormal cases in around 50% of the cases:

```
> temp<-abs(data$Stage1_RM2_RequiredQty -
data$Stage1_RM2_ConsumedQty)
> temp<-ifelse(temp>data$Stage1_RM2_ToleranceQty,
 "Abnormal","Normal")
> data$Stage1_RM2_Consumption_Flag <-as.factor(temp)

> summary(data$Stage1_RM2_Consumption_Flag)

  Abnormal    Normal
      489       511
```

Apart from the raw material consumption details and quality parameters, we have the quality parameters for the resultant mixture in Stage 1 (also in all other stages). There are in all four quality parameters measured for the mixture. The lower and higher threshold of each quality parameter is also provided. Let's have a look at the data:

```
head(data[,32:34],3)
  Stage1_QP1_Low Stage1_QP1_Actual Stage1_QP1_High
1        180.000          250.0000          280.00
2        181.035          231.3225          281.61
3        182.070          242.7600          283.22
```

As we can see, for each quality parameter, we have the actual value along with the lower and higher threshold for each row. Similar to the previous transformations, we can create a new feature that represents whether the quality parameter was in the normal range or outside the range:

```
> temp<-ifelse(data$Stage1_QP1_Actual > data$Stage1_QP1_Low &
data$Stage1_QP1_Actual > data$Stage1_QP1_High,"Normal","Abnormal")
> summary(as.factor(temp))

Abnormal    Normal
   976        24
```

However, what we see here is that more than 90% of the readings are abnormal. Then it wouldn't really add value if we just classify them as normal and abnormal. In such scenarios, we can add more intelligence to the variable by showcasing the percentage of deviation from the normal range. Let's say that the expected value was between 90 and 110 and the actual value was 140, then the % deviation from normal is mean (90,110) = 100 and deviation from 100 is 40, therefore 40%.

Let's calculate the % deviation for Quality Parameter 1 for Stage1:

```
> temp<-(data$Stage1_QP1_High + data$Stage1_QP1_Low)/2
> temp<-abs(data$Stage1_QP1_Actual-temp)/temp
> data$Stage1_QP1_deviation<-temp
> summary(data$Stage1_QP1_deviation)

    Min.  1st Qu.  Median    Mean  3rd Qu.    Max.
 0.00000  0.04348 0.11300 0.13180 0.13040  9.67800
```

We do see outliers, ~900% deviation; we can process them in the same way that we did earlier using the 98th percentile cutoff:

```
> threshold<-quantile(data$Stage1_QP1_deviation,0.98)
> temp<-data$Stage1_QP1_deviation
> temp<-ifelse(temp>threshold,threshold,temp)
> summary(temp)

   Min. 1st Qu.  Median    Mean 3rd Qu.    Max.
0.00000 0.04348 0.11300 0.11280 0.13040 0.26090

> data$Stage1_QP1_deviation<-temp
```

Similarly, based on the conditions, we can create features for the other three quality parameters for the Stage 1 final mixture. The following code creates similar features for the remaining three quality parameters in Stage 1:

```
#Extract the required column names
col_matrix<-t(matrix(colnames(data)[32:43],ncol=4,nrow=3))
#Iterate through loop for all the remaining 3 parameters
for(x in 2:nrow(col_matrix))
                        {
                            low<-col_matrix[x,1]
                            high<-col_matrix[x,3]
                            actual<-col_matrix[x,2]
                            temp<-(data[,low] + data[,high])/2
                            temp<-abs(data[,actual]-temp)/temp
                            var<-paste0("Stage1_QP",x,"_deviation")
                            print(var)
                            data[,var]<-temp

                        }
```

In a similar way, we can explore each dimension at the stage-level granularity and transform the dimension to suit our needs better for all other stages (2, 3, 4, and 5).

 It is recommended that you explore the remaining stage data dimensions using a similar approach.

Finally, it's time to study the final outcome. The final mixture that is an output from Stage 5 is measured using four quality parameters. The end product is discarded or accepted on the basis of these four parameters. Let's have a look at the output:

```
#Collecting all the 4 output parameters together
> a<-c("Output_QualityParameter1","Output_QualityParameter2",
"Output_QualityParameter3","Output_QualityParameter4")
> head(data[,a])
```

| | Output_QualityParameter1 | Output_QualityParameter2 | Output_QualityParameter3 | Output_QualityParameter4 |
|---|---|---|---|---|
| 1 | 380.0000 | 15625.00 | 39000.00 | 7550.000 |
| 2 | 391.0821 | 14202.98 | 36257.61 | 7151.502 |
| 3 | 386.1621 | 16356.87 | 39566.61 | 8368.513 |
| 4 | 392.7473 | 12883.11 | 36072.71 | 7164.511 |
| 5 | 386.8247 | 12485.48 | 34779.19 | 8256.930 |
| 6 | 394.4137 | 13013.65 | 36613.40 | 7257.613 |

From these four parameters, we have the final judgement on the manufactured product, whether it can be accepted or rejected:

```
> sample<-data[,a]
> t(apply(sample,2,function(x)
c(min=min(x),max=max(x),mean=mean(x),sd=sd(x))))
```

```
                          min        max       mean          sd
Output_QualityParameter1   368.5864   478.445   414.2725    25.13131
Output_QualityParameter2 12127.8443 20796.288 15278.1903  1258.28580
Output_QualityParameter3 29222.8600 47995.730 37320.7930  3063.96085
Output_QualityParameter4  5724.6521 10595.364  8029.0012   643.45730
```

As we can clearly guess, the output quality parameters also have a standard deviation lower than the mean.

From these four output quality parameters, we have the final quality of the detergent being determined using some weighted algorithm. The final outcome can be viewed as follows:

```
> summary(data$Detergent_Quality)
 Bad Good
 225  775
```

# Summarizing this section

In the entire exercise, we explored the different data dimensions in the IoT ecosystem in a more granular way. We now have a more detailed understanding of what each dimension has to offer and how we can use them further in our analysis. Next, we will explore the relationships that exist between these different dimensions.

# Studying relationships

The end result of the produce from the manufacturing plant is whether it can be **accepted** as a good quality product or **discarded** due to bad quality. This status for each manufacturing exercise is identified in the data using the 'Detergent_Quality' dimension, which is calculated using some weighted algorithm by taking into account the four output quality parameters of the end detergent produced. Our end goal is to find out the reasons why the final product was not accepted, which shows that we need to study why the output quality was bad. The reasons could be many, but how do we identify them? This is when the task of studying relationships is presented to the decision scientist. We have with us plenty of independent variables that are either continuous or categorical. Trying to understand how these independent dimensions eventually contribute to the end output is where we start studying the relationship between them. The entire exercise can be simply defined as **bivariate analysis**, that is, simultaneous analysis of two dimensions. Before getting into the data, let's understand a few basic constructs and prerequisites required for bivariate analysis.

# So what is correlation?

Correlation is a statistical technique that can show whether and how strongly pairs of variables are related. For example, height and weight are related-taller people tend to be heavier than shorter people. The relationship isn't perfect, but with the results you can understand how these two dimensions are related. In the example of height and weight, we can say 'weight increases as height increases' and this will be true for most cases (exceptions are inevitable).

The result of the correlation test is called the correlation coefficient (or "r"). It ranges from -1.0 to +1.0. The closer r is to +1 or -1, the more closely the two variables are related. Interpreting the correlation coefficient is straightforward. If the correlation coefficient between height and weight is 0.8, we can infer that there is strong positive correlation between the two; as height increases, weight also increases and vice versa.

The relationship between a student's absence records in school and his grades is, say, 0.75, so we infer that there is a negative correlation between the student's absence record and his grades. An increase in absence records will decrease his grades.

Before we begin finding the correlation between the output quality parameters and independent dimensions, let's take a step back and try to understand how we can interpret the parameter as good or bad. In our use case, we have four output quality parameters for the detergent manufactured. Let's try to understand how the output parameter compares with the accept/reject flag:

```
> library(reshape2)
> library(dplyr)
  #Selecting the required variables
> sample<-select(data,
                Output_QualityParameter1,
                Output_QualityParameter2,
                Output_QualityParameter3,
                Output_QualityParameter4,
                Detergent_Quality)
> melted <- melt(sample, id.vars = c("Detergent_Quality"))

#Calculating the mean of the Quality parameter
#across the Detergent Quality

> dcast(melted,variable~Detergent_Quality,mean)

                   variable        Bad        Good
1 Output_QualityParameter1    432.2532    409.0523
2 Output_QualityParameter2  16008.0896  15066.2840
3 Output_QualityParameter3  39101.2648  36803.8819
4 Output_QualityParameter4   8381.1793   7926.7560

#Calculating the Standard Deviation of the Quality parameter
#across the accept flag

> dcast(melted,variable~Detergent_Quality,sd)

                   variable        Bad         Good
1 Output_QualityParameter1     6.430605     26.11407
2 Output_QualityParameter2   533.959565   1327.09995
3 Output_QualityParameter3  1401.156940   3218.63850
4 Output_QualityParameter4   285.606162    681.37160
```

If we observe the mean and standard deviations of the quality parameters across the Detergent Quality, then we can see that standard deviation between Good and Bad is quite high. Just observing the mean values across the accept flag, we might conclude that the lower the value of the parameter, the higher the chances of the produce being accepted. If we closely observe the standard deviation, we can study that the relationship might not be a simple and straightforward one. Consider Quality Parameter 1; looking at the mean, we can assume that the higher the value of the parameter, the lower the chances of quality being good, which means bad = 432 and good = 409. However, if we look at the standard deviation, we can understand that there is a huge variation in the records that were Good, that is, 26. This infers that approximately the range of good quality detergent can be 383 and 435, and "bad" can be approximately be identified in the range of 426 and 438. There is a clear overlap between the good and bad records for the Output Quality Parameter1. A similar story can be observed for the other three parameters also.

Moving on to the other variables, let's try to understand the main relationships between our independent variables and the end outcome.

We have two main categories of independent dimensions: manufacturing process-level and individual stage-/phase-level dimensions. In each of these categories, we have created a couple of features that can help us gather more information than the individual dimensions. Whenever we come across some interesting results, we will add the result to our hypotheses list; this will eventually create our **Data-driven Hypotheses Matrix**.

For the manufacturing process, the most important dimensions that we have are Assembly Line ID, total manufacturing time, and the feature that we created-order quantity deviation. We'll start with the Assembly Line ID that is a categorical variable with two levels. Let's see the percentage distribution of good and bad produce across the assembly lines. The following code aggregates the count of records of Good/Bad quality produce across the assembly line and then calculates the percentage of bad quality produce in each category:

```
> temp<- as.data.frame(
tapply(data$Material_ID,
list(data$AssemblyLine_ID,data$Detergent_Quality), length))
> temp$bad_perc<-temp$Bad/(temp$Bad + temp$Good)
> temp

        Bad Good   bad_perc
Line 1  183  602  0.2331210
Line 2   42  173  0.1953488
```

As we can see,the percentage of bad quality of produce is slightly higher in Line 1 than Line 2. The difference is not really high and we can't be very sure whether the following observation is true or a data anomaly outcome. Irrespective of this, let's add this point to our DDH matrix; we can later validate the result by digging deeper into this.

Let's understand the relationship of the other two dimensions:

```
#Studying the average time across Detergent Quality
> tapply(data$Total_Manufacturing_Time_mins,
data$Detergent_Quality,mean)
      Bad       Good
  251.4667 244.1806

#Studying the Standard Deviation in time across Detergent Quality
> tapply(data$Total_Manufacturing_Time_mins,
data$ Detergent_Quality,sd)
      Bad       Good
  90.06981 82.18633
```

The results do not show any significant relationship between the two. To confirm, let's study the relationship between the two along with the four output quality parameters. The following code visualizes the relationship between the manufacturing time and four output quality parameters. The good and bad quality produce is distinguished with two different colors:

```
> ggplot(data,
    aes(x=Total_Manufacturing_Time_mins,
 y=Output_QualityParameter1)) +
    geom_point(aes(color=Detergent_Quality))

> ggplot(data,
    aes(x=Total_Manufacturing_Time_mins,
 y=Output_QualityParameter2)) +
    geom_point(aes(color= Detergent_Quality))

> ggplot(data,
    aes(x=Total_Manufacturing_Time_mins,
 y=Output_QualityParameter3)) +
    geom_point(aes(color=Detergent_Quality))

> ggplot(data,
    aes(x=Total_Manufacturing_Time_mins,
 y=Output_QualityParameter4)) +
    geom_point(aes(color= Detergent_Quality))
```

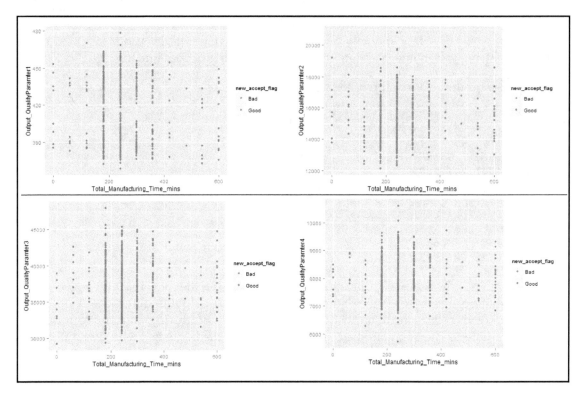

The results clearly show that there isn't any strong relationship between the two dimensions. Let's explore the next dimension, order deviation (the feature we created in the previous section):

```
> #Aggregating the data over Quantity_Deviation + Detergent_Quality
> # and creating a dataframe
> temp<-as.data.frame(
+      tapply(data$Material_ID,
+             list(data$Quantity_Deviation,data$Detergent_Quality),
+             length))
> #Calculating the percentage of Bad records in each category
> temp$Bad_Perc<- temp$Bad/(temp$Bad + temp$Good)

> temp

        Bad Good  Bad_Perc
High     89  221 0.2870968
Low      74  293 0.2016349
Medium   62  261 0.1919505
```

The results look very promising! We can observe that, when the deviation is high, the percentage of bad produce is significantly high. Let's add this hypotheses to our DDH matrix.

Moving on, let's study the stage-wise dimension. The following is the list of dimensions that we explored in previous exercises. We'll begin with studying the dimensions stage-wise:

| Stage | Dimensions explored/created (features) |
|---|---|
| Stage 1 | Previous Product, Product Change Flag, Delay Flag, Processing Time, Resources, Two x 2 quality parameters for two raw materials, four Stage 1 output quality parameters ( features) |
| Stage 2 | Product Change Flag, Delay Flag, Processing Time, four Stage 2 output quality parameters (features) |
| Stage 3 | Delay Flag, Resources used, Two x 2 quality parameters for two raw materials used, four Consumption Flags for four Products (Features), Four Stage 3 output quality parameters |
| Stage 4 | Previous Product, Delay Flag, Processing Time, Resources used |
| Stage 5 | Product Change Flag, Delay Flag, Processing Time, three Stage 5 output quality parameters (features) |

# Exploring Stage 1 dimensions

Previously, we created two features for the Previous Product category, Stage1_PrevProduct_1 and Stage1_PrevProduct_2:

```
> summary(data$Stage1_PrevProduct_1)
    Others Product_545
       531         469
> summary(data$Stage1_PrevProduct_2)
  Others Product_543 Product_545 Product_546 Product_547 Product_555
     105         352         469          26          30          18
```

The difference between the two was only the number of categories. We'll study the feature with more levels first and, based on the results, we can take a call on the next one. Similar to the previous exploration, we'll try to study the percentage of bad records in each category:

```
> #Aggregating the data over Stage1_PrevProduct_2 + Detergent_Quality
> # and creating a dataframe
> temp<-as.data.frame(
+      tapply(data$Material_ID,
+             list(data$Stage1_PrevProduct_2,data$Detergent_Quality),
+             length))
> #Calculating the percentage of Bad records in each category
> temp$Bad_Perc<- temp$Bad/(temp$Bad + temp$Good)
> temp
             Bad Good  Bad_Perc
Others        14   91 0.1333333
Product_543   85  267 0.2414773
Product_545  113  356 0.2409382
Product_546    3   23 0.1153846
Product_547    5   25 0.1666667
Product_555    5   13 0.2777778
```

The maximum records belong to the `Product_543` and `Product_545` categories; both have no interesting trends. Therefore, we can move on without exploring the other feature.

The following code snippet aids in studying the relation between Delay Flag for Stage 1 and Good/Bad Quality of the end produce:

```
> summary(data$Stage1_DelayFlag)
 No Yes
637 363
> #Aggregating the data over Stage1_DelayFlag + Detergent_Quality
> # and creating a dataframe
> temp<-as.data.frame(
+      tapply(data$Material_ID,
+             list(data$Stage1_DelayFlag,data$Detergent_Quality),
+             length))
> #Calculating the percentage of Bad records in each category
> temp$Bad_Perc<- temp$Bad/(temp$Bad + temp$Good)
> temp
    Bad Good  Bad_Perc
No  147  490 0.2307692
Yes  78  285 0.2148760
```

Again, we can see no promising results. The percentage difference for bad quality produce is low between the two categories.

Let's now study the influence of raw materials used over the end quality of the detergent. This was one of our most important hypotheses in our heuristics-driven hypotheses. The raw material property is a continuous variable, so let's study the relationship between the raw material and output quality parameter by computing the correlation between them:

```
> cor(data$Stage1_RM1_QParameter1,data$Output_QualityParameter1)
[1] 0.5653402
> cor(data$Stage1_RM1_QParameter1,data$Output_QualityParameter2)
[1] 0.4431995
> cor(data$Stage1_RM1_QParameter1,data$Output_QualityParameter3)
[1] 0.3992361
> cor(data$Stage1_RM1_QParameter1,data$Output_QualityParameter4)
[1] 0.4460737
```

The correlation tests indicate that there is barely any relationship between the two. To investigate further, let's visualize the results to see if we could find something intuitive. The following code plots the scatterplot between the two with the bad and good quality records distinguished by color:

```
#Plotting a scatter plot of Raw Material Quality parameter and all 4 output
quality parameters
> ggplot(data,
      aes(x=Stage1_RM1_QParameter1,y=Output_QualityParameter1)) +
      geom_point(aes(color=Detergent_Quality))

> ggplot(data,
      aes(x=Stage1_RM1_QParameter1,y=Output_QualityParameter2)) +
      geom_point(aes(color= Detergent_Quality))

> ggplot(data,
      aes(x=Stage1_RM1_QParameter1,y=Output_QualityParameter3)) +
      geom_point(aes(color=Detergent_Quality))

> ggplot(data,
      aes(x=Stage1_RM1_QParameter1,y=Output_QualityParameter4)) +
      geom_point(aes(color= Detergent_Quality))
```

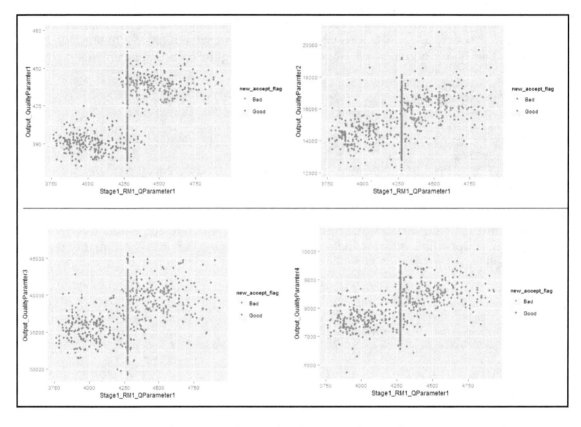

As we can see, there is definitely a relationship between the quality parameters of Raw Material 1 and output quality parameters of the end product. In a nutshell, we can understand that most bad quality products are observed beyond a threshold in the data. There is definitely an overlap between the good and bad products, and this could possibly be due to some latent features that we have not observed till now. However, with the preceding results, we can definitely add the observations to our DDH matrix.

If we observe the same visuals for the second quality parameter for Raw Material 1 across the four different output quality parameters, we can see something very similar. The relationship may not be really strong from a correlation perspective, but there definitely exists some patter that can be useful for us to identify the root cause in our further analysis:

```
> ggplot(data,
    aes(x=Stage1_RM1_QParameter2,y=Output_QualityParameter1)) +
    geom_point(aes(color=Detergent_Quality))

> ggplot(data,
```

```
    aes(x=Stage1_RM1_QParameter2,y=Output_QualityParameter2)) +
    geom_point(aes(color= Detergent_Quality))

> ggplot(data,
    aes(x=Stage1_RM1_QParameter2,y=Output_QualityParameter3)) +
    geom_point(aes(color= Detergent_Quality))

>  ggplot(data,
    aes(x=Stage1_RM1_QParameter2,y=Output_QualityParameter4)) +
    geom_point(aes(color= Detergent_Quality))
```

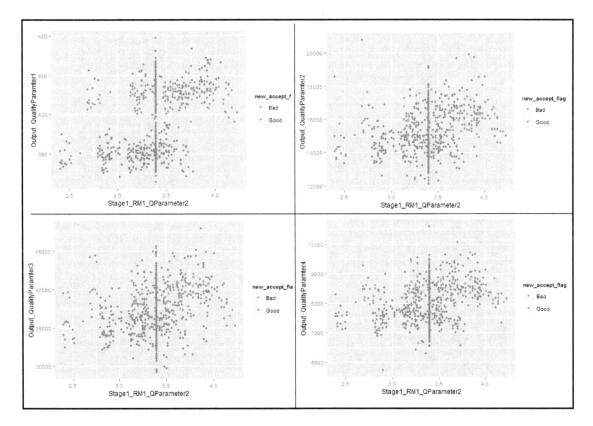

Another feature that we created to understand how much deviation was observed in the stage-level final quality parameters, that is, `Stage1_QP1_deviation` and others. Let's quickly compute the correlation tests to observe whether there is any significant relationship:

```
> cor(data$Stage1_QP1_deviation,data$Output_QualityParameter1)
[1] 0.05035061
```

```
> cor(data$Stage1_QP1_deviation,data$Output_QualityParameter2)
[1] -0.05433026

> cor(data$Stage1_QP1_deviation,data$Output_QualityParameter3)
[1] -0.0584961

> cor(data$Stage1_QP1_deviation,data$Output_QualityParameter4)
[1] -0.03834813
```

As we can notice, the correlation tests indicate that there is absolutely no relationship between the two dimensions. The same holds true for the other three Stage 1 quality parameters. To be on the safer side, let's validate whether there is any pattern visible from the scatterplots. The following visual showcases the scatterplot for Stage 1 Quality Parameter 1 against the final output quality parameters (all four of them) and we can conclude that there is no clear relationship or interesting pattern that can be studied:

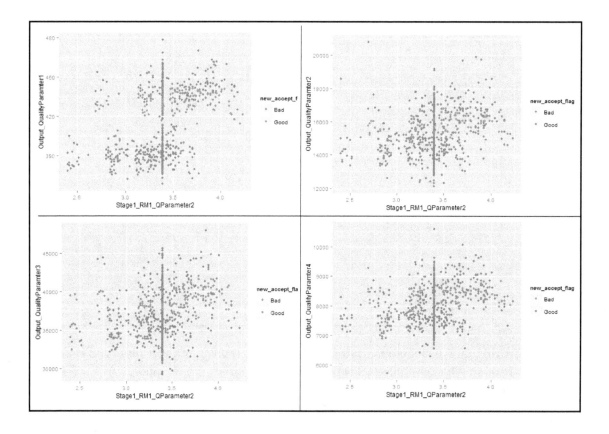

# Revisiting the DDH matrix

As of now, we have explored in depth and studied all the important dimensions that were at the manufacturing level as well as from Stage 1. The same approach can be extended to study the dimensions in Stages 2,3,4, and 5.

Next, we have come across some results that were interesting and some that were not interesting at all. We now take a pause to revisit the DDH to list all the hypotheses that we collected during the data exploration and studying relationships phase:

| Dimension | Hypotheses |
|---|---|
| **Order Deviation** | As the deviation between Order Quantity and actual Produced Quantity increases, the chance of the bad quality detergent being manufactured also increases |
| **Assembly Line ID** | Line 1 has an overall higher chance of manufacturing more number of bad quality detergent products |
| **Stage 1 Raw Materials properties** | Raw material quality parameters have an impact on the end quality of the detergent |
| **Stage 3 Raw Materials properties** | Raw material quality parameters have an impact on the end quality of the detergent |
| **Stage 3 Resources** | Resources used during manufacturing in Stage 3 have an impact on the end quality of the detergent |
| **Stage 3 Delay** | A delay in manufacturing during Stage 3 has an impact on the end quality of the detergent |
| **Stage 3 Resources** | Resources used during manufacturing in Stage 4 have an impact on the end quality of the detergent |

 The insights regarding Stage 3 and others that were not discussed earlier were gathered while studying relationships in Stages 2, 3, 4, and 5. Discussing each stage in depth is out of the scope for the book. It is recommended that you explore these exercises before moving ahead.

The preceding hypotheses generated as a result of the data surfacing and studying relationships exercises have rendered few hypotheses. However, these hypotheses are still not concrete results. To get to a more realistic and confident answer, we need to prove these results statistically. In the next section, we will take a closer look at how to validate these findings.

# Exploratory data analysis

This part of the problem solving stack is also called "**Confirmatory data analysis**". Generally, the problems that we touch base over the Internet and other learning resources explain a stack called "ECR" that can be extended as **E**xploratory Data Analysis + **C**onfirmatory Data Analysis + **R**oot Cause Analysis. This is the same approach that we have considered-**Exploratory Data Analysis (EDA)**-where we understand "What" happened, then CDA, that is, Confirmatory Data Analysis, where we cement the results from our exercises using statistical tests. Finally, we will answer the "Why" question using Root Cause Analysis. In our current approach, we have the same approach but a slightly different naming convention. We have broken down the steps into more granular ones:

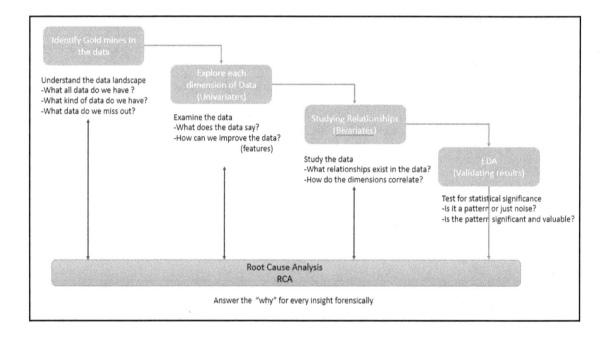

We have now reached the EDA phase, that is, we will now validate the insights and patterns that we observed in the data. Let's start with understanding how we are going to approach this. If we look back at the journey, we defined the problem, hypothesized the different factors that could be a reason for the problem to exist, created a framework where we can iterate, solve, and evolve the problem, explored and studied the data, and found patterns that could be answers to our questions. We now need to validate our findings using a variety of statistical techniques.

# So how do we validate our findings?

We use a statistical technique called hypothesis testing, which will help us determine the probability that the concerned hypothesis is true.

# So how does hypothesis testing work?

A hypothesis test basically evaluates two mutually exclusive statements about a scenario to determine whether the statement is best supported by the sample data. When we say that a finding is statistically significant, it indicates that our hypothesis is true and not observed by just an anomaly.

In our use case, we have identified a bunch of hypotheses/scenarios from the earlier exercises. We'll test these hypotheses to understand whether they are valid or whether they appear just due to mere noise in the data.

The techniques for hypothesis testing depend on the following points:

- The type of outcome variable being analyzed (continuous or categorical)
- The number of comparison groups in the investigation
- Whether the comparison groups are independent

Let's understand this better. We can have dimensions that are either continuous or categorical, that is, `Delay_Flag` with values (Yes/No) is categorical whereas the manufacturing time in minutes is continuous. For two independent categorical/continuous or categorical + continuous variables, the kind of test that we would perform would be different. Similarly, based on the number of comparison groups in the categorical variable, the test would differ. For example, `Delay_Flag` has two values, that is, Yes/No whereas the resource variable has multiple levels, say Resource 1, Resource 2, and so on. Finally, it is also based on the comparison groups-whether they are independent or dependent. In our use case, the data dimensions are independent. We can study dependent and independent variables using the following example. Let's say that a drug company wants to test the effectiveness of a new drug in reducing blood pressure; they would collect data from blood pressure recordings of the same people before and after they receive a dose. These dimensions are dependent as they are collected from the same people before and after the test. When the data is collected from two separate groups-one from people who consumed the drug and the other from people who have not consumed-the dimensions would be an example of independent groups.

A cheat sheet to understand which statistical test should be used for our use case will look like the following:

|  |  | Dependent Variable | |
|---|---|---|---|
|  |  | Categorical | Continuous |
| Independent Variable | Categorical | Chi Square | T Test/Anova |
|  | Continuous | LDA/QDA | Regression |

We'll get into the details of the required tests as and when required. Let's begin with a simple one. The following table lists the different hypotheses along with their dependent and independent variable type and the respective test required to validate them:

| Hypothesis | Independent Dimension | Dependent Dimension | Test |
|---|---|---|---|
| Line 1 has an overall higher chance of manufacturing more number of bad quality detergent products | **Assembly Line** categorical (2 levels) | Accept Flag Categorical (2 Levels) | Chi Square |
| | **Assembly Line** categorical (2 levels) | Output Quality Parameters Continuous Variable | T Test |
| As the deviation between Order Quantity and actual Produced Quantity increases, the chance of the bad quality detergent being manufactured also increases | **Order Deviation** categorical (3 levels) | Accept Flag Categorical (2 Levels) | Chi Square |
| | **Order Deviation** categorical (3 levels) | Output Quality Parameters Continuous Variable | Anova |
| Stage 1 Raw Material quality parameters have an impact on the end quality of the detergent | **2x2 Quality Parameters for Raw Materials** Continuous Variable | Output Quality Parameters Continuous Variable | Regression |
| Stage 3 Raw Material quality parameters have an impact on the end quality of the detergent | **2x2 Quality Parameters for Raw Materials** Continuous Variable | Output Quality Parameters Continuous Variable | Regression |
| Resources used during manufacturing in Stage 3 have an impact on the end quality of the detergent | **Resource ID** Categorical variable (>2 levels) | Accept Flag Categorical (2 Levels) | Chi Square |
| A delay in manufacturing during Stage 3 has an impact on the end quality of the detergent | **Stage 3 Delay Flag** Categorical Variable 2 levels | Accept Flag Categorical (2 Levels) | Chi Square |

# Validating hypotheses – category 1

We'll start with the first one; Line 1 has an overall higher chance of manufacturing more number of bad quality detergent products. To validate this test, we need to prove that there exists a relationship between the two dimensions, that is, the Assembly Line dimension and the End Quality of the Detergent are not two independent dimensions; instead there exists some relationship between the two. Once, we have the relationship proved, we can affirmatively say that the Assembly Line used in the manufacturing process does have an impact on the quality of the detergent.

Here, we have both dimensions as categorical variables, that is, Assembly Line ID has two distinct values Line 1 and Line 2. Similarly, the quality of the detergent also is a categorical variable with values Good/Bad. In such scenarios, where the dependent as well as independent variables are categorical, we will use a statistical test called **Chi Squared Test of Independence**. To perform the statistical test, we will need to build a null hypothesis and alternative hypothesis. The null hypothesis H0 would essentially be the devil's advocate as it always assumes that whatever we are trying to prove did not happen. Whereas the alternative hypothesis (H1) assumes exactly the opposite of the null hypothesis.

In our test, we have the following features:

- **H0**: There is no relationship between the Assembly Line used for the manufacturing and the end quality of the detergent manufactured
- **H1**: There is a relationship between the Assembly Line used for the manufacturing and the end quality of the detergent manufactured

# How does the chi-squared test work in a nutshell?

Let's say that we have an outcome and a variable that we think might have an effect. (In our case, the outcome is the quality of the detergent and the variable of interest is the Assembly Line used.) We look at the observed values of the outcome, with and without our variable of interest. We then calculate the expected values using a statistically derived formula. From the result, we calculate the deviations from what we observed and it is highly likely that we observe some deviations. We scale the deviations based on the expected values and adjust for the number of sets of samples. The chi-square statistic is one measure of that deviation, where we try to prove whether whatever we are observing is random or unlikely to be random.

Renowned statisticians around the globe have already calculated a look-up table called the chi-squared table. For an observed deviation, we can use the table to calculate the probability that this deviation is due to chance. If that probability (p value) is very small, then we can affirmatively conclude that the deviation can't be due to chance. There is indeed some relationship between the variable of interest and outcome. We consider any p value below 5% to be very small. On the other hand, if the p-value is greater than 5%, then we conclude that the observations/relationship that we see is purely by chance and hence there wouldn't be any relationship between the two. To summarize, we can say that the chi-squared test is a measure of deviation compared against precomputed values that tell us how probable these deviations are.

The test is entirely automated in R; we don't need to code the process for the test. We will use the `chisq.test()` function available in the `stats` package of R:

```
> #Creating a table of the frequency count for the two variables
> #that is, Outcome v/s Variable of Interest
> sample<-table(data$AssemblyLine_ID,data$Detergent_Quality)
> sample     #View the actual table
          Bad Good
   Line 1 183  602
   Line 2  42  173
>
> #Perform the Chi Squared Test of Independence
> chisq.test(sample)

    Pearson's Chi-squared test with Yates' continuity correction

data:  sample
X-squared = 1.1728, df = 1, p-value = 0.2788
```

As we can see, the result is p value = 0.27, that is, 27%, which is very high. We can easily conclude that the null hypothesis is true, which means that the Assembly Line and Quality of the Detergent produced are independent dimensions and there exists no relationship between the two. Therefore, we can chuck one of the hypothesis from our DDH.

Before we move on, we need to perform a few more checks. The end quality of the detergent is computed by combining the four output quality parameters of the detergent using some weighted algorithm (which we are not aware about). The end result may be 'Bad' or 'Good' if one parameter gives an extremely out-of-range value. So, instead of trying to find out whether there is a relationship between the end quality, that is, Good/Bad, and Assembly Line, we can actually go ahead and find out whether there is a relationship between Assembly Line and any of the Output Quality Parameters. Here, the kind of test that we need to perform will be different as the type of dimension has also changed. We have the same independent variable, that is, Assembly Line ID (categorical with 2 levels) and a dependent variable Output Quality Parameter (continuous). You can consider any one of the four. The chi-squared test that we used earlier will not be of use here. In such cases, we perform the two-sample T test. (Refer to the cheat sheet in the previous section.)

## So what is the two-sample T Test?

The two-sample t-test is one of the most commonly used hypothesis tests. It is performed to compare whether the average difference between two groups is really significant or if it is due to random chance. In our case, the two groups are the one referring to the two different Assembly Lines (Line 1 and Line 2). Using the test, we try to validate whether the two dimensions are actually independent with no relation between them or whether they are related and therefore Assembly Line has an impact on the respective output quality parameter. The process of getting started with any hypothesis testing is exactly similar to the one shown in the chi-squared test; we define a null hypothesis and alternate hypothesis. As we have four different output quality parameters, we can individually test whether there is a relationship between Assembly Line and any one of the output quality parameters.

Hence, in our test, we have (for now consider Output Quality Parameter 1) the following features:

- **H0**: There is no relationship between the Assembly Line used for the manufacturing and Quality Parameter 1 of the detergent manufactured
- **H1**: There is a relationship between the Assembly Line used for the manufacturing and Quality Parameter 1 of the detergent manufactured

Similar to the chi-squared test, we have the T test also automated with the `t.test()` function in the stats package of R:

```
> t.test(data$Output_QualityParameter1~data$AssemblyLine_ID)

Welch Two Sample t-test

data:  data$Output_QualityParameter1 by data$AssemblyLine_ID

t = -0.87375, df = 341.76, p-value = 0.3829

alternative hypothesis: true difference in means is not equal to 0

95 percent confidence interval:
 -5.478854  2.108418

sample estimates:
mean in group Line 1 mean in group Line 2
          413.9102              415.5954
```

The result shows an extremely high p value; therefore, H0 is true and thus Assembly Line and Quality Parameter 1 are two independent dimensions; that is, Assembly Line does not impact Quality Parameter 1.

Let's try performing T-tests for the other three output quality parameters in the same way as we performed for Quality Parameter 1:

```
> t.test(data$Output_QualityParameter2~data$AssemblyLine_ID)

Welch Two Sample t-test

data:  data$Output_QualityParameter2 by data$AssemblyLine_ID

t = -5.2088, df = 307.57, p-value = 3.487e-07

alternative hypothesis: true difference in means is not equal to 0

95 percent confidence interval:
 -742.4911 -335.3277
sample estimates:
mean in group Line 1 mean in group Line 2
           15162.32               15701.23


> t.test(data$Output_QualityParameter3~data$AssemblyLine_ID)

Welch Two Sample t-test

data:  data$Output_QualityParameter3 by data$AssemblyLine_ID

t = -6.4768, df = 315.18, p-value = 3.596e-10

alternative hypothesis: true difference in means is not equal to 0
95 percent confidence interval:
 -2067.649 -1104.125

sample estimates:
mean in group Line 1 mean in group Line 2
           36979.83               38565.71


> t.test(data$Output_QualityParameter4~data$AssemblyLine_ID)

    Welch Two Sample t-test

data:  data$Output_QualityParameter4 by data$AssemblyLine_ID

t = -3.1554, df = 309.4, p-value = 0.001761

alternative hypothesis: true difference in means is not equal to 0

95 percent confidence interval:
 -272.34233  -63.13942
```

```
sample estimates:
mean in group Line 1 mean in group Line 2
              7992.937               8160.678
```

If you glance through the results and focus on the p value, we can see that it is very low (much lower than 5%), which can be inferred as, the null hypotheses can be rejected. Therefore, we can conclude that there is indeed an impact of Assembly Line over the Output Quality Parameters 2, 3, and 4.

Therefore, we have validated our first and second hypothesis in the preceding matrix. Let's move on to the third and fourth.

# Validating hypotheses – category 2

The hypothesis is as the deviation between Order Quantity and actual Produced Quantity increases, the chance of the bad quality detergent being manufactured also increases.

Similar to the previous hypothesis, we have two categories here: first, where the dependent variable is the end outcome Good/Bad and second, where the dependent variable is one of the four output quality parameters (continuous). The first scenario is exactly similar to the previous hypothesis, that is, the independent and dependent variable both are categorical. We can straightaway define our H0 and H1 and perform the chi-squared test using the function available in R.

The null and alternate hypothesis can be defined as follows:

- **H0**: There is no relationship between the Quantity deviation from Order quantity and Produced quantity and end Quality of the detergent manufactured
- **H1**: There is a relationship between the Quantity deviation from Order quantity and Produced quantity and end Quality of the detergent manufactured:

```
> #Creating a table of the frequency count for the two variables
> #that is, Outcome v/s Variable of Interest
> sample<-table(data$Quantity_Deviation,data$Detergent_Quality)
> sample    #View the actual table

           Bad Good
  High      89  221
  Low       74  293
  Medium    62  261
>
> #Perform the Chi Squared Test of Independence
> chisq.test(sample)

        Pearson's Chi-squared test
```

```
data:   sample
X-squared = 10.027, df = 2, p-value = 0.006646
```

The p value is a little above our desired cutoff, that is, 5%, which indicates that our null hypothesis is true. Deviation in the quantity of the order produced has no impact on the quality of the manufactured detergent. The essential problem with the chi-squared test is that the way in which we categorize data needs multiple thoughts. Let's say that the variable of interest was "age" and we have categorized age as five segments-0-18, 18 -35, and so on. Chi-square will never be able to highlight whether the segments are meaningful or not; it will only test based on the values in the provided segments.

If you recollect the data surfacing exercise, we have created this feature on the basis of percentile values, that is, below 30 percentile is low, ~30 – 70 percentile is medium, and so on. Let's adjust these numbers a bit, such that they are still in the approximate percentile range but may be more meaningful in order to study the pattern:

```
> #Calculating the deviation between Order and Produced Quantity
> temp<-(abs(data$Order_Quantity - data$Produced_Quantity))
> data$Quantity_Deviation_new <-
as.factor(ifelse(temp<= 140,"Low",
                        ifelse(temp<= 280,"Medium","High")))
#View the frequency of each category
> summary(data$Quantity_Deviation_new)
  High    Low Medium
   351    365    284
```

Now that we have slightly modified the rule for creating the segments in the Quantity deviation, let's perform a Chi Squared Test on the newly created dimension.

```
> #Creating a table of the frequency count for the two variables
> #that is, Outcome v/s Variable of Interest
> sample<-table(data$Quantity_Deviation_new,data$Detergent_Quality)
> sample     #View the actual table
         Bad Good
  High   100  251
  Low     74  291
  Medium  51  233
>
> #Perform the Chi Squared Test of Independence
> chisq.test(sample)

        Pearson's Chi-squared test

data:   sample
X-squared = 11.62, df = 2, p-value = 0.002998
```

Now, we can clearly see that the p value has dipped below 5% and therefore we can reject the null hypothesis. Thus, we can conclude that there is indeed a relation between the Quantity deviation between order quantity and Produced Quantity and the end quality of the detergent manufactured.

Moving to a more detailed view, we can now try to understand whether there is any relation between the Qunatity_Deviation (new) dimension and each of the individual output quality parameters for the detergent. When we explore the dimensions, we understand that we have a categorical independent variable and continuous dependent variable. The instant thought would be that we can try t-tests to validate it like the previous hypotheses. Unfortunately, this won't work. Let's try it out after defining our H0 and H1.

Looking at the hypothesis, we can build our null and alternative hypothesis as follows:

- H0: There is no relationship between the Quantity deviation from Order quantity and Produced quantity and Quality Parameter 1 of the detergent manufactured
- **H1**: There is a relationship between the **Quantity deviation** from Order quantity and Produced quantity and Quality Parameter 1 of the detergent manufactured

If we try to perform a simple two-sample t test like the earlier scenario, we'll get the following error:

```
> t.test(data$Output_QualityParameter1~data$Quantity_Deviation_new)
Error in t.test.formula(data$Output_QualityParameter1 ~
data$Quantity_Deviation_new) :
  grouping factor must have exactly 2 levels
```

Yes, t test can be performed only if the variable of interest has two levels, but in our case we have three levels (high / medium / low). So how do we move ahead?

One simple trick would be to create three different dummy variables, that is, one for High, another for Medium, and so on. Then perform three separate tests on each of the variables and try to conclude whether our null hypothesis can be rejected. However, there is a huge flaw in this method that deals with the issue of Type 1 error.

# What does a Type 1 error mean?

In the process of hypothesis testing, there are chances that, due to data issues, we might end up rejecting a null hypothesis even when it is right or we might fail to reject a null hypothesis even when it false. These two cases can be called as Type 1 and Type 2 errors:

|  | Given the Null Hypothesis Is | |
|---|---|---|
|  | True | False |
| Reject | Type I Error | Correct Decision |
| Do Not Reject | Correct Decision | Type II Error |

Your Decision Based On a Random Sample

Two Types of Errors in Decision Making

T-tests are easier to perform, but Type I error is the reason that we need to move on to a better technique because the more hypothesis tests you use, the more you risk making a Type I error and the less power a test has. There is no disputing that the t-test changed statistics with its ability to find significance with a sample, but for cases where our variable of interest has more than two means, we need to use ANOVA.

# So what is ANOVA?

**Analysis of Variance (ANOVA)** is a statistical method used to test differences between two or more means. In fact, we can also use ANOVA instead of t test when the variable of interest has only two levels (with some assumptions).

To perform the anova test, we can use the `aov()` function provided with the stats package of R:

```
> #Output Quality Parameter 1
> anova_model<-
aov(data$Output_QualityParameter1~data$Quantity_Deviation_new)
> summary(anova_model)
                    Df Sum Sq Mean Sq F value Pr(>F)
```

```
data$Quantity_Deviation_new   2    2007   1003.5   1.591   0.204
Residuals                   997  628944    630.8
```

When we test ANOVA for the Quantity deviation and Output Quality Parameter 1, we can see that the p value is higher than our acceptance range. Therefore, we can infer that there is no relationship between the two dimensions, Quantity Deviation and Output Quality Parameter 1:

```
> #Output Quality Parameter 2
> anova_model<-
aov(data$Output_QualityParameter2~data$Quantity_Deviation_new)
> summary(anova_model)
                             Df    Sum Sq Mean Sq F value Pr(>F)
data$Quantity_Deviation_new   2 1.061e+07 5306477   3.367 0.0349 *
Residuals                   997 1.571e+09 1575814
---
Signif. codes:  0 '***' 0.001 '**' 0.01 '*' 0.05 '.' 0.1 ' ' 1
>


> #Output Quality Parameter 3
> anova_model<-
aov(data$Output_QualityParameter3~data$Quantity_Deviation_new)
> summary(anova_model)

                             Df    Sum Sq  Mean Sq F value Pr(>F)
data$Quantity_Deviation_new   2 6.913e+07 34563909   3.702  0.025 *
Residuals                   997 9.309e+09  9337352
---
Signif. codes:  0 '***' 0.001 '**' 0.01 '*' 0.05 '.' 0.1 ' ' 1
>


> #Output Quality Parameter 4

> anova_model<-
aov(data$Output_QualityParameter4~data$Quantity_Deviation_new)
> summary(anova_model)
                             Df    Sum Sq Mean Sq F value  Pr(>F)
data$Quantity_Deviation_new   2   4815985 2407992   5.873 0.00291 **
Residuals                   997 408807280  410037
---
Signif. codes:  0 '***' 0.001 '**' 0.01 '*' 0.05 '.' 0.1 ' ' 1
```

The preceding code performs the anova test on the variable of interests: Quantity Deviation with three levels and the remaining three Output Quality Parameters. Observing the p value from the result of ANOVA, we can reject the null hypothesis and can affirmatively say that Quantity Deviation impacts the Output Quality Parameters 2, 3, and 4 for the detergent manufactured.

# Validating hypotheses – category 3

The hypothesis is *Stage 1 Raw Material quality parameters have an impact on the end quality of the detergent*.

We have completed performing statistical tests for two out of four categories that we have assimilated till now. In each category, we came across a different type of test as we had different kinds of independent and dependent variables. In the current category, we have both independent as well as dependent variables as continuous. Therefore, we cannot use the tests we have explored till now to validate our current hypothesis. If you refer to the cheat sheet, we can find that we have to use regression to solve these set of problems.

## So what is regression?

Regression analysis is a statistical process to estimate the relationships among variables. More specifically, regression analysis helps one understand how the typical value of the dependent variable changes when any one of the independent variables is varied while the other independent variables are held fixed.

Thus, if we limit the scope to our current use case scenario, we can understand that regression helps us identify whether there is any relationship between the independent variables and dependent variable. We will be exploring regression in more depth, but for the current scenario, let's limit the scope of regression as just a means to study the relationships between our variables of interest.

For our hypothesis, we have two raw materials in Stage 1-each with two individual quality parameters, that is, altogether four raw material quality parameters. Similarly, our second hypothesis surfaces on the raw material parameters from Stage 3. Unlike stage 1, stage 3 has four raw materials, but the quality parameters are available for only three of them. We have (2+1+2) = 5 quality parameters for the raw materials.

We can combine all of these dimensions together into one single equation and then study whether there exists a relationship between the dependent and independent variables. Also, as we have four different output quality parameters as the dependent variable, we will perform the test four times to gather the results:

```
> #Performing a regression model with
> #4 quality parameters from Stage 1 and
> #5 quality parameters from Stage 3
>
> regression_model<-lm(Output_QualityParameter1~
data$Stage1_RM2_QParameter1 +
                        data$Stage1_RM2_QParameter2 +
```

```
                                    data$Stage1_RM1_QParameter1 +
                                    data$Stage1_RM1_QParameter2 +
                                    data$Stage3_RM1_QParameter1 +
                                    data$Stage3_RM1_QParameter2 +
                                    data$Stage3_RM2_QParameter1 +
                                    data$Stage3_RM3_QParameter1 +
                                    data$Stage3_RM3_QParameter2 ,
                        data=data)
> anova(regression_model)
Analysis of Variance Table
```

**Response: Output_QualityParameter1**

|  | Df | Sum Sq | Mean Sq | F value | Pr(>F) | |
|---|---|---|---|---|---|---|
| data$Stage1_RM2_QParameter1 | 1 | 489966 | 489966 | 6551.5908 | < 2.2e-16 | *** |
| data$Stage1_RM2_QParameter2 | 1 | 696 | 696 | 9.3112 | 0.002338 | ** |
| data$Stage1_RM1_QParameter1 | 1 | 1671 | 1671 | 22.3399 | 2.615e-06 | *** |
| data$Stage1_RM1_QParameter2 | 1 | 1307 | 1307 | 17.4746 | 3.169e-05 | *** |
| data$Stage3_RM1_QParameter1 | 1 | 38932 | 38932 | 520.5839 | < 2.2e-16 | *** |
| data$Stage3_RM1_QParameter2 | 1 | 471 | 471 | 6.2975 | 0.012250 | * |
| data$Stage3_RM2_QParameter1 | 1 | 6253 | 6253 | 83.6113 | < 2.2e-16 | *** |
| data$Stage3_RM3_QParameter1 | 1 | 10512 | 10512 | 140.5668 | < 2.2e-16 | *** |
| data$Stage3_RM3_QParameter2 | 1 | 7105 | 7105 | 95.0078 | < 2.2e-16 | *** |
| Residuals | 990 | 74038 | 75 | | | |

```
---
Signif. codes:  0 '***' 0.001 '**' 0.01 '*' 0.05 '.' 0.1 ' ' 1
>
Signif. codes:  0 '***' 0.001 '**' 0.01 '*' 0.05 '.' 0.1 ' ' 1
```

As we can observe from the results of the regression model, all the nine dimensions-five raw material quality parameters from Stage 3 and four quality parameters from stage 1-have a p value less than 5%, which means that we can reject our null hypothesis and confirm that there is definitely an impact of raw material properties on the Output Quality Parameter 1 for the detergent.

In the same way, let's study the relationship with the remaining three output quality parameters:

The same preceding code with a different dependent variable, that is, Output Quality Parameters 2, 3, and 4, can be used to view the results shared here.

```
#For Output_QualityParameter2
> anova(regression_model)
Analysis of Variance Table
```

**Response: Output_QualityParameter2**

|  | Df | Sum Sq | Mean Sq | F value | Pr(>F) | |
|---|---|---|---|---|---|---|
| data$Stage1_RM2_QParameter1 | 1 | 679471149 | 679471149 | 807.4247 | < 2.2e-16 | *** |

```
data$Stage1_RM2_QParameter2      1     220054      220054   0.2615  0.609210
data$Stage1_RM1_QParameter1      1    7626898     7626898   9.0631  0.002674 **
data$Stage1_RM1_QParameter2      1       1865        1865   0.0022  0.962466
data$Stage3_RM1_QParameter1      1   28665642    28665642  34.0638  7.222e-09 ***
data$Stage3_RM1_QParameter2      1      16686       16686   0.0198  0.888048
data$Stage3_RM2_QParameter1      1    7902621     7902621   9.3908  0.002240 **
data$Stage3_RM3_QParameter1      1   21963781    21963781  26.0999  3.889e-07 ***
data$Stage3_RM3_QParameter2      1    2717698     2717698   3.2295  0.072628 .
Residuals                      990  833113480      841529
---
Signif. codes:   0 '***' 0.001 '**' 0.01 '*' 0.05 '.' 0.1 ' ' 1
```

#Performing a regression model for Output_QualityParameter3
```
> anova(regression_model)
Analysis of Variance Table

Response: Output_QualityParameter3
                              Df       Sum Sq     Mean Sq  F value     Pr(>F)
data$Stage1_RM2_QParameter1    1   4040239678  4040239678 802.2017 < 2.2e-16
***
data$Stage1_RM2_QParameter2    1       928873      928873   0.1844   0.66769
data$Stage1_RM1_QParameter1    1      1806552     1806552   0.3587   0.54937
data$Stage1_RM1_QParameter2    1       154571      154571   0.0307   0.86097
data$Stage3_RM1_QParameter1    1    223809743   223809743  44.4381  4.354e-11
***
data$Stage3_RM1_QParameter2    1     14285485    14285485   2.8364   0.09246 .
data$Stage3_RM2_QParameter1    1     83651956    83651956  16.6093  4.960e-05
***
data$Stage3_RM3_QParameter1    1     23903953    23903953   4.7462   0.02960 *
data$Stage3_RM3_QParameter2    1      3612936     3612936   0.7174   0.39722
Residuals                    990   4986074467     5036439
---
Signif. codes:   0 '***' 0.001 '**' 0.01 '*' 0.05 '.' 0.1 ' ' 1
```

#Performing a regression model for Output_QualityParameter4
```
> anova(regression_model)
Analysis of Variance Table

Response: Output_QualityParameter4
                              Df      Sum Sq    Mean Sq  F value     Pr(>F)
data$Stage1_RM2_QParameter1    1   188207474  188207474 883.5117 < 2.2e-16 ***
data$Stage1_RM2_QParameter2    1      187981     187981   0.8824  0.347761
data$Stage1_RM1_QParameter1    1     1472674    1472674   6.9132  0.008689 **
data$Stage1_RM1_QParameter2    1       50382      50382   0.2365  0.626845
data$Stage3_RM1_QParameter1    1     8718238    8718238  40.9265  2.434e-10 ***
data$Stage3_RM1_QParameter2    1        4720       4720   0.0222  0.881697
data$Stage3_RM2_QParameter1    1     2559058    2559058  12.0131  0.000551 ***
data$Stage3_RM3_QParameter1    1      789099     789099   3.7043  0.054558 .
```

```
data$Stage3_RM3_QParameter2   1     741804    741804   3.4823  0.062324 .
Residuals                     990 210891835    213022
---
Signif. codes:  0 '***' 0.001 '**' 0.01 '*' 0.05 '.' 0.1 ' ' 1
```

Unlike Output Quality Parameter 1, we have only a few relationships between the remaining output quality parameters and the raw material quality parameters.

In an nutshell, output quality parameter 2 is impacted by five of the raw material properties, Output quality parameter 3 by four of the raw material properties, and Output quality parameter 4 only by three of the raw material quality parameters.

Therefore, we now have a more detailed picture of the issues as we understand how the raw material quality parameters impact the overall quality of the detergent and how they impact the individual output quality parameters.

# Hypotheses – category 3

- Resources used during manufacturing in Stage 3 have an impact on the end quality of the detergent
- A delay in manufacturing during Stage 3 has an impact on the end quality of the detergent

Validating these hypotheses is now straightforward. Each of these cases have already been encountered earlier. Both the hypotheses can be validated using the chi-squared test. Let's quickly look at the results of these tests.

**Hypothesis #1**: Resources used during manufacturing in Stage 3 have an impact on the end quality of the detergent:

```
> #Creating a table of the frequency count for the two variables
> #that is, Outcome v/s Variable of Interest
> sample<-table(data$Stage3_ResourceName,data$Detergent_Quality)
> sample    #View the actual table
              Bad Good
  Resource_105   8   68
  Resource_106  15   55
  Resource_107   9   65
  Resource_108  88  298
  Resource_109 105  289

> #Perform the Chi Squared Test of Independence
> chisq.test(sample)
```

```
Pearson's Chi-squared test

data:   sample
X-squared = 14.741, df = 4, p-value = 0.005271
```

We see a similar issue like the one we encountered earlier, that is, the results are slightly above 5%. To make our results more interpretable for the test, we can try to reduce the number of groups and give it another try. As the number of records in Resources 105,106, and 107 are comparatively low, we can club them together and perform the test again:

```
> #Transforming the variable
> data$Stage3_ResourceName_new<-
as.factor(ifelse(data$Stage3_ResourceName
%in% c("Resource_105","Resource_106",
 "Resource_107"),
"Others",
as.character(data$Stage3_ResourceName )))
> sample<-table(data$Stage3_ResourceName_new,
data$Detergent_Quality)
> sample     #View the actual table
               Bad Good
  Others        32  188
  Resource_108  88  298
  Resource_109 105  289
> #Perform the Chi Squared Test of Independence
> chisq.test(sample)
      Pearson's Chi-squared test
data:   sample
X-squared = 11.894, df = 2, p-value = 0.002614
```

As we can see, we now have the p value lower than our cutoff threshold, which can help us in rejecting our null hypothesis. Therefore, the resources used in Stage 3 can have an impact on end quality of the detergent.

**Hypothesis #2**: A delay in manufacturing during Stage 3 has an impact on the end quality of the detergent:

```
> #Creating a table of the frequency count for the two variables
> #that is, Outcome v/s Variable of Interest
> sample<-table(data$Stage3_DelayFlag,data$Detergent_Quality)
> sample     #View the actual table
       Bad Good
  No   115  437
  Yes  110  338
>
> #Perform the Chi Squared Test of Independence
> chisq.test(sample)
```

```
   Pearson's Chi-squared test with Yates' continuity correction
data:   sample
X-squared = 1.7552, df = 1, p-value = 0.1852
```

The p value is very high, therefore we accept our null hypothesis-delay in stage 3 does not impact the end quality of the detergent.

# Summarizing Exploratory Data Analysis phase

We have now finished the EDA phase, that is, validating results by performing a variety of statistical tests on the various hypotheses or insights that we touch on during our initial exercise. In the entire course, we have found a lot of different results; some were drafted with our heuristics and some were drafted with our observation from the data. All of these insights or observations are signals of what could be the problem. We went a step ahead and validated statistically the fact that the signals that we see are real signals and not just due to random data points. Now we have a list of dimensions that we are confident about having an impact on the end outcome, that is, the quality of the detergent, but we still miss out on one important thing. We need to study how these different dimensions affect the problem, that is, the quality of the detergent. To understand this, we need to revisit the previous four milestones in the current chapter's exercise (refer to the diagram in the Exploratory Data Analysis section) and stich together the results by studying with a forensic mindset to understand the why in the big picture. In the next section, we will connect the dots by assimilating all our learnings from the exercise to stitch the results and answer the why question of the problem.

# Root Cause Analysis

We now begin our journey with answering the why question from all the insights we have gathered till now. Let's assimilate all our results that we have validated in our EDA exercise. Once we have all the results, let's try to simplify it to create a simple story that helps us in answering the questions in a more lucid way.

The following figure is an extended version of the DDH matrix we designed in the previous section along with the results we found during our exercise:

| Hypothesis | Result | Insight |
|---|---|---|
| Line 1 has an overall higher chance of manufacturing more number of bad quality detergent products | FALSE | Assembly Line has no impact on the end quality of the detergent |
| Line 1 has an overall higher chance of deteriorating the Output Quality Parameters in the detergent | TRUE | Assembly line has an impact on Output Quality Parameter 2,3, and 4 |
| As the deviation between Order Quantity and actual Produced Quantity increases, the chance of the bad quality detergent being manufactured also increases | TRUE | The orders with "High" deviation of produced quantity have higher chances for bad quality |
| As the deviation between Order Quantity and actual Produced Quantity increases, the output quality parameters deteriorates | TRUE | The orders with "High" deviation of produced quantity have an impact on the Output Quality Parameters 2,3, and 4 |
| Stage 1 Raw Material quality parameters have an impact on the end quality of the detergent | TRUE | *Results shared in the following text |
| Stage 3 Raw Material quality parameters have an impact on the end quality of the detergent | TRUE | |
| Resources used during manufacturing in Stage 3 have an impact on the end quality of the detergent | TRUE | Resources used during manufacturing in Stage 3 have an impact on the end quality of the detergent |
| A delay in manufacturing during Stage 3 has an impact on the end quality of the detergent | FALSE | Stage 3 delay has no impact on the quality of the detergent |

For the raw material quality parameters, the results can be summarized as follows:

- For Output Quality Parameter 1: All nine raw material quality parameters have an impact on the quality.
- For Output Quality Parameter 2: Stage 1 RM1_QParameter1 and RM2_QParameter1 have an impact. Stage 3 RM1_QParameter1, RM2_QParameter1, and RM3_QParameter1 have an impact.
- For Output Quality Parameter 3: Stage 1 RM2_QParameter1 has an impact. Stage 3 RM1_QParameter1, RM2_QParameter1, and RM3_QParameter1 have an impact.
- For Output Quality Parameter 4: Stage 1 RM1_QParameter1, and RM2_QParameter1 have an impact. Stage 3 RM1_QParameter1 and RM2_QParameter1 have an impact.

The results overall look very interesting; except for two, all the other hypotheses that we framed have been validated statistically and the results are positive.

# Synthesizing results

So let's start simple; we'll first synthesize the results that we have on our plate one by one.

The problem statement revolves around the quality of the detergent manufactured in a plant. The quality can be tagged as Good or Bad by combining the four final Output Quality Parameters from the manufacturing unit. The Assembly Line used for the manufacturing impacts three out of the four final output quality parameters, but still does not affect the final end quality of the detergent. A very important point to notice. The algorithm used to combine the four output quality parameter into the final Good/Bad is a weighted one (as mentioned earlier). The fact that Assembly Line impacts three output parameters and still does not impact the end quality could be a cue to understand that Output Quality Parameter 1 has a higher weightage than all others. It could also be the scenario that the impact that the 'Assembly Line' dimension has on the three output quality parameters might not be strong enough to make a final impact on the quality. Let's make a note of this point and move ahead.

There is usually a deviation between the planned quantity for the manufacturing order and the actual quantity produced. The quantity deviation for a particular manufacturing order is featured as High, Medium, or Low. The quantity deviation dimension has a heavy impact on the end quality of the detergent. The orders with High deviation have higher chances to produce a bad quality detergent. Similarly, the quantity deviation has an impact on three out of the four quality parameters similar to the Assembly Line dimension.

The quality of the raw materials used in Stage 1 and Stage 3 have a strong impact on the end quality. All the nine raw material quality parameters have an impact on Output Quality Parameter 1. From the nine raw material quality parameters, the most important ones are Stage1_RM1_QParameter1, Stage1_RM2_QParameter1, Stage3_RM1_QParameter1, and Stage3_RM2_QParameter1. These four raw material quality parameters have major impact on quality among the entire list. If we look at our previous section, "Studying Relationships", and refer to the visuals showcasing the correlation plots for Raw material Quality parameters and output quality parameters, we can easily notice that all the errors, that is, bad quality detergent, are produced when the value of the raw material quality parameter exceeds a certain threshold. For example, refer to the "Exploring Stage 1 dimensions" subsection in "Studying Relationships". If we observe the correlation plots for all four output quality parameters and Stage1_RM1_QParameter1, we can clearly see that the maximum number of data points have a value of ~4275 and majority of the bad quality cases appear beyond the value 4275 for this parameter. A simple rule enforcing the value of Quality Parameter 1 for Raw Material 1 from Stage 1 can be an easy approach to improve the quality of detergent produced. The same can be studied for the other eight raw material parameters.

The following can be noted as a thumb rule for raw material quality parameters. The ones featured as important have been added here:

 The following values are jotted by merely observing the correlation visuals like the ones studied earlier.

| Raw Material Quality Parameter | Max quality threshold |
|---|---|
| Stage 1- Raw Material 1 – Quality Parameter 1 | 4275 |
| Stage 1- Raw Material 2 – Quality Parameter 1 | 145 |
| Stage 3-Raw Material 1 – Quality Parameter 1 | 210 |
| Stage 3-Raw Material 2 – Quality Parameter 1 | 540 |

Lastly, the 'Resources used in Stage 3' dimension also impacts the end quality of the detergent. If we look back at the results of the EDA section, we can understand that Resource_109 has major propensity toward bad quality produce. A thumb rule to fix Resource_109 for cleanliness or any other domain-related attribute that we would not be aware about or worst case scenario to avoid Resource_109 for the manufacturing process will also help in reducing the bad quality produce.

# Visualizing insights

To aid in faster root cause analysis, let's create a simple tree diagram that would simplify visualizing all insights in one view. Once we have all our insights and recommendations condensed and improved in one place, stitching a story would be an extremely easy task.

The following diagram represents the factors that cause the bad quality of the produce. The text below the factors elucidate how the factor affects the produce and what can be done to reduce the perils of bad produce:

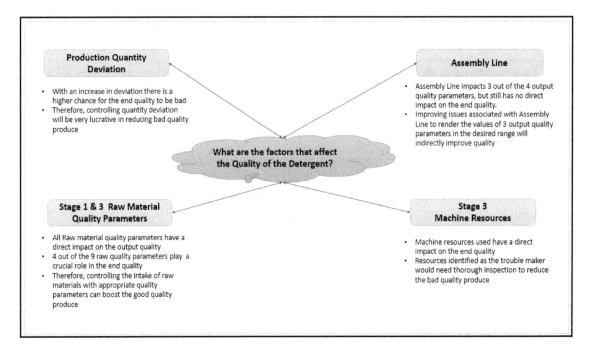

If we study the visual, we can quickly connect our initial steps of the problem solving framework. In case you find it hard to recollect, it was called the SCQ-Situation Complication and Question. Referencing the same old diagram, let's juxtapose our findings and results to see how far we have reached.

The following diagram overlays our results and insights over the initial framework design. It seems like we have everything we need to solve the problem:

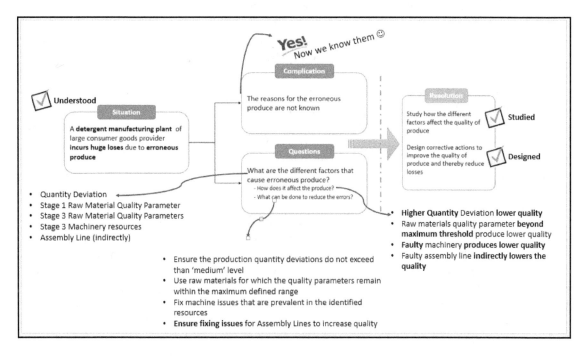

Yay, it looks very accomplished! Doesn't it?

# Stitching the Story together

We have covered everything that we planned to. The last thing that would be left on our plate is to stich the final story together. So John (operations head) had initially approached us with the problem where he mentioned that his manufacturing unit was facing huge losses due to the bad produce of detergent.

We brainstormed on how we could help him and finally designed an SCQ that set the context and objective of the problem to be solved. We then proceeded in a structured way to explore, study, experiment, and visualize data to find out why the problem was happening.

In our analysis, we found that the major culprits for bad quality produce of detergents are defined by four simple dimensions, namely, Production Quantity deviation, Quality of the raw materials used, the Assembly Line used for production, and the machinery used for the manufacturing during Stage 3 of the process. In an attempt to study how these factors affect the quality, we understood that there is a positive relationship between the production deviation and probability of a bad quality produce. In a nutshell, the chances of manufacturing bad quality detergent are very high if the deviation between the produced quantity and order quantity is also high. Also, the quality of the raw materials used in Stage 1 and Stage 3 have a direct impact on the end quality of the detergent. Four of the nine quality parameters measured have very high relationship with the end quality. There are clear signals of bad quality produce when the quality of the raw materials are accepted beyond a threshold.

The machinery used in stage 3 of the manufacturing process seems to be a troublemaker. There are a few faulty operations in the machine that need to be fixed quickly to reduce bad quality produce. Finding the issues associated with the entire machine will be an arduous task, but as we know that one of the machines has a higher chance of producing a bad quality product, we can now narrow down our fixes in the differences associated between the machines used. Finally, the Assembly Line used for the manufacturing also has an indirect impact on the quality. It could be a case where we have the assembly line impacting the processing time or any of the above mentioned factors that then ultimately impacts the quality. Identifying these intricacies and fixing them will further improve the detergent quality.

# Conclusion

We now have a simplified story in front of us for the problem that we are trying to solve. The answers to the questions we framed in our initial problem definition phase have helped us study the reasons for the problem. Let's quickly summarize the different actions we need to suggest to John so that he can solve the problem and reduce the losses by mitigating the perils of producing bad quality detergent.

# Production Quantity

There is often a huge gap between the quantities of detergent planned to be manufactured and the actual quantity manufactured. The deviation has a huge impact on the end quality of the detergent. An increase in deviation significantly increases the chances of manufacturing bad quality detergent. Appropriate measures to plan out manufacturing detergent in the required quantity rather than deviating from the proposed quantity to incorporate eleventh-hour changes is highly recommended.

# Raw material quality parameters

The quality of the raw materials used to manufacture detergent has an extremely high impact on the quality of the detergent. It is clearly observed in the data that the quality of raw materials beyond an identified threshold have an extremely high chance to produce bad quality detergent. It is therefore recommended to use raw materials with quality ranging within the standard/observed threshold range.

# Resources/Machinery used in Stage 3

Resources used in the third stage of manufacturing have an impact on the quality of the detergent manufactured. Identifying the exhaustive list of issues associated with the machine may not be a feasible solution. However, as one specific resource demonstrates higher propensity to produce bad quality, we can investigate the mere differences by comparing the machines with the others that produce better quality detergent and then fix them.

# Assembly Line

The assembly line does not directly impact the end quality of the detergent, but still has a strong impact on three of the four quality parameters. A study of the impact of Assembly Line on other vital factors is highly recommended so that we could fix them and further improve the detergent quality.

These recommendations can definitely help John in quickly taking actions to improve the detergent quality and thereby reduce losses.

# Summary

In this chapter, we moved one step ahead in solving a real-life IoT business use case. Using the blueprint of the problem that we defined in the previous chapter, we attempted solving the problem in a structured way guided by the problem solving framework. After having the business problem well-defined, we got our hands dirty by solving the business problem using R. We started our journey with identifying gold mines in the data for decision making, where we examined the data sources to understand what hypotheses can we prove to solve our problem. We then validated the fact that we have a good amount of data to solve the problem and studied more about the data to understand how the data can be used in our use case. After gathering a fair amount of data and domain context, we explored each dimension in the IoT ecosystem and studied what the data has to say. We performed univariate analysis and also transformed the dimensions to create more powerful and valuable dimensions. We then studied the relationships that exist in the data to understand how different dimensions relate with the quality of the detergent manufacture by performing bivariate analysis. After studying the relationships and collecting signals/insight from the data, we validated our observations statistically to cement our insights using a variety of statistical techniques such as hypothesis testing using Chi-square tests, T tests, regression ANOVA, and so on With our results being validated, we thoroughly synthesized our results and stitched together a story and designed recommendations to mitigate the hurdles and thus answered all the key business questions that we had drafted while defining the problem.

Thus, using a structured and matured methodology and combining multiple disciplines such as math, business, and technology, we finally solved the problem. However, we are not done yet. As we discussed earlier, the problem always evolves. The current problem can be explored further by asking more powerful questions like 'When'. This is when we will explore a different area of analytics called 'Predictive Analytics'. In the next chapter, we take our problem solving skills one step ahead by answering the question when and therefore explore predictive analytics in more depth.

# 4
# Experimenting Predictive Analytics for IoT

Humans solve a problem by asking a series of nested questions to themselves. When a problem arises, asking Why, What, and How more and more number of times until all our questions are answered helps us solve a problem. Decision Science is no different. The entire stack of decision science, that is, Descriptive + Inquisitive + Predictive + Prescriptive, is designed on the basis of the different kinds of questions we ask. The solutions we develop get more and more powerful with the depth of the questions we frame Initially, we surface the problem space by understanding 'what' has happened, then we get in deeper by understanding how it happened. The solution to the problem becomes even more powerful when you have an answer to the question when, and this is when we touch base with Predictive Analytics. The ability to look into the future and then solve a problem is way more powerful and effective than any other alternative.

In this chapter, we begin our journey with predictive analytics using a variety of statistical techniques. We will continue on the same use case solved in the previous chapter and delve deeper into the solution with the 'when' question. In the course of the problem's solution, we'll explore a variety of techniques to predict the outcome based on the type of the outcome event. We will start approaching the problem by understanding what problem we are solving and what algorithm to use and why. You will then learn the fundamentals of the statistical technique and practically solve a prediction problem. Finally, we'll assimilate the results and tie back the insights to the story to strengthen the solution.

In this chapter, we will explore few simple algorithms such as linear regression, logistic regression, and decision trees. In the next chapter, we will explore more advanced and sophisticated machine learning techniques for predictive analytics. The current chapter will focus on the following topics:

- Resurfacing the problem – what's next?
- Linear regression – predicting a continuous outcome
- Decision trees – predicting the intuitive way
- Logistic regression – predicting a binary outcome

# Resurfacing the problem – What's next?

Before exploring the different techniques for predictive analytics, let's take a step back and understand what's next in order to solve the problem better. After finding out the reasons for the bad quality produce in the previous chapter, we assimilated all our learnings to draft a story. John seemed to be very impressed with the solution. His team studied the different factors that affected the quality of the detergent manufactured and brainstormed for countermeasures to alleviate bad quality produce before manufacturing the detergent. The team identified one critical output quality parameter-Output Quality Parameter 2-that affects the end outcome the most and reached out to us to check whether we could build a solution that would aid them in understanding the quality of detergent before the manufacturing process. Had the team been aware beforehand about the end quality of the detergent going to be manufactured, they could immediately have taken countermeasures to improve the quality, if bad. The team could benefit a lot with visibility into the predicted value of Output Quality Parameter 2 (critical quality parameter) or the actual end outcome of the detergent-Good/Bad-before initiating the manufacturing process.

These are actually two separate problems. Let's understand the situation in a more layman way by again taking the analogy of cooking. Let's say that you are cooking pasta and you have all the necessary ingredients in the required amount readied on a plate before cooking. Your friend, Rick, an expert chef with phenomenal experience in cooking a variety of cuisines, visits your place while you are about to cook. Rick takes a closer look at the different ingredients you have readied for the dish along with the quantity. He assumes that you would be cooking as per the recipe, but based on the quantity and quality of the ingredients, he makes an estimate on the rating for the taste of the dish that will be prepared on a scale of 1-9 (9 being the best). After a close examination, he estimates that the rating for the dish would be around 6.5 (average). You feel heartbroken and ask him why? He smiles and points towards the turmeric powder and chilly powder that seems to be of a little lower grade. Based on his suggestion, you change the turmeric and chilly powder by borrowing some of a better quality from your neighbor. He then takes a closer look again and says, *Yes, this seems perfect! An 8.5 on 9* (excellent) You now feel confident and start cooking for a delicious dinner.

Intuitive, isn't it? We wish we had a friend like Rick for every problem we try to solve.

John is also in need of such an expert who can assist the technician responsible for manufacturing the detergent. The expert would examine upfront the readied ingredients, that is, raw materials, and estimate the quality of the detergent that will be manufactured in order to take preventive measures before the first step (if bad quality). The expert could tell the technician that in case he plans to use the existing set of raw materials with the defined quantities, then the end quality of the detergent will be around 670 units (assume). The technician realizes that with such quality parameters, the chances that the detergent being manufactured will be rejected are very high. He would quickly summon the person in charge of the storehouse to replace some of the raw materials or probably change some settings in the machine. This entire process can be boiled down to one simple word-prediction. Having a view into the future helps everyone avoid getting into a problem. John reached out to us to check whether we could build a system that could help the team with answers to a few questions regarding the quality of the end produce. The answer is **yes**! We can definitely help him in building a system that can predict the quality of the detergent before being manufactured. Let's understand how we can do this.

There are two different types of problems that we can solve here based on the end outcome. For the prediction method, we can predict either each individual quality parameter or the end outcome-Good/Bad. The latter is a categorical outcome whereas the former is a continuous outcome. Let's take a shot at solving both of these problems separately. Based on the results, we can take a call on which would be a better model. We'll begin by trying to solve the first problem: predicting as a critical one.

# Linear regression – predicting a continuous outcome

There are a variety of statistical techniques available that can be used for prediction. Their usage is defined by the type of the dependent variable (continuous/categorical). A different technique or algorithm is required to solve these two different categories. We can use linear regression to predict a continuous variable and logistic regression for a categorical variable. A plethora of other techniques are available for these cases, but let's start solving the problem of predicting a continuous variable using linear regression.

## Prelude

Before we begin understanding what we are going to build, let's take a moment to clearly understand the requirements from John's team and also study about how they plan to use the results. The team needs our help in building a system that can predict the actual quality parameter (Output Quality Parameter 2) before the manufacturing process. The team of technicians and store managers plan the production a day in advance by preparing and staging the required raw materials and machinery to manufacture the detergent. The system that we build should be capable of predicting the quality parameter (continuous) of the end produce based on the available information, namely, raw material quantity and quality dimensions, machine/resources identified, assembly line to be used, time/day for the planned manufacturing, and so on. The operational data dimensions cannot be captured while staging. The prediction of the end produce quality parameter before the manufacturing process can aid the technician in taking quick countermeasures to mitigate the chances of a bad quality produce. A comparison of the quality parameter prediction with the benchmark along with the estimated impact from different factors can aid the technician in implementing quick fixes such as changing raw materials with better quality alternatives or fixing issues associated with machinery or the assembly line or any other dimension identified as highly influential to improve the quality and thereby reduce losses.

## Solving the prediction problem

To predict the quality parameter of the detergent manufactured, which is a continuous variable, we can use a very famous and easy-to-use statistical technique called Linear Regression. There are many other alternatives (even more powerful), but let's start with a fundamental algorithm.

# So what is linear regression?

Linear regression is a statistical technique that models the relationship between a dependent variable and one or multiple independent variables by fitting a linear equation to the observed data. It is the study of linear, additive relationships between variables. When there is only one independent variable, it is called 'Simple Linear Regression', and when multiple independent variables are studied together, it is called 'Multiple Linear Regression'. In general, simple linear regression is rarely used; most use cases we deal with in business will be for multiple linear regression. Therefore, from here onward, all references made to linear regression will be a use case referring to multiple linear regression. Let's quickly move on to solving the problem that we have on our plate. You'll learn new concepts related to linear regression as and when we come across them.

The end outcome or dependent variable is Output Quality Parameter 2. The input variables we choose need to be carefully selected as we are trying to build a prediction model that will consider data points available before the manufacturing process has started. The use case we are solving captures data dimensions throughout the manufacturing process. Referring to the' Understanding data landscape' subsection in `Chapter 3`, *The What and Why – Using Exploratory Decision Science for IoT*, will give you a more detailed idea about which data dimensions are captured before, during, and after the manufacturing process.

From all the dimensions available, we can narrow down our selection to the following dimensions: the manufacturing date, order quantity and produced quantity, (Production quantity changes are made usually at the last minute before beginning the manufacturing process.) assembly line and machine/resources used for the manufacturing process, raw material quantity and quality, and so on. We will not be able to use dimensions such as delay flags, overall and stage-wise processing time, stage-wise resultant mixture output quality parameters, and others as these dimensions will only be available during or after the manufacturing process. The other manufacturing process-level dimensions such as the site, location, product, and so on can ideally be used, but in our case, as the data is a subset for just one location and one product, it will not be valuable to consider them in the model building exercise.

So, in a nutshell, we have to model a relationship to predict 'Output Quality Parameter 2' as a function of raw material quantity and quality parameters, production quantity deviation (feature), assembly line and machine/resources used at each stage, previous product-related features, and manufacturing date- and time-related features.

To build a linear regression model, we can use the 'lm' function in the stats package.

The lm function is used to fit linear models. The following example shows you how to use the function using R:

```
> # Linear Regression Example
> fit <- lm(y ~ x1 + x2 + x3, data=mydata)
> summary(fit) # show results
```

Here, y is the independent variable and x1, x2, and x3 are the independent variables. Once a model is created, the results can be summarized using the summary function. Let's try solving our use case using the dependent variable 'Output Quality Parameter 2' and a few independent dimensions that we have:

 Using a few random independent dimensions in the first step is not the best method to start with. This is more to get you acquainted with the technique. We will discuss about best practices and alternatives in the coming exercises.

```
#Performing Linear Regression on a few independent variables
> fit<-lm(Output_QualityParameter2~
                #The Production Quantity deviation feature
                data$Quantity_Deviation_new +
                #The Production Quantity deviation feature
                data$Stage1_PrevProduct_1 +
                #Stage 1 Raw Material Quality Parameters
                data$Stage1_RM2_QParameter1 +
                data$Stage1_RM2_QParameter2 +
                data$Stage1_RM1_QParameter1 +
                data$Stage1_RM1_QParameter2 +
                #Machine/Resources used in a Stage
                data$Stage3_ResourceName_new +
                data$Stage1_ProductChange_Flag+
                #Flag indicating Normal/Abnormal consumption
                data$Stage1_RM2_Consumption_Flag
            ,
            data=data
        )
> summary(fit)
```

```
#Result Output
Call:
lm(formula = Output_QualityParameter2 ~ data$Quantity_Deviation_new +
    data$Stage1_PrevProduct_1 + data$Stage1_RM2_QParameter1 +
    data$Stage1_RM2_QParameter2 + data$Stage1_RM1_QParameter1 +
    data$Stage1_RM1_QParameter2 + data$Stage3_ResourceName_new +
    data$Stage1_ProductChange_Flag + data$Stage1_RM2_Consumption_Flag,

    data = data)

Residuals:
    Min      1Q  Median      3Q     Max
-2632.6  -591.7     4.0   503.2  5064.6

Coefficients:
                                               Estimate Std. Error t value Pr(>|t|)
(Intercept)                                   2299.1744   795.2243   2.891  0.00392 **
data$Quantity_Deviation_newLow                  97.1952    70.6117   1.376  0.16899
data$Quantity_Deviation_newMedium              -70.0664    75.0060  -0.934  0.35046
data$Stage1_PrevProduct_1Product_545           252.0285   106.6254   2.364  0.01829 *
data$Stage1_RM2_QParameter1                     84.1166     5.5395  15.185  < 2e-16 ***
data$Stage1_RM2_QParameter2                    -16.5414     8.9058  -1.857  0.06356 .
data$Stage1_RM1_QParameter1                      0.3223     0.1823   1.768  0.07735 .
data$Stage1_RM1_QParameter2                     15.4425   115.4700   0.134  0.89364
data$Stage3_ResourceName_newResource_108       384.2826    96.5075   3.982 7.34e-05 ***
data$Stage3_ResourceName_newResource_109      -149.8731    96.1707  -1.558  0.11946
data$Stage1_ProductChange_FlagYes              -29.5209   105.0881  -0.281  0.77883
data$Stage1_RM2_Consumption_FlagNormal        -367.6675    77.3153  -4.755 2.27e-06 ***
---
Signif. codes:  0 '***' 0.001 '**' 0.01 '*' 0.05 '.' 0.1 ' ' 1

Residual standard error: 923.4 on 988 degrees of freedom

Multiple R-squared:  0.4673,  Adjusted R-squared:  0.4614

F-statistic: 78.81 on 11 and 988 DF,  p-value: < 2.2e-16
```

Too many results to interpret? No worries if the preceding output was difficult to interpret. We'll explore the important aspects of the results step by step. Take a look at the different components highlighted; we'll start with them and eventually understand others in depth.

Let's begin by understanding what exactly we will achieve. In linear regression, we are identifying a relationship between one dependent variable and multiple independent variables. The relationship will help us determine the value of the dependent variable when we have the values of the corresponding independent variables and the impact of each independent variable on the dependent variable. In a nutshell, we have two simple results: the predicted value of dependent value and the quantified impact from each individual independent variable.

So how do we get this?

The linear regression equation is as follows:

$$Y = \beta_0 + \beta_1 X_1 + \beta_2 X_2 + \cdots\cdots + \beta_n X_n + \varepsilon$$

Where:

- $y$ – Dependent variable
- $\beta_0$ – Intercept
- $\beta_1$ – Estimate for $X_1$
- $X_1$ – Independent variable 1
- $\varepsilon$ – Error term

For any specific scenario, if we have the values of the independent variables (say, raw material quality parameters) and their estimates, that is, the impact of the variable on the dependent variable (Output Quality), we can predict the value of the output quality. The intercept is a constant that is the value at which the fitted line crosses the y axis.

There are a few broad areas such as the formula, residual deviance, intercept, estimates, standard error, t value and p value of the independent variables and intercept, residual standard error, and R-squared and F Statistic that we need to understand so that we can interpret the output. We'll first understand these topics before we delve into the regression exercise.

# Interpreting the regression outputs

The whole process of linear regression is based on the fact that there exists a relation between the independent variables and dependent variable. In case this is not true, then there is absolutely no need to move ahead. However, if there exists at least one variable that has a relationship with the dependent variable, then we need to find the estimates for the independent variable to construct the equation. With the estimates (coefficient) and intercept calculated, we can construct the equation that can aid us in predicting the dependent variable.

Before we predict the value of the dependent variable, we need to know a few important points: how correct are the estimates and how accurate are the predictions. To help us understand these important questions, the regression output provides us with a variety of test results and estimates. Examining the results of these tests and estimates, we can understand the goodness of fit, that is, how well has the relationship between the dependent variable and independent variable been defined. The broad topics that we discussed in the previous section are a part of the results that help us understand the goodness of fit. Let's explore these results one by one.

# F statistic

The first step in linear regression is to check whether there is a relationship between independent variables and the dependent variable. This is tackled using the same approach we saw in the previous chapter-hypothesis testing. We will define a null hypothesis and alternate hypothesis as follows:

- **H0**: No relationship exists between the dependent and independent variables
- **H1**: At least one of the independent variables are related

To test the hypothesis, we calculate the F statistic. The F statistic is used to test whether a group of variables are jointly significant (similar to the t statistic from t test, which confirms whether a single variable is statistically significant). From the results of the regression, you can notice the last highlighted result, "F-statistic: 78.81 on 11 and 988 DF, p-value: < 2.2e-16". The overall p value is way lower than our desired cutoff-5%-and F statistic can be interpreted as the higher the better. If the F statistic is closer to 1, then there is a very high chance that the null hypothesis is true. In this case, as the F statistic is larger than 1, we can comfortably reject the null hypothesis. A quick question that would arise while interpreting the F statistic is, how large should the F statistic be to reject the null hypothesis?

As a thumb rule, we can call out (n = number of rows of data, p = number of independent variable); when n is very large that is, n > (p*20) [at least 20 cases for each independent variable;: if the F statistic is even a little above 1, it is enough for us to reject the null hypothesis. With a lower n, we need a higher F statistic to reject the null hypothesis.

Moreover, the F statistic is always studied along with the overall p value. With the preceding results, we can conclude that it is highly unlikely for the null hypothesis to be true. Therefore, we can reject the null hypothesis and affirmatively mention that there exists a relation between at least one of the independent variables and dependent variable and move ahead to model the relationship.

# Estimate/coefficients

Once we establish the fact that there is scope for the relationship to be modeled, we move on to the most important part of the results, that is, estimates for each independent variable that help us quantify how much does each independent variable impact the end dependent variable:

```
Coefficients:
                                                     Estimate
(Intercept)                                         2299.1744
data$Quantity_Deviation_newLow                        97.1952
data$Quantity_Deviation_newMedium                    -70.0664
data$Stage1_PrevProduct_1Product_545                 252.0285
data$Stage1_RM2_QParameter1                           84.1166
data$Stage1_RM2_QParameter2                          -16.5414
data$Stage1_RM1_QParameter1                            0.3223
data$Stage1_RM1_QParameter2                           15.4425
data$Stage3_ResourceName_newResource_108             384.2826
data$Stage3_ResourceName_newResource_109            -149.8731
data$Stage1_ProductChange_FlagYes                    -29.5209
data$Stage1_RM2_Consumption_FlagNormal              -367.6675
```

The preceding code shows you a small part of the regression output result shared earlier. The estimates show how much and how do they impact the dependent variable. A positive estimate indicates that, for every unit increase of the respective independent variable, there is a corresponding increase in the result and vice versa. As we can see, all the independent variables used in the regression equation (formula) have an individual estimate computed, but we can see that for the categorical variables like Stage 3 Resource name, the dimension has internally converted them to binary flags with the respective estimates. This is because linear regression only handles continuous variables, and therefore every categorical variable is internally coded as a binary flag. Along with the independent variables, we also see 'Intercept'. Intercept can be simply called the point where the regression line meets the y axis that can also be interpreted as the expected mean value of Y when Xs are 0. To understand this better, let's say that you are modeling height as a function of age and gender. Gender is a categorical variable (which will be coded internally as 1 and 0), say gender =1 for male and 0 for female. Therefore, the variance when the values of X is zero is taken care by the intercept.

## Standard error, t-value, and p value

Looking at the estimates, we may not be able to directly assert the results even though we have confirmed that there exists a relationship between the independent variables and dependent variable. We are not sure whether each variable has an impact. To confirm whether the estimates of each of these variables are significant, we have results from a variety of tests performed over the estimates such as standard error, t test, p value, and others. Let's look at how to interpret them:

```
Coefficients:
                                           Estimate Std. Error t value Pr(>|t|)
(Intercept)                               2299.1744   795.2243   2.891  0.00392  **
data$Quantity_Deviation_newLow              97.1952    70.6117   1.376  0.16899
data$Quantity_Deviation_newMedium          -70.0664    75.0060  -0.934  0.35046
data$Stage1_PrevProduct_1Product_545       252.0285   106.6254   2.364  0.01829  *
data$Stage1_RM2_QParameter1                 84.1166     5.5395  15.185  < 2e-16  ***
data$Stage1_RM2_QParameter2                -16.5414     8.9058  -1.857  0.06356  .
data$Stage1_RM1_QParameter1                  0.3223     0.1823   1.768  0.07735  .
data$Stage1_RM1_QParameter2                 15.4425   115.4700   0.134  0.89364
data$Stage3_ResourceName_newResource_108   384.2826    96.5075   3.982 7.34e-05  ***
data$Stage3_ResourceName_newResource_109  -149.8731    96.1707  -1.558  0.11946
data$Stage1_ProductChange_FlagYes          -29.5209   105.0881  -0.281  0.77883
data$Stage1_RM2_Consumption_FlagNormal    -367.6675    77.3153  -4.755 2.27e-06  ***
```

The objective in using all these results is to validate whether there exists a relationship between the dependent variable and each independent variable. In order to prove this, standard errors are calculated and the null hypothesis is framed as: no relationship exists between x and y. We then determine whether the **estimate** is truly far away from 0. If the standard error of the estimate is small, then relatively small values of the estimate can reject the null hypothesis. If the standard error is large, then the estimate should also be large enough to reject the null hypothesis. To prove the hypothesis, we compute the t statistic, which measures the number of standard deviations that the estimate is away from 0. Alternatively, we compute the p value for each individual independent variable that will help us confirm whether there was any relationship between x and y. The entire process is made easy to interpret by examining the presence of '*' at the right-hand side of the result. Take a closer look at Stage 1 RM2 Quality Parameter 1 and 2. More number of asterisks indicate a lower p value that cues for higher chances for a relationship between the variable and output as well as the estimates to be true.

Similarly, once we have details about which dimension has a stronger relationship with the outcome as well as how it impacts, we need few more overall statistics that can help us understand the goodness of fit. If we glance at the results of regression (provided at the beginning of this section), we can see Residuals, Multiple R Squared, Residual Standard Error, and Adjusted R Squared. Let's understand these results better.

# Residuals, multiple R squared, residual standard error and adjusted R squared

Residuals can be defined as the difference between the actual and predicted value for the dependent variable. The lower the residuals will tend to be, the closer we make the predictions. The first result shown in the output (after the formula) is the percentile distribution of residuals. After predicting the value on the existing data, if we look at the percentile distribution of the residuals-errors-we can understand how they look:

Residuals:

```
    Min        1Q     Median      3Q      Max
-2632.6    -591.7       4.0    503.2   5064.6
```

The residual ranges from -2632 to 5064, that is, approximately a range of 7,500 units. The dependent variable has a mean of ~15000 and if the prediction can have an error of 7500, it will barely add any value. However, if we take a closer look, we can see a clearer picture; Median = 4 and additionally, the 25th percentile to 75th percentile has a maximum range of ~1000 units. Therefore, we can understand that a major chunk of our data is predicted with a maximum error of 1,000 units, which seems a fair prediction (definitely not the best; this experiment was just the first iteration of an exercise). The same can be studied better with the residual standard error showcased toward the end:

```
Residual standard error: 923.4 on 988 degrees of freedom
```

Residual standard error is the standard error on the residuals that represent the average distance that the observed values fall from the regression line. In a nutshell, it is the standard deviation for regression that helps us understand how wrong the regression model is on average using the units of the response variable. Smaller values are better because that indicates that the observations are closer to the fitted line. Therefore, we can infer from the preceding results that, for the response variable with a mean value of 15000, we predict with approximately 923 units of error. These results are decent enough as there is a tangible portion of variance being explained with lower residuals.

Multiple R-squared is another measure for the overall goodness of fit. Sometimes it is preferred more than the residual standard error due the interpretation advantages, although it completely depends on the persona. R-squared is the statistical measure of how close the data is to the fitted regression line. It is also known as the coefficient of determination or coefficient of multiple determination for multiple regression; R-squared = Explained variation / Total variation. It is calculated by taking the residual from predictions into account, but the results are independent of the scale of the response variable. Like previously, we had 923 units of error on an average for the response variable; here, if we do not know the scale of the response variable, we can make no sense from the result and sometimes we may even misinterpret the error impact while mentally calculating the error scale. R-squared, however, is independent of the scale of the response variable and therefore intuitive and easy to interpret:

```
Multiple R-squared:  0.4673,    Adjusted R-squared:  0.4614
```

As we can see, the value of R-squared is 0.46, that is, 46%, which is not a great score. We can infer that only 46% of the entire variance is actually explained by the regression model. (A ballpark figure for a good R-squared value will completely depend on the business use case.) Along with the R-squared value, we can also spot the adjusted R-squared value that is slightly lower than R-squared.

# What is the adjusted R-squared value?

The adjusted R-squared examines the variance explanatory power of regression models that contain different numbers of independent dimensions.

Suppose you compare a 10 independent dimension model with a high R-squared to a model with one independent dimension. Does the first model have a higher R-squared because it's better? Or is the R-squared higher because it has more independent variables/dimensions? This is where we use the adjusted R-squared value. The adjusted R-squared is a modified version of R-squared that has been adjusted for the number of independent dimensions in the model. The adjusted R-squared increases only if the new dimension improves the model more than would be expected by chance. It decreases when a predictor improves the model by less than expected by chance. The adjusted R-squared can be negative (very rare). It is always lower than the R-squared. A huge difference in the R-squared and adjusted R-squared shows that many dimensions considered in the regression exercise are not aiding in explaining the variance for the dependent variable.

So far, we have explored in depth about linear regression with the use case that we touched base on in the previous chapters. We understood in detail when and why is linear regression used and we studied about how to use it in R. We also interpreted the outputs to study the overall goodness of fit as well as the smaller individual dimensions. We will now dig deeper into linear regression for the same use case to improve the results by improving the goodness of fit and thereby amplifying the overall prediction power.

# Improving the predictive model

The preceding exercise was an attempt to understand the regression model. We can now move ahead to get a better and more accurate version of the prediction model. To understand the overall goodness of fit, we will consider R-squared along with adjusted R-squared and the residual standard error.

# Let's define our approach

There are multiple ways to approach the modeling problem. Let's say that from a list of 25 odd dimensions/predictors, we can begin by adding the predictors one by one and observe the differences and improvements to the overall model. This is called 'Forward selection'. We can also go the other way round, by starting with all the variables in a first iteration and then eliminating the less valuable predictors based on the results retrieved. This approach is called Backward Elimination. There is another approach where a combination of both the methods are used to build the best model. Either options are good; we'll use the backward elimination approach.

# How will we go about it?

We'll select all the variables that have been identified as important in the previous chapter. We'll then run an iteration of linear regression with all independent predictors and then try to improve the results. Using the p-value and estimate, we can identify how important each predictor is in defining a relationship with the dependent outcome and then eliminate the ones that add zero or low value. We will perform some data transformations on the predictors to further improve the results, and finally we will test our results on an unseen dataset to check how good the model in prediction is.

# Let's being modeling

We'll start by executing an iteration with all possible predictors for the use case:

For this specific use case, we won't be using every possible variable available in the data. The reason being the nature of the solution to be used. John's team needs a solution where they can predict the output quality parameter of the detergent before the manufacturing process. A couple of dimensions that we used in the previous chapter are dimensions that are captured during the manufacturing process. To build a solution that caters to John's needs, we need to consider only those dimensions as predictors that will be available before the manufacturing process.

For example, stage-wise processing time, delay flags, and Raw Material Consumption Flags are captured only after the manufacturing process has completed the respective stages. We can use raw material quality parameters, resource details, product details, planned quantity and to-be-produced quantity, product change flags, and so on.

```
#Building a Linear Regression Model
fit<-lm (Output_QualityParameter2~
        #Overall Process dimensions
        data$Quantity_Deviation_new
        +data$AssemblyLine_ID
        +data$Stage1_PrevProduct_1

        #Stage 1 Raw Material Parameters
        + data$Stage1_RM1_QParameter2
        + data$Stage1_RM1_QParameter1
        + data$Stage1_RM2_QParameter2
        + data$Stage1_RM2_QParameter1

        #Stage 3 Raw Material Parameters
        + data$Stage3_RM1_QParameter1
        + data$Stage3_RM1_QParameter2
        + data$Stage3_RM2_QParameter1
        + data$Stage3_RM3_QParameter2
        + data$Stage3_RM3_QParameter1

        +data$Stage3_ResourceName_new
        +data$Stage1_ProductChange_Flag
                        ,
    data=data
    )
```

```
Call:
lm(formula = Output_QualityParameter2 ~ data$Quantity_Deviation_new +
    data$AssemblyLine_ID + data$Stage1_PrevProduct_1 +
    data$Stage1_RM1_QParameter2 +
    data$Stage1_RM1_QParameter1 + data$Stage1_RM2_QParameter2 +
    data$Stage1_RM2_QParameter1 + data$Stage3_RM1_QParameter1 +
    data$Stage3_RM1_QParameter2 + data$Stage3_RM2_QParameter1 +
    data$Stage3_RM3_QParameter2 + data$Stage3_RM3_QParameter1 +
    data$Stage3_ResourceName_new + data$Stage1_ProductChange_Flag,
    data = data)

Residuals:
    Min      1Q  Median      3Q     Max
-2691.4  -548.8   -19.4   502.0  4683.3

Coefficients:
                                          Estimate Std. Error t value Pr(>|t|)
(Intercept)                             -362.94335  628.70591  -0.577  0.56388
data$Quantity_Deviation_newLow            17.23158   68.39549   0.252  0.80114
data$Quantity_Deviation_newMedium        -58.52954   72.01983  -0.813  0.41659
data$AssemblyLine_IDLine 2               485.81219   71.17584   6.826 1.53e-11 ***
data$Stage1_PrevProduct_1Product_545     417.65117  104.71284   3.989 7.14e-05 ***
data$Stage1_RM1_QParameter2               -7.30299  113.12474  -0.065  0.94854
data$Stage1_RM1_QParameter1               -0.07852    0.18680  -0.420  0.67433
data$Stage1_RM2_QParameter2              -35.21957    8.79188  -4.006 6.64e-05 ***
data$Stage1_RM2_QParameter1               39.07678    9.50374   4.112 4.26e-05 ***
data$Stage3_RM1_QParameter1               19.65419    8.70462   2.258  0.02417 *
data$Stage3_RM1_QParameter2             -894.10622  740.63916  -1.207  0.22764
data$Stage3_RM2_QParameter1                6.58343    3.40376   1.934  0.05338 .
data$Stage3_RM3_QParameter2                9.26441    3.36309   2.755  0.00598 **
data$Stage3_RM3_QParameter1             -156.44916   32.92914  -4.751 2.32e-06 ***
data$Stage3_ResourceName_newResource_108 505.08622   93.90030   5.379 9.36e-08 ***
data$Stage3_ResourceName_newResource_109 210.10217  104.66425   2.007  0.04498 *
data$Stage1_ProductChange_FlagYes       -104.08007  101.62313  -1.024  0.30600
---
Signif. codes:  0 '***' 0.001 '**' 0.01 '*' 0.05 '.' 0.1 ' ' 1

Residual standard error: 884.6 on 983 degrees of freedom
Multiple R-squared:  0.5137,    Adjusted R-squared:  0.5058
F-statistic: 64.89 on 16 and 983 DF,  p-value: < 2.2e-16
```

As we can see, compared to the previous results, we have a fairly better goodness of fit. The residual standard error has reduced from 923 to 884 and the R-squared has increased from 0.46 to 0.51. The results are still not great, though better than the previous iteration.

# So how do we move ahead?

The significant variables in the list have been highlighted; as the next step, we can either drop the insignificant variables and fine-tune the significant variables further to improve the goodness of fit or we can take a shot at improving both insignificant as well as significant predictors. The results may or may not be fruitful, but if something turns significant, that's a huge value add. Data transformation is a trial and error approach. Applying transformations on the predictors or dependent variable in some cases helps the variance to be more intuitively captured. The transformations can be in any form, such as square($x^2$), cube ($x^3$), exponential ($e^x$), log transformations, and so on. These transformations can be applied to the predictors or dependent variable or both.

If we take a closer look at the results, we can observe that only five of the nine raw material quality parameters are significant. Data transformations may or may not be valuable; the results can be validated only with a trial and error approach. We can try all combinations of data transformations on the predictors, dependent variable, or both and finally choose the combination that renders the best results.

It is recommended that you execute various linear regression iterations to see the differences in results with different transformations. The following showcased result is the output for one of the various iterations executed for different types of mathematical data transformations.

Unfortunately, in our use case, data transformations are not really boosting the results. Even if we try a variety of combinations of different data transformation operations, we barely see a big difference. Here is the best result captured from multiple iterations:

```
Call:
lm(formula = log(Output_QualityParameter2) ~ data$Quantity_Deviation_new +
    data$AssemblyLine_ID + data$Stage1_PrevProduct_1 + (data$Stage1_RM2_QParameter2)^3 +
    (data$Stage1_RM2_QParameter1)^3 + (data$Stage3_RM1_QParameter1)^3 +
    (data$Stage3_RM3_QParameter2)^3 + (data$Stage3_RM3_QParameter1)^3 +
    data$Stage3_ResourceName_new + data$Stage1_ProductChange_Flag,
    data = data)

Residuals:
     Min        1Q    Median        3Q       Max
-0.174552 -0.035115 -0.000359  0.033994  0.256303

Coefficients:
                                              Estimate Std. Error t value Pr(>|t|)
(Intercept)                                  8.6040707  0.0340016 253.049  < 2e-16 ***
data$Quantity_Deviation_newLow               0.0020019  0.0043999   0.455 0.649219
data$Quantity_Deviation_newMedium           -0.0036540  0.0046184  -0.791 0.429026
data$AssemblyLine_IDLine 2                   0.0306491  0.0045500   6.736 2.76e-11 ***
data$Stage1_PrevProduct_1Product_545         0.0260981  0.0066912   3.900 0.000103 ***
data$Stage1_RM2_QParameter2                 -0.0022017  0.0005660  -3.890 0.000107 ***
data$Stage1_RM2_QParameter1                  0.0028370  0.0005889   4.818 1.68e-06 ***
data$Stage3_RM1_QParameter1                  0.0016332  0.0005376   3.038 0.002443 **
data$Stage3_RM3_QParameter2                  0.0007464  0.0001899   3.931 9.05e-05 ***
data$Stage3_RM3_QParameter1                 -0.0088619  0.0019895  -4.454 9.37e-06 ***
data$Stage3_ResourceName_newResource_108     0.0337991  0.0059072   5.722 1.40e-08 ***
data$Stage3_ResourceName_newResource_109     0.0139059  0.0066806   2.082 0.037643 *
data$Stage1_ProductChange_FlagYes           -0.0046708  0.0064988  -0.719 0.472486
---
Signif. codes:  0 '***' 0.001 '**' 0.01 '*' 0.05 '.' 0.1 ' ' 1

Residual standard error: 0.05718 on 987 degrees of freedom
Multiple R-squared:  0.5177,  Adjusted R-squared:  0.5118
F-statistic: 88.28 on 12 and 987 DF,  p-value: < 2.2e-16
```

The raw material quality parameters for Stage 1 and Stage 3 have been transformed using a cubic operation and finally the dependent variable has been transformed using a log operation. Over the iterations, while performing these transformations, a few continuous predictors that were not significant were eliminated from the model. The elimination of categorical variables can be tricky and would again need a trial and error combination. In case the elimination of insignificant categorical variables leads to the deterioration of results, they are added back to the list. (The concept has been elaborated in interpretation of the Intercept results in the previous section.) We can see that two raw material quality parameter predictors have been eliminated. Finally, we can notice that the results have improved by a very small margin. We have adjusted R-squared that is slightly better than the previous version. (The residual standard error is 0.057, which is very different from the previous version. This is because we have performed a log operation on the dependent variable.)

Apart from improving the goodness of fit, data scientists also take efforts to reduce multicollinearity. A statistical phenomenon in which two or more predictor variables in a multiple regression model are highly correlated. The presence of multicollinearity would result in the misinterpretation of estimates for each of the predictors. Let's say that if estimate of A is 5 and estimate of B is 7 and say A and B are correlated, then the estimate of 5 doesn't represent the true impact of A on the dependent variable. The estimate would be a shared variance of A and B. In cases where one is interested in studying the impact of each dimension on the end outcome, removing multicollinearity is a must. However, in this exercise, we are more focused on the accuracy of the prediction.

To further improve the goodness of fit or accuracy of the prediction, we'll need to study and observe interaction effects. An interaction occurs when an independent variable has a different effect on the outcome depending on the values of another independent variable; that is, a situation in which the simultaneous influence of two variables on a third is not additive.

It can be understood from the following equation:

$$Y = \beta_0 + \beta_1 A + \beta_2 B + \beta_n(A\,B) + \varepsilon$$

There are scenarios where two independent variables may not define much variance, but when considered together, explain significant amount of variance. In our exercise, we can consider the raw material properties on a higher priority for interaction study. There are more sophisticated techniques to detect automated variable interaction (discussing this in detail would be beyond the scope of the book). For now, we can consider the raw material quality parameters as a combination. We can try multiple combinations from the list of nine raw material quality parameters and check whether the interaction is significant (using p value) and then study the overall model accuracy improvement.

The following results showcase the results of the best modeling iteration from a variety of combinations for interaction variables tried out. We have considered interaction between multiple raw material quality parameter combinations and chosen the iteration that gave the best accuracy. A few insignificant variables have been eliminated and a few have still been retained. The residual standard error is the least and the adjusted R-squared is the highest. In the following showcased iteration, we have considered a combination of interaction variables in the raw materials quality parameters, transformed processing time, base raw material quality parameters, and the log transformed dependent variable.

The interaction variables have been highlighted in yellow:

```
Call:
lm(formula = log(Output_QualityParameter2) ~
    data$Quantity_Deviation_new +
    data$AssemblyLine_ID +
    data$Stage1_PrevProduct_1 +
    (data$Stage1_RM1_QParameter2) * (data$Stage3_RM1_QParameter2) +
    (data$Stage1_RM1_QParameter1) * (data$Stage3_RM1_QParameter1) +
    (data$Stage1_RM2_QParameter1) * (data$Stage3_RM1_QParameter1) +
    log(data$Stage1_RM1_QParameter1) +
    log(data$Stage1_RM2_QParameter2) +
    log(data$Stage1_RM2_QParameter1) +
    log(data$Stage3_RM1_QParameter1) +
    log(data$Stage3_RM1_QParameter2) +
    log(data$Stage3_RM2_QParameter1) +
    log(data$Stage3_RM3_QParameter2) +
    log(data$Stage3_RM3_QParameter1) +
    data$Stage3_ResourceName_new +
    data$Stage1_ProductChange_Flag, data = data)
Residuals:
     Min       1Q    Median       3Q      Max
-0.185280 -0.032139  0.000059  0.032401  0.271451

Coefficients:
```

| | Estimate | Std. Error | t value | Pr(>\|t\|) | |
|---|---|---|---|---|---|
| (Intercept) | -2.254e+02 | 5.903e+01 | -3.818 | 0.000143 | *** |
| data$Quantity_Deviation_newLow | 9.018e-05 | 4.344e-03 | 0.021 | 0.983444 | |
| data$Quantity_Deviation_newMedium | -2.330e-03 | 4.555e-03 | -0.511 | 0.609177 | |
| data$AssemblyLine_IDLine 2 | 3.542e-02 | 4.526e-03 | 7.825 | 1.31e-14 | *** |
| data$Stage1_PrevProduct_1Product_545 | 3.102e-02 | 6.768e-03 | 4.584 | 5.15e-06 | *** |
| data$Stage1_RM1_QParameter2 | -4.167e-02 | 2.208e-02 | -1.888 | 0.059389 | . |
| data$Stage3_RM1_QParameter2 | -5.699e-01 | 5.174e-01 | -1.102 | 0.270942 | |
| data$Stage1_RM1_QParameter1 | -3.156e-03 | 1.221e-03 | -2.584 | 0.009915 | ** |
| data$Stage3_RM1_QParameter1 | -2.514e-01 | 6.970e-02 | -3.606 | 0.000327 | *** |
| data$Stage1_RM2_QParameter1 | 2.462e-03 | 6.244e-02 | 0.039 | 0.968556 | |
| log(data$Stage1_RM1_QParameter1) | 5.974e+00 | 2.746e+00 | 2.176 | 0.029816 | * |
| log(data$Stage1_RM2_QParameter2) | -8.538e-02 | 2.863e-02 | -2.983 | 0.002930 | ** |
| log(data$Stage1_RM2_QParameter1) | -4.941e-01 | 4.670e+00 | -0.106 | 0.915752 | |
| log(data$Stage3_RM1_QParameter1) | 4.536e+01 | 1.038e+01 | 4.368 | 1.39e-05 | *** |
| log(data$Stage3_RM1_QParameter2) | -4.264e-02 | 2.279e-02 | -1.871 | 0.061657 | . |
| log(data$Stage3_RM2_QParameter1) | 1.579e-01 | 1.179e-01 | 1.340 | 0.180661 | |
| log(data$Stage3_RM3_QParameter2) | 3.974e-01 | 1.152e-01 | 3.450 | 0.000585 | *** |
| log(data$Stage3_RM3_QParameter1) | -6.773e-02 | 1.389e-02 | -4.875 | 1.27e-06 | *** |
| data$Stage3_ResourceName_newResource_108 | 1.586e-02 | 6.785e-03 | 2.338 | 0.019594 | * |
| data$Stage3_ResourceName_newResource_109 | 6.830e-03 | 6.640e-03 | 1.029 | 0.303887 | |
| data$Stage1_ProductChange_FlagYes | -6.145e-03 | 6.393e-03 | -0.961 | 0.336629 | |
| data$Stage1_RM1_QParameter2:data$Stage3_RM1_QParameter2 | 2.650e-01 | 1.240e-01 | 2.136 | 0.032905 | * |
| data$Stage1_RM1_QParameter1:data$Stage3_RM1_QParameter1 | 8.360e-06 | 2.839e-06 | 2.945 | 0.003311 | ** |
| data$Stage3_RM1_QParameter1:data$Stage1_RM2_QParameter1 | 1.293e-05 | 1.497e-04 | 0.086 | 0.931177 | |

```
---
Signif. codes:  0 '***' 0.001 '**' 0.01 '*' 0.05 '.' 0.1 ' ' 1

Residual standard error: 0.05554 on 976 degrees of freedom
Multiple R-squared:  0.55,   Adjusted R-squared:  0.5394
F-statistic: 51.87 on 23 and 976 DF, p-value: < 2.2e-16
```

The results have improved but still not reached an ideally good model. We would need at least 70% of the variance to be explained so that we can consider this a good model (the more the merrier). We see a small increase in the number of significant variables and fairly improved overall results, that is, the residual standard error has reduced (comparing the previous iteration) and the adjusted R-squared has also increased. Though the results are still early, let's take a pause and understand what we have learned.

# The important points to ponder are as follows:

- We are now aware that the results we saw in the previous chapter are useful and also significant in understanding the relationship between the independent and dependent variables
- A few variables that were not significant were transformed mathematically to boost significance
- There is a scope for interaction variables and it helps in explaining more variance

While we have looked into the results separately from the regression exercise, we have not validated it on a new unseen dataset. This is an important step as we may fail to get the same results when the model is scored on a new dataset. If that is the case, we need to rework to get a more improved version of the model that works similar to the trained datasets. To validate the model in the new dataset, usually a test and train approach is taken where the data is split randomly into 70:30, 80:20, or 90:10 train and test samples. The current exercise has been performed on the entire dataset, so let's keep a sample of 10% aside for the testing and rerun the same model for prediction.

To test the results on the new data, we can use **Mean Absolute Percentage Error** (**MAPE**) and calculate the R-squared on the test dataset. These results together will help us in assessing the model on new datasets:

```
set.seed(600)
#Creating a 10% sample for test and 90% Train
test_index<-sample(1:nrow(data),floor(nrow(data)*0.1))
train<-data[-test_index,]
test<-data[test_index,]

#new_fit :We fit the model 'new_fit' on the train dataset using the same
formula used in the previous iteration. Codes have been ignored here.

#Define functions to calculate MAPE and R Squared
mape <- function(y, yhat)
return(mean(abs((y - yhat)/y)))
```

```
r_squared<-function(y,yhat)
                return(1 - sum(abs(y-yhat)^2)/sum((y-mean(y))^2))

#Predict the output from the Model
#Since, we performed a log operation on the dependent variable,
We would need to take a exponential of the prediction to get the end
Predcition

predicted<-exp(predict(new_fit,test))

#Calculate R Squared
> r_squared(test$Output_QualityParameter2,predicted)
[1] 0.4837209

> mape(test$Output_QualityParameter2,predicted)
[1] 0.04446882
```

From the results, we can see that the MAPE is around 4% and the overall R-squared value on the test dataset is 0.48, which is a bit less compared with the results that we had for the training sample, but still the difference is not huge. The results indicate that they are almost in sync with the results we expected (in comparison to the training data). This indicates that the model has overall good generalization capabilities that infers that the model will fairly work as per expectations on any new unseen data. However, the overall results are still not great enough to tell John that we have nailed it. We still need much better accuracy and lower errors in prediction so that his team can extract value from the results.

## What should we take care of?

- Attempts to improve results further using the same technique will require strenuous efforts; we can instead use a more powerful algorithm or technique that can give us better results
- Data transformation, feature engineering, and study of interaction among variables can further help in boosting accuracy power
- Alternative options to change the modeling outcome, that is, predicting the end outcome (Good or Bad Quality) or predicting each individual quality parameter needs to be evaluated and considered

# So what next?

The results that we have achieved so far-even though incrementally have been favorable-but at an overall level, we are able to explain just ~55% of the overall variance. This is probably just an inch higher than random probability (50%). To improve the results further, there are a variety of options where we can reach a notch further using linear regression, but the efforts will be strenuous. To get better results using a more fast-paced and agile method, we can explore using a more powerful technique for the same prediction exercise. Using a new techniques helps getting more favorable results in most cases as it uncovers some latent relationships that may not have been straightforward in linear regression. Therefore, to improve results further, we'll explore another new technique, decision trees, for the same use case.

# Decision trees

Decision trees is a commonly used technique in data mining to create a model that predicts the value of a target (or dependent variable) based on the values of several input (or independent variables). There is a variety of decision tree algorithms available with small changes here and there. We will be using a very popular version of a decision tree called **Classification and Regression Trees** (**CART**). It was introduced in 1984 by Leo Breiman, Jerome Friedman, Richard Olshen, and Charles Stone as an umbrella term to refer to classification and regression types of decision trees. Using decision trees, we can predict either a categorical variable or continuous variable. Based on the type of dependent variable, we use a regression tree (for a continuous outcome variable) or classification tree (for a categorical outcome). The CART has a small variation in the internal working of the algorithm. For our current exercise, we will be using regression trees. Later, we'll look into the differences between classification and regression trees. So let's begin by understanding the nuances of decision trees.

# Understanding decision trees

Let us understand decision tress in more detailed way.

# So what is a decision tree?

In a nutshell, it is a data mining algorithm that is used to predict categorical or continuous outcomes based on training samples. It does so by creating a flowchart-like structure in which each internal node represents a "test" on an attribute (for example, whether flipping a coin results in heads or tails), each branch represents the outcome of the test, and each leaf node represents a class label (decision taken after computing all attributes). The path from root to leaf represents the rules.

# How does a decision tree work?

A decision tree implements a very simple algorithm. The following image can be a simple visualization for decision trees:

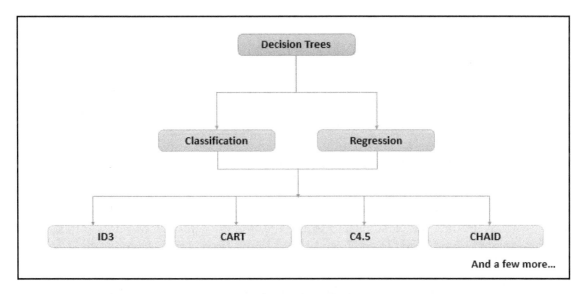

It works by breaking data from the root node into smaller and smaller subsets while incrementally building an associated decision tree. The final result is a tree with a root node, decision nodes, and leaf nodes, as shown in the preceding image. Decision nodes create a rule and leaf nodes deliver a result. The final result is a simple and intuitive flowchart that can be mentally mapped to a list of questions and rule-based answers.

# What are different types of decision trees?

There is a wide variety of decision tree types. Each have small variations in the way they approach the problem. We will be using the most popular and widely-used decision tree called CART:

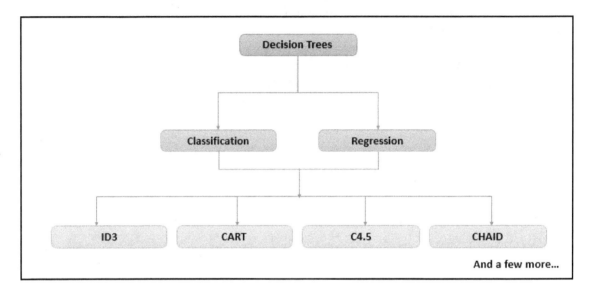

The differences are minimum; in most cases, one technique is an updated version of the other one. ID3 or Iterative Dichotomiser 3 was one of the earlier versions that was then followed by C4.5 and so on. The differences were the incremental updates and improvements in most cases. For example, the earlier versions couldn't handle numeric variables, and the updated versions had support for the same and a few other optimization improvements.

# So how is a decision tree built and how does it work?

The overall algorithm can be explained in five simple steps:

1. Select the root node
2. Partition the data into groups
3. Create a decision node
4. Partition data into respective groups
5. Repeat until node size > threshold or features = empty

Let's consider a very simple example to understand the algorithm. Consider a case where you are trying to predict the average number of working hours for an employee when you are provided with the dimensions 'Dress code' and 'Gender' for each employee. The example can be visualized using the following image:

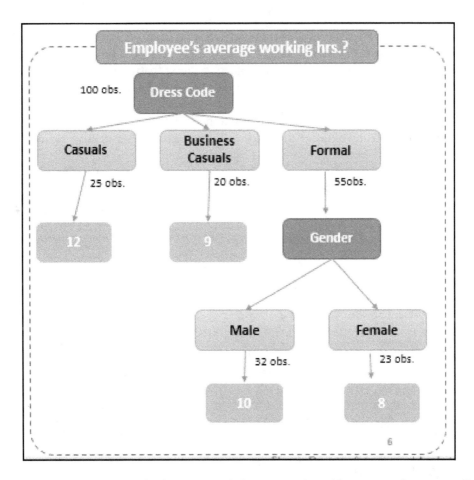

The root node is the 'Dress code' feature, and the grey-colored boxes are the groups/levels for each feature. The yellow-colored box gives the average value of the working hours for all the data dimensions in the respective partition.

Let's say that there are 100 observations for the training in all. We set a threshold of 30 data points or more in each node for further splitting. Therefore, the partitioning stops when there are 30 or less data points in a node or the features (independent variables) are empty. The root node-Dress code-is selected algorithmically (we'll explore how in detail later) and the data is partitioned into respective groups. So we have 25 for 'Casuals', 20 for 'Business Casuals', and 55 for Formals. Once a feature is assigned and data is partitioned, then we move on to the respective group that can be split. In this case, we have 'Casuals' and 'Business Casuals' with < 30 observations, and so it won't be considered for further splitting. 'Formal' has >30 node size and therefore we place the next feature Gender under 'Formal'. These 55 observations are further partitioned into Male and Female. This process continues till the features are empty or node size is less than a predefined threshold. Each of the grey boxes is a terminal node where the result is calculated. In regression trees, as the outcome is continuous, the result is the average of all the data points in the respective terminal nodes. The average number of working hours for a partition is showcased in amber color. In the preceding example, let's say that we have an employee whose Gender is 'Male' and Dress Code is 'Casual', then if we traverse through the tree we can find that the average number of working hours for the employee is 12. Similarly, if dress code = 'Formal' and Gender = 'Female', then the average number of working hours = 8. This is how a decision tree is built and works to predict the end outcome. We are still left with a couple of questions that need clarity to understand how the decision trees work in detail.

A few questions that would surface in our thoughts would be as follows:

- How to select the root node?
- How are the decision nodes ordered/chosen?
- How does the tree treat continuous variables?
- How different is the process for classification and regression?

Answers to these questions will help us understand the entire process of decision trees in more detail. Let's tackle them one by one.

## How to select the root node?

The algorithm to calculate the root node in regression trees and classification trees is different. For regression trees, the algorithm calculates the **Standard Deviation Reduction** (**SDR**) of the feature with respect to the dependent variable. Take a look at the following example. Consider the following data as the training data for the algorithm:

| Sr. No | Dress code | Gender | Working hours |
|--------|-----------|--------|---------------|
| 1 | Formal | Male | 10 |

| 2 | Business Casual | Female | 11 |
|---|---|---|---|
| 3 | Casual | Male | 12 |
| 4 | Formal | Male | 9 |
| 5 | Business Casual | Female | 14 |
| 6 | Casual | Male | 9 |
| ....... | | | |
| 100 | Casual | Male | 15 |

We have two features and one continuous outcome, Working Hours.

**Standard Deviation Reduction (SDR)** can be calculated as follows:

(SDR)= Standard Deviation(Outcome) – Standard Deviation(Outcome, Feature)

Calculating the standard deviation of a single numeric variable is straightforward. The standard deviation of two variables can be calculated as the multiplicative sum of probability of each group and standard deviation of each group.

Let's say that we are calculating the standard deviation, Sd(Dress Code, Working Hours):

Sd(Dress Code, Working Hours) = P(Formal) * Sd(Formal) + P(Casual) * Sd(Casual) + P(Business Casual) * P(Business Casual)

Let's assume that Sd(Working Hours) = 15, and the frequency count of dress code across groups and the respective standard deviation is as follows:

| Dress Code | Working Hours Standard Deviation | Count |
|---|---|---|
| Formal | 1.4 | 55 |
| Business Casual | 1.9 | 20 |
| Casual | 2.8 | 25 |
| Total | | 100 |

Then, Sd(Dress Code, Working Hours) = P(Formal) * Sd(Formal) + P(Casual) * Sd(Casual) + P(Business Casual) * P(Business Casual) = (55/100) * 1.4 + (20/100) * 1.9 + (25/100) * 2.8

Therefore, Sd(Dress Code, Working Hours) = **1.85.**

**Now calculating SDR is straightforward:**

(SDR)= Standard Deviation (Outcome) – Standard Deviation (Outcome, Feature)

= 15 – 1.85

**SDR = 13.15**

Similarly, the SDR for other features are also calculated and the root node is chosen as the one with the largest SDR.

# How are the decision nodes ordered/chosen?

Once the root node is selected and data is partitioned across its groups, the next feature is placed under eligible groups of the root node. Eligibility is calculated based on the node size threshold. The feature selected is the next feature with the highest SDR. The node is terminated if it has lesser number of data points than the threshold. The following image shows you the flow of features based on the SDR:

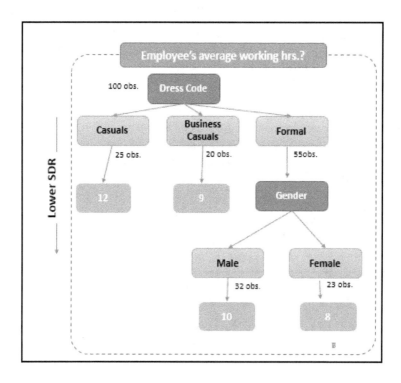

**How does the tree treat continuous variables?**

Continuous variables are a special case. Ideally, the decision trees work only on categorical features, but the continuous features can be added to the decision by converting it to a categorical feature. This is done by an algorithm called binning and is done automatically in the R packages we use. Binning can be easily understood by taking into consideration the Age dimension. Age can have any values between 0 and 100 (assume). We can easily categorize the age dimension into five bins or groups such as 0-18 years, 19-35 years, 36-65 years, and above 65 years. The same can be extended to other numeric features.

# How different is the process for classification and regression?

The main difference between the classification tree and regression tree algorithm is the means used to select the root node and order the decision nodes. In regression trees, we use SDR, whereas in classification trees, we use **Entropy**. Similarly, the node termination rule for a regression tree is a finite number of data points, whereas in classification trees, it is the homogeneity of the outcome, which means that all data points in the partition should have the same outcome. We'll explore more about entropy and the working of the classification tree in the next chapter.

# Predictive modeling with decision trees

Now that we have a detailed understanding about decision trees, let's continue solving the same problem (solved in the previous section) with the new algorithm. There is a variety of packages available in R that can help in building decision trees; we'll use the RPART package (an extension of CART).

# So how do we approach?

Unlike linear regression, decision tree execution in R will not give us clear results of how accurately the model predicts the outcome. We will need to test and find the results on our own. We can use the MAPE and **R-squared value** to understand how accurately the models are built. Moreover, the biggest advantage of decision trees is the ability to visualize the constructed tree. It becomes extremely simple and intuitive for a layman to consume the results. We'll first execute one simple iteration with the initial list of features that we used in linear regression. Decision trees cannot handle interaction variables (Though we can indirectly create a new interaction variable and add it to the decision tree model, the interpretation will not be intuitive.):

```
#Building a Decision Tree in R using rpart package
library(rpart)
fit<-rpart(Output_QualityParameter2~

          #The Production Quantity deviation feature
          Quantity_Deviation_new +

          #The Production Quantity deviation feature
          Stage1_PrevProduct_1 +

          #Raw Material Quality Parameters
           Stage1_RM1_QParameter2 +
          Stage1_RM1_QParameter1 +
          Stage1_RM2_QParameter2 +
          Stage1_RM2_QParameter1 +
          Stage3_RM1_QParameter1 +
          Stage3_RM1_QParameter2 +
          Stage3_RM2_QParameter1 +
          Stage3_RM3_QParameter2 +
          Stage3_RM3_QParameter1 +

          #Machine/Resources used in a Stage
          Stage3_ResourceName_new +
          Stage1_ProductChange_Flag
          ,
     data=train,control=rpart.control(minsplit=20,cp=0.1)
     )

#Predicting the values from the newly created model
predicted<-predict(fit,test)
mape(test$Output_QualityParameter2,predicted)
[1] 0.0449977

r_squared(test$Output_QualityParameter2,predicted)
[1] 0.4308113
```

The parameter control in the rpart function helps in defining additional details. minsplit = 20 is defined so that if a node has less than or equal to 20 training samples, then the node will not be split further. Similarly, cp is defined as a complexity parameter. Any split that does not decrease the overall lack of fit by a factor of cp is not attempted. For instance, with regression trees, this means that the overall R-squared must increase by cp at each step. The main role of this parameter is to save computing time by pruning off splits that are obviously not worthwhile.

If we observe the results, we can clearly see that the results have actually deteriorated compared to the previous model-a tiny decrease in the MAPE and overall R-squared for the test dataset.

But why?

Let's try to visualize the tree that was constructed by the model:

```
#Installing the required packages
install.packages('rattle')
install.packages('rpart.plot')
install.packages('RColorBrewer')

#Loading the installed packages
library(rattle)
library(rpart.plot)
library(RColorBrewer)

#Plotting the Regression Tree
fancyRpartPlot(fit)
```

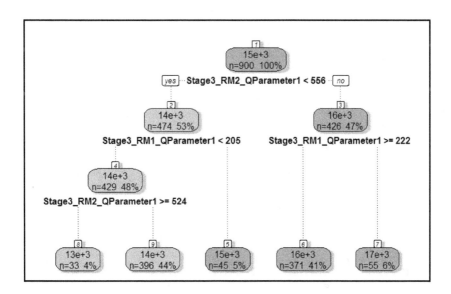

As we can see, the tree has selected only two distinct nodes in all-Stage3_RM2_QParameter1 and Stage3_RM1_QParameter1. Therefore, the algorithm has internally dropped other features as it couldn't find a feature and an optimal split where it was also adding value to explain the overall variance.

# So what do we do to improve the results?

If we plan to fine-tune the regression tree, we can play around with parameters such as cp, minsplit, maxdepth, minbucket, and a few more. Let's try tuning the cp parameter. Ideally, the cp parameter is a threshold to decide whether a particular feature should be added to the tree or not. The algorithm internally executes iterations to find the amount that the R-squared has improved when the feature was added. If the value is not significant, then we move ahead. One would wonder that if adding a feature to the tree may add only a small improvement to the R-squared, then why ignore it? Won't multiple small increments be a valuable one?

This is where we need to understand the concept of overfitting. Overfitting is a scenario where the model works perfectly on trained data compared to a simple model, but fails miserably on test data. Such scenarios occur when the model fails to generalize patterns. Failing to ignore noise in the data, that is, generalizing the model, will result in extremely complicated rules. Let's look into this. We'll rerun an iteration of the decision tree model with the cp parameter value set to 0.001. Now the features that the algorithm dropped while constructing the tree will be considered:

```
#Executing another Decision Tree Iteration
library(rpart)

fit<-rpart(Output_QualityParameter2~

        #The Production Quantity deviation feature
        Quantity_Deviation_new +

        #The Production Quantity deviation feature
        Stage1_PrevProduct_1 +

        #Raw Material Quality Parameters
        Stage1_RM1_QParameter2 +
        Stage1_RM1_QParameter1 +
        Stage1_RM2_QParameter2 +
        Stage1_RM2_QParameter1 +
        Stage3_RM1_QParameter1 +
        Stage3_RM1_QParameter2 +
        Stage3_RM2_QParameter1 +
        Stage3_RM3_QParameter2 +
        Stage3_RM3_QParameter1 +

        #Machine/Resources used in a Stage
        Stage3_ResourceName_new +
        Stage1_ProductChange_Flag
                ,
        data=train,control=rpart.control(minsplit=20,cp=0.001)
```

```
        )
predicted<-predict(fit,test)

mape(test$Output_QualityParameter2,predicted)
[1] 0.04104942

r_squared(test$Output_QualityParameter2,predicted)
[1] 0.53973
```

There seems to be a small improvement in the R-squared and MAPE, but is this for real?

Let's have a look at the tree that is constructed by the algorithm:

```
> fancyRpartPlot(fit)
```

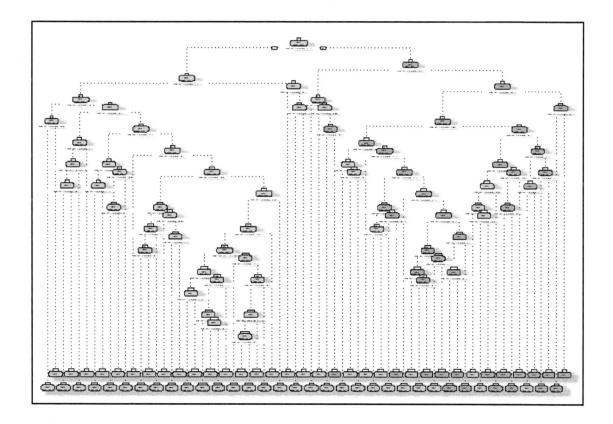

As expected, the algorithm has added almost all the features available, but we can barely see anything. The results showcase improvement compared to the previous iteration, but this is purely due to chance. If we consider another 90:10% random sample for the training and testing, we might get completely opposite results. The following code performs the tenfold cross-validation exercise to validate whether the results we got in one of our iterations is actually better or purely by chance.

A tenfold cross-validation exercise is basically a process where we divide the data into 10 equal partitions and then use nine partitions, that is, 90% to train and the remaining partition, that is, 10% to test. The process is repeated 10 times with a different partition chosen every time for the testing. In case we observe spurious results, the same can be validated using the k fold cross-validation exercise (k is any number, say 10):

```
#Creating 10 fold cross validation sample
k=10 #Defining the number of partitions

#Creating an identifier to assign a partition index
set.seed(100)
data$id <- sample(1:k, nrow(data), replace = TRUE)

list <- 1:k

results<-vector()
for (i in 1:k){
    # remove rows with id i from dataframe to create training set
    # select rows with id i to create test set
    trainingset <- subset(data, id %in% list[-i])
    testset <- subset(data, id %in% c(i))

    fit<-rpart(Output_QualityParameter2~
            #The Production Quantity deviation feature
            Quantity_Deviation_new +

            #The Production Quantity deviation feature
            Stage1_PrevProduct_1 +

            #Raw Material Quality Parameters
            Stage1_RM1_QParameter2 +
            Stage1_RM1_QParameter1 +
            Stage1_RM2_QParameter2 +
            Stage1_RM2_QParameter1 +
            Stage3_RM1_QParameter1 +
            Stage3_RM1_QParameter2 +
            Stage3_RM2_QParameter1 +
            Stage3_RM3_QParameter2 +
            Stage3_RM3_QParameter1 +
```

```
            #Machine/Resources used in a Stage
            Stage3_ResourceName_new +
            Stage1_ProductChange_Flag,
        data=trainingset,control=rpart.control(minsplit=20,cp=0.001)
            )

    yhat<-predict(fit,newdata = testset)
    y<-testset$Output_QualityParameter2
    a<-r_squared(y,yhat)

    #Appending the R Squared results to a vector
    results<-as.vector(c(results,a))
}

mean(results)
[1] 0.4526883

min(results)
[1] 0.1588772

max(results)
[1] 0.6123546
```

Have a look at the results; after performing tenfold cross-validation on the model, we can clearly see the huge variation in results. The overall R-squared could be something as low as 0.15 or as high as 0.61. Therefore, we need a more stable value for cp.

Fortunately, the model output gives a CP table as one of its parameters:

```
head(fit$cptable)
            CP nsplit rel error     xerror       xstd
1 0.471497076      0 1.0000000 1.0011024 0.05081692
2 0.015820550      1 0.5285029 0.5309135 0.03556166
3 0.015320589      3 0.4968618 0.5209064 0.03475611
4 0.010957717      4 0.4815412 0.5108439 0.03451988
5 0.008642251      6 0.4596258 0.5081714 0.03460857
6 0.007985705      7 0.4509835 0.4938715 0.03388218
```

The cptable showcases the results of various internal iterations with the values of cp and the corresponding error terms captured. We can choose the value of cp that has the least error among others and then we can prune the tree. Pruning is a process where specific branches or nodes are removed from the tree to reconstruct an optimized tree. You learned that there is a high chance of overfitting and getting poor results with a higher number of nodes (branches) in a tree. Therefore, choosing the most optimized value of cp and reconstructing the tree by pruning the nodes that do not add enough importance can help overcome overfitting to a small extent. Let's give it a shot:

```
#Find the CP parameter value with the least error
best_cp<-fit$cptable[which.min(fit$cptable[,"xerror"]),"CP"]
best_cp
[1] 0.004459267

#Prune the exisitng model
new_fit<-prune(fit,cp=best_cp)

#Predict using the new model
yhat<-predict(new_fit,newdata = testset)
y<-testset$Output_QualityParameter2

r_squared(y,yhat)
0.5461565

mape(y,yhat)
0.04234978
```

Again, we do see a better R-squared than the previous iteration and almost similar MAPE, but is this still good?

No, we are almost at the same position where we were in linear regression. The results haven't shown any significant improvement.

# So, what next? Do we try another modeling technique that could give us more powerful results?

We probably can, but hold on. There are many use cases where we can find the best results by changing the modeling technique than to keep tuning to improve the existing one. Of course, it doesn't mean that we keep changing modeling techniques without looking into the details of how the existing model can be improved and why it is failing. However, in some cases, we can achieve better results faster by trying out a new technique rather than exhaustively tuning the same existing model. In our use case, we did this already. We started solving our prediction problem with a simple linear regression technique and after a few experiments with poor results, we moved on to explore decision trees and experimented further. We still haven't reached satisfactory results, so what's next? Shall we try another technique that is more powerful and may give us better results?

As mentioned earlier, yes we can, but let's wait a bit more. Rather than trying a new machine learning technique or exhaustively trying to tune the exiting models, why don't we try something different?

Recalling John's request, he had mentioned that his team needs a solution where they can predict the outcome before the manufacturing process so as to take corrective countermeasures. We have four output quality parameters and one resultant detergent quality outcome (calculated algorithmically from the four output parameters)-Good or Bad. Instead of predicting the numeric outcome, Output Quality Parameter 2, we can try to predict a categorical outcome, Detergent Quality.

The overall exercise will be slightly different as we would be predicting a categorical outcome rather than a numeric or continuous outcome. Let's park the experiments to try a more powerful machine learning technique to predict the numeric outcome for the time being (we'll try this in the next chapter) and meanwhile let's attempt to create a simple model where we can predict a categorical outcome.

# Logistic Regression – Predicting a categorical outcome

Let's shift our focus to building a predictive model that will now take a different step. We started by solving the prediction problem that can predict a continuous outcome, but we didn't achieve great results. John's team requires a solution that they can leverage to predict the end quality of the detergent being manufactured. It could be achieved in multiple ways; the first one was to predict the most critical output quality parameter and the second was to predict the actual end outcome, Good or Bad. Both the methods have their own advantages and disadvantages. Predicting the continuous outcome, Output Quality Parameter 2, actually gives us a sneak peek to understand the actual quantified deviation from the benchmark, say below or above 60%. Such crisp information aids the technician in taking more accurate corrective countermeasures.

On the other hand, predicting the categorical outcome, Good/Bad Quality, has its interpretational advantage. A layman can easily interpret the results without any benchmark comparison or relative measurement. However, at the same time, it doesn't give a quantified measure of how good or bad the quality is. To build a predictive model for a binary categorical outcome, we will use a very simple and popular algorithm called logistic regression.

## So what is logistic regression?

Logistic regression is a statistical technique used to develop predictive models with categorical dependent variables having dichotomous or binary outcomes. (In our use case, the dependent variable is detergent quality). Similar to linear regression, the logistic regression models the relationship between the dependent variable and one or more independent variables. Logistic regression measures the relationship between the categorical dependent variable and one or more independent variables by estimating probabilities using a logistic function, which is the cumulative logistic distribution. There are other variants of logistic regression that focus on modeling a categorical variable with three or more levels, say X, Y, and Z and a few others. For now, let's focus on the scenario where we model an outcome that is binary-Good or Bad.

Unlike linear regression, logistic regression models for the log of odds ratio or the probability of the event to happen. Let's understand this better. Everything starts with the concept of probability. Let's say that the probability of success of some event is 0.8. Then the probability of failure is 1 – 0.8 = 0.2. The odds of success are defined as the ratio of the probability of success over the probability of failure. In our example, the odds of success are 0.8/0.2 = 4. That is to say that the odds of success are 4 to 1. If the probability of success is 0.5, that is, a 50-50 percent chance, then the odds of success are 1 to 1.

The equation for logistic regression can be defined as follows:

$$\mathrm{Ln}\left(\frac{P}{1-P}\right) = \beta_0 + \beta_1 X_1 + \beta_2 X_2 + \cdots .. + \beta_n X_n$$

Here, $\mathrm{Ln}\left(\frac{P}{1-P}\right)$ is the log of odds ratio.

To predict the probability of the event to happen, we can further solve the preceding equation as follows:

Discussing the mathematical background and derivation of the equations is out of scope for the book. Before we begin getting our hands dirty on logistic regression, we'll take a pause and try to contemplate a few important and things. We did mention at the beginning of the section that we cannot use linear regression to model categorical variables, but why? What if we could encode the outcome as 1 for Good and 0 for Bad?

Suppose that we are trying to predict the winning chances of a basketball team for a tournament based on the team's attributes. In this simplified example, there are three possible diagnoses: yes, no, and maybe. We can consider encoding these values as a quantitative response variable Y, as follows:

1: Yes

2: No

3: Maybe

With this coding, we can perform linear regression to predict Y as a function of the predictors X1, . . .,Xn. However, the biggest problem with this coding technique is interpreting the ordering of the outcomes. With 'no' between 'yes' and 'maybe', the model will infer that the difference between 'Yes' and 'No' is the same as the difference between 'No' and 'Maybe', which is not something we can be sure of. Moreover, if the sequence is reversed or changed for 'Yes', 'No', and 'Maybe', it would completely change the interpretation for the model in which case it wouldn't make sense to use linear regression for categorical variables.

On the other hand, for our use case, we have a binary flag where the preceding argument can somehow be abstracted, saying that the prediction values between 0 and 1 can be used as a proxy for the probability. This scenario will also not hold true as there would be predictions outside the range of 0 and 1, say -5, which would make the overall interpretation very difficult.

# So how does the logistic regression work?

Keeping aside mathematical complications, we'll touch base on one simple topic-Maximum Likelihood. In statistics, **maximum-likelihood estimation (MLE)** is a method of estimating the parameters of a statistical model with given data. To put it simply, we can say that for a fixed set of data points and statistical model, the method of maximum likelihood selects the set of values of the model parameters that maximizes the likelihood function, that is, it maximizes the "agreement" of the selected model with the observed data. Once the parameters of the model are determined, we can plug the values into the equation and get our predictions in no time. The process of MLE is iterative.

Let's now quickly get our hands dirty by building logistic regression models. We'll touch base on new topics and unknown results as we proceed. To perform logistic regression on the existing data, we'll use the `glm()` function available in the stats package of R. To start, we'll use the same set of predictors that we used in the previous exercise:

```
fit<-glm(Detergent_Quality~
        #The Production Quantity deviation feature
        Quantity_Deviation_new +

        #The Production Quantity deviation feature
        Stage1_PrevProduct_1 +

        #Raw Material Quality Parameters
        Stage1_RM1_QParameter2 +
        Stage1_RM1_QParameter1 +
        Stage1_RM2_QParameter2 +
        Stage1_RM2_QParameter1 +
```

```
        Stage3_RM1_QParameter1 +

        #Machine/Resources used in a Stage
        Stage1_ProductChange_Flag,
        data=train,
        family = "binomial"
    )
```

The `family = "binomial"` command tells R to use the `glm` function to fit a logistic regression model. (The `glm()` function can fit other models too; we'll look into this later.)

Similar to linear regression and regression trees, we can use the summary command to see the model results:

```
summary(fit)

Call:
glm(formula = Detergent_Quality ~ Quantity_Deviation_new +
Stage1_PrevProduct_1 +
    Stage1_RM1_QParameter2 + Stage1_RM1_QParameter1 +
 Stage1_RM2_QParameter2 +
    Stage1_RM2_QParameter1 + Stage3_RM1_QParameter1 +
 Stage1_ProductChange_Flag,
    family = "binomial", data = train)

Deviance Residuals:
     Min        1Q     Median        3Q       Max
 -3.15433   0.09734   0.13489   0.88196   1.36402

Coefficients:
                                     Estimate  Std. Error  z value  Pr(>|z|)
(Intercept)                        44.8389526   5.0582122    8.865   < 2e-16 ***
Quantity_Deviation_newLow           0.1205316   0.2382435    0.506     0.613
Quantity_Deviation_newMedium        0.2632456   0.2599262    1.013     0.311
Stage1_PrevProduct_1Product_545    -0.3469915   0.2224928   -1.560     0.119
Stage1_RM1_QParameter2             -0.6242709   0.3973832   -1.571     0.116
Stage1_RM1_QParameter1             -0.0005502   0.0006402   -0.859     0.390
Stage1_RM2_QParameter2             -0.0416442   0.0284004   -1.466     0.143
Stage1_RM2_QParameter1              0.0103492   0.0330121    0.313     0.754
Stage3_RM1_QParameter1             -0.1763619   0.0314876   -5.601  2.13e-08 ***
Stage1_ProductChange_FlagYes       -0.1831766   0.3778035   -0.485     0.628
---
Signif. codes:  0 '***' 0.001 '**' 0.01 '*' 0.05 '.' 0.1 ' ' 1

(Dispersion parameter for binomial family taken to be 1)

    Null deviance: 840.51  on 799  degrees of freedom
Residual deviance: 569.85  on 790  degrees of freedom
```

```
AIC: 589.85

Number of Fisher Scoring iterations: 7
```

Let's study the results from the logistic regression one by one. The first part shown in the result is the regression call (formula), that is, expressing the regression of the dependent variable over the independent variables.

Model checking (goodness of fit) is just as important in logistic regression as it is in classical linear models or any other model. The ingredients for goodness of fit are again the residuals or differences between observed and fitted values. Unlike the case of linear models, we now have to make allowance for the fact that the observations have different variances. There are different types of residuals used, such as the 'Pearson Residual', 'Deviance Residual', and so on. The `glm()` function computes the Deviance Residual. For the ith observation, the deviance residual is the signed square roots of the ith observation to the overall deviance:

```
Deviance Residuals:
      Min         1Q      Median         3Q        Max
  -3.15433    0.09734    0.13489    0.88196    1.36402
```

It is calculated as follows:

$$d_i = sgn(y_i - \widehat{y}_i) \left\{ 2y_i \, log\left(\frac{y_i}{\widehat{y}_i}\right) + 2(n_i - y_i)log\left(\frac{n_i - y_i}{n_i - \widehat{y}_i}\right) \right\}^{1/2}$$

Observations with a deviance residual in excess of two may indicate lack of fit. The output in logistic regression by default calculates the deviance residuals, and the first part of the results is the summary of distribution of deviance residuals.

Moving on, we have the most important part of the results-estimates for each independent variable-that helps us quantify how much does each of the independent variable impact the end dependent variable:

```
Coefficients:
                                       Estimate Std. Error z value Pr(>|z|)
(Intercept)                          44.8389526  5.0582122   8.865  < 2e-16 ***
Quantity_Deviation_newLow             0.1205316  0.2382435   0.506    0.613
Quantity_Deviation_newMedium          0.2632456  0.2599262   1.013    0.311
Stage1_PrevProduct_1Product_545      -0.3469915  0.2224928  -1.560    0.119
Stage1_RM1_QParameter2               -0.6242709  0.3973832  -1.571    0.116
Stage1_RM1_QParameter1               -0.0005502  0.0006402  -0.859    0.390
Stage1_RM2_QParameter2               -0.0416442  0.0284004  -1.466    0.143
Stage1_RM2_QParameter1                0.0103492  0.0330121   0.313    0.754
Stage3_RM1_QParameter1               -0.1763619  0.0314876  -5.601 2.13e-08 ***
```

```
Stage1_ProductChange_FlagYes    -0.1831766  0.3778035  -0.485    0.628
---
```

The preceding figure shows a small part of the logistic regression output results shared earlier. The estimates show how much and how they impact the dependent variable; that is, the coefficients give the change in the log odds of the outcome for a one-unit increase in the predictor variable. A positive estimate indicates that, for every unit increase of the respective independent variable, there is a corresponding increase in the log of odds ratio and the other way for a negative estimate. We can note that all the independent variables used in the regression equation (formula) have an individual estimate computed, but for the categorical variables like Stage 1 Product Change Flag, the dimension has internally converted them to binary flags with the respective estimate. This is because logistic regression handles only continuous variables, and therefore every categorical variable is internally coded as a binary flag. Along with the independent variables, we also see 'Intercept'. Intercept is the log of odds of the event (Good or Bad Quality) when we have all the categorical predictors having a value as 0.

To understand how good the estimates are, we have a series of results calculated by the `glm` function and provided along with the estimates. We can see the standard error, z value, and p-value along with an asterisk indication to easily identify significance. The ultimate goal in using all these results is to validate whether there exists a relationship between the log odds of the event and independent variable. In order to prove this, standard errors are calculated and the null hypothesis is framed as: no relationship exists between x and log odds of the event. We then determine whether the **estimate** is truly far away from 0. If the standard error of the estimate is small, then relatively small values of the estimate can reject the null hypothesis. If the standard error is large, then the estimate should also be large enough to reject the null hypothesis. To test the significance, we use the 'Wald Z Statistic' to measure how many standard deviations the estimate is away from 0. Alternatively, the p value helps in interpreting the results more intuitively. The significance of the estimate can be determined if the probability of the event happening by chance is less than 5%.

The reason to use Wald Z statistic instead of T Statistic (used in linear regression) is based on the way we have calculated the estimates. In linear regression, the estimates were calculated using the technique called OLS (Ordinary Least Squares), but in logistic regression, we use the MLE technique (as discussed earlier). The choice of the test statistic depends on how the standard error of the coefficients has been calculated.

Looking at our results, we can see that only the intercept and the Stage3 RM1 QParameter 1 predictor is significant but not the rest. The reasons can be easily studied by comparing the estimates and standard error. If the standard error of the estimate is small, then relatively small values of the estimate can reject the null hypothesis, and we see many cases that have higher standard errors for smaller estimates:

```
    Null deviance: 840.51  on 799  degrees of freedom
Residual deviance: 569.85  on 790  degrees of freedom
```

Moving on, we can see two types of deviance results shown below the estimates for the predictors, namely, Null Deviance and Residual Deviance. Deviance is actually the measure of goodness of fit of a generalized linear model (logistic regression in our case) or rather, it's a measure of badness of fit-higher numbers indicate a worse fit. The glm function in R reports two forms of deviance-the null deviance and residual deviance. The null deviance shows how well the response variable is predicted by a model that includes only the intercept (grand mean), and the residual deviance shows how well the response variable is predicted by the proposed model (the model we submitted). Interpreting the deviances is very easy; a very small null deviance indicates that the null model explains the data very well. This is the same with the residual deviance as well. The difference between the null deviance and residual deviance indicates how much value the independent variables add to the goodness of fit. A higher difference between the two clearly indicates that the independent predictors help in explaining the data to a great extent. In our example, we see that null deviance is 840 on 799 degrees of freedom whereas the residual deviance is 569 on 790 degrees of freedom. This indicates that with the addition of nine predictors, there was a huge drop in the overall residual, which shows that there is a good amount of variance being explained by the predictors.

Below the null and residual deviance, we can see the AIC results, that is, Akaike Information criterion, another metric used to study the goodness of fit across models:

```
AIC: 589.85
```

In our example, we can see that the AIC value is 589, which can be used as a comparison metric with the AIC of the other iterations of the model building exercise. If the other model has a lower AIC value, we can infer that the new model has a better goodness of fit compared to the current one.

Lastly, we can see the number of Fisher scoring iterations used for the model to converge. The logistic regression calculates the estimates using the MLE, which requires multiple iterations. It starts with a tentative estimate and tries to improve it based on the results of each iteration. The algorithm then looks around to see if the fit can be improved using different estimates instead. If so, it moves in that direction (say, using a higher value for the estimate) and then fits the model again. The algorithm stops when it doesn't perceive that moving again would yield much additional improvement. This line tells you how many iterations were executed before the process stopped and output the results:

```
Number of Fisher Scoring iterations: 7
```

We have by far explored the various results showcased in the logistic regression's output, which helped us in understanding the estimate or impact of the predictors in predicting the outcome-detergent quality. However, have we missed out something? Unlike linear regression, we didn't have any overall goodness of fit metric for logistic regression, such as the R-squared and F statistic. We didn't have any metric or statistic that could give us a holistic picture for the model built.

## How do we assess the goodness of fit or accuracy of the model?

We definitely cannot use MAPE and we also cannot calculate R-squared for logistic regression. To have a holistic view about the picture, we need to calculate a few additional things. We'll use the confusion matrix and ROC curve to solve our problem.

What is the confusion matrix and ROC curve and how does it help?

A confusion matrix is a table used to analyze the performance of a model (classification). Each column of the matrix represents the instances in a predicted class while each row represents the instances in an actual class or vice versa. Similarly, the **Receiver Operating Characteristic (ROC)** curve is a standard technique to summarize classification model performance over a range of trade-offs between **true positive (TP)** and **false positive (FP)** error rates. The ROC curve is a plot of sensitivity (the ability of the model to predict an event correctly) versus 1-specificity for the possible cutoff classification probability values.

# Too many new terms?

Let's tackle them one by one. We'll start with exploring the confusion matrix. To build the confusion matrix, we will need to predict the outcomes for a sample test dataset. We can use the 'predict' function in R to predict the probability of getting a 'Good' quality outcome for the detergent. If the probability is > 0.5, we assume that it is Good; otherwise, we assume that it is Bad:

```
predicted_probability<-predict(fit,newdata=test,type="response")
summary(predicted_probability)

   Min. 1st Qu.  Median    Mean 3rd Qu.    Max.
 0.3417  0.5376  0.7065  0.7599  0.9913  0.9961

predicted<-as.factor(ifelse(predicted_probability>0.5,"Good","Bad"))
actuals<-test$Detergent_Qualitytable(actuals,predicted)
        predicted
actuals Bad Good
    Bad  15   35
    Good  16  134
```

We can see the quantile distribution of the probabilities; the 25th percentile shows us 53%, which indicates that a majority of our results are predicted as Good and very few as Bad. This is also aligned with the data as we had only around 20% of the data with Bad quality cases.

The following image shows the sample confusion matrix for the preceding prediction:

|  |  | Predicted | |
|---|---|---|---|
|  |  | Bad | Good |
| Actual | Bad | 15 | 35 |
|  | Good | 16 | 134 |

Here, each row indicates the actual value and each column indicates the predicted value. We can read each row of the matrix as the sum of actuals; the first row can be read as out of all the 'Bad', 15 were correctly predicted as 'Bad' and another 35 were predicted incorrectly as 'Good'. Similarly, each column can be read as the sum of predicted, that is, the first column can be inferred as out of all the predicted 'Bad', 15 were correctly predicted as 'Bad' and 16 were incorrectly predicted as 'Bad'. Based on the actual and predicted values, there is another name given for each of the columns in the confusion matrix as follows:

- **True Positive (TP)**: When it is predicted as TRUE and is actually TRUE
- **False Positive (FP)**: When it is predicted as TRUE and is actually FALSE
- **True Negative (TN)**: When it is predicted as FALSE and is actually FALSE
- **False Negative (FN)**: When it is predicted as TRUE and is actually FALSE

The preceding confusion matrix is overlaid with the nomenclature and is showcased here:

| | | Predicted | |
|---|---|---|---|
| | | Bad | Good |
| Actual | Bad | TN= 15 | FP = 35 |
| | Good | FN=16 | TP =134 |

An exhaustive list of metrics that are usually computed from the confusion matrix to aid in interpreting the goodness of fit for the classification model are as follows:

- **Overall accuracy**: Overall, how often is the classifier correct?

  (TP+TN)/total = (15+134)/200 = 0.75

- **Misclassification rate** or **error rate**: Overall, how often is it wrong?

  (FP+FN)/total = (16+35)/200 = 0.25 *[equivalent to 1 – Accuracy]*

- **True positive rate**: When it's actually true, how often does it predict true?

  TP/(TP + FN) = 134/(16+134) = 0.89

  Also known as **Sensitivity** or **Recall**

- **False positive rate**: When it's actually False, how often does it predict True?

  FP/(TN+FP) = 35/(15+35) = 0.7

- **Specificity** or **true negative rate**: When it's actually no, how often does it predict no?

  TN/actual no = 15/(15+35) = 0.3 [equivalent to 1 – False Positive Rate]

- **True precision**: When it predicts yes, how often is it correct?

  TP/total predicted 'Good' = 134/(35+134) = 0.79

- **False precision**: When it predicts 'Bad', how often is it correct?

  FN/total predicted 'Bad' = 15/(15+16) = 0.48

With the preceding results, we get a fair holistic view of the model performance. We can clearly understand where our model performs poorly and where it performs well. Based on the results, we can further take a call on how to optimize our model. For the current results, we can clearly see that even though we have a decent **overall accuracy**, we fail to predict correctly most 'Bad' cases. In context to our use case, our main objective is to predict the 'Bad' as well as 'Good' quality detergent beforehand correctly. An equal priority for both is defined.

In a nutshell, our model has a very high **False Positive Rate** (FPR) and low TNR (True Negative Rate). We can clearly see that the model predicts many 'Bad' cases incorrectly as 'Good'. How can we improve this? We chose the probability cutoff at 0.5 for Good and Bad; does this have an impact on the results?

Yes, it does. Let's see how it affects. In most average cases, the probability cutoff for the True and False scenario is chosen as 0.5, but we can definitely choose a higher or lower cutoff based on the use case. These use cases are very industry- and domain-specific. It all depends on what is more important to you-True Positive Rate (Sensitivity) or True Negative Rate (Specificity) or both. There are use cases where predicting the True events as True becomes increasingly important for business; say, a retail chain trying to identify their high-value customers. It may be relatively okay for the model to predict a non-high-value customer as a high-value customer, but predicting a high-value customer as a non-high-value customer may cause huge losses to their business. In such cases, the demand is for higher Sensitivity. Similarly, there are use cases when predicting 'False' events as False becomes extremely important for business; say, a healthcare center is predicting cancer patients. It may be relatively fine to predict a patient without cancer as True, but predicting a patient with cancer as False will be life-threatening! In such cases, there is a very high demand for Specificity. A study of Specificity and Sensitivity is used to choose the optimum cutoff for any use case.

In our use case, we have an equal importance for both the events. For John's business, it is equally important to predict a True event as True and False event as False. Therefore, we will need higher overall accuracy without a big compromise over Sensitivity or Specificity. To understand the best probability cutoff value in order to get the highest accuracy, we can use the accuracy function in R to get a visual of how overall accuracy fares for different cutoff levels:

```
library(AUC)
actuals<-test$Detergent_Quality
plot(accuracy(predicted_probability,actuals))
```

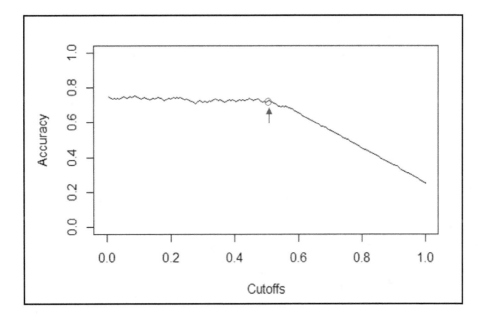

The plot showcases the overall accuracy for the model across different probability cutoffs. As we can see, there is a gradual dip in the overall accuracy after ~0.5. Therefore, our initial probability cutoff was more or less the best chosen cutoff.

Similarly, to understand visually how our model is performing, we can use the ROC curve. As mentioned earlier, the ROC curve is a plot of sensitivity (the ability of the model to predict an event correctly) versus 1-specificity for the possible cutoff classification probability values. Interpreting the ROC curve is again straightforward. The ROC curve visually helps us understand how our model compares with a random prediction. The random prediction will always have a 50% chance of predicting correctly; after comparing with this model, we can understand how much better is our model.

The following code plots the ROC curve for the model fitted previously:

```
library(AUC)
plot(roc(predicted_probability,actuals))
```

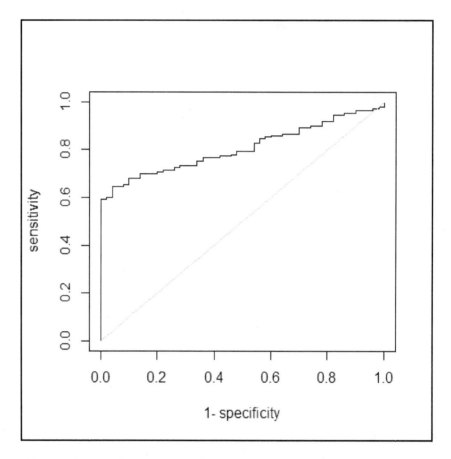

The diagonal line indicates the accuracy of random predictions and the lift from the diagonal line towards the left upper corner indicates how much improvement our model has in comparison to the random predictions. Observing the preceding plot, we can see that the model is quite above the diagonal and has much better accuracy than a random model. Models having a higher lift from the diagonals are considered to be more accurate models.

# Recap to the model interpretation

So far, we have delved deep into the logistic regression modeling exercise. We executed a basic iteration and learned how to interpret the results. You learned how we can quantify the impact of each independent predictor on the net outcome, that is, log odds ratio of the event, and studied other metrics that would help us in understanding the holistic picture of the model's goodness of fit. We calculated the confusion matrix and also visualized the ROC curve. By far, the results that we got are not great. Though we have a decent overall accuracy, our model has a very high False Positive Rate and therefore fails in correctly predicting the 'Bad' outcomes. We would now try tuning the model to improve its performance and predict with better True Positive Rate and True Negative Rate.

# Improving the classification model

The preceding exercise was an attempt to understand the logistic regression model. We'll now focus on improving our model to get better and more accurate results. To understand the overall goodness of fit, we'll consider the overall accuracy, TPR, and TNR.

## Let's define our approach

Similar to linear regression, we can start modeling using the 'Forward Selection', 'Backward Elimination', or a combination of both. We'll use the backward elimination method.

## How do we go about it?

We'll start with the final list of predictors that have been identified as important in our overall analysis till now. We'll then run an iteration of logistic regression with all independent predictors and then try to improve the results. Using the p-value and estimates, we can identify how important each predictor is in defining a relationship with the dependent outcome and then eliminate the ones that add zero or low value. We will perform some data transformations on the predictors to further improve the results and finally, we will test our results on a dataset to check the goodness of fit of our data using a variety of metrics and tests.

# Let's begin modeling

We'll start with the list of predictors that have been identified as important in our overall analysis. After fitting the model, we'll predict the outcomes with probability cutoff as 0.5 and calculate the different measures for goodness of fit:

```
fit<-glm(Detergent_Quality~

        #The Production Quantity deviation feature
        Quantity_Deviation_new +
        AssemblyLine_ID     +

        #The Production Quantity deviation feature
        Stage1_PrevProduct_1 +

        #Raw Material Quality Parameters
        Stage1_RM1_QParameter2 +
        Stage1_RM1_QParameter1 +
        Stage1_RM2_QParameter2 +
        Stage1_RM2_QParameter1 +
        Stage3_RM1_QParameter1 +
        Stage3_RM1_QParameter2 +
        Stage3_RM2_QParameter1 +
        Stage3_RM3_QParameter2 +
        Stage3_RM3_QParameter1 +

        #Machine/Resources used in a Stage
        Stage3_ResourceName_new +
        Stage1_ProductChange_Flag,
        data=train,
        family = "binomial"
    )
summary(fit)
```

```
Call:
glm(formula = Detergent_Quality ~ Quantity_Deviation_new +
AssemblyLine_ID +
    Stage1_PrevProduct_1 + Stage1_RM1_QParameter2 +
    Stage1_RM1_QParameter1 +
    Stage1_RM2_QParameter2 + Stage1_RM2_QParameter1 +
    Stage3_RM1_QParameter1 +
    Stage3_RM1_QParameter2 + Stage3_RM2_QParameter1 +
    Stage3_RM3_QParameter2 +
    Stage3_RM3_QParameter1 + Stage3_ResourceName_new +
    Stage1_ProductChange_Flag,
    family = "binomial", data = train)

Deviance Residuals:
    Min       1Q    Median       3Q      Max
-3.3815   0.0645   0.1213   0.6787   1.5129

Coefficients:
                                           Estimate Std. Error z value Pr(>|z|)
(Intercept)                              46.7480396  5.4505701   8.577  < 2e-16 ***
Quantity_Deviation_newLow                 0.1106493  0.2545713   0.435 0.663817
Quantity_Deviation_newMedium              0.3149165  0.2683646   1.173 0.240609
AssemblyLine_IDLine 2                     0.2079202  0.2689347   0.773 0.439448
Stage1_PrevProduct_1Product_545           0.4152689  0.4153397   1.000 0.317393
Stage1_RM1_QParameter2                   -0.4453806  0.4082431  -1.091 0.275287
Stage1_RM1_QParameter1                    0.0003624  0.0007384   0.491 0.623575
Stage1_RM2_QParameter2                   -0.0148075  0.0311087  -0.476 0.634080
Stage1_RM2_QParameter1                    0.0245136  0.0357919   0.685 0.493412
Stage3_RM1_QParameter1                   -0.1307426  0.0393105  -3.326 0.000881 ***
Stage3_RM1_QParameter2                   -2.9851588  2.5515944  -1.170 0.242034
Stage3_RM2_QParameter1                   -0.0255049  0.0134841  -1.891 0.058560 .
Stage3_RM3_QParameter2                   -0.0064451  0.0123199  -0.523 0.600870
Stage3_RM3_QParameter1                   -0.1592651  0.1173381  -1.357 0.174680
Stage3_ResourceName_newResource_108      -0.7249357  0.3926719  -1.846 0.064869 .
Stage3_ResourceName_newResource_109      -1.2094513  0.4141960  -2.920 0.003500 **
Stage1_ProductChange_FlagYes             -0.2346322  0.3997010  -0.587 0.557191
---
Signif. codes:  0 '***' 0.001 '**' 0.01 '*' 0.05 '.' 0.1 ' ' 1

(Dispersion parameter for binomial family taken to be 1)

    Null deviance: 840.51  on 799  degrees of freedom
Residual deviance: 545.17  on 783  degrees of freedom
AIC: 579.17

Number of Fisher Scoring iterations: 7
```

```
#Creating a Function to predict and calculate TPR,TNR, Overall accuracy
from the confusion matrix

prediction_summary<-function(fit,test)
    {
    #Predicting results on the test data, using the fitted model
    predicted_probability<-predict(fit,newdata=test,
type="response")
    print("Distribution of Probability")
    print("")

    print(summary(predicted_probability))
    predicted<-as.factor(ifelse(predicted_probability>0.5,
"Good","Bad"))

    actuals<-test$Detergent_Quality

    confusion_matrix<-table(actuals,predicted)
    print("Confusion Matrix :-")
    print(confusion_matrix)
    print("")

    #Calcualting the different measures for Goodness of fit
    TP<-confusion_matrix[2,2]
    FP<-confusion_matrix[1,2]
    TN<-confusion_matrix[1,1]
    FN<-confusion_matrix[2,1]

    #Calcualting all the required
    print(paste("Overall_accuracy ->
                ",(TP+TN)/sum(confusion_matrix)))
    print(paste("TPR -> ",TP/(TP+FN)))
    print(paste("TNR -> ",TN/(TN+FP)))
    print(paste("FP -> ",FP/(TN+FP)))


    }

#Viewing the results together

#Calling the function to view results
prediction_summary(fit,test)

#Results
[1] "Distribution of Probability"
[1] ""
   Min. 1st Qu.  Median    Mean 3rd Qu.    Max.
 0.2747  0.5274  0.7977  0.7527  0.9927  0.9982
```

```
[1] "Confusion Matrix :-"
          predicted
actuals Bad Good
    Bad    20   30
    Good   24  126
[1] ""

[1] "Overall_accuracy ->   0.73"
[1] "TPR ->   0.84"
[1] "TNR ->   0.4"
[1] "FP ->   0.6"
```

The highlighted predictors have been identified as the significant ones. We can see that only the intercept and two other predictors-Stage 3 RM1 QParameter 1 and Stage3 ResourceName-are significant. The overall results have improved slightly compared to our first exercise.

We have an additional significant variable; the residual deviance has reduced from 569.85 on 790 degrees of freedom to 545.17 on 783 degrees of freedom. The overall AIC has improved from 589 to 579. The overall accuracy seems to have reduced but the True Negative Rate has increased from 0.3 to 0.4, the overall FPR (False Positive Rate) has reduced from 0.7 to 0.6, and the improvement is relatively better. We will need to continuously improve our overall accuracy, TPR, and TNR and thereby reduce FPR.

# So how do we move ahead?

The significant variables in the list have been highlighted; as a next step similar to linear regression, we can either drop the insignificant variables and fine-tune the significant variables further to improve the goodness of fit or we can take a shot at improving both insignificant as well as significant predictors. We will also try data transformations on the continuous predictors using a trial and error approach as applying transformations to the predictors or the dependent variable helps the variance to be more intuitively captured in some cases. The transformations can be in any form, such as square($x2$), cube ($x3$), exponential ($ex$), log transformations, and so on. These transformations can be applied only to the predictors.

If we take a closer look at the results, we can observe that only one of the nine raw material quality parameters is significant. Data transformations may or may not be valuable; the results can be validated only with a trial and error approach. We can try all combinations of data transformations on the predictors and finally choose the combination that renders the best results.

 It is recommended that you execute various logistic regression iterations to see the differences in results with different transformations. The following showcased result is the output for one of the various iterations executed for different types of mathematical data transformations.

Similar to linear regression, we do not see any specific improvement from data transformations. Moreover, data transformations has only deteriorated the goodness of fit to a certain extent. The following result showcases one of the iterations where data transformations were tried:

```
> #the variable fit has the best iteration in the experiments
> summary(fit)
```

```
Call:
glm(formula = Detergent_Quality ~ Quantity_Deviation_new +

AssemblyLine_ID +
   Stage1_PrevProduct_1 +
log(Stage1_RM1_QParameter2) +
Stage1_RM1_QParameter1 +
   (Stage1_RM2_QParameter2)^2 +
log(Stage1_RM2_QParameter1) +
   log(Stage3_RM1_QParameter1) +
log(Stage3_RM1_QParameter2) +
   (Stage3_RM2_QParameter1)^3 +
log(Stage3_RM3_QParameter2) +
   (Stage3_RM3_QParameter1)^2 +
Stage3_ResourceName_new +
Stage1_ProductChange_Flag,
    family = "binomial", data = train)

Deviance Residuals:
    Min      1Q   Median      3Q      Max
-3.4029   0.0640   0.1193   0.6977   1.5571

Coefficients:
                                    Estimate Std. Error z value Pr(>|z|)
(Intercept)                         1.769e+02  4.250e+01   4.162 3.15e-05 ***
Quantity_Deviation_newLow           1.972e-01  2.441e-01   0.808  0.41916
Quantity_Deviation_newMedium       -7.100e-02  3.030e-01  -0.234  0.81471
AssemblyLine_IDLine 2               1.715e-01  2.685e-01   0.639  0.52288
Stage1_PrevProduct_1Product_545     4.102e-01  4.118e-01   0.996  0.31910
log(Stage1_RM1_QParameter2)        -1.466e+00  1.431e+00  -1.025  0.30538
Stage1_RM1_QParameter1              4.724e-04  7.362e-04   0.642  0.52103
Stage1_RM2_QParameter2             -1.226e-02  3.103e-02  -0.395  0.69287
log(Stage1_RM2_QParameter1)         4.273e+00  5.451e+00   0.784  0.43309
log(Stage3_RM1_QParameter1)        -2.983e+01  8.427e+00  -3.540  0.00040 ***
log(Stage3_RM1_QParameter2)        -2.802e-01  2.511e-01  -1.116  0.26442
Stage3_RM2_QParameter1             -2.475e-02  1.349e-02  -1.834  0.06665 .
log(Stage3_RM3_QParameter2)        -3.360e+00  6.901e+00  -0.487  0.62629
Stage3_RM3_QParameter1             -1.396e-01  1.159e-01  -1.205  0.22812
Stage3_ResourceName_newResource_108 -7.462e-01  3.927e-01  -1.900  0.05742 .
Stage3_ResourceName_newResource_109 -1.249e+00  4.160e-01  -3.002  0.00269 **
Stage1_ProductChange_FlagYes       -1.996e-01  4.023e-01  -0.496  0.61981
---
Signif. codes:  0 '***' 0.001 '**' 0.01 '*' 0.05 '.' 0.1 ' ' 1

(Dispersion parameter for binomial family taken to be 1)

    Null deviance: 840.51  on 799  degrees of freedom
Residual deviance: 545.47  on 783  degrees of freedom
AIC: 579.47

Number of Fisher Scoring iterations: 7
```

```
#Calling the Prediction Summary Function, we created earlier
prediction_summary(fit,test)
[1] "Distribution of Probability"
[1]
    Min. 1st Qu.  Median    Mean 3rd Qu.    Max.
  0.2780  0.5291  0.7953  0.7526  0.9927  0.9983

[1] "Confusion Matrix :-"
        predicted
actuals Bad Good
    Bad  19   31
   Good  24  126
[1]
[1] "Overall_accuracy ->  0.725"
[1] "TPR ->  0.84"
[1] "TNR ->  0.38"
[1] "FP ->  0.62"
```

We have tried square operation, cubic operation, and many log operations on the data. Overall, we can clearly see a small drop in the TNR and increase in the TPR compared to our previous iteration. The results are comparatively bad. The overall accuracy has also dropped by a small margin.

# Adding interaction terms

As we didn't get any better results with the data transformation exercise, let's try adding interaction variables. Interaction variables, as discussed in linear regression, occur when an independent variable has a different effect on the outcome depending on the values of another independent variable, that is, a situation in which the simultaneous influence of two variables on a third is not additive.

This can be understood from the following equation:

$Y = \beta 0 + \beta 1A + \beta 2B + \beta(A\ B) + $ &#55349;

The following iteration showcases the result of one of the comparatively better models from a variety of combinations for the interaction variables tried out. We have considered interaction between multiple raw material quality parameter combinations and chosen the iteration that gave the best accuracy. A few insignificant variables have been eliminated and a few have been retained. We can see that the AIC has reduced significantly and the residual deviance has also reduced:

```
>#fit contains the Logistic Regression iteration with Interaction variables
>summary(fit)
```

```
Call:
glm(formula = Detergent_Quality ~ Quantity_Deviation_new + AssemblyLine_ID +
    Stage1_PrevProduct_1 + Stage1_RM1_QParameter2 + Stage1_RM1_QParameter1 +
    Stage1_RM2_QParameter2 + Stage1_RM2_QParameter1 + Stage3_RM2_QParameter1 +
    Stage3_RM3_QParameter1 +
    Stage1_RM1_QParameter2 * Stage3_RM3_QParameter1 +
    Stage1_RM2_QParameter2 * Stage3_RM2_QParameter1 +
    Stage1_RM2_QParameter1 * Stage3_RM2_QParameter1 +
    Stage3_RM1_QParameter1 * Stage1_RM2_QParameter1 +
    Stage3_ResourceName_new +
    Stage1_ProductChange_Flag,
    family = "binomial",   data = train)

Deviance Residuals:
    Min      1Q    Median      3Q      Max
-3.5814   0.0033   0.0427   0.6614   1.8348


Coefficients:
                                                 Estimate Std. Error z value Pr(>|z|)
(Intercept)                                      6.973e+02  1.736e+02    4.017  5.9e-05 ***
Quantity_Deviation_newLow                        1.768e-01  2.508e-01    0.705  0.48086
Quantity_Deviation_newMedium                    -1.426e-01  3.137e-01   -0.455  0.64928
AssemblyLine_IDLine 2                            -1.782e-01  2.890e-01   -0.616  0.53763
Stage1_PrevProduct_1Product_545                  6.680e-02  4.277e-01    0.156  0.87589
Stage1_RM1_QParameter2                          -1.151e-01  3.925e+00   -2.934  0.00335 **
Stage1_RM1_QParameter1                           3.055e-04  7.587e-04    0.403  0.68721
Stage1_RM2_QParameter2                           5.888e+00  1.851e+00    3.181  0.00147 **
Stage1_RM2_QParameter1                          -6.180e+00  1.554e+00   -3.976  7.0e-05 ***
Stage3_RM2_QParameter1                          -7.761e-01  3.870e-01   -2.005  0.04493 *
Stage3_RM3_QParameter1                          -5.407e+00  1.890e+00   -2.861  0.00422 **
Stage3_RM1_QParameter1                          -1.004e+00  9.497e-01   -1.057  0.29060
Stage3_ResourceName_newResource_108             -6.769e-01  4.102e-01   -1.650  0.09890 .
Stage3_ResourceName_newResource_109             -1.307e+00  4.169e-01   -3.135  0.00172 **
Stage1_ProductChange_FlagYes                    -2.773e-01  4.150e-01   -0.668  0.50401
Stage1_RM1_QParameter2:Stage3_RM3_QParameter1    1.553e+00  5.509e-01    2.818  0.00483 **
Stage1_RM2_QParameter2:Stage3_RM2_QParameter1   -1.026e-02  3.220e-03   -3.185  0.00145 **
Stage1_RM2_QParameter1:Stage3_RM2_QParameter1    8.557e-03  3.043e-03    2.812  0.00492 **
Stage1_RM2_QParameter1:Stage3_RM1_QParameter1    6.026e-03  6.224e-03    0.968  0.33289
---
Signif. codes:  0 '***' 0.001 '**' 0.01 '*' 0.05 '.' 0.1 ' ' 1

(Dispersion parameter for binomial family taken to be 1)

    Null deviance: 840.51  on 799  degrees of freedom
Residual deviance: 516.87  on 781  degrees of freedom
AIC: 554.87

Number of Fisher Scoring iterations: 8
```

```
#Calling the Prediction Summary Function, we created earlier
prediction_summary(fit,test)
```

```
[1] "Distribution of Probability"
[1]
    Min. 1st Qu.  Median    Mean 3rd Qu.    Max.
  0.2780  0.5291  0.7953  0.7526  0.9927  0.9983

[1] "Confusion Matrix :-"
        predicted
actuals Bad Good
    Bad   19   31
    Good  24  126
[1]
[1] "Overall_accuracy ->   0.725"
[1] "TPR ->   0.84"
[1] "TNR ->   0.38"
[1] "FP ->   0.62"
```

In spite of having a comparatively better model with the goodness of fit measure, we still get similar results for TPR, TNR, and overall accuracy. Again, we do not see any good results. We don't see any improvements in our results and the confusion matrix remains exactly the same. Our model still has a very high FPR and low TNR.

# What can be done to improve this?

One issue with the data is that the distribution of Good and Bad detergent quality samples is skewed. Around 80% of our data is Good quality and the remaining is Bad quality. Our prediction models are failing with a high FPR because it is not able to identify the Bad quality samples clearly. The training is skewed toward Good quality samples and hence the model does fairly good in predicting them, but fails when it comes to predicting Bad quality samples correctly.

The following code shows the distribution of "Good" and "Bad" quality samples across the overall dataset:

```
tapply(data$Detergent_Quality,data$Detergent_Quality,length)

Bad Good
225  775

#We can see only ~20% of the data belongs to "Bad" samples.
```

One way in which we can try fixing this is by oversampling or taking a stratified balanced sample to train. The problem for high false positive and low true negative is probably due to the skewed training of Good quality samples. We can provide a stratified training sample to the logistic regression model, rather than providing the existing 80% training sample, to see whether it makes any difference.

The new stratified training sample will have 50% Good quality and 50% Bad quality samples. The following code creates a stratified training sample from the existing training sample. Once the new model is fit, we will validate the results using the same old test dataset:

```
#Function to create a stratified sample
#Here, df = Dataframe,
#        group = The variable on which stratification needs to be done.
#     maximum number of sample for each level in group

stratified = function(df, group, size) {
  require(sampling)
  temp = df[order(df[group]),]
  if (size < 1) {
    size = ceiling(table(temp[group]) * size)
  } else if (size >= 1) {
    size = rep(size, times=length(table(temp[group])))
  }
  strat = strata(temp, stratanames = names(temp[group]),
                 size = size, method = "srswor")
  (dsample = getdata(temp, strat))
}

#Counting the number of "Good" and "Bad" rows in the data
a<-tapply(train$Detergent_Quality,train$Detergent_Quality,length)
size<-a["Bad"]
print(size)

#We create a new training sample, with the same number of "Good" and "Bad"
Quality samples.

stratified_train<-stratified(train,"Detergent_Quality",size)

#Checking the frequency of Good and Bad samples
summary(stratified_train$Detergent_Quality)
 Bad Good
 175   175

#Fitting the model on the new stratified Training sample

#Ignoring the codes to fit

#Printing summary
> summary(fit)
```

```
Call:
glm(formula = Detergent_Quality ~ Quantity_Deviation_new + AssemblyLine_ID +
    Stage1_PrevProduct_1 + Stage1_RM1_QParameter2 + Stage1_RM1_QParameter1 +
    Stage1_RM2_QParameter2 + Stage1_RM2_QParameter1 + Stage3_RM2_QParameter1 +
    Stage3_RM3_QParameter1 + Stage1_RM1_QParameter2 * Stage3_RM3_QParameter1 +
    Stage1_RM2_QParameter2 * Stage3_RM2_QParameter1 + Stage1_RM2_QParameter1 *
    Stage3_RM2_QParameter1 + Stage1_RM2_QParameter1 * Stage3_RM1_QParameter1 +
    Stage3_ResourceName_new + Stage1_ProductChange_Flag, family = "binomial",
    data = stratified_train)

Deviance Residuals:
    Min       1Q   Median       3Q      Max
-3.1899  -0.6528  -0.0746   0.1756   2.2304

Coefficients:
                                                  Estimate Std. Error z value Pr(>|z|)
(Intercept)                                     493.706052 217.491971   2.270  0.02321 *
Quantity_Deviation_newLow                         0.456392   0.395030   1.155  0.24795
Quantity_Deviation_newMedium                     -0.020023   0.494143  -0.041  0.96768
AssemblyLine_IDLine 2                            -0.553821   0.449905  -1.231  0.21833
Stage1_PrevProduct_1Product_S45                  -0.681547   0.594820  -1.146  0.25188
Stage1_RM1_QParameter2                           -9.039760   5.801280  -1.558  0.11918
Stage1_RM1_QParameter1                            0.001025   0.001226   0.835  0.40350
Stage1_RM2_QParameter2                            6.856833   2.551667   2.687  0.00721 **
Stage1_RM2_QParameter1                           -5.203091   1.999460  -2.602  0.00926 **
Stage3_RM2_QParameter1                           -0.871920   0.530776  -1.643  0.10044
Stage3_RM3_QParameter1                           -4.308830   2.802132  -1.538  0.12412
Stage3_RM1_QParameter1                            0.166045   1.192918   0.139  0.88930
Stage3_ResourceName_newResource_108             -1.105921   0.568190  -1.946  0.05161 .
Stage3_ResourceName_newResource_109             -0.894735   0.616154  -1.452  0.14647
Stage1_ProductChange_FlagYes                     -0.185957   0.645186  -0.288  0.77318
Stage1_RM1_QParameter2:Stage3_RM3_QParameter1    1.214459   0.821106   1.479  0.13913
Stage1_RM2_QParameter2:Stage3_RM2_QParameter1   -0.011976   0.004447  -2.693  0.00707 **
Stage1_RM2_QParameter1:Stage3_RM2_QParameter1    0.009651   0.004338   2.225  0.02609 *
Stage1_RM2_QParameter1:Stage3_RM1_QParameter1   -0.001565   0.007849  -0.199  0.84194
---
Signif. codes:  0 '***' 0.001 '**' 0.01 '*' 0.05 '.' 0.1 ' ' 1

(Dispersion parameter for binomial family taken to be 1)

    Null deviance: 485.20  on 349  degrees of freedom
Residual deviance: 247.26  on 331  degrees of freedom
AIC: 285.26

Number of Fisher Scoring iterations: 8|
```

```
> prediction_summary(fit,test)

[1] "Distribution of Probability"
[1]
   Min. 1st Qu.  Median    Mean 3rd Qu.    Max.
0.01273 0.22640 0.49960 0.58490 0.99580 1.00000

[1] "Confusion Matrix :-"
        predicted
actuals Bad Good
    Bad  49    1
    Good 52   98

[1]
[1] "Overall_accuracy ->  0.735"
```

```
[1] "TPR ->   0.653333333333333"
[1] "TNR ->   0.98"
[1] "FP ->   0.02"
```

The model summary looks pretty much the same, except for the AIC and residual deviance, for which the differences are huge. It seems like there has been a drastic improvement in the results. However, when we take a look at the prediction summary, we'll be surprised.

The overall accuracy has increased by a small fraction and the TPR has dropped by quite some range, but the TNR rate has reached almost 100% and the FPR has reached 0.02. The results look very surprising.

# What just happened?

Our earlier models were trained on a sample that was skewed in the distribution of 'Good' and 'Bad' samples (80:20). The model that learned from this data learned how to predict the 'Good' sample quite well, but miserably failed to predict the 'Bad' quality samples. This indicates that our understanding about the model's learning limitation was true. Due to a skewed training sample for "Good", the model could not learn the patterns for "Bad" easily. With a stratified sample in place, we can see that there is a huge difference in the results. The model now predicts almost 100% 'Bad' quality samples correctly. However, a major problem is that the preceding results can't be justified as better because there is a huge drop in the TPR; moreover, the results may be overfitting. If we try the model iteration using a different test sample, we might probably see a different result. We'll temporarily set aside the overfitting issue and learn about it in the next chapter. We now need to improve the TNR and overall accuracy while having the TPR also intact or at least good. The current iteration of the model has improved the overall accuracy and TNR, but there is a huge compromise in the TPR.

# What can be done to improve the TNR and overall accuracy while keeping the TPR intact?

Using a stratified training sample has helped us improve the TNR, but we need to achieve high TNR along with a high TPR. Our model needs to learn the nuances of the 'Bad' sample more intuitively. Stratification helped, but not completely. Can we have our model learn the prediction of 'Bad' and 'Good' better without compromising the TPR and goodness of fit? This is when we need to step into machine learning. With machine learning, we have a variety of cutting-edge and state-of-the-art algorithms that can help us in achieving better results. We'll explore a few of these interesting techniques in the next chapter.

However, there are alternative ways to improve the same in logistic regression with a little extra effort. We would need to explore regularization in more depth and achieve the same with quite a lot of effort. However, the regularization topic in logistic regression is extremely vast and would make it difficult to do justice in a small section of a chapter.

# Summary

In the current chapter, we took our problem solving skills one step ahead by trying to answer the question 'When'. In an attempt to provide John's team with a more powerful and actionable solution, we touched base on the predictive stack of data science. We analyzed the problem and found two different ways to solve the same problem-one being a regression problem (predicting a continuous outcome) and the other being a classification problem (predicting a categorical outcome). We started by solving the problem to predict the output quality parameter for the detergent before being manufactured. We used Linear Regression and also experimented the same problem with CART, that is, Decision trees. You learned about the functioning of the algorithm in detail (keeping the mathematical aspect aside) and experimented with a variety of techniques to improve the accuracy, but didn't achieve favorable results.

We then experimented with the alternative approach, where the same problem was defined in a new way that then changed the overall type of the problem statement-classification. We attempted to solve the problem using a very famous and easy-to-implement statistical technique, Logistic Regression. You learned the nuances of the algorithm and understood how to interpret the results using R. We experimented with a variety of iterations to improve the results and, toward the end, we got some promising signals. We have still not achieved good results, but we see a ray of hope where we can improve. To improve the results further, we will require more powerful algorithms that can learn latent signals and give more accurate results. To achieve this, we'll use a bunch of machine learning techniques in the next chapter. We'll try to build a valuable and actionable solution for John's team and create an impact in the manufacturing firm.

In the next chapter, we'll focus on cutting-edge machine learning algorithms that can take our results to a more accurate level. With machine learning, we'll take our decision science and analytical skills to a more sophisticated level.

# 5
# Enhancing Predictive Analytics with Machine Learning for IoT

The predictive stack for analytics is an extremely wide and varied domain. Many ambiguous buzz words and disciplines can be associated with this field. Statistical modeling, machine learning, artificial intelligence, neural networks, deep learning, cognitive computing, and the list goes on. The variety of definitions available for each of these disciplines makes it difficult to articulate the similarities and differences between them. Our initial exercises were aligned towards statistical modeling; we will now focus more on machine learning. The difference between the two is mainly the school that they originate from. Statistical modeling comes from the mathematical school whereas machine learning evolved from computer science.

In this chapter, we'll enhance our predictive analytics skills using cutting-edge machine learning algorithms that will help us predict with better accuracy. From the time we started solving the problem, we have made incremental progresses in the solution, but our solutions still haven't reached the maturity level, which John's team can leverage to take action. Our focus in this chapter will be to get our solutions more mature so that they can solve the problem better and add value to John's team. The current chapter will cover the following topics:

- A brief introduction to machine learning
- Ensemble modeling – random forest
- Ensemble modeling – XGBoost
- Neural networks and deep learning

# A Brief Introduction to Machine Learning

Machine learning is not a very well-defined term in the industry. There is a variety of definitions available in multiple textbooks and e-resources. The general difference between statistical modeling and machine learning is a much talked about topic but is still a very ambiguous term. At a high level, we can call machine learning an advanced layer in the predictive stack of decision science; an area where powerful algorithms and techniques use data to learn patterns and relationships to predict an outcome.

We started our predictive journey using statistical modeling. You learned how to implement and use various statistical models such as linear regression, logistic regression, and decision trees. We'll now try solving the same problem using more advanced algorithms that will give us better results. Before we start, we still want to know: what is machine learning and how is it different from statistical modeling?

In a single sentence, machine learning can be defined as an **algorithm that can learn from data without relying on rules-based programming,** whereas statistical modeling can be defined as the **formalization of relationships between variables in the form of mathematical equations**. Machine learning has more relaxed rules when compared to statistical modeling. In machine learning, there are relatively less assumptions made about the underlying data. (We didn't give much focus on assumptions about the data in our previous exercises.)

Also, Machine learning is comparatively powerful in leveraging the learning with the increasing amount of data. However, statistical models have a learning saturation. Let's take a simple example to understand this better. Let's say that you have built a model using 1,000 training samples (assuming that 1,000 is a good enough number for a model to learn) and get around 60% overall accuracy for a classification scenario. If you add more training samples, 2,000 instead of 1,000, in most cases, we can normally expect to get a slightly better accuracy than previously. Let's assume that the overall improvement is around 3%. The issue with statistical models is that this improvement doesn't scale with the addition of more and more training samples beyond a point. Let's say that you achieved the best results with 10 K training samples, then there is a very high chance that the overall accuracy will barely improve in case you add another 10 K samples to the training set. This is where we say models reach a learning saturation. There isn't a mathematical proof for the reason but it is a general observation while modeling. Machine learning techniques, however, are much better in leveraging the large datasets for improved prediction. There are fairly high chances that you will observe better results with an increased training data size compared to statistical models to a great extent.

A special area in machine learning and statistics is called **Ensemble modeling**, that is, the art of using multiple learning algorithms to obtain better predictive performance. A major reason for machine learning techniques to improve accuracy with more and more training samples is through ensemble modeling. Let's explore ensemble modeling a bit more.

# What exactly is ensemble modeling?

*An ensemble is a learning technique to combine multiple weak learners/models to produce a strong learner.* In a nutshell, it is the art of building multiple models and then combining the results from all models algorithmically to get a better result. A simple example of an ensemble model is the **Random Forest** algorithm *(having multiple CART models; we will explore more of this in the next section).* The performance is much better compared to an individual CART or decision tree model. The algorithm classifies a new object where each tree gives "votes" for that class and the forest chooses the classification having the most votes (over all the trees in the forest). In the case of regression, it takes the average of the outputs of different trees.

# Why should we choose ensemble models?

In real life, we often see that a group of people are more likely to make better decisions compared to individuals, especially when group members come from diverse backgrounds. The analogy holds true for machine learning too. An ensemble basically combines multiple weak learners/models to produce a strong learner. The diversity in each model is introduced through **bootstrapping**-the process of randomly sampling with replacement. On a general note, each model will be provided with a different sample to train; therefore, each model learns in a slightly different way and thus reduces variance error.

The major benefits of ensemble modeling are as follows:

- Improved prediction
- Improved stability in the model

The fact that many weak learners together deliver more accurate results than one strong model alone holds true in majority of the cases. Secondly, bringing in diversity through bootstrap aggregation-taking random samples with replacement for each model-helps reducing noise and improves generalization capabilities of the model to a great extent. With better generalization capabilities, the results from the ensemble model help in giving better accuracy and more stability.

# So how does an ensemble model actually work?

In a theoretical scenario, we can create an ensemble-multiple models for the same task that are completely heterogeneous, say a group of classification trees and logistic regression models or some other technique. However, mostly we develop an ensemble using the same class of technique, say an ensemble of only classification trees or only logistic regression models. We can decide on the number of models we plan to create and then combine the results from each model using some method (mostly voting).

Consider our current scenario, where we are building a classification model using a universe of 1,000 training samples. Instead of building one model, let's build 100 models of the same type, say classification trees. Firstly, a bootstrap aggregation process creates 100 training sets from the 1,000 training samples using random selection with replacement. Each training set can be created with around 60% of the original size (not a fixed number; it can be defined by the user). Therefore, we'll have 100 different training sets each having around 600 training samples. We can then build 100 models using the training set assigned to the respective models. Each model built using the bootstrapped training set will have small variations in the way the tree gets constructed. The overall process remains exactly the same like we discussed in the previous chapter, but as the training data for each tree will be slightly different, each tree will have a slight difference in its overall construction.

After all the models are built, we can then use them to classify the testing sample. For each test, we'll have 100 results instead of one, which we can combine using votes. Let's assume that we tried to classify a test case for 'Good' or 'Bad' and while testing it, used the 100 trees we built; we get 70 trees with 'Good' and the rest 20 with 'Bad' as the outcome. Then we can affirmatively conclude that the end quality for the test case is 'Good'. A general voting algorithm is considered to get the maximum voted outcome as the end outcome. In the case of regression, where we predict a continuous outcome, the results from all the models can be averaged to give the final answer. This process can also be called **Bagging.** The overall process can be visualized in the following image:

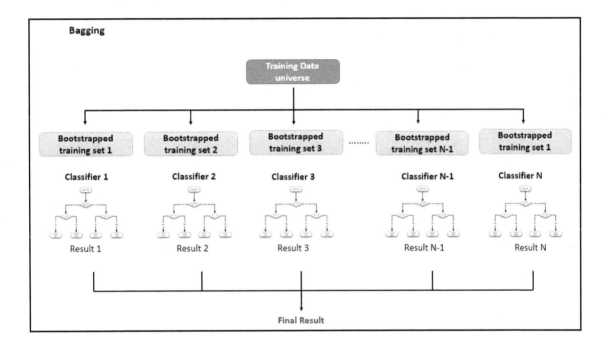

In some cases, we have another technique used for ensemble modeling called '**Boosting**'. Unlike bagging, the boosting process works iteratively and improves each model to learn the previously misclassified samples in a better way. In the process of boosting, rather than building all the models in parallel, the models are built iteratively. The first model is built using the entire training data and the next model runs on a random sample and weighted training dataset. The weighting is done in such a way that the misclassified samples by the previous model are given an added weight so that the model learns to predict the misclassified samples better. The process continues and iterates for a definite number of times. The resultant model will ideally have the lowest misclassification rate. There is a variety of boosting algorithms developed by statisticians across the globe. The differences among most of them is in the method used to calculate weights for the misclassified cases. The overall boosting process can be visualized in the following image:

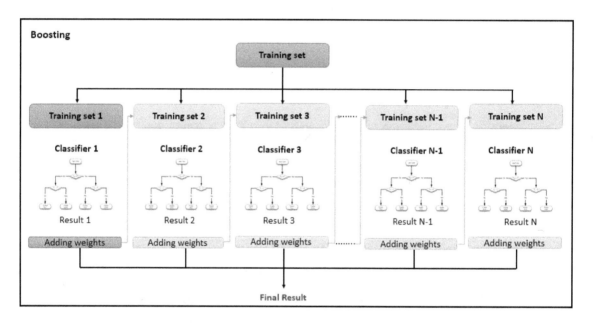

Another means of creating an ensemble model is '**Stacking**'. The stacking process is very similar to boosting. Initially, the models are trained using the available data, then a combiner model is trained to make a final prediction using all the predictions of the other models as additional inputs.

# What are the different ensemble learning techniques?

There are many popular ensemble techniques used for classification and regression:

- **Bagging**: Bagging and random forest
- **Boosting**: Adaboost, gradient boosted machines, and XGBoost

The most popular ones are **Random Forest** and **XgBoost**. Random forest is basically an advanced version of bagging, whereas XgBoost is based on the principles of boosting and is an advanced version of Gradient Boosted Machines (GBM). Both have been widely used in the industry for a variety of use cases and have delivered improved results in accuracy and stability.

In this chapter, you'll learn and implement predictive modeling using random forest and xgboost.

## Quick Recap – Where were we previously?

In the previous chapter, we tried to build a classification model using logistic regression. In a series of experiments, we used a stratified balanced training sample to increase the TNR, that is, True Negative Rate. We did achieve this, but at the cost of a lower TPR, that is, True Positive Rate. We need to improve our results by increasing the TNR and TPR and therefore increasing the overall accuracy. In this chapter, we take our predictive analytics skills one notch higher by learning and implementing two very popular machine learning techniques in ensemble modeling.

# Ensemble modeling – random forest

Random forest is an extremely popular machine learning technique that is used mainly for classification and regression. As the algorithm builds multiple decision trees, we have already covered a substantial part of the foundation required for random forest. Let's quickly understand the algorithm and solve our previous problem better.

# What is random forest?

Random forest is a machine learning technique built on the principle of ensemble modeling. It builds an ensemble of decision trees with each tree having a randomly chosen subset of features; hence the name Random + Forest. Random forest is basically an advanced version of the bagging algorithm. In bagging, we build multiple decision trees with a bootstrapped training sample selected with replacement from the entire training set. In random forest, the addition of randomness is taken one step further. Here, from the entire list of features only a predefined number of features are chosen randomly for each tree. Let's say that we have a total of 15 features in all, then each tree will be assigned randomly selected five or six (a fixed predefined number) features along with a bootstrap training sample chosen with replacement. The addition of randomness in features for each tree helps random forest achieve better stability than decision trees and bagging algorithms.

A new degree of randomness associated with the features as well as the training sample helps the random forest algorithm to deliver more powerful results and leverage the surplus training data in the most effective way. At the crux of the algorithm, we have decision trees being built to form a forest. The process of building a decision tree is exactly the same as we discussed in Chapter 4, *Experimenting Predictive Analytics for IoT*. Once all the trees are trained with their respective features and training samples, we can now predict results from n trees rather than one (n being the number of trees built in the forest, a finite number). To get the final result, the results from n trees is converted to a single result by majority voting.

Moving on, let's understand how a **classification tree** is constructed in the random forest algorithm. By the way, there is no difference in how a classification tree is built in a normal circumstance and in the random forest algorithm. Overall, the entire process is exactly the same as we studied for the **regression trees** except for the selection of root nodes and subsequent decision nodes. In the previous chapter, we studied how regression trees are constructed in CART in detail. It calculates the Standard Deviation Reduction (SDR) of all the features with respect to the dependent variable. The root node is chosen as the feature that has the maximum SDR and the feature with the next highest SDR as the next node and so on. For the classification tree, as the dependent variable is **categorical**, we cannot calculate the SDR; instead we calculate **entropy** and the **information gain** for each feature with respect to the dependent variable. The root node is selected as the feature that has the **maximum information gain** with respect to the dependent variable.

A decision tree, as discussed earlier, is built top-down from a root node and involves partitioning the data into subsets that contain instances with similar values (homogenous). The algorithm uses entropy to calculate the homogeneity of a sample. If the sample is completely homogeneous, the entropy is zero and if the sample is equally divided, it has an entropy of one.

Let's understand in detail how the root node and the other nodes are selected for the construction of the classification tree.

Consider the following sample dataset. It is similar to the example we considered in the regression tree in `Chapter 4`, *Experimenting Predictive Analytics for IoT*. The difference being the dependent variable; here, it is **categorical,** that is, 'Employee Type' with two levels-Techie and Corporate:

| Sr. No. | Dress code | Gender | Employee type |
|---------|------------|--------|---------------|
| 1 | Formal | Male | Techie |
| 2 | Business Casuals | Female | Corporate |
| 3 | Casuals | Male | Techie |
| 4 | Formal | Female | Corporate |
| 5 | Business Casuals | Female | Techie |
| 6 | Casuals | Male | Corporate |
| ......... | | | |
| 100 | Casuals | Male | Techie |

To build a decision tree, we need to calculate two types of **entropy-**the entropy of the dependent variable and entropy of each independent variable with respect to the dependent variable. This can be done using frequency tables.

- Entropy using the frequency table of one attribute:

*Here, c is the number of different classes in the variable.*

Consider the distribution of Employee type in the overall dataset looks like the following table:

| Employee Type | | Probability |
|---------------|-----|-------------|
| Techie | 73 | 0.73 |
| Corporate | 27 | 0.27 |

Then, we can calculate the entropy of the dependent variable as follows:

Entropy (Employee type) = Entropy(27,73)

$= - (0.27) * \log2 (0.27) - (0.73) * \log2(0.73)$

$= -(- 0.51 ) - (- 0.33) = 0.84$

Similarly, to calculate the entropy of a feature variable with respect to the dependent variable, assume the following distribution of Employee Type across the 'Dress Code' variable:

| | Employee Type | | | |
|---|---|---|---|---|
| **Dress Code** | Techie | Corporate | Total | Probability |
| Formal | 10 | 14 | 24 | 0.24 |
| Business Casuals | 21 | 8 | 29 | 0.29 |
| Casuals | 42 | 5 | 47 | 0.47 |

We can then calculate the entropy of the feature variable as follows:

E(Employee type, Dress Code)

= P(Formal)*E(10,14) + P(Business Casuals)*E(21,8) + P(Casuals)*E(42,5)

= 0.24 * 0.98 + 0.29*0.85 + 0.47*0.48

= 0.71

With the two types of entropies, we can now calculate the information gain for each feature using the following formula:

**Information Gain (Y,X) = Entropy(Y) – Entropy(Y,X)**

Therefore, Information Gain (Employee Type, Dress Code)

=Entropy(Employee Type) – Entropy(Employee Type, Dress Code)

= 0.84 – 0.71 = 0.13

In a similar way, the information gain for all other features are calculated and the feature with the maximum information gain with respect to the dependent variable is chosen as the root node, the next highest feature as the next node, and so on. Information gain aids the tree in defining the best node to be chosen as the root node and the subsequent decision nodes.

The overall process for classification trees remains very similar to regression trees.

# How do we build random forests in R?

R has a package built exclusively for the random forest algorithm and is called 'randomforest'. It comes with the required functions to build the entire model with a few lines of code. Let's build a rudimentary random forest model to learn the know-how and then move on to build better and improved versions.

The following code builds a random forest model for the same training dataset that we used in the previous chapter for logistic regression experiments and showcases the summary of the model. Take a closer look at the highlighted section in the codes and results:

```
library(randomForest)
set.seed(600)
#Creating a 20% sample for test and 80% Train
test_index<-sample(1:nrow(data),floor(nrow(data)*0.2))
train<-data[-test_index,]
test<-data[test_index,]

#Building a random forest model
fit<-randomForest(Detergent_Quality~
            #The Production Quantity deviation feature
            Quantity_Deviation_new +

            #The Production Quantity deviation feature
            Stage1_PrevProduct_1 +

            #Raw Material Quality Parameters
            Stage1_RM1_QParameter2 +
            Stage1_RM1_QParameter1 +
            Stage1_RM2_QParameter2 +
            Stage1_RM2_QParameter1 +
            Stage3_RM1_QParameter1 +
            Stage3_RM1_QParameter2 +
            Stage3_RM2_QParameter1 +
            Stage3_RM3_QParameter2 +
            Stage3_RM3_QParameter1 +
```

```
               #Machine/Resources used in a Stage
               Stage3_ResourceName_new +
               Stage1_ProductChange_Flag,
               data=train,
               ntree=50,mtry=5,replace=TRUE,importance=TRUE
      )

> fit
Call:
 randomForest(formula = Detergent Quality ~ Quantity_Deviation_new +
Stage1_PrevProduct_1 + Stage1_RM1_QParameter2 + Stage1_RM1_QParameter1 +
Stage1_RM2_QParameter2 + Stage1_RM2_QParameter1 + Stage3_RM1_QParameter1 +
Stage3_RM1_QParameter2 + Stage3_RM2_QParameter1 + Stage3_RM3_QParameter2 +
Stage3_RM3_QParameter1 + Stage3_ResourceName_new +
Stage1_ProductChange_Flag,       data = train, ntree = 50, mtry = 5, replace
= TRUE, importance = TRUE)

               Type of random forest: classification

                    Number of trees: 50

No. of variables tried at each split: 5

          OOB estimate of  error rate: 16.25%

Confusion matrix:

      Bad Good class.error
Bad   107   68   0.3885714
Good   62  563   0.0992000
```

Let's try to understand what we have done here. Most of the codes and results seem pretty much the same. Let's look at the new things one by one.

We use the inbuilt randomForest function in the package by the same name to build the model. The calling style remains exactly the same. However, we see a few parameters that we didn't touch on earlier, that is, ntree=50, mtry=5, replace=TRUE, and importance=TRUE.

# What are these new parameters?

At a high level, random forest provides us with an option to choose the number of trees we would like to build in the ensemble model and also gives us an option to choose the number of features that should be randomly chosen for each tree. We chose five, that is, mtry =5. A good ballpark number for the mtry hyperparameter will be to consider the nearest number to the square root of the total number of features. In our exercise, we have around 14 features and the dependent variable, so ideally three or four would have been a better choice. We can choose the best value using a trial and error method, but the randomForest package internally provides us with a tool to play around and select the most optimum value for mtry. We'll explore this in a while. Similarly, the next set of hyperparameters that are new in the code are **replace=TRUE** and **importance=TRUE.** The replace option provides us with the choice of whether sampling should be done with or without replacement. As a thumb rule, it is always good to have the replacement set to TRUE while sampling. The model is bound to be more stable in most cases. (There are also cases where this might not be the best choice.) The **importance = TRUE** parameter provides the importance score (GINI index as well Mean Decrease in accuracy) for each feature used in the model. Using the variable importance, we can more easily identify which features are adding more value to the overall model. In case we have too many features, say quite a few of them are barely adding any value, we can use the variable importance plot (a function provided by the random forest package) to visualize the variable importance and therefore take a better choice in elimination of variables.

Apart from the parameters used in the preceding model iteration, there are a few more that we'll be using in further iterations such as bag fraction, class weight, and a few more. We'll explore these options as and when we use them. There are many more parameter options available that you can explore using the R help command (?randomforest).

Let's move on to interpret the summary results. The first part showcases the **calling style formula** used for the model. Next, we see a statement that mentions the **type of modeling** used in the iteration. We are building a classification model and hence the type of random forest is **classification**. Next, it calls out the **number of trees** built in the model. We chose 50 trees; we can actually choose a higher number as the dataset we are using is quite small in size and can be easily handled by a normal machine with decent RAM. Choosing an extremely high number of trees for the model won't add an equivalent incremental value to the accuracy, but still around 1,000-2,000 trees is a good number to have. We see the **number of variables** used to split the data into partitions in each tree as five. Finally, we see two important measures used in the model, that is, **OOB estimate** and the **confusion matrix** built from predictions made on the training dataset. The OOB estimate is nothing but the out-of-bag estimate. Each tree is trained on around $2/3^{rd}$ of the training set sampled randomly with replacement. The remaining $1/3^{rd}$ can be used for cross-validation. The OOB error estimates showcase the results from cross-validation done on all the trees internally. Lastly, we see the confusion matrix along with class error rates.

In random forest, there is actually no need to test the model on an unseen data as internally, the OOB error estimate provides a fair and unbiased metric to infer the model's prediction capability. Still, let's try to check the results on our remaining 20% data set aside for the testing.

The following code is a `prediction_rf_sumary` function similar to the `prediction_summary` function that we built in the previous chapter. The only difference here is that we directly take the prediction rather than predicting the probability and then classifying it as 'Good' or 'Bad'. The function finally outputs the metrics we have been using so far, that is, Overall Accuracy, **True Positive Rate (TPR)**, **True Negative Rate (TNR)**, and **False Positive Rates (FPR)**:

```
prediction_rf_summary<-function(fit,test)
{
    #Predicting results on the test data, using the fitted model
    predicted<-predict(fit,newdata=test,type="response")
    actuals<-test$Detergent_Quality
    confusion_matrix<-table(actuals,predicted)
    print("Confusion Matrix :-")
    print(confusion_matrix)
    print("")
    #Calcualting the different measures for Goodness of fit
    TP<-confusion_matrix[2,2]
    FP<-confusion_matrix[1,2]
    TN<-confusion_matrix[1,1]
    FN<-confusion_matrix[2,1]
    #Calcualting all the required
    print(paste("Overall_accuracy ->",(TP+TN)/sum(confusion_matrix)))
```

```
    print(paste("TPR -> ",TP/(TP+FN)))
    print(paste("TNR -> ",TN/(TN+FP)))
    print(paste("FP  -> ",FP/(TN+FP)))
}

#Viewing the results together
>prediction_rf_summary(fit,test)
```

[1] **"Confusion Matrix :-"**

```
         predicted
actuals Bad Good
    Bad   29    21
    Good  17   133
```

[1] **""**
[1] **"Overall_accuracy -> 0.81"**
[1] **"TPR ->  0.8866666666666667"**
[1] **"TNR ->  0.58"**
[1] **"FP ->  0.42"**

As we can see, the results in random forest are relatively better than the results from logistic regression. Compare the iteration in logistic regression, where we used the normal training sample and not the stratified balanced training sample. We had an overall accuracy of 0.72, TPR of 0.84, TNR of 0.38, and FPR of 0.62.

The first iteration in building a random forest model has given us an increased overall accuracy of 0.81, TPR of 0.88, TNR of 0.58, and reduced FPR of 0.42. The results seem far better, but have we still reached our goal? Not yet, but we are close and the results definitely look promising.

What do we need to do to further improve the overall accuracy, TPR, and TNR and reduce the FPR? Remember the point where we halted our experiments in logistic regression? We used a stratified balanced sample for the training and saw a phenomenal improvement in the TNR but a huge dip in the TPR. We understood that the model was previously not able to learn the patterns to predict the TNR effectively. We therefore used a stratified balanced training sample and noticed that the model was able to predict TNR much better but it came at the cost of reduced TPR. To improve TNR while not compromising on the TPR, we can leverage a machine learning technique that could help us in achieving this.

In random forest, we have a parameter option called class weight that is used to signify an added weight to the training samples where the distribution of a particular class is skewed. It helps in learning the class with a lower number of samples better without compromising the other class.

So let's build an improved version of the random forest model. Where do we start? What parameter settings would give us the best results? Let's discuss this one by one.

# Mtry

We discussed that the best value for mtry is the square root of the overall number of features in the model. In our case, we have around 14 features. So do we choose 3, 4, or 5? We can move further using either a trial and error method or an inbuilt tool in the same package where we can see the results for each value of mtry:

```
#Creating a vector with all the predictors
x<-c('Quantity_Deviation_new','Stage1_PrevProduct_1',
    'Stage1_RM1_QParameter2', 'Stage1_RM1_QParameter1',
    'Stage1_RM2_QParameter2', 'Stage1_RM2_QParameter1',
    'Stage3_RM1_QParameter1', 'Stage3_RM1_QParameter2',
    'Stage3_RM2_QParameter1', 'Stage3_RM3_QParameter2',
    'Stage3_RM3_QParameter1', 'Stage3_ResourceName_new',
    'Stage1_ProductChange_Flag')

#Tune the model
mtry <- tuneRF(train[x],train$Detergent_Quality, ntreeTry=200,
stepFactor=1.5,improve=0.01, trace=TRUE, plot=TRUE)

#Since the sampling is done randomly, different iterations might #render
different results

mtry = 3   OOB error = 14.25%
Searching left ...
mtry = 2      OOB error = 15.75%
-0.1052632 0.05
Searching right ...
mtry = 4      OOB error = 17%
-0.1929825 0.05
```

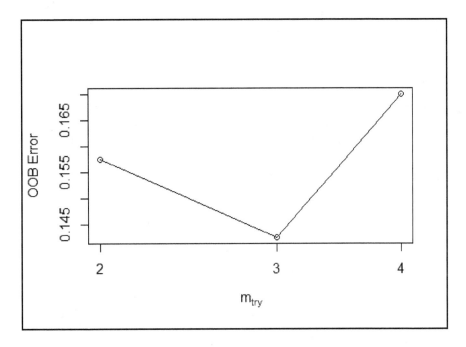

We can see that with mtry =3, we get the best results, that is, the lowest OOB error rate. So let's freeze the value of mtry at 3.

# Building a more tuned version of the random forest model

To improve our model further, we can have a few things fixed easily. The ntree parameter decides the number of trees in our forest. As our dataset size is relatively small and most computers have relatively high computing power, we'll set this to 5,000. Maybe such a high number won't add an appropriate value but still won't cause any harm.

Secondly, our dataset is an unbalanced sample, that is, we have Good and Bad samples in the ratio 80:20. As we saw previously, our model failed to have a good TPR with a balanced stratified sample. Therefore, we need to think about a better approach to train our models. As using a 50:50 ratio reduced the TPR to a great extent, why don't we change the training sample ratio to something like 60:40 or 70:30? Increasing the Bad samples by a small margin and decreasing the Good samples ratio by a small margin will definitely help us achieve a better performance than the highly unbalanced samples. We can achieve this by creating a modified training dataset.

Lastly, even though **replacement** works really well in most cases for random forest, it may not be the most recommended step when we have a highly unbalanced training sample. Sampling without replacement in unbalanced samples will be useful; otherwise, samples from the smaller classes will contain many more repetitions and the class will still be underrepresented.

Finally, **classwt** helps us set the prior probabilities for the training samples of the classes in each tree while sampling. Setting this value helps us stratify the training sample for each tree in a more strategic way.

Let's build a model with the newly tuned settings:

```
set.seed(600)
data$y<-ifelse(data$Detergent_Quality=="Good",1,0)
test_index<-sample(1:nrow(data),floor(nrow(data)*0.2))
train<-data[-test_index,]
test<-data[test_index,]

#Creating a modified training dataset with Good:Bad ratio as 66:33
new_train<-stratified(train,"Detergent_Quality",175)
subset<-train[sample(rownames(train[train$y==1,]),350),]
new_train<-rbind(new_train[new_train$y==0,1:ncol(train)],subset)

#Building a random forest model
fit<-randomForest(Detergent_Quality~
                #The Production Quantity deviation feature
                Quantity_Deviation_new +
                #The Production Quantity deviation feature
                Stage1_PrevProduct_1 +
                #Raw Material Quality Parameters
                Stage1_RM1_QParameter2 +
                Stage1_RM1_QParameter1 +
                Stage1_RM2_QParameter2 +
                Stage1_RM2_QParameter1 +
                Stage3_RM1_QParameter1 +
                Stage3_RM1_QParameter2 +
                Stage3_RM2_QParameter1 +
                Stage3_RM3_QParameter2 +
                Stage3_RM3_QParameter1 +
                #Machine/Resources used in a Stage
                Stage3_ResourceName_new +
                Stage1_ProductChange_Flag,
            data=new_train, classwt = c(0.4, 0.6),
            ntree=5000,mtry=3,replace=FALSE)

#.Training sample: Approximately 66:33 ratio for Good:Bad
```

```
> fit

Call:
 randomForest(formula = Detergent_Quality ~ Quantity_Deviation_new +
Stage1_PrevProduct_1 + Stage1_RM1_QParameter2 + Stage1_RM1_QParameter1 +
Stage1_RM2_QParameter2 + Stage1_RM2_QParameter1 + Stage3_RM1_QParameter1 +
Stage3_RM1_QParameter2 + Stage3_RM2_QParameter1 + Stage3_RM3_QParameter2 +
Stage3_RM3_QParameter1 + Stage3_ResourceName_new +
Stage1_ProductChange_Flag,        data = new_train, ntree = 5000, mtry = 3,
replace = FALSE,       classwt = c(0.4, 0.6))
                Type of random forest: classification
                     Number of trees: 5000
No. of variables tried at each split: 3

        OOB estimate of  error rate: 21.71%

Confusion matrix:
      Bad Good class.error
Bad   131   44   0.2514286
Good   70  280   0.2000000


> prediction_rf_summary(fit,test)

[1] "Confusion Matrix :-"

         predicted
actuals Bad Good
    Bad   42    8
    Good  29  121

[1] ""
[1] "Overall_accuracy -> 0.815"
[1] "TPR ->  0.806666666666667"
[1] "TNR ->  0.84"
[1] "FP ->  0.16"
```

We can clearly see that our results have fairly improved. We have above 80% accuracy for TPR and TNR as well as the overall accuracy. This is by far the best result that we have achieved in our predictive modeling and machine learning experiments.

Let's take a pause and contemplate whether the current results add value to the overall business and can we showcase the results to John?

By all means, Yes. We have certainly created valuable and actionable results for John's team to go ahead.

# How?

For simplicity, let's assume that the data we have is the universal set of data for detergent manufacturing orders. We have 1,000 orders where 225 cases had Bad quality detergent produce and the rest, Good quality. So, in a nutshell, the 225 Bad quality cases resulting to around 20% of the overall quantity of detergent manufactured had to be discarded resulting in operational losses. With our predictive solution in place, the team responsible for the manufacturing can achieve reduced operational losses by taking counter measures for the cases where Bad quality produce was identified before manufacturing.

Let's nail this in simple math.

We have 80% TPR, that is, from all the actual Good quality produce, we correctly predicted that 80% of them were going to yield Good quality after manufacturing.

We have 80% TNR, which shows that from all the actual Bad Quality Produce, we have correctly predicted 80% of them. Therefore, we have given actionable means to reduce 80% of the overall 20% bad quality produce-16%. This means that for the remaining 4% bad quality produce, our model predicted incorrectly as Good quality. These 4% cases are what we have missed in the overall picture.

Therefore, we can see a tangible value addition to John's team where they can take actionable measures to reduce the bad quality produce.

# Can we improve this further?

Even though we have achieved relatively good results, we still have a scope for improvement. Our solutions can be enhanced further if we can drop the FPR and FNR, that is, False Negative Rate.

# What can we do to achieve this?

There is a variety of measures associated with improving a model to a better extent. This includes more and more feature engineering, adding new data dimensions if possible, capturing more and more data, that is, increasing training sample size, tuning the model, and calibrating the hyperparameters to generalize better. Discussing these topics would require more advanced statistical and domain skills that will be difficult to elaborate in the scope of this book. Hence, we pause our results here momentarily.

As a next step, you will learn and build a few more powerful and popular machine learning and artificial intelligence modeling techniques.

# Ensemble modeling – XGBoost

XGBoost, that is, Extreme Gradient Boosting, is a very popular machine learning ensemble technique that has helped data scientists across the globe to achieve great results with phenomenal accuracy. XGBoost is built on the principles of ensemble modeling and is an improved version of the Gradient Boosted Machine algorithm. In general, the XgBoost algorithm creates multiple classifiers that are weak learners, which means a model that gives a bit better accuracy than just a random guess. The learner in the ensemble model can be a linear or tree model that is built iteratively with random sampling along with an added weight from the learnings of the previously built model. At each step, a tree is built and the cases where the tree has failed to classify an outcome correctly is assigned a corresponding weight. The next iteration of model building learns from the mistakes of the previous model. At each step, the weight of an incorrect prediction is calculated using an algorithm, say mean squared error for regression or a logistic loss for classification. The next iteration makes an attempt to reduce the loss and so on. Eventually, the last iteration would probably have the best results for the prediction problem.

# What is different in XgBoost?

Boosting in ensembles has always been a very hot and favorite topic for data scientists, but is also usually criticized for overfitting. Gradient Boosted Machines (GBM) were among the popular choices for classification and regression problems as they provide the analyst an extensively customizable framework to build predictive models. XgBoost is an enhanced version of GBM where it builds more stable models by reducing the chances of overfitting to a great extent. It does so by leveraging an inbuilt penalty logic for complexity. It is a simple mechanism to heavily penalize complexity at every iteration and therefore reduce complexity about as much as reducing the bias. This heavily reduces the chances for the model to overfit. Basically, regularization is a feature that was newly added to XgBoost when compared to the legacy GBM to render favorable results. Moreover, the speed of converging in Xgboost has been greatly improved and therefore allows one to iterate and tune faster.

Let's quickly build an xgboost model for the same problem that we tried in random forest. We'll use the 'xgboost' package that will have the necessary functions to build the model.

The xgboost package in R provides us with a function with the same name to train the model. This function, however, accepts only numeric values. Therefore, the categorical variables in our dataset such as Quantity Deviation, Product Change flag, and others all have to be converted to a numeric variable. We can do this using one-hot coding, that is, a binary flag for the respective class.

Also, as we previously saw our results being favored for a weighted balanced sample for the training, we'll continue to use the same-a training sample with 66.66% 'Good' and the rest as 'Bad':

```
#Modelling for XgBoost

#Importing the required libraries
library(xgboost)
library(Matrix)
set.seed(600)

#Converting the target variable to a binary 1/0 flag
        # that is, 1 = Good and 0 = Bad
data$y<-ifelse(data$Detergent_Quality=="Good",1,0)

#Collecting all numeric features together
features<-c(
'Stage1_RM1_QParameter2', 'Stage1_RM1_QParameter1',
'Stage1_RM2_QParameter2',
'Stage1_RM2_QParameter1', 'Stage3_RM1_QParameter1',
'Stage3_RM1_QParameter2',
'Stage3_RM2_QParameter1', 'Stage3_RM3_QParameter2',
'Stage3_RM3_QParameter1')

#Collecting all categorical features together
categorical<-c('Quantity_Deviation_new','Stage1_PrevProduct_1',
               'Stage1_ProductChange_Flag','Stage3_ResourceName_new')

#Creating a 20% sample for test and 80% Train
test_index<-sample(1:nrow(data),floor(nrow(data)*0.2))
train<-data[-test_index,]
test<-data[test_index,]

#Stratifying the training sample to get 50:50 training samples
new_train<-stratified(train,'Detergent_Quality',175)

#Creating a 66:33 ration training sample for Good:Bad
subset<-train[sample(rownames(train[train$y==1,]),350),]
new_train<-rbind(new_train[new_train$y==0,1:ncol(train)],subset)

#Converting the training and test datasets into sparse datasets
    #This takes care of creating binary variables for each categorical
variable
train.sparse<-sparse.model.matrix(y~.-1,
data=new_train[,c(features,'y',categorical)])
test.sparse<-sparse.model.matrix(y~.-1,
data=test[,c(features,'y',categorical)])
#Training an XGBoost model with the resampled training data
```

```
xgb <- xgboost(data = train.sparse,
               label = new_train$y,
               objective="binary:logistic",
               eta = 0.1,
               max_depth = 12,
               nround=100,
               subsample = 0.8,
               colsample_bytree = 0.6,
               random.seed = set.seed(100),
               nfold=20,
               eval_metric = "error",
               nthread = 3,booster="gbtree",
               early.stop.round = 10,
               verbose = TRUE
)
```

The preceding code pretty much follows the same process as earlier. Additionally, it converts the training and testing datasets to a sparse matrix so as to work with the xgboost implementation in R. Let's have a closer look at the model building code. We see quite a few new hyperparameters in the model building function call, such as objective, eta, max_depth, eval_metric, and so on. Let's discuss them step by step.

XGboost's implementation in R is a very customizable framework. It allows the data scientist to choose and customize a couple of parameters for improved performance. Most of these parameters have default values if the data scientist doesn't wish to tune.

The first few options are exactly as they seem to be; **data** indicates the option for the training set and **label** indicates the target/dependent variable. The **Objective** function helps us define the type of model we are building; here, we attempt to build a classification model and therefore we set objective as *"binary:logistic"*. For regression, we would have set it to *"reg:linear"*. The **eta** parameter helps us control the learning rate, that is, it scales the contribution of each tree by a factor of $0 < eta < 1$ when it is added to the current approximation. This is used to prevent overfitting by making the boosting process more conservative. A lower value for eta implies a larger value for **nrounds**, that is,the number of iterations. Similarly, a low eta value means that the model is more robust to overfitting but slower to compute. The default value is set to 0.3; in our experiment, we have set it to 0.1 and taken a considerably higher value for the number of iterations. **Max_depth** defines the maximum depth for the tree; the default value is set to 6 and we have chosen a slightly higher value of 12.

**Subsample** defines the ratio of the training instance, that is, the fraction of observations to be randomly sampled for each tree. Setting it to 0.5 means that xgboost will randomly collect half of the data instances to grow trees that eventually aid in preventing overfitting. **Colsample_bytree** decides the maximum number of features to be randomly selected for each tree. The default value is 1; we have set it to a slightly lower value of 0.6 to add randomness to each tree. The **eval_metric** parameter defines the metric to be used for the validation data. The default option set for classification is 'error' and 'rmse' for regression. The boosting process is improved based on the results of the evaluation metric. The **booster** parameter defines the type of the model for each iteration. We have two options to choose for now: *gbtree* for a tree or *gblinear* for linear models. For most scenarios, we can blindly use gbtree as a better option to build the ensemble model.

The **early.stop.round** helps xgboost decide when to stop iterating in the case of bad results for a defined number of rounds. In some cases, boosting iterations deliver poor results compared to the previous iteration. In such scenarios, it is better to kill the further iterations and choose the recent best iterations for the model. Early.stop.iteration defines the number of iterations to observe before stopping in the case of poorer results. After each iteration, the xgboost algorithm prints the stats on the screen for us to interpret the model improvements. We can disable this by setting **Verbose** = 0. Similarly, we also have an option to set the number of parallel threads to be selected for the xgboost algorithm to process. Ignoring this parameter will result in xgboost taking an automatically selected optimum value for parallel processing.

Now that we have an understanding of how to build the algorithm, let's use the model to predict the outcomes in our test dataset:

```
#Creating a function to predict the outcome
#And also calculate the TPR, TNR, FPR and overall accuracy
print_xgb_summary<- function(xgb,test.sparse,test)
    {
        y_pred <- predict(xgb, newdata=test.sparse)
        y_pred<-ifelse(y_pred>0.5,"Good","Bad")
        print(a<-table(test$Detergent_Quality,y_pred))
        print(paste("Overall accuracy ->",(sum(a[1,1],a[2,2])/sum(a))))
        print(paste("TPR ->",(a[2,2]/sum(a[2,1],a[2,2]))))
        print(paste("TNR ->",(a[1,1]/sum(a[1,1],a[1,2]))))
        print(paste("FPR ->",(a[1,2]/sum(a[1,1],a[1,2]))))
    }

#Showcasing the results
print_xgb_summary(xgb,test.sparse,test)

        y_pred
        Bad Good
    Bad    45    5
```

```
   Good  30  120
```

```
[1] "Overall accuracy -> 0.825"
[1] "TPR -> 0.8"
[1] "TNR -> 0.9"
[1] "FPR -> 0.1"
```

Have the results improved when compared to the random forest results?

Hmm, looks like it.

If we take a closer look at all the metrics-overall accuracy, TPR, FPR, and TNR-we can see that the TNR has improved quite a bit. The solution can still be concluded as a fairly improved result or at par with the previous results.

Tuning our results further would need exploring the variables better and playing around with the hyperparameters for more regularization. Xgboost provides us with a plethora of options to tune and regularize; discussing all of them is beyond the scope of the book. We'll try another attempt by changing a few parameters. We'll increase the scope of early.stop.iteration and eta, and we'll try playing around with maximum depth, subsampling, and column sample parameters:

```
#Training an XGBoost model with the resampled training data
xgb <- xgboost(data = train.sparse,
               label = new_train$y,
               objective="binary:logistic",
               eta = 0.1,
               max_depth = 15,
               nround=200,
               subsample = 0.6,
               colsample_bytree = 0.8,
               random.seed = set.seed(100),
               nfold=20,
               eval_metric = "error",
               nthread = 3,booster="gbtree",
               early.stop.round =20,
               verbose = TRUE
)
print_xgb_summary(xgb,test.sparse,test)
      y_pred
        Bad Good
  Bad    42    8
  Good   30  120
[1] "Overall accuracy -> 0.81"
[1] "TPR -> 0.8"
[1] "TNR -> 0.84"
[1] "FPR -> 0.16"
```

We don't see any further improvement; instead, we see a slight dip in the overall accuracy. We can keep exploring other tuning parameters available in the xgboost implementation in R and execute a series of experiments on a trial and error basis to see where we can improve our results. Moreover, before affirmatively concluding that the results we received in xgboost by far are good, we need to do a simple check to validate whether this holds true in most cases.

## Are we really getting good results?

Boosting algorithms are prone to overfitting; xgboost has, however, improved this immensely compared to its predecessors but still there are chances for overfitting, especially when the data is imbalanced.

To validate this, we'll quickly check the results using the prediction on the training dataset:

```
#Using the previously define function to predict on the training dataset
print_xgb_summary(xgb,train.sparse,new_train)
```

```
           y_pred
          Bad Good
  Bad     173    2
  Good      0  350

[1] "Overall accuracy -> 0.996190476190476"
[1] "TPR -> 1"
[1] "TNR -> 0.988571428571429"
[1] "FPR -> 0.0114285714285714"
```

We can clearly see that the results are highly overfitting. Even though we got favorable results in the test dataset, but there seems to be a huge difference between the results of the training and testing dataset. With this overfitting model, we can't really leverage the results we achieved in the test dataset as it is highly prone to give completely different results if we use another small test sample.

Similarly, boosting algorithms may also be highly unstable, which means getting different results while iteratively building a model using the same data and parameters.

Therefore, taking this model ahead will result in a very unstable prediction power as we might see completely different results with another testing sample. Therefore, we conclude the results from random forest as the best results by far and move ahead.

# What next?

The first step to get the best results in predictive analytics is delving deeper into the data like we did in `Chapter 3`, *The What and Why – Using Exploratory Decision Science for IoT*-in fact even more. Exploring really deep into the data coupled with strong business domain knowledge will aid a data scientist in creating new features that will draft the story. Taking these learnings to the modeling technique and improving the results by regularizing and calibrating the model using a variety of methods will help us get the best.

Before we conclude our results and convey it to John, we will give one last attempt with an advanced and very promising area in the field of machine learning and artificial intelligence-**Neural Networks and Deep Learning**. Inspired from the model of the human brain, neural networks and deep learning have proven the capability to render robust solutions by studying complicated relationships in the data at ease. Limiting the scope of our book, we'll study the nuances of neural networks and deep learning and also understand its different types and applications in today's world. Once we have a sound understanding of the topic, we'll build a few simple deep learning models on our existing use case and see if there are any improvements.

## A cautionary note

Neural networks and deep learning are extremely vast and complicated topics. Exploring and experimenting such a vast topic in depth will be beyond the scope of this book. The following section will be a preliminary and early introduction to the topic. The objective of introducing the topic and experimenting our use case is solely to give you a fair idea on how to get started. You are encouraged to further explore and learn these topics.

# Neural Networks and Deep Learning

Neural networks and deep learning have been a promising area in machine learning and artificial intelligence over the last two decades. The recent growth has been phenomenal as we can see the industry using them to solve a variety of problems that were previously difficult. We have been knowingly or unknowingly using applications in our daily life that have been built using these sophisticated technologies. The **Google Now, Apple's Siri,** or **Microsoft Cortana** voice-enabled digital assistant applications have all been developed using powerful deep learning techniques. Similarly, the face detection feature that you would have noticed while uploading your photos to Facebook, real-time language translation tools, and so on have been developed using the latest and most powerful neural networks and deep learning techniques.

# So what is so cool about neural networks and deep learning?

Essentially, we have always used a computer to build software and applications to ease our lifestyle. The predictive algorithms that we build have taken a step ahead by solving problems that were relatively complicated for a human being to solve. However, there is a class of problems that is easily solved by humans but gets extremely difficult for a computer to solve. These problems were initially focused mainly on the vision- and speech-related use cases. When we do a Google search on "cars in yellow color", it shows us results with many images of a car in yellow color. For a human being to distinguish and classify an image with this criteria, that is, "car in yellow color", is a very easy task, but it used to be an extremely challenging task for aiding the ability for a computer to recognize and distinguish.

It all starts with how a human brain processes information received in the form of visuals and speech/audio. A human brain is composed of an extremely dense network of biological neurons that process and pass information to other connected neurons in a fraction of a second. Many such interconnected neurons together help in solving a set of problems.

The initial attempts to aid the computer in recognizing image/video visuals or speech/audio clips have failed miserably. The process of training a computer to learn these patterns was a mammoth and extremely complicated task. Neural networks and deep learning was an attempt to solve such problems by mimicking a highly simplified version of the human brain. In recent years, the advancement in these areas has been colossal and we have tangibly seen how it impacts our day-to-day life. Let's understand these complicated terms in a more simplified way.

# What is a neural network?

A neural network, in the simplest form, can be defined as "a computing system made up of a number of simple, highly interconnected processing elements, which process information by their dynamic state response to external inputs". In a nutshell, neural networks create a network of highly interconnected neurons-simple processing units-by mimicking a highly simplified version of the human brain to solve problems. These neurons are usually arranged into a number of layers. A typical feedforward neural network will have at a minimum an input layer, hidden layer, and output layer. The input layer nodes correspond to the number of features or attributes you wish to feed into the neural network. These are similar to the features/dimensions we would use in the linear and logistic regression models. The number of output nodes correspond to the number of items you wish to predict or classify. The hidden layer nodes are generally used to perform nonlinear transformations on the original input attributes.

Neural networks were initially built to solve problems in the area of speech and visuals, but has now been leveraged in almost every other field for phenomenal problem solving capabilities.

The following image shows a simple neural network with a single hidden layer:

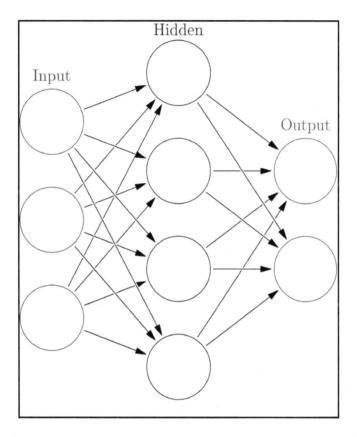

It's a simple neural network with three inputs, two outputs, and one hidden layer (multiple hidden layers are also possible) with four neurons. Each connection in the preceding image has a weight associated with it. Each neuron receives an input from the preceding node, processes some information based on a function, and passes the information to the next node. The final output nodes will have the result. The learning process for the neural network is done using a simple algorithm like backpropagation, where it tries to reduce the error by changing the weights associated with each connection between the neurons.

To simplify the overall process, compare the preceding image with the example we used earlier to learn decision trees, that is, predicting whether an employee is a Techie or Corporate. The three input nodes can be features such as dress code, age, and gender and the final output will have one node for Techie and one node for Corporate. Based on the value in the final node, we can take a call for yes or no.

# So what is deep learning?

In a nutshell, deep learning can be defined as a neural network with many more hidden layers (it is definitely a lot more than this; we'll discuss this in a while). As you can see, in the previous example, we have a neural network with a single hidden layer. Most neural networks have 2-3 hidden layers at the most. Deep neural networks, however, are much deeper than neural networks in the real sense. They can be as deep as 25-30 layers to solve a complex voice recognition problem.

Deep learning is an advancement in the field of neural networks. A quick question would arise to many of us: what is the actual need to classify a neural network with many hidden layers as deep learning; aren't they pretty much the same?

The answer would be a 'yes' as well as 'no'. Let me explain. The initial attempts to build a neural network had the sole vision of solving complex problems that were not achievable using the existing techniques. The highly simplified model of the human brain built using programming helped the model learn complicated features and patterns that helped in early success. A simple thought that triggered was that having more numbers of hidden layers will help the model learn more complicated features and patterns and therefore solve more complex problems. This was, however, not true. Attempts to train and build neural networks with multiple layers for almost two decades have rarely been successful. There was absolutely no benefit leveraged from the addition of more than one hidden layer, mainly because of the "vanishing gradient" effect.

The discovery of a different approach in training the lower layers in a neural network that then passes on the processed information to the upper layers in a problem-agnostic manner helped leverage the power of multiple layers in solving more complex problems. This advancement helped neural networks achieve a different level of success in solving problems with huge complexities. This is how deep learning was born, taking the name from the deep layers built in the neural network to learn complex functions.

The following diagram shows a deep neural network with three hidden layers along with one input and output layer:

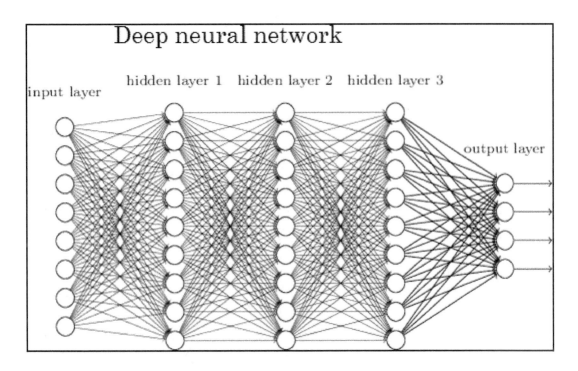

## So what problems can neural networks and deep learning solve?

Neural networks and deep learning together have solved revolutionary problems. The benefits have been clearly seen in our day-to-day activities. All of us have benefitted from the problems solved by deep learning in some way or the other. Here are a few broad examples of the areas where neural network and deep learning technologies have solved problems:

- Regression: Our plain old vanilla problems have been taken a notch further by leveraging deep learning techniques to solve the problems
- Classification: The classification problems for binary and multiclass classification have seen phenomenal improvements by leveraging the deep learning techniques

- Pattern recognition:
    - Finding patterns in text, videos, and images
    - Speech detection, that is, conversion of speech to text and text to speech
    - Language translation for speech and text
    - Video analytics for sports and forensics

Some major milestones can been seen recently in the advancement of the software applications that we use on a daily basis.

Google Translate with video helps you use your phone to view a signboard or other boards in a different language to convert it to another language in real time. Accuracy of speech-to-text conversion has seen phenomenal improvement. Image analysis and pattern detection have made tools like Google Photos very intelligent. Sequenced photographs are automatically detected to create short animated movies. Searching your image gallery has now options to search by image, background, or person.

Enhancements in sports videos such as real-time path tracing of the ball in cricket and augmentation of extra information in the video aids the audience to consume information at ease. The autonomous cars and drones, auto-pilot feature in planes, self-guided missiles, and so on have been enhancing our life in one way or the other.

Suggestions while shopping on an e-commerce website, autocompletion features while typing text in your phone, the spellcheck and grammar check tools in different software, and so on all leverage deep learning techniques.

A variety of features that you might have missed out like your smart AC that reduces power consumption, the brightness of your smartphone's screen being auto-adjusted, and the auto-enhancements to your selfies and photos all have a touch of deep learning in it.

We will, however, use deep learning techniques to continue the problem solving exercise on the same page where we left Xgboost. We'll try to see whether we get any enhanced results for our use case using neural networks and deep learning.

# So how does a neural network work?

We'll start understanding the different components in a neural network in brief. A simple neural network can fundamentally be broken into four main areas:

- Neurons
- Edges (connections)
- Activation function
- Learning

Let's discuss them one by one.

# Neurons

The following image shows you the representation of a biological neuron in the brain. Looking at the most important parts, we have axons, dendrites, and neurons:

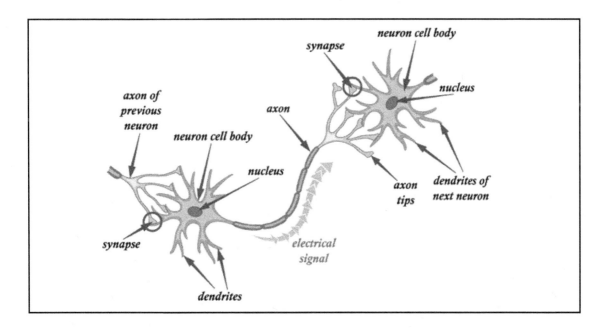

Biological neurons pass signals or messages to each other via electrical signals or impulses. Adjacent neurons receive these signals through their dendrites. Information flows from the dendrites to the main cell body-the axon-to the axon terminals. In simple words, biological neurons are computation machines passing messages between each other about various biological functions. The preceding image represents two neurons connected to each other.

The crux of a neural network is a mathematical node, unit, or **neuron,** which is a simple processing element. The information received in the input layer neurons is processed using a mathematical function and then passed to the neurons in the hidden layer. This information is again processed by the hidden layer neurons and passed to the output layer neurons. An important point to note is that the information or message is processed via an activation function. The activation function mimics brain neurons where it may or may not send a signal based on the strength of the input signal. The result from the activation function is then weighted and sent across to each connection in the next layer.

The whole process can be visualized in the following diagram:

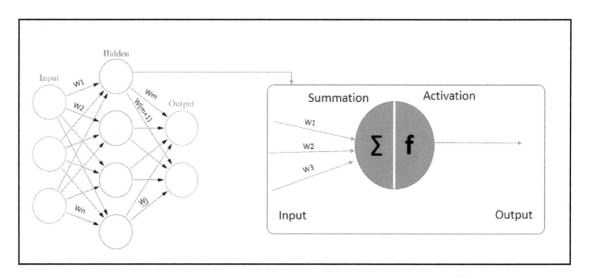

The image on the right-hand side represents one of the neurons from the neural network's hidden layer. It receives three input connections and each connection has a weight associated with it. The values from the input nodes are multiplied with the weight and a summation of all the weights and inputs is then passed to the activation function.

The summation function can be represented as follows:

$$f(u) = \sum_{i=1}^{n} w_{ij}x_{ij} + b_{ij}$$

Where:

- n is the total number of incoming neurons
- $W_{ij}$ is the weight of the connection from ith neuron to the current neuron, that is, j
- $X_{ij}$ is the output from the input neuron (ith neuron)
- $B_{ij}$ is the bias

Bias is similar to the concept of intercept that you learned earlier in a linear and logistic regression model. It allows the neural network model to shift the activation function "upward" or "downward". This helps the neural network be more flexible and therefore deliver more robust and stable results.

# Edges

Edges represent the connection between two neurons in two adjacent layers. It could be between an input layer and hidden layer, between two hidden layers, or between a hidden layer and output layer. Each edge carries a weight that is equivalent to the relevance of the input neuron in deciding the feature:

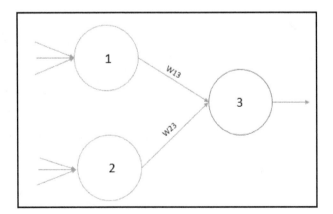

# Activation function

The activation function helps the neurons in the hidden layer introduce non-linearity into the network. The activation function is applied to the result of the summation function and the output passed to the next neuron or neurons in the next layer. It stimulates the firing or non-firing nature of the biological neuron. The biological neuron basically passes an electrical signal to the next neuron based on the input signals it has received. To get a similar functioning in the neurons in a neural network, we can design it to limit the output of the neuron, usually to values between 0 to 1 or -1 to +1. In most cases, the same activation function is used for every neuron in a network. Almost any nonlinear function does the job; although for the backpropagation algorithm, it must be differentiable and it helps if the function is bounded.

Among many choices, the sigmoid function is the most widely-used activation function. It is an S-shaped differentiable activation function. It is popular mainly due to the computational efficiency it delivers as it is easily differentiated.

Apart from the sigmoid function, a few other popular activation functions used are the linear function, hyperbolic tangent function, softmax function, Rectified Linear unit (ReLU), and others.

# Learning

Unlike the algorithms that we explored previously, neural networks have a slightly different learning process. The learning process is iterative in nature, and with each iteration, it tries to improve the weight of the edges so as to reduce the error and get closer to the result. The process continues until the results fall below a prespecified threshold.

One of the most popular learning algorithms used for neural networks is the backpropagation algorithm. (There are many more.) It was developed during the early days and is still used widely. It uses **gradient descent** as the core learning mechanism. The algorithm starts by assigning random weights to each edge in the network. It then calculates the edge weights by making small changes and gradually making adjustments determined by the error between the result produced by the network and the desired outcome.

The algorithm applies error propagation from outputs to inputs and gradually fine-tunes the network weights to minimize the sum of error using the gradient descent technique.

The algorithm for backpropagation learning can described as follows:

- **Initialize the weights for edges**: Each edge is randomly assigned a weight to get started. This can also be defined by the user.
- **Feedforward**: The message is processed and passed forward through the network from the input to hidden and output layer via node activation functions and weights.
- **Calculate error**: The result from the network is compared to the actual known output. If the error is lower than a predefined threshold, the neural network is trained and the algorithm terminated; otherwise, it is propagated.
- **Propagate**: The weights of the edges are modified based on the error calculated at the output layer. The algorithm propagates the error backward through the network (therefore the name backpropagation) and computes the gradient of the change in error with respect to changes in the weight values.
- **Adjust**: The weights of the edges are adjusted using the gradients of change with the sole objective of reducing the error. The weights and biases of each neuron are adjusted by a factor based on the derivative of the activation function.

This is how the neural network learns while it is trained. Each cycle through this learning process is called an epoch.

## So what are the different types of neural networks?

Based on the architecture of the neural network, there is a variety of neural networks established by scientists over the globe. The most popular ones that we have are as follows:

- Feedforward neural network: A feedforward neural network is an artificial neural network where connections between the units do not form a cycle. It was the first and simplest type of artificial neural network devised. The information moves in only one direction, forward, from the input nodes through the hidden nodes (if any) and to the output nodes; for example, Perceptrons and MLP.

- Recurrent neural network: A Recurrent Neural Network (RNN) contains at least one feedback connection so that the activations can flow round in a loop. This enables the networks to do temporal processing and learn sequences, for example, performing sequence recognition/reproduction or temporal association/prediction. Examples of RNN are Elman Networks, Jordan Networks, and others:

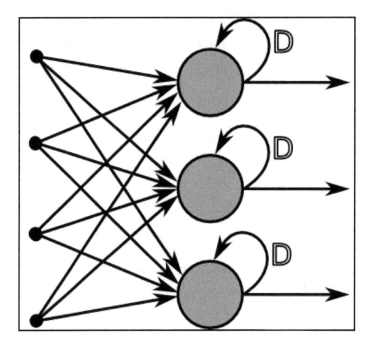

- Convolutional neural network: In convolutional neural networks (CNN), every layer acts as a detection layer for the presence of specific features or patterns present in the original data. The first layers in a CNN detect features that can be recognized and interpreted relatively easy. The later layers detect smaller features that are more abstract and usually present in many of the larger features detected by the earlier layers. The last layer of the CNN is able to make classification by combining all the specific features detected by the previous layers in the input data.

# How do we go about modeling using a neural network or deep learning technique?

The R programming language has numerous packages where we can get started to build deep learning models. The most popular ones are neuralnet, AMORE, H20, RSNNS, and a few more. For our use case, we'll use a very popular implementation of a feedforward neural network called Multilayer Perceptron (MLP) available in the **RSNNS** package.

MLP is an advanced and improved implementation of a perceptron, that is, an algorithm that is the simplest form of feedforward neural networks. A perceptron has only one hidden layer of neurons whereas MLP, as the name suggests, has multiple hidden layers. MLP has a lot of advantages over perceptrons; it can handle data better and model complex relations more easily as it can distinguish data that is not linearly separable. Moreover, a two-layer backpropagation network with sufficient hidden nodes has been proven to be a universal approximator.

Occasionally, the multilayer perceptron fails to settle into the global minimum and instead finds itself in one of the local minima. This is due to the gradient descent strategy followed. Additionally, due to this, sometimes we get very unstable models. Unstable models can be defined as a scenario where each iteration of the model with exactly the same parameter settings on the same data gives very different results.

We'll start building the MLP deep learning models and try to see whether they render better results than our previous solutions.

An MLP handles only numeric data. Therefore, we will be creating binary flags separately and also normalizing the numeric data points before training the neural network:

```
library(RSNNS)

#creating a binary flag for the categorical variables
data$Quantity_Deviation_new_High<-
ifelse(data$Quantity_Deviation_new=="High",1,0)
data$Quantity_Deviation_new_Medium<-
ifelse(data$Quantity_Deviation_new=="Medium",1,0)
data$Quantity_Deviation_new_Low<-
ifelse(data$Quantity_Deviation_new=="Low",1,0)

data$Stage1_PrevProduct_1_Product_545<-ifelse(data$Stage1_PrevProduct_1 ==
"Product_545",1,0)
data$Stage1_PrevProduct_1_Others<-ifelse(data$Stage1_PrevProduct_1 ==
"Others",1,0)

data$Stage3_ResourceName_new_Resource_108<-
ifelse(data$Stage3_ResourceName_new=="Resource_108",1,0)
```

```
data$Stage3_ResourceName_new_Resource_109<-
ifelse(data$Stage3_ResourceName_new=="Resource_109",1,0)
data$Stage3_ResourceName_new_Others<-
ifelse(data$Stage3_ResourceName_new=="Others",1,0)

data$Stage1_ProductChange_Flag_Yes<-
ifelse(data$Stage1_ProductChange_Flag=="Yes",1,0)

#Creating the test and train sample
set.seed(600)
#Creating a 20% sample for test and 80% Train
test_index<-sample(1:nrow(data),floor(nrow(data)*0.2))
train<-data[-test_index,]
test<-data[test_index,]


#Collecting the newly created variables together
binary_categorical<-
c("Quantity_Deviation_new_High","Quantity_Deviation_new_Medium",
"Quantity_Deviation_new_Low","Stage1_PrevProduct_1_Product_545",
"Stage1_PrevProduct_1_Others","Stage3_ResourceName_new_Resource_108",
"Stage3_ResourceName_new_Resource_109","Stage3_ResourceName_new_Others",
                   "Stage1_ProductChange_Flag_Yes")

#Collecting all the numeric features together
features<-c(
'Stage1_RM1_QParameter2', 'Stage1_RM1_QParameter1',
'Stage1_RM2_QParameter2',
'Stage1_RM2_QParameter1', 'Stage3_RM1_QParameter1',
'Stage3_RM1_QParameter2',
'Stage3_RM2_QParameter1', 'Stage3_RM3_QParameter2',
'Stage3_RM3_QParameter1')

#Taking a 66:33 training sample for Good:Bad
new_train<-stratified(train,"Detergent_Quality",175)
subset<-train[sample(rownames(train[train$y==1,]),350),]
new_train<-rbind(new_train[new_train$y==0,1:ncol(train)],subset)

#Normalizing all the numeric columns in the data and then combining with
the cateogrical data
train.numeric<-normalizeData(new_train[,features])
train.numeric<-cbind(train.numeric,new_train[,binary_categorical])

#Normalizing all the numeric columns in the data and then combining with
the cateogrical data
test.numeric<-normalizeData(test[,features])
test.numeric<-cbind(test.numeric,test[,binary_categorical])
```

```
Y<-new_train$y
X=train.numeric


fit<-mlp(x=train.numeric, y=Y, size = c(5,3),
        maxit = 100,
        initFunc = "Randomize_Weights",
     initFuncParams = c(-0.3, 0.3),
        learnFunc = "Std_Backpropagation",
        learnFuncParams = c(0.1, 0),
        updateFunc = "Topological_Order",
        updateFuncParams = c(0),
        hiddenActFunc = "Act_Logistic",
        shufflePatterns = TRUE,
        linOut = FALSE)
```

The codes used are pretty much the same; we have added a few extra snippets to manually create the binary flags for the four categorical variables in our selection as MLP handles only numeric data. Also, we have normalized the continuous variables in the dataset using an inbuilt function available in the RSNNS package.

Finally, we take a rebalanced 66:33 ratio training sample for the Good:Bad like our previous experiments. The function call for the mlp neural network is highlighted in the preceding code. We'll quickly touch base on the newly seen parameters here. The **size** parameter defines the number of neurons in each hidden layer. For the current iteration, we have defined two hidden layers with five and three neurons in the respective layers. The **maxit** parameter defines the upper limit for the maximum iterations that the neural network should execute to find the best estimates for the weights of the edges. The **initFunc** parameter defines the initialization function to initialize the weights of the edges in the network. In most cases, it is best to go ahead with random weights. Assigning the function as "Randomize_Weights" tells the **mlp** function to take care of the process.

The **learnFunc** parameter defines the learning algorithm for the network. We can choose "Std_Backpropagation", that is, the learning algorithm you learned a while back. It is the most popular and widely-used learning function. There are a few other options also available within the package, which you can give a try. We need to define the activation function for the neurons in the hidden layer. We have a few other options such as SCG (Scaled Conjugate Gradient), Rprop, Quickprop, and others. Each learning technique comes with its own advantages and disadvantages that can be leveraged based on the variations in the data. Lastly, the **linout** option is set to false as we are modeling for a classification case and not a linear regression use case.

We have selected the number of neurons and layers pretty randomly. A general thumb rule can be defined as the lower the number of neurons in each layer, the lower are the chances of overfitting. We can use a trial and error method to see and validate what number of layers and neurons will be best suited for the neural network. As mentioned earlier, a network with two layers have been universally showing great results. Therefore, we also choose two hidden layers for the network.

Let's now try to see how good our model predicts on the test data. We'll construct a function similar to the previous model that will predict and calculate our metrics of interest, that is, TPR, TNR, FPR, and overall accuracy:

```
print_mlp_summary<-function(fit,test.numeric, test)
{
    yhat<-predict(fit,test.numeric)
    yhat<-ifelse(yhat>0.5,1,0)
    confusion_matrix<- table(test$y,yhat)
    print("Confusion Matrix :-")
    print(confusion_matrix)
    TP<-confusion_matrix[2,2]
    FP<-confusion_matrix[1,2]
    TN<-confusion_matrix[1,1]
    FN<-confusion_matrix[2,1]
    print(paste("Overall_accuracy ->",(TP+TN)/sum(confusion_matrix)))
    print(paste("TPR -> ",TP/(TP+FN)))
    print(paste("TNR -> ",TN/(TN+FP)))
    print(paste("FP -> ",FP/(TN+FP)))

}

print_mlp_summary(fit,test.numeric,test)

    yhat
       0   1
  0   40  10
  1   42 108

[1] "Overall_accuracy -> 0.74"
[1] "TPR ->  0.72"
[1] "TNR ->  0.8"
[1] "FP ->  0.2"
```

We don't really see great results. The results are relatively poor when we compare it with our previous iteration. Our overall accuracy, TPR, and TNR all have dipped by a small fraction in comparison with our previous results. Before we go ahead and finalize our results, we still need to finalize whether the model is stable and whether it overfits.

We'll need to test the prediction results with our training data to check whether there is a huge difference in the result:

```
> print_mlp_summary(fit,train.numeric,new_train)

[1] "Overall_accuracy -> 0.811428571428571"
[1] "TPR ->   0.768571428571429"
[1] "TNR ->   0.897142857142857"
[1] "FP ->   0.102857142857143"
```

We can observe that the results are slightly overfitting, but still better than what we previously saw in Xgboost. Probably, the results are also unstable. We can check this by iterating the model execution a couple of times using the same parameter setting and data. If the results vary too much, we can conclude that the model is also unstable.

The following result is the output of another iteration of the model building exercise with the same training dataset and hyperparameters:

```
[1] "Confusion Matrix :-"

   yhat
       0   1
  0   43   7
  1   43 107

[1] "Overall_accuracy -> 0.75"
[1] "TPR ->   0.713333333333333"
[1] "TNR ->   0.86"
[1] "FP ->   0.14"
```

The results are fairly similar; therefore, we can say that the model is relatively stable, does not overfit to a great extent, and has an overall average performance. However, we can't publish the preceding results as the best results and hand it over to John's team. They are not the best results that we have got so far; we have another model-random forest-that gives us the best result for the current exercise. We can either tune our deep learning model further to deliver better and more stable results or we can go back and choose any of the previous experiments and tune the model better.

# What next?

We will now take a break in our predictive analytics experiments and assimilate our learnings from all the exercises and put forward our best results. The experiments to tweak and tune can go on forever. We will, therefore, take the best results we have achieved by far in the predictive analytics stack.

# What have we achieved till now?

We started solving the problem by surfacing the predictive stack in analytics. We started solving the problem in the previous chapter using linear regression to predict one of the critical output quality parameters for the detergent manufactured. We then tried using a more powerful yet simple algorithm to predict the continuous variable. We still didn't see any major improvements in our results, and so we alternatively tried modeling for a binary outcome. We built classification models using a very simple technique called logistic regression and saw promising results to experiment more. We saw a ray of hope to improve the model accuracy using a balanced sample.

We then leveraged cutting-edge algorithms in machine learning to learn the patterns in order to predict the chances of a 'Bad' quality detergent better. We used ensemble machine learning models such as random forest and XgBoost. We got the best results in our entire journey with random forest-above 80% TPR, TNR, and overall accuracy. The boosting algorithms, however, didn't favor good results as they couldn't fit the data in a generalized way. Finally, we explored and experimented with the basics of neural networks and deep learning to take a shot at improving results. We got fairly good results, but not better than random forest.

We can, therefore, take our random forest model to John's team for the prediction problem they are trying to solve in order to reduce the bad quality detergent produce in the plant.

# Packaging our results

Let's quickly package our findings and learnings as a solution for John's team. We'll have a quick recap for the entire problem solving journey for the detergent quality use case.

# A quick recap

It all started when the manufacturing plant for a giant consumer goods company located in Pune, India faced heavy losses in business due to frequent bad quality detergent being manufactured. John, the operational head, reached out to us to check whether we could help him find out the reasons for the bad quality detergent manufactured. We used the art of problem solving and studied in detail the dynamics of the problem. We spent quality time understanding the problem and then defined the problem using a very famous industry artefact, SCQ.

After defining the problem, we brainstormed on the different factors and designed various hypotheses that could help us in solving the problem. We designed the high-level yet exhaustive solution/blueprint for the problem using a structured framework-the problem solving framework. We then dived into the data and validated the different hypotheses we designed using the problem solving framework. Finally, we assimilated all our learning from the hypotheses testing exercise and laid out the reasons to the problem to John.

John was impressed by the solution and his team had a better understanding of the problem and reasons that played a pivotal role in it. John's team further reached out to us to check whether we could help his team even better by building a predictive solution that could help them take better and more targeted decisions before the manufacturing process and thereby reduce losses.

We then surfaced the predictive stack of analytics for problem solving. We discussed, experimented, and practically implemented linear regression, logistic regression, decision trees, machine learning techniques such as random forest and xgboost, and deep learning techniques such as multilayer perceptrons. From all our experiments, we got the best results from the random forest model. We achieved above 80% overall accuracy, above 80% True Positive Rate (predicting Good quality detergent correctly), and above 80% True Negative Rate (correctly predicting a Bad quality detergent produce).

# Results from our predictive modeling exercise

With our predictive model in place, we can help John's team take countermeasures in 80% of the cases where the chances of a bad quality produce is high. Therefore, the operational team now has an opportunity to tackle and mitigate 80% of the overall 20% bad quality detergent manufactured. This will directly help them reduce the bad quality detergent produce from ~20% to 4% that can translate to approximately 16% increment in the $ revenue.

# Few points to note

In the entire problem solving journey, we took a very simple approach. There could be many different or even better alternative paths. The differences could be in the way we defined the problem or even in the techniques and statistical tests used in the solution. When our results from a machine learning or statistical technique were not encouraging, we quickly moved on to experiment with another one. This approach definitely works but may not be the best or most ideal way. There is a variety of methods to fine-tune a model further by regularizing and calibrating the models to a great extent without choosing another technique. Drafting these approaches is a very vast topic to which we can't do justice with a small section in our chapter. The learning path taken during the book was focused on engaging and building a variety of skillsets to solve a problem.

Similarly, in our use case, we saw the best results from the random forest model; this doesn't imply that the random forest model will always surpass the other techniques we discussed or are available in the industry. The results were purely a function of the data we used for our use case. Different use cases will have different dimensions in data and altogether different patterns for which a different technique might fit the best. It is always recommended to explore the data to a great extent to understand the patterns and test with different techniques to see which one delivers the best results. Trial and error testing has always given a very easy and fast means for many data scientists to achieve great results.

Lastly, the iterations required in a predictive modeling exercise to see good results and improve it further are very high. The iteration we studied here is just a glimpse of many iterations tried, which failed. It is highly recommended that you practice and experiment exhaustively to improve the results and master predictive analytics.

# Summary

In this chapter, we took our predictive analytics skillset to a notch higher. You learned and practically implemented sophisticated cutting-edge machine learning and deep learning algorithms to improve our results in the predictive power. We studied ensemble modeling techniques in machine learning such as random forest and extreme gradient boosting, xgboost. You also learned the basics of neural networks and deep learning using Multilayered Perceptrons, that is, MLP. In the overall exercise, we achieved better and improved results for our use case to predict the end quality of the detergent before the manufacturing process. We built a valuable solution for John and his team with an opportunity where they could take immediate actions to mitigate the bad quality produce and reduce the overall losses by 16%.

In the next chapter, we will reinforce our problem solving and decision science skills by solving another IoT use case in a fast-track mode. We'll revisit the decision science journey within a single chapter and ace the problem solving skillsets by the end of the chapter. In the next chapter, we will focus on solving an IoT use case for a renewable energy industry giant pioneering in producing solar energy.

# 6
# Fast track Decision Science with IoT

Decision science differs from data science in the path of problem solving on a variety of factors. Though this can be a never-ending debate, decision science can be aligned more on the front of solving problems using a structured framework that is *inquisitively driven by business questions*, and data science can be defined as a more sophisticated version of data-driven analytics and modeling. Our problem solving approach is more aligned with decision science.

In Chapter 2, *Studying the IoT Problem Universe and Designing a Use Case* you learned in depth about an IoT business use case. We then defined the problem and designed an approach to solve it using the '*problem solving framework*'. It helped us build the blueprint for the problem solving task in detail. In Chapter 3, *The What and Why -Using Exploratory Decision Science for IoT* we practically tried solving the problem using the approach drafted in Chapter 2, *Studying the IoT Problem Universe and Designing a Use Case*. We had answers to our 'what' and 'why' questions and therefore designed a simplified solution for the problem. In Chapter 4, *Experimenting Predictive Analytics for IoT* we touched base with predictive analytics to take the solution one step ahead and answer the question 'when'. In Chapter 5, *Enhancing Predictive Analytics with Machine Learning for IoT* we used cutting-edge machine learning algorithms to improve our predictive accuracy and solve the problem better.

The entire exercise for problem solving took us four chapters, where we took a detailed step in each phase to understand the different means to solve it. In this chapter, we will solve an all new IoT use case from a new domain. We'll wrap up the solution for the entire use case by the end of the chapter and assimilate our learnings to draft the solution. We will go through the same fashion of problem solving, that is, defining the problem and approach using the structured problem solving framework. We'll then get our hands dirty with the data exploration phase and solve the problem in a very quick and agile way. By the end of the chapter, we will reinforce our learnings on problem solving in decision science in a fast-track mode.

This chapter will cover the following topics:

- Setting the context for the problem
- Defining the problem and designing the approach
- Performing exploratory data analysis and feature engineering
- Building a predictive model for the use case
- Packaging the solution

# Setting context for the problem

Let's start fresh with another new IoT use case from the renewable energy domain. Let's assume that a multinational conglomerate giant has forayed into the field of renewable energy to provide solar energy as a service for off-grid locations. The company aims to provide end-to-end solar energy setup in areas where drawing an electric cable for power is much more expensive than arranging diesel for a generator. Tropical countries in Africa will be a perfect example for this scenario. Consider a small village in Uganda where there is an abundance of solar energy but no electricity; many small to medium organizations rely on diesel-powered generators for daily operations. The operational expenses for these organizations would go beyond break-even as a huge cost is incurred in transporting and arranging diesel, maintaining and servicing the diesel generators time to time, and purchasing the required diesel to generate electricity.

The company engineered a solution where an organization of any size and power requirements can be self-sustained by generating clean and cost-effective energy from the sun for their daily operations. Solar panels are set up on the roof of the building or in the premises of the organization. The remaining infrastructure is set up in one of the rooms of the building to connect the battery, inverters, and other logistics. During the day, solar panels charge the battery and provide power for the lighting and powering of the instruments and other devices in the building.

# The real problem

The major hurdle in the solution is the certainty whether the solar energy generated will be enough to power the operation for the next day.

The admin head of the company is responsible for taking care of everything that would be required for smooth operations during the day. As the generation of solar energy is completely dependent on the weather conditions, it is important to make arrangements for diesel to operate the generator if there isn't enough energy produced. Business will incur huge losses if the solar panels are unable to produce sufficient energy due to bad weather conditions or the operations that consumed more than usual energy to serve urgent business requirements.

To solve the problem, there are multiple ways one could use. The company could either overengineer the infrastructure so that the chances of running out of energy is the least, that is, doubling the capacity than required. However, this solution is not at all viable. It will not be a profitable deal to overengineer every solar tech installed. Alternatively, the admin head could be asked to be prepared with a tank of diesel in advance to provide backup using generators in events of low energy generation. This would also not be a viable solution for the admin head as keeping backups everyday would also be an expensive deal.

To solve the problem intuitively, the company has reached out to us to help them close the open ends with a cost-effective and viable option. A simple solution would be a tool that predicts whether the solar energy produced for a day will be sufficient for the day's operation-at least one day in advance.

In a nutshell, if the admin head is informed today that tomorrow it is highly likely that the energy generated will not suffice the activities for the day, he will be in a better position to make arrangements for the diesel required to operate the generator without incurring business losses.

# What next?

Now that we have enough context about the problem, we need to define the problem and design it in a more detailed way using the frameworks that we studied earlier. Unlike the previous use case, the problem here is much more focused and clear. We know pretty much what exactly we need to solve. Here, more specifically, we will be answering the question 'when' and therefore our data exploration and research will be slightly different than the previous use case. Further, to design the approach and study the problem landscape, we will need access to a subject matter expert who can help us understand the problem better and provide answers to our questions from a more domain-intrinsic view.

# Defining the problem and designing the approach

To define the business problem, we'll use the SCQ framework that we used in `Chapter 2,` *Studying the IoT Problem Universe and Designing a Use Case*. It will help us clearly define the current situation, complications, and key question. After defining the problem, we'll research, ideate, and brainstorm to design the approach for the problem.

## Building the SCQ: Situation – Complication – Question

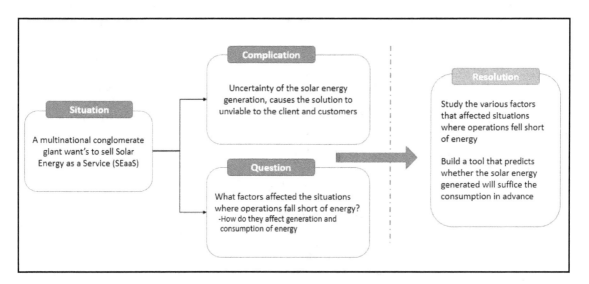

With the SCQ, we have clearly defined the problem by detailing the situation, complications, and questions that need answers along with the 'resolution'.

To design the approach in more detail, we will need to research and ideate a lot of things related to the domain. Moreover, we will need access to an SME who can provide us with insights about how the internal system works in a location where the infrastructure is deployed.

# Research

To study the problem in detail, we need to study the dynamics of the problem better. We need to study how solar panel setups work in general, the different types of solar panel installations, problems that are faced during normal operations, and so on. Also, a fair understanding about the solar panel ecosystem and different components will be an added advantage.

Here is a curated list of questions along with a brief explanation. *(The discussions with an SME and Internet research will help in curating the following results.)*

## How does a solar panel ecosystem work?

A solar panel ecosystem consists of different assets such as a solar panel that converts solar energy to electric energy when exposed to sunlight, a battery to store the energy when charged by the panel, an inverter to convert the DC power from the battery to AC, and so on. A few components could directly use the DC power from the battery; the rest would use the AC power via the inverter.

## Functioning

When the sun rays are incident on the solar panel, it allows the photons, or particles of light, to knock electrons free from atoms, generating a flow of electricity. Solar panels actually comprise of many small units called photovoltaic cells. Many cells linked together make up a solar panel. The electricity generated is stored in the battery or sometimes directly provided for use (when the battery is fully charged or generation is in surplus). A charge controller prevents the battery from overcharging. The required power for an operation could be DC or AC, based on the type of the device. In case of an AC load, the required power can be drawn from the inverter (which converts DC power from the battery to AC) or directly from the battery for DC power.

The following image showcases an overview of a basic:

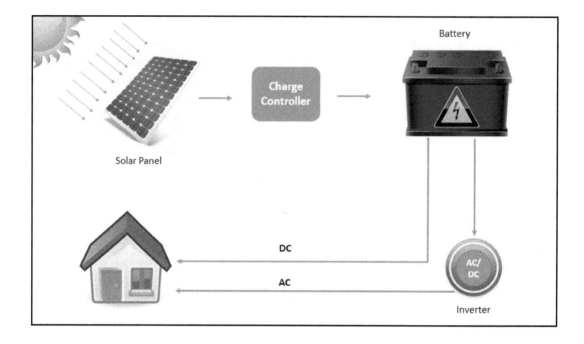

# What are the different kinds of solar panel installations?

The differences in the different types of solar panel installations can be basically be identified by the support of the grid. Some setups may be completely off-grid solutions, that is, there is no support of the grid at all. So if the battery dries off, then there is no other source of energy.

Some have grid support; they can be configured to charge the battery from the grid in cases where there is no battery power or energy or can also send the surplus energy generated to the grid when the battery is fully charged and no other loads require additional energy.

# What challenges are faced in operations supported by solar panels?

Off-grid solutions face the biggest challenges when the system has no other means of generating energy other than the sun. In case the battery dries up, the only alternative is to set up a generator wait till the next sunrise.

The other versions where there is grid support, the battery can be charged using the grid for surplus requirement in cases of low energy generation or heavy consumption. Also, the surplus energy generated can be fed back to the grid when the battery is fully charged.

Similarly, regular cleaning of panels is required to keep the panels non-dusty. Accumulation of dust and other dirt particles reduces the exposure of sun rays and therefore reduces the amount of energy generated

# Domain context

The preceding research notes give us a high-level idea about the solar panel setups. You are encouraged to explore and research more. Now that we have a fair idea about the solar panel and its infrastructure, let's get deep into the domain to understand the finer details about the problem.

The company has set up solar panel installations at multiple locations in the tropical countries as a part of their early experiments. These locations are basically catering to small to mid-size organizations where 2-3 kilowatt capacity panels are enough for their daily operations. We have data from one such plant located in a tropical country in a completely off-grid area. The plant is a hospital that has around 20 beds for patients and can cater to basic medical amenities for around 50 patients a day. There are in all three loads drawing power from the solar infrastructure in the hospital. The AC load provides power to the medical instruments, computers, and other equipment, the DC load powers the external lights, and another DC load powers the internal lights. The solar panels are placed on the roof of the building that is two-story high. A room on the first floor houses the remaining infrastructure for the setup, that is, the inverter, battery, charge controller, and cables.

There are sensors installed in various components of the solar infrastructure to measure a variety of parameters. The solar panel is equipped with sensors to measure the voltage, instantaneous power, current, and energy generated. Similarly, the battery is also equipped with a sensor to measure voltage, power, and current parameters. The inverter has another sensor that measures similar parameters. An ambient sensor measures the temperature of the panel and an irradiance sensor measures irradiance on the panel. Irradiance is nothing but the total amount of sunlight incident on the panel. The panel is a 3 KW panel that is off-grid and has no support for grid charging or discharging. Maintenance of the battery, inverter, and panels happens in scheduled intervals.

In case the battery dries up, the admin in charge of the hospital makes arrangements for diesel to operate the generator. The nearby locations have no fuel stations and therefore it takes around 1-2 hours for an individual to arrange diesel from a distant fuel station.

# Designing the approach

With sufficient domain context, we can now start brainstorming and ideating the different factors that would affect the situation where there was no power to support the routine operations in the clinic. Let's capture the factors in a map similar to Chapter 2, *Studying the IoT Problem Universe and Designing a Use Case*:

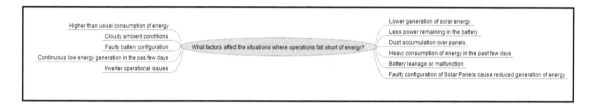

There could be a variety of reasons for which the solar energy generated falls short for consumption on a particular day, that is, power outages. The preceding factor map captures the reasons that could potentially be a cause for the issue. It might be due to low solar energy generated either due to faulty configuration of the panels, dust accumulation, or cloudy ambient conditions. Similarly, the consumption could also be on the higher end for that particular day or the previous 3-4 days, or it could be a combined effect of both, that is, low generation of solar energy and higher consumption of energy for the current day or past few days. The inverter could also be a potential cause for the sudden discharge of power due to faulty operations; similarly, issues could also arise due to faulty batteries or low battery energy remaining for the previous day.

As the problem is more focused on a predictive track, we probably need not create a hypotheses matrix to prioritize and collect all our hypotheses. Instead, we can use the preceding list of factors to understand how to solve the predictive problem. We can leverage each and every data dimension we have to build a predictive model for the solution. A few dimensions or factors that we brainstormed and captured in the preceding image may not be available in the data. We will refurbish our factor/dimension list once we have a complete understanding about the data landscape.

Next, as a part of designing our approach, we can lay out the steps that we need to execute to solve the problem. We have defined the problem and identified the factors that could be a potential reason for the issue. We should now explore the data landscape to understand what kind of data we have and how we can use it. We will then conduct exploratory data analysis on the data to uncover patterns that can be leveraged to build the predictive model better. Our domain knowledge and results from the exploratory data analysis can be further leveraged to create features, that is, feature engineering. With a variety of features and predictors for the model in place, we can engineer the data specifically for the use case. As the data granularity is at a sensor level and data is being captured at a minute level, we will require data engineering to tame the data. We will finally build machine learning/predictive models for our use case where we will try to predict whether the next day will be '0', that is, energy sustained or '1', that is, no energy sustained; therefore, cueing the admin head that backup would be required for the next day's operation.

The whole approach can be visualized in the following flow diagram:

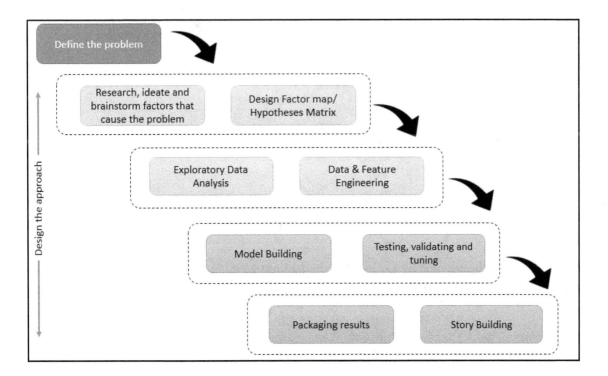

# Studying the data landscape

The data for our use case is captured from various sensors installed in the different assets of the solar panel ecosystem. These sensors capture data at every minute level and push it to the cloud. We have a dump of the sensor data for a variety of parameters from the cloud for four months from one location.

The following diagram can be used to visualize the solar panel architecture and the sensors that capture different data points:

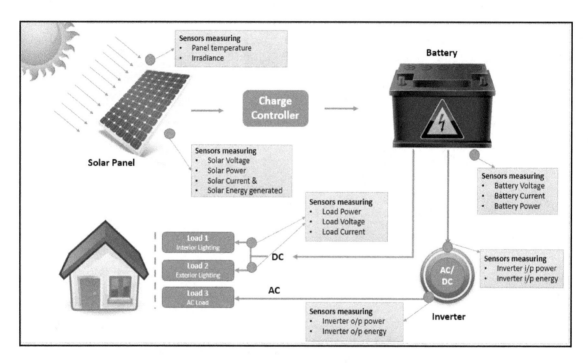

The sensors are installed above and below the solar panels, in the battery, before and after the inverter, and finally in the loads. *(A load is similar to one endpoint of energy consumption measured as an individual unit. Say, in a four-story building, each floor could be considered as a load.)* Altogether, these sensors help in capturing the voltage, instantaneous power, current of the solar panel, battery, and individual DC loads. The amount of energy consumed by the AC loads and two DC loads and the amount of energy generated by the solar panel is also captured. The sensor above the solar panel captures the solar panel temperature and the irradiance (insolation). As mentioned earlier, the current solar panel installation considered in our use case does not have grid support and therefore, there is no charging or discharging of energy to the grid.

The sensors measuring energy generated by the solar panel and consumed by the AC and DC loads measure the amount of energy generated/consumed in the respective time interval between two records, that is, ~1 minute.

# Exploratory Data Analysis and Feature Engineering

We will now focus on diving deep into the data and performing exploratory data analysis. The following code downloads the data from my public Git repository and creates a data frame. We'll start by exploring the data at a high level:

```
>#Read Solar Panel IoT use case CSV data from public repository

>url<-
"https://github.com/jojo62000/Smarter_Decisions/raw/master/Chapter%206/Data
/Final_SolarData.csv"

>#Load the data into a dataframe
>data<-read.csv(url)

>#Check the dimensions of the dataframe
>dim(data)
[1] 119296      23

>#Take a glimpse into each column of the dataframe
>str(data)

'data.frame':     119296 obs. of   23 variables:
 $ location           : Factor w/ 1 level "Peru":  1 1 1 ...
 $ date_time          : Factor w/ 119308 levels "2015-12-02
00:01:40",...
 $ solarvoltage       : num  0 0 0 0 0 0 0 0 0 0 ...
 $ solarcurrent       : num  0 0 0 0 0 0 0 0 0 0 ...
 $ solarenergy        : num  0 0 0 0 0 0 0 0 0 0 ...
 $ solarpower         : num  0 0 0 0 0 0 0 0 0 0 ...
 $ batteryvoltage     : num  98.8 98.5 98.6 98.6 ...
 $ batterycurrent     : num  0 0 0 0 0 0 0 0 0 0 ...
 $ batterypower       : num  0 0 0 0 0 0 0 0 0 0 ...
 $ load_energy1       : num  0.01 0 0 0.01 0 ...
 $ load_power1        : num  192 185 176 189 179 ...
 $ load_current1      : num  1.01 0.98 0.93 1.01 ...
 $ load_voltage1      : num  189 188 188 189 189 ...
 $ load_energy2       : num  0.01 0 0 0 0 ...
 $ load_power2        : num  71.7 81.3 87.8 78.3 ...
```

```
$ load_current2       : num  0.38 0.43 0.46 0.46 ...
$ load_voltage2       : num  189 188 188 189 189 ...
$ inverter_input_power  : num  0.52 0.52 0.66 0.42 ...
$ inverter_output_power : num  0.32 0.32 0.45 0.22 ...
$ inverter_input_energy : num  0.01 0 0.03  0.01 ...
$ inverter_output_energy: num  0 0.01 0.01 0.01 0 ...
$ irradiance          : int  0 15 0 0 0 30  0 0 ...
$ temperature         : num  38.4 38.4 38.4 38.4 ...
```

The data loaded is a data frame with 119,266 rows and 23 columns of data. If we look at what kind of data we have in these columns using the str command, we can see that, except for date_time and 'location', all other variables are numeric. The location contains only value, that is, 'Peru' and we have date_time capturing the timestamp and is unique for each row.

Let's see how many days' data we have and how they are distributed:

```
>#Load the R package required for date operations
>library(lubridate)

>#Convert the string to a timestamp format
>data$date_time<-ymd_hms(data$date_time)

>min(data$date_time)
[1] "2015-12-02 00:00:27 UTC"

>max(data$date_time)
[1] "2016-03-14 22:26:52 UTC"
```

We have data for approximately 3.5 months. However, do we have data for everyday between this time period? Let's have a look:

```
>#Counting the number of distinct days in the data
>length(unique(date(data$date_time)))
[1] 104

>#Calculating the difference between min and max date time values
> difftime(ymd_hms(max(data$date_time)),ymd_hms(min(data$date_time)))
Time difference of 103.9342 days
```

Yes, we do have data for everyday for the time period.

Let's move on to the core parameters in the data one by one. To visualize the data, let's consider a sample for a single day to see how the parameters behave over time. Based on our findings, we'll further explore for a longer time period.

We'll start with solar panel parameters, that is, Solar Voltage, Solar Power, Solar Energy, and Solar Current:

```
>#Selecting the Solar panel related parameters
>cols<- c("solarpower","solarvoltage","solarenergy","solarcurrent")
>summary(data[,cols])
```

```
    solarpower         solarvoltage        solarenergy        solarcurrent
Min.    :   0.0    Min.    :  0.00    Min.    :0.000000    Min.    : 0.000
1st Qu.:   0.0    1st Qu.:  0.00    1st Qu.:0.000000    1st Qu.: 0.000
Median :   0.0    Median :  0.00    Median :0.000000    Median : 1.170
Mean    : 508.3    Mean    : 81.55    Mean    :0.008706    Mean    : 3.123
3rd Qu.:1130.6    3rd Qu.:182.39    3rd Qu.:0.020000    3rd Qu.: 6.300
Max.    :2981.0    Max.    :198.75    Max.    :3.230000    Max.    :18.350
```

We can see that the minimum is zero for all solar panel parameters and the maximum can be seen as varying for different parameters. The data looks somewhat sparse and this is expected. The solar panels will be active only in the presence of the sun, which is around 10-12 hours a day. Let's try to visualize how the parameters behave over the time of a day:

```
>#Select any one day for a sample
>day<-"2015-12-12"

>#Subset the data for the sample day
>sample<-data[date(data$date_time)==day,]
>summary(sample[,cols])
```

```
    solarpower         solarvoltage        solarenergy        solarcurrent
Min.    :   0.0    Min.    :  0.00    Min.    :0.000000    Min.    : 0.000
1st Qu.:   0.0    1st Qu.:  0.00    1st Qu.:0.000000    1st Qu.: 0.000
Median :   0.0    Median :  0.00    Median :0.000000    Median : 0.000
Mean    : 459.1    Mean    : 85.21    Mean    :0.007726    Mean    : 2.522
3rd Qu.: 993.3    3rd Qu.:184.02    3rd Qu.:0.010000    3rd Qu.: 5.370
Max.    :2173.6    Max.    :191.62    Max.    :0.090000    Max.    :12.790
```

The summary of the solar panel parameters for a single day looks pretty much in sync with the overall dataset. Let's look at the distribution of these parameters for a single day:

```
>library(ggplot2)

>#Plotting 4 line charts for the 4 different parameters
>ggplot(sample,aes(x=date_time,y=solarvoltage))+geom_line()
>ggplot(sample,aes(x=date_time,y=solarcurrent))+geom_line()
>ggplot(sample,aes(x=date_time,y=solarpower))+geom_line()
>ggplot(sample,aes(x=date_time,y=solarenergy))+geom_line()
```

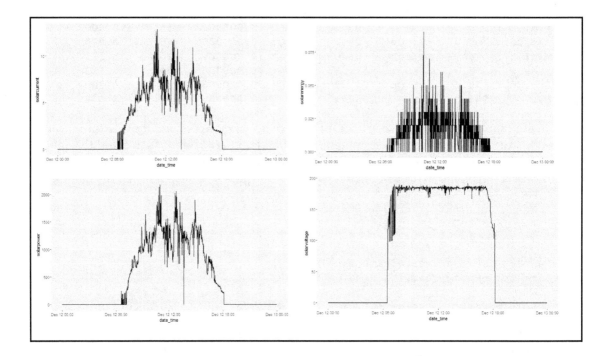

The preceding plot uses a sample day's data, that is, 12th December, 2015. As expected, we can see that the parameters have a finite value only when the sun shines. The x axis plots the time of the day, and we can see that the sun shines and the solar panel is active for around 12 hours, that is, approximately 6 A.M. to 6 P.M. The amount of energy generated (top row of the plot on the right-hand side) is calculated for every one-minute interval. Let's plot a pareto chart to study the cumulative generation across the day:

```
> sample$solarenergy_cumsum<-cumsum(sample$solarenergy)
> ggplot(sample,aes(x=date_time,y=solarenergy_cumsum))+geom_line()
```

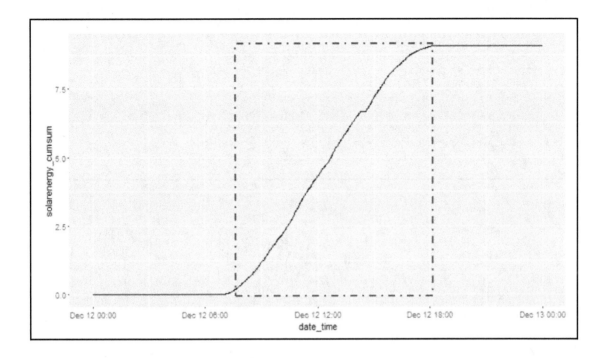

The generation starts at 6 A.M. and continues till 6 P.M. in the evening. Overall for a day, we can see around 9-10 units of energy being generated. The generation curve is highlighted in the plot using the red dashed box.

So we see that all solar panel parameters are alive when the sun shines enough to generate some finite energy from the panel. Approximately, we can conclude that for the considered location, the sun shines for around 12 hours. Let's see how the energy generation varies across days in the time period:

```
>library(dplyr)

>#Calculate Total Solar energy generated for each day
>data$date<-as.Date(data$date_time)
>new<-data %>% group_by(location,date) %>%
            summarise(total_senergy=sum(solarenergy))

>summary(new$total_senergy)
  Min. 1st Qu.  Median    Mean 3rd Qu.    Max.
 4.960   9.275  10.030   9.987  10.900  13.020
```

The distribution clearly shows that most days we have around 9-10 units of energy generated. Let's plot a line chart for the entire time period. This will help us understand seasonality and trend in the time period:

```
> ggplot(new,aes(x=date,y=total_senergy)) +
    geom_line(colour="blue",size=1)+
    theme(axis.text=element_text(size=12),
        axis.title=element_text(size=15,face="bold")) +
    geom_hline(yintercept = 11,colour="red") +
    geom_hline(yintercept = 8,colour="red")
```

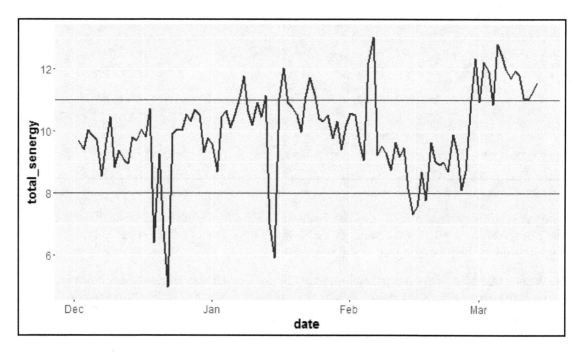

We can see that for a major time period, solar energy generated is between 8 and 11 (taking a slightly wider window) units. There are surges (sudden increase) and sags (sudden decrease) without a consistent pattern. However, overall we see a small dip from February to March and then a steep increase.

# So how does the consumption fare in comparison with the generation?

We have three different loads for consumption-two DC loads and one AC load. Let's study how the consumption data looks. Similar to solar energy, the load energy is also calculated for a one-minute time interval. We can aggregate this data to a day level to study the patterns. First, let's try to study how the consumption looks at a minute-level distribution:

 Load is a term used to define an identified source for consumption. In a four-storied building, one could define each floor as one load. In our use case, the AC consumption and DC consumption is segregated and the DC consumption is further segregated as interior and exterior lighting.

```
>cols<-c("load_energy1","load_energy2","inverter_input_energy")
>summary(data[,cols])
```

```
      load_energy1            load_energy2           inverter_input_energy
 Min.    :0.00000      Min.    :0.00000      Min.    :0.000000
 1st Qu.:0.00000      1st Qu.:0.00000      1st Qu.:0.000000
 Median :0.00000      Median :0.00000      Median :0.000000
 Mean    :0.00298      Mean    :0.00161      Mean    :0.004202
 3rd Qu.:0.01000      3rd Qu.:0.00000      3rd Qu.:0.007000
 Max.    :2.01000      Max.    :0.27000      Max.    :1.162000
```

The overall distribution for consumption parameters is comparable to the solar energy generation patterns. The data overall seems very sparse.

The following codes takes a sample day's data to study the distribution:

```
>day<-"2015-12-12"

>#Collecting the consumption related parameters
>cols<-c("load_energy1","load_energy2","inverter_input_energy")

>#Taking a sample day's data
>sample<-data[date(data$date_time)==day,]

>#Calaculating cumulative sum for the consumption parameters
>sample$load_energy1_cumsum<-cumsum(sample$load_energy1)
>sample$load_energy2_cumsum<-cumsum(sample$load_energy2)
>sample$inverter_input_energy_cumsum<-
    cumsum(sample$inverter_input_energy)

>library(reshape2)
>a<-melt(sample,id.vars="date_time",
        measure.vars=c("load_energy1_cumsum","load_energy2_cumsum",
```

```
        "inverter_input_energy_cumsum"))

>#Plotting all 3 consumption trends for a day together
>ggplot(a,aes(x=date_time,y=value,group=variable,colour=variable)) +
    geom_line(size=1) +
    theme(axis.text=element_text(size=12),
    axis.title=element_text(size=15,face="bold"))
```

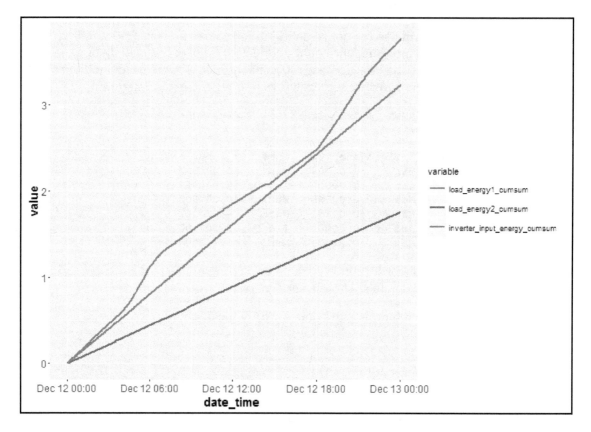

The consumption trends for load 1 and load 2 and the AC inverter load can be seen as a linearly increasing trend. The highest consumption can be observed for load 1 and the lowest for load 2; the inverter fares in-between. Let's also see how energy generation compares with the combined consumption from all three loads together:

```
>#Calculating the energy consumed and generated at a day level
>new<-data %>% group_by(location,date) %>%
    summarise(total_solarenergy=sum(solarenergy),
              total_load1energy=sum(load_energy1),
              total_load2energy=sum(load_energy2),
```

```
                  total_invenergy=sum(inverter_input_energy)
                )

>#Calculating the total consumption from all 3 loads together
>new$total_consumption<-new$total_load1energy+
                        new$total_load2energy+
                        new$total_invenergy

>summary(new$total_consumption)
    Min. 1st Qu.  Median    Mean 3rd Qu.    Max.
   5.830   8.743   9.979  10.090  11.360  14.820

>#Creating a melted dataframe for combined plot
>a<-melt(new,id.vars="date",measure.vars =
     c("total_solarenergy","total_consumption"))

>#Plotting the generation and consumption trends at a day level
>ggplot(a,aes(x=date,y=value,colour=variable)) +
    geom_line(size=1.5) +
    theme(axis.text=element_text(size=12),
    axis.title=element_text(size=15,face="bold"))
```

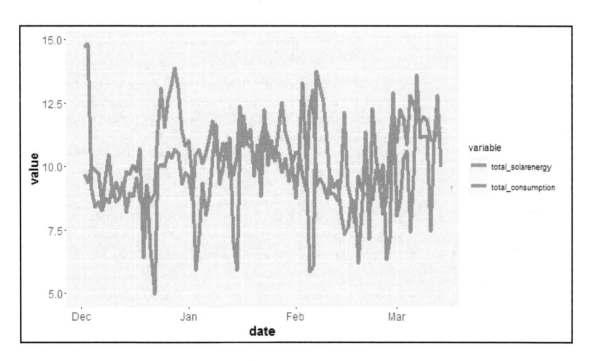

We can see that there are enough cases when the generation was more than the consumption and vice versa. In the scenarios when the overall generation was lower than the combined consumption, the surplus energy from the battery is used. There would have definitely been cases when the remaining battery energy also wouldn't have sufficed. In such cases, it's a power outage situation.

# Battery

Let's move on to explore the battery parameters. We have the battery voltage, current, and power. Similar to the previous exercise, we'll start with the study of the distribution of the parameters:

```
#Collecting the battery related parameters
>cols<-c("batterypower","batteryvoltage","batterycurrent")
>summary(data[,cols])
```

```
   batterypower          batteryvoltage        batterycurrent
Min.    :    0.00    Min.    :   0.00    Min.    : 0.000
1st Qu.:    0.00    1st Qu.:  97.02    1st Qu.: 0.000
Median :   94.13    Median :  98.77    Median : 0.970
Mean    :  421.16    Mean    :  98.69    Mean    : 4.171
3rd Qu.:  885.87    3rd Qu.: 100.53    3rd Qu.: 8.840
Max.    : 2526.64    Max.    : 112.07    Max.    :23.990
```

The *battery voltage* parameter seems pretty different when compared to the other parameters of the solar panel and other battery parameters. It is comparatively less sparse. This is expected as the battery voltage is alive throughout the life of the battery unless it dries off. Battery Power and Battery current on the other hand are very similar to the behavior of the solar panel parameters. They are active in the presence of sunlight (when the panel charges the battery). Let's study the trend of the battery parameters for a sample day's data:

```
>day<-"2016-01-31"
>sample<-data[date(data$date_time)==day,]

>#Plot Battery Power across Time
>ggplot(sample,aes(x=date_time,y=batterypower)) +
    geom_line() +
    theme(axis.text=element_text(size=12),
    axis.title=element_text(size=15,face="bold"))

>#Plot Battery Voltage across Time
>ggplot(sample,aes(x=date_time,y=batteryvoltage)) +
    geom_line() +
    theme(axis.text=element_text(size=12),
    axis.title=element_text(size=15,face="bold"))
```

```
>#Plot Battery Current across Time
>ggplot(sample,aes(x=date_time,y=batterycurrent)) +
    geom_line() +
    theme(axis.text=element_text(size=12),
    axis.title=element_text(size=15,face="bold"))
```

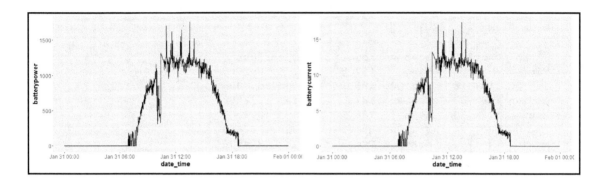

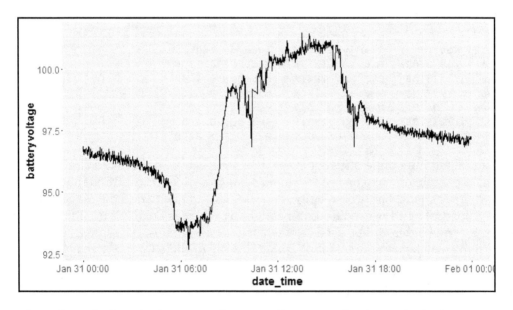

If we take a closer look at the battery voltage trend, we can clearly study the battery discharge and charge cycle. The x axis plots the time from morning 12 A.M. to 11.59 P.M. for a particular day. We can see that the battery voltage decreases consistently from midnight to sunrise. After sunrise, the battery voltage increases and decreases intermittently till evening 5 P.M. This indicates simultaneous charge and discharge. After sunset, the battery again continues to discharge consistently.

# Load

Let's now take a look at the load parameters. We have two DC loads and one AC inverter load. We have already seen the distribution of energy consumed by the loads, therefore we'll explore the remaining parameters:

```
>cols<-c("load_power1","load_voltage1","load_current1")
>summary(data[,cols])

    load_power1        load_voltage1         load_current1
 Min.    : 55.03    Min.    :127.8      Min.    :0.2900
 1st Qu.:134.18     1st Qu.:186.1       1st Qu.:0.7000
 Median :165.37     Median :187.3       Median :0.8800
 Mean    :174.80    Mean    :186.7      Mean    :0.9307
 3rd Qu.:204.62     3rd Qu.:188.1       3rd Qu.:1.0800
 Max.    :461.43    Max.    :190.9      Max.    :2.4800
```

Similarly, we'll take a look at the distribution of the parameters for Load 2:

```
>cols<-c("load_power2","load_voltage2","load_current2")
>summary(data[,cols])

    load_power2        load_voltage2         load_current2
 Min.    :  0.00    Min.    :127.8      Min.    :0.1300
 1st Qu.: 75.29     1st Qu.:186.1       1st Qu.:0.4100
 Median :  97.33    Median :187.3       Median :0.5100
 Mean    : 94.92    Mean    :186.7      Mean    :0.5043
 3rd Qu.:113.06     3rd Qu.:188.1       3rd Qu.:0.6000
 Max.    :242.00    Max.    :190.9      Max.    :1.3300
```

Load 1 and Load 2 are quite different in the data perspective. If we take a closer look at the load power parameters, we can see that Load 1 has been live almost throughout the time period whereas Load 2 has been relatively sparse. This can be tied to the usage of the respective loads. Load 1 is used for internal lighting whereas Load 2 is used for external lighting. External lights will be used only when it is dark, that is, post sunset, whereas internal lights will be used almost throughout the day in some form or the other, say, for the operation theatre or others. Also, the voltage for Load 1 as well as Load 2 is exactly the same. This is because both the loads are DC loads and are drawing power from the same battery.

Let's plot the trend for the DC load's current and power parameters together for a sample day's data:

```
>#Consider the sample dataset with 1 day's data
>#Create a melted dataframe for Load Current 1 and 2
>a<-melt(sample,id.vars="date_time",
        measure.vars=c("load_current1","load_current2"))

>#Plotting Load 1 and Load 2 parameters across time
>ggplot(a,aes(x=date_time,y=value,group=variable,colour=variable)) +
    geom_line() +
    theme(axis.text=element_text(size=12),
    axis.title=element_text(size=15,face="bold"))

>#Create a melted dataframe for Load Power 1 and 2
>a<-melt(sample,id.vars="date_time",
        measure.vars=c("load_power1","load_power2"))

>#Plotting Load 1 and Load 2 parameters across time
>ggplot(a,aes(x=date_time,y=value,group=variable,colour=variable)) +
    geom_line() +
    theme(axis.text=element_text(size=12),
    axis.title=element_text(size=15,face="bold"))
```

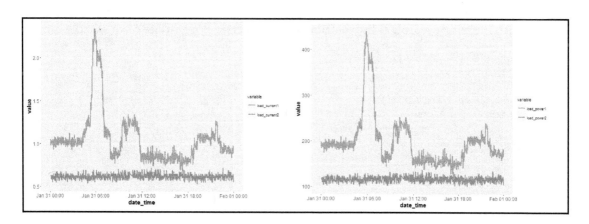

The power and current trends for the same load are very much comparable. Though on a different scale altogether, the trends look very similar for the same load. This is because the power has a linear relationship with the current when voltage is constant.

# Inverter

Last but not least, we need to study the inverter parameters. The inverter has energy- and power-related parameters captured. For both the parameters, we have input as well as output metrics captured. This is provided because there would be a difference in the parameter values that are provided as an input and output. Firstly, the inverter will require some finite amount of energy for its operations and secondly there would be some losses occurred during the conversion from DC to AC. We'll study the input power parameters as we have already studied the energy consumption parameter:

```
>cols<-c("inverter_input_power")
>summary(data[,cols])
   Min. 1st Qu.  Median    Mean 3rd Qu.    Max.
 0.0000  0.1900  0.1900  0.2936  0.3300  2.3200
```

We can see small amounts of sparsity in the inverter power data and this usually happens when the supply is completely cutoff or there is absolutely no consumption. The AC loads are used by the instruments and other equipment for the clinic. The usage patterns may be intermittent. Let's have a look at the distribution of inverter power data for a sample day:

```
>cols<-c("inverter_input_power")
>summary(data[,cols])
>ggplot(sample,aes(x=date_time,y=inverter_input_power)) +
    geom_line(size=1) +
    theme(axis.text=element_text(size=12),
    axis.title=element_text(size=15,face="bold"))
```

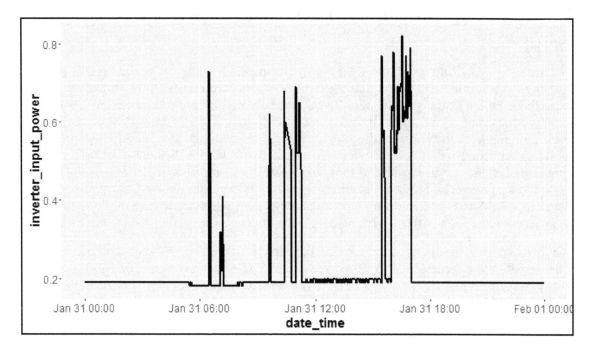

The preceding plot of inverter input power for a sample day's data can help us understand how intermittent the AC load consumption can be. It can vary on the basis of patient treatment requirements.

# Assimilate learnings from the data exploration exercise

So far, we have explored the different parameters in the data landscape. In the exploratory data analysis phase, we deep-dived into the different parameters for the solar panel, battery, and DC and AC loads. What have we learned till now?

# Let's assimilate all our findings and learnings in brief

We studied the distribution of the solar panel parameters such as power, voltage, current, and energy generated and found that the pattern is in accordance with the sun as we expected from the sparsity in the data. To take our understanding to a better level, we explored the time series trend of the parameters for a sample day's data. The behavior of all these patterns were in sync with the sunrise and sunset patterns. Most parameters are active while the sun shines, that is, approximately 6 A.M. to 6 P.M. We also looked at the cumulative energy generation trend for a sample day across time and also across the time period at a day level and found that energy generation increases almost linearly during daytime (6 A.M. to 6 P.M.); additionally, the energy generation trend on a day-to-day basis lacks consistency for a pattern. Around 8-11 units of energy are generated on a daily basis.

We then explored the energy consumption patterns from the two DC loads and one AC load and all of them combined together. We saw that the maximum consumption was mostly seen from Load 2 and the least from Load 1. AC loads were more or less in the middle throughout. The study of total energy generated and total energy consumed on a day-to-day basis revealed that there have been enough cases where energy generated for a day was lower than the energy consumed and vice versa.

While studying the battery parameters, we saw that, except for battery voltage, the other parameters behave in accordance with the solar panel behavior. The voltage of the battery decreases while discharging and increases while charging that was seen consistent for a normal day during the sun hours. Also, the power, current, and voltage parameters for the DC loads are intermittent and completely depend on the kind of devices consuming energy. As power is in a linear relationship with current, we can see a similar trend for both the parameters.

Lastly, exploring the inverter parameters, we studied that the inverter power trends are very intermittent again due to the sporadic use of the AC load during the day.

# Solving the problem

Now that we have a decent overview of the data, we'll take a pause to contemplate what problem we are solving and how we will solve it.

The **major problem** or the pain point faced by the clinic with the solar panel installations is the **uncertainty about the sustenance of energy for the next day**. So basically, we need to predict whether there will be enough energy for the next day or not. Finding which day there was a power outage is something we cannot directly calculate from the data. This is because, apart from the energy consumed and energy generated difference, there is also a finite amount of energy stored in the battery from the past generation.

We have a separate dataset that has recorded the power outage scenario for the same time period and location. The data is a power outage flag, say 1 or 0 (1 indicating that there was a power outage) for each day. We therefore need to build a model where we can have all the metrics or features at day level. With data at this level, we can engineer the data to predict the condition for the next day based on different features, metrics, and other data points for the current day.

Now the question is, what kind of features can we define/engineer to represent a day in the considered location?

This is where we need to get our hands dirty with feature engineering. Let's see what information/features we can draft firsthand from the data.

# Feature engineering

First and foremost, the easiest and most important features we can create are as follows:

- Total solar energy generated for a day
- Total energy consumed for a day

Similarly, the behavior of many parameters has a close relationship with the sun's activity, that is, the solar panel activity. There would be variations in the behavior of the solar panel on a day-to-day basis as it is completely dependent on the sun. It will be important to engineer features to condense this information in the most appropriate way.

Let's start with simple features that should add value. The **maximum value** for most parameters on a day level will have relatively good variations. The minimum, however, will be 0 for most of the parameters, so let's chuck this for now.

Similarly, the **duration** for which these parameters were active, such as the solar current will be 0 in the absence of the sun, but will have values beyond the threshold when the sun rays are powerful enough to generate energy, is valuable. It may happen that, due to cloudy weather, the duration for which the solar panel received sufficient sunlight was comparatively less, which affects generation and therefore could be a potential reason for power outage the next day.

Additionally, the amount of **energy present in the battery** at the start of the day and end of the day will be helpful in deciding the chances for a power outage the next day. We have battery voltage values for every minute. This can be used to find out the percentage of energy left in the battery at a particular instant.

The battery's maximum voltage is 112 and minimum is 88V. The battery is never allowed to drop below 30% of its capacity for performance reasons. Here, 112V indicates 100% energy and 88V indicates 30% energy. We can therefore calculate the percentage of energy left in the battery at any given instant with the voltage alone.

We have not touched base on the irradiance and temperature readings till now. Ideally, a solar panel is designed to work best when it receives an irradiance of 1,000 w/m$^2$ at 25° C. An increase or decrease in temperature causes a small reduction in the energy generated; similarly, an irradiance value below 1,000 w/m$^2$ will also reduce the generation of energy. We can encode this information as features for a day. Say, the duration for which we had an irradiance of at least 1,000 w/m$^2$ and if deviated, then how much? The average absolute deviation of panel temperature from 25° C during the day will also be valuable.

The insight about the effect of temperature and irradiance on solar energy generation, and thereby other parameters, is ideally assumed to be an outcome of the research or domain context conversations with the SME.

Let's quickly build these features for the data.

We'll first try to find out the duration for which a parameter was above the specified threshold. We have defined thresholds for different parameters. We have chosen 5 Amperes for Solar Current, 120V for Solar Voltage, 1,000 Watts for Solar Power, 10 Amperes for battery current, and 800 Watts for battery power. These values have been considered after a small deep-dive into the data and SME consultation:

```
>a<- data %>%
    mutate(
        s_current_ts = ifelse(solarcurrent > 5,as.numeric(date_time),NA),
        s_voltage_ts = ifelse(solarvoltage > 120,as.numeric(date_time),NA),
        s_power_ts = ifelse(solarpower > 1000,as.numeric(date_time),NA),
        b_current_ts = ifelse(batterycurrent >
10,as.numeric(date_time),NA),
        b_power_ts = ifelse(batterypower > 800,as.numeric(date_time),NA)
            )
```

We can now create a couple of features at a day level like the ones we discussed earlier:

```r
>a<-a %>% group_by(location,date) %>%
        summarise(
                #Calculating the maximum values at a day level
                max_solarpower=max(solarpower),
                max_solarcurrent=max(solarcurrent),
                max_solarvoltage=max(solarvoltage),

                #Calculating the mean/avg values at a day level
                mean_solarpower=mean(solarpower),
                mean_solarcurrent=mean(solarcurrent),
                mean_solarvoltage=mean(solarvoltage),

                #Calculating the min and max of date_time
                    #for conditional parameters
                s_current_min=min(s_current_ts,na.rm=T),
                s_current_max=max(s_current_ts,na.rm=T),
                s_voltage_min=min(s_voltage_ts,na.rm=T),
                s_voltage_max=max(s_voltage_ts,na.rm=T),
                s_power_min=min(s_power_ts,na.rm=T),
                s_power_max=max(s_power_ts,na.rm=T),
                b_power_min=min(b_power_ts,na.rm=T),
                b_power_max=max(b_power_ts,na.rm=T),
                b_current_min=min(b_current_ts,na.rm=T),
                b_current_max=max(b_current_ts,na.rm=T),

                #Calculating total energy at a day level
                  s_energy=sum(solarenergy),
                  l1_energy=sum(load_energy1),
                  l2_energy=sum(load_energy2),
                  inv_energy=sum(inverter_input_energy),

                  #Calculating first and last battery Voltages
                fbat=first(batteryvoltage),
                lbat=last(batteryvoltage)
                )

>#Converting the data time to the proper required format
>a <- a %>%
     mutate(
        s_current_min=
as.POSIXct(s_current_min,origin="1970-01-01",tz="UTC"),
        s_current_max=
as.POSIXct(s_current_max,origin="1970-01-01",tz="UTC"),
        s_voltage_min=
as.POSIXct(s_voltage_min,origin="1970-01-01",tz="UTC"),
        s_voltage_max=
```

```
            as.POSIXct(s_voltage_max,origin="1970-01-01",tz="UTC"),
         s_power_min= as.POSIXct(s_power_min,origin="1970-01-01",tz="UTC"),
         s_power_max= as.POSIXct(s_power_max,origin="1970-01-01",tz="UTC"),

         b_power_min= as.POSIXct(b_power_min,origin="1970-01-01",tz="UTC"),
         b_power_max= as.POSIXct(b_power_max,origin="1970-01-01",tz="UTC"),
         b_current_min=
as.POSIXct(b_current_min,origin="1970-01-01",tz="UTC"),
         b_current_max=
as.POSIXct(b_current_max,origin="1970-01-01",tz="UTC"),
         weekdays=weekdays(date)
              )

>#Adding final changes to the dataset
>a<-a %>%
     mutate(
     #Calculating the time duration in mins for the parameters with active
     #Value above threshold
s_current_duration=as.numeric(difftime(s_current_max,s_current_min),units="
mins"),
s_voltage_duration=as.numeric(difftime(s_voltage_max,s_voltage_min),units="
mins"),
s_power_duration=as.numeric(difftime(s_power_max,s_power_min),units="mins")
,
b_power_duration=as.numeric(difftime(b_power_max,b_power_min),units="mins")
,
b_current_duration=as.numeric(difftime(b_current_max,b_current_min),units="
mins"),

     #Calculating % battery remaining from the voltage
     fbat_perc=(100-(112-fbat)*2.916),
     lbat_perc=(100-(112-lbat)*2.916),

     #Calculating
     total_consumed_energy=inv_energy+l1_energy+l2_energy
   )
```

Now that we have created most of our features, let's have a look at their distribution.

We have already studied the trend of energy consumed and generated on a day-to-day basis. Let's have a look at the maximum and average values of the solar panel and battery parameters at a day level:

```
>cols<-c("max_solarpower","max_solarcurrent","max_solarvoltage",
         "mean_solarpower","mean_solarcurrent","mean_solarvoltage")

>summary(a[,cols])
```

| max_solarpower | max_solarcurrent | max_solarvoltage | mean_solarpower | mean_solarcurrent | mean_solarvoltage |
|---|---|---|---|---|---|
| Min.    :1379 | Min.    : 7.60 | Min.    :186.0 | Min.    :304.0 | Min.    :1.748 | Min.    :61.03 |
| 1st Qu.:2068 | 1st Qu.:12.29 | 1st Qu.:189.0 | 1st Qu.:466.3 | 1st Qu.:2.643 | 1st Qu.:75.04 |
| Median :2226 | Median :13.53 | Median :192.6 | Median :513.0 | Median :2.967 | Median :84.72 |
| Mean   :2193 | Mean   :13.44 | Mean   :192.3 | Mean   :507.6 | Mean   :3.117 | Mean   :81.49 |
| 3rd Qu.:2331 | 3rd Qu.:14.77 | 3rd Qu.:194.9 | 3rd Qu.:552.9 | 3rd Qu.:3.376 | 3rd Qu.:85.83 |
| Max.   :2981 | Max.   :18.35 | Max.   :198.8 | Max.   :659.9 | Max.   :5.023 | Max.   :98.97 |

Except for maximum solar voltage, we can see a relatively good spread in the distribution. This means that considering the maximum or mean value for a parameter at a day level, we can expect some variation in the values that will eventually help us collate a few signals to predict whether a power outage will happen the next day.

Moving on, we'll study the distribution of data for the duration of different parameters above the defined threshold:

```
>cols<-c("s_current_duration","s_voltage_duration","s_power_duration",
        "b_power_duration","b_current_duration")
>summary(a[,cols])
```

| s_current_duration | s_voltage_duration | s_power_duration | b_power_duration | b_current_duration |
|---|---|---|---|---|
| Min.    :243.7 | Min.    :646.3 | Min.    :207.7 | Min.    :201.7 | Min.    : 40.02 |
| 1st Qu.:461.2 | 1st Qu.:697.5 | 1st Qu.:438.7 | 1st Qu.:437.6 | 1st Qu.:367.50 |
| Median :481.8 | Median :702.5 | Median :455.1 | Median :448.6 | Median :406.20 |
| Mean   :482.4 | Mean   :705.1 | Mean   :451.1 | Mean   :447.4 | Mean   :388.81 |
| 3rd Qu.:516.0 | 3rd Qu.:715.1 | 3rd Qu.:468.7 | 3rd Qu.:465.7 | 3rd Qu.:432.90 |
| Max.   :544.8 | Max.   :743.7 | Max.   :540.0 | Max.   :508.1 | Max.   :463.20 |

Also, let's look at how the distribution of data looks for the battery percentage remaining at the start and end of the day:

```
>cols<-c("fbat_perc","lbat_perc")
>summary(a[,cols])
```

| fbat_perc | lbat_perc |
|---|---|
| Min.    :39.11 | Min.    :38.56 |
| 1st Qu.:54.81 | 1st Qu.:54.77 |
| Median :58.75 | Median :59.04 |
| Mean   :57.95 | Mean   :57.69 |
| 3rd Qu.:62.70 | 3rd Qu.:62.47 |
| Max.   :71.83 | Max.   :68.89 |

Similar to the previous features, we can see that there is a relatively good spread across the data for the remaining battery percentage at the start and end of the day.

Now, let's take a look at the data that was recorded by the clinic owner regarding power outages while using the solar infrastructure:

```
>url<-
"https://github.com/jojo62000/Smarter_Decisions/raw/master/Chapter%206/Data
/outcome.csv"
>outcome<-read.csv(url)

>dim(outcome)
[1] 104    2

>head(outcome)
        date flag
1 2015-12-02    1
2 2015-12-03    1
3 2015-12-04    0
4 2015-12-05    0
5 2015-12-06    0
6 2015-12-07    0

>summary(as.Date(outcome$date))

        Min.      1st Qu.       Median         Mean      3rd Qu.
Max.
"2015-12-02" "2015-12-27" "2016-01-22" "2016-01-22" "2016-02-17"
"2016-03-14"

>#Check the distribution of 0's and 1's in the data
>table(outcome$flag)

  0   1
 68  36
```

As we can see, the outcome data has recorded the outcome for power outages at a day level. 1 indicates that there was a *power outage* and 0 indicates *no power outage*, and we have data for the same time period as our solar panel sensor data. From the entire 104 days' data, there was a power outage for 36 days, that is, ~35% of the cases had unplanned power outages when the consumption exceeded the energy generated and surplus energy in the battery.

Let's get the complete data under one roof, that is, one data frame:

```
>columns<-
    c(
    "location","date",
    "s_current_duration","s_voltage_duration","s_power_duration",
    "b_power_duration","b_current_duration",
    "max_solarpower","max_solarcurrent","max_solarvoltage",
    "mean_solarpower","mean_solarcurrent","mean_solarvoltage",
    "fbat_perc","lbat_perc",
"s_energy","l1_energy","l2_energy","inv_energy","total_consumed_energy",
    "weekdays"
    )

>#Convert the Date variable in Outcome data to a 'Date' format
>outcome$date<- as.Date(outcome$date)

>day_level<-a[,columns]
>day_level<-merge(day_level,outcome,on="date",how="inner")

>dim(day_level)
[1] 104  22
```

We have collected all the important variables/features that we created at a day level and also merged the outcome for the day, that is, the flag indicating whether there was a power outage for the day or not.

As we will be modeling to predict whether there would be a power outage the next day, let's create a new variable that will indicate whether there was a power outage the immediate next day. This can be easily done with a lead operation, that is, shifting all the rows up by one. As the last row will have a missing value, we will remove the last row from the data:

The data in the outcome dataset will indicate only whether there was a power outage for the current day as per the dataset. However, we need to predict the condition for the next day. We therefore take a lead operation to get the cross-sectional data at the same level with access to the next day's outcome.

```
>day_level$outcome<-lead(day_level$flag)
>day_level<-day_level[1:(nrow(day_level)-1),]
```

Next, we can probably start building predictive models and validate them using techniques similar to the previous version.

There are multiple methods to solve the problem. As the data is in time series format, most data scientists and statisticians would leverage ARIMA or ARIMAX models for the same problem. We have chosen the following method for convenience. Either methods can be leveraged.

# Building predictive model for the use case

So far, we have defined the problem and designed the approach. We explored the data and studied the patterns across a variety of parameters captured through the sensors. We then engineered the data and created a couple of features that depict the day-level activities in an enriched dimension. We now have the data with multiple predictors and the dependent variable **outcome** (created by taking a lead operation on the flag, that is, indicator whether there was a power outage the next day).

We are challenged with the vanilla classification problem with a binary outcome, that is, 1 and 0.

As a part of the modeling exercise, we need to explore in depth the variables for the classification model, study correlation, multicollinearity, and other tests, and so on Covering the entire journey of getting data aware for the predictive model building exercise would be out of scope for the chapter. It is highly recommended to execute all the required checks before modeling.

As it is a binary classification problem, we can choose any one of the algorithms that you learned in the previous chapters, such as decision trees, random forest, logistic regression, or even xgboost. In the current use case, though we initially had a huge dump of data, after engineering and transforming the data, we are left with only ~100 days of data that translates to 100 training samples in all. The number is quite low; it would have been great if we had at least 500 training samples. A thumb rule can be considered as, for every predictor, we should have at least 30 training samples, that is, if we have six predictors, >180 training samples.

To build the model, we will start with the random forest model and give a try with one more algorithm if required.

# Building a random forest model

From the entire list of predictors that we have engineered, not all will be a real value add. The variables chosen here are considered randomly; we'll try to improve the model accuracy with backward selection.

Step 1: Start with all the variables:

```
>set.seed(600)
>train_sample<-sample(1:nrow(day_level),floor(0.7*nrow(day_level)))
>train<-day_level[train_sample,]
>test<-day_level[-train_sample,]
>library(randomForest)
>fit<-randomForest(    as.factor(outcome)~
s_current_duration +  total_consumed_energy + s_voltage_duration +
s_power_duration + b_power_duration + b_current_duration +
fbat_perc + lbat_perc + s_energy + l1_energy + l2_energy+
inv_energy + max_solarpower + max_solarcurrent +
max_solarvoltage + mean_solarpower + mean_solarcurrent+
mean_solarvoltage,
data=train,mtry=4,ntree=500,replace=TRUE)

Call:
 randomForest(formula = as.factor(outcome) ~ s_current_duration +
total_consumed_energy + s_voltage_duration + s_power_duration +
b_power_duration + b_current_duration + fbat_perc + lbat_perc +
s_energy + l1_energy + l2_energy + inv_energy + max_solarpower +
max_solarcurrent + max_solarvoltage + mean_solarpower + mean_solarcurrent +
mean_solarvoltage, data = train, mtry = 4, ntree = 500, replace = TRUE)
               Type of random forest: classification
                     Number of trees: 500
No. of variables tried at each split: 4
```

```
          OOB estimate of  error rate: 26.39%
Confusion matrix:
    0 1 class.error
0 45 5   0.1000000
1 14 8   0.6363636

>#Creating a function to summarise the prediction
>prediction_summary<-function(fit,test)
    {
    #Predicting results on the test data, using the fitted model
    predicted<-predict(fit,newdata=test,type="response")
    actuals<-test$outcome
    confusion_matrix<-table(actuals,predicted)
    print("Confusion Matrix :-")
    print(confusion_matrix)
    print("")
    #Calcualting the different measures for Goodness of fit
    TP<-confusion_matrix[2,2]
    FP<-confusion_matrix[1,2]
    TN<-confusion_matrix[1,1]
    FN<-confusion_matrix[2,1]
    #Calcualting all the required
    print(paste("Overall_accuracy -> ",(TP+TN)/sum(confusion_matrix)))
    print(paste("TPR -> ",TP/(TP+FN)))
    print(paste("TNR -> ",TN/(TN+FP)))
    print(paste("FP -> ",FP/(TN+FP)))
    }

>prediction_summary(fit,test)

[1] "Confusion Matrix :-"
        predicted
actuals  0   1
      0 15   3
      1 10   3
[1] ""
[1] "Overall_accuracy ->  0.580645161290323"
[1] "TPR ->  0.230769230769231"
[1] "TNR ->  0.833333333333333"
[1] "FP ->  0.166666666666667"
```

With the first iteration using all the variables, we can clearly see that we get very bad results. In this exercise, we would like to predict the maximum correct cases for power outages, thus we need to focus on TPR and a relatively good TNR.

As the TPR is extremely low, we can check with the distribution of the training data:

```
>table(train$outcome)

 0  1
50 22
```

The training samples are skewed toward 0 and therefore we have less samples for 1s. This is somewhat similar to our previous use case; however, we had a skewed sample for 1s there. To improve our learning rate, we can try a variety of techniques such as oversampling, stratified sampling, boosting, and so on. For now, let's take a sample with a similar distribution of the dependent variable so that the model learns to predict a 1 and 0 with equal weightage. With this step, we are basically adding some extra weight to the 1s as we have very less training samples:

```
>#Doubling the number of 1's
>new_train<-rbind(train,train[train$outcome==1,])

>table(new_train$outcome)

 0  1
50 44

#we have added more number of 1's to get the training sample almost
balanced
```

Let's now try to run the same model with all the variables on the new oversampled training dataset:

```
>#Codes have been ignored for the model call
Call:
 randomForest(formula = as.factor(outcome) ~ s_current_duration +
total_consumed_energy + s_voltage_duration + s_power_duration +
b_power_duration + b_current_duration + fbat_perc + lbat_perc +
s_energy + l1_energy + l2_energy + inv_energy + max_solarpower +
max_solarcurrent + max_solarvoltage + mean_solarpower + mean_solarcurrent +
mean_solarvoltage, data = new_train, mtry = 4, ntree = 500,        replace =
TRUE)
               Type of random forest: classification
                     Number of trees: 500
No. of variables tried at each split: 4

        OOB estimate of  error rate: 9.57%

Confusion matrix:
    0  1 class.error
0 41  9        0.18
```

```
1   0 44          0.00

> prediction_summary(fit,test)
[1] "Confusion Matrix :-"

          predicted
actuals   0   1
      0  14   4
      1   5   8
[1] ""
[1] "Overall_accuracy ->  0.709677419354839"
[1] "TPR ->  0.615384615384615"
[1] "TNR ->  0.777777777777778"
[1] "FP ->  0.222222222222222"
```

Studying the results from the test data, we can see relatively better results. We have improved the TPR and overall accuracy with a small sacrifice on TNR. Let's try to drop the predictors that are not adding much value. This can be studied using the varImpPlot tool in the randomForest package:

```
>varImpPlot(fit)
```

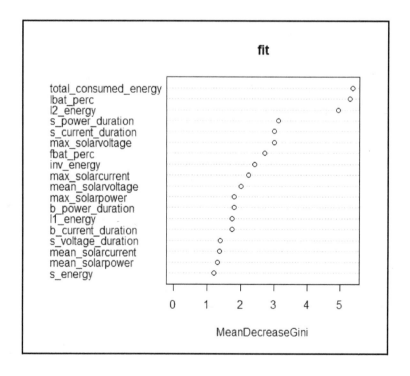

Studying the MeanDecreaseGini from the variable importance plot, we can study the least important variables defined by the random forest model. The top variables are the most important ones for the model whereas the bottom ones are the least significant variables. To improve the model, we'll eliminate a few less important variables and try tuning the model. This step will be completely iterative and a trial and error experiment.

The following result is the outcome from one such iteration:

```
Call:
 randomForest(formula = as.factor(outcome) ~ s_current_duration +
total_consumed_energy + s_power_duration + b_power_duration +
b_current_duration + fbat_perc + lbat_perc + l1_energy +        l2_energy +
inv_energy + max_solarpower + max_solarcurrent +       max_solarvoltage +
mean_solarvoltage, data = new_train, mtry = 3,       ntree = 100, replace =
TRUE, nodesize = 5, maxnodes = 5)
                Type of random forest: classification
                     Number of trees: 100
No. of variables tried at each split: 3

        OOB estimate of  error rate: 20.21%
Confusion matrix:
    0  1 class.error
0 36 14   0.2800000
1  5 39   0.1136364

> prediction_summary(fit,test)
[1] "Confusion Matrix :-"
        predicted
actuals  0  1
      0 13  5
      1  3 10
[1] ""
[1] "Overall_accuracy ->  0.741935483870968"
[1] "TPR ->  0.769230769230769"
[1] "TNR ->  0.722222222222222"
[1] "FP ->  0.277777777777778"
```

We can see small improvements in our results. The TPR, TNR, and overall accuracy have improved by a small margin. However, as the number of samples used in the testing sample is relatively low, we can't affirmatively conclude the results. There is scope for the results to vary with another testing sample. The chances of such an event happening is quite high as, with lower training samples, misclassification of even one or two samples can bring about 10-20% change in the overall results. To get a better idea, we'll test the model using the entire dataset and study the results:

```
>prediction_summary(fit,day_level)

[1] "Confusion Matrix :-"
        predicted

actuals  0  1
      0 54 14
      1  3 32


[1] ""
[1] "Overall_accuracy ->  0.83495145631068"
[1] "TPR ->  0.914285714285714"
[1] "TNR ->  0.794117647058823"
[1] "FP ->  0.205882352941176"
```

We can see that overall we achieved good results. There is a relatively good mix of TPR and TNR along with the overall accuracy for the tuned version. If we consider an average version, that is, neither as good as the results from the entire dataset, nor as low as the test dataset, we can say that we have TPR ~ 70 and TNR ~ 75% and thus, ~75% overall accuracy.

 There is humongous scope for improvements in the current model building activity. However, the current exercise is restricted with the preceding results for the solution. You are encouraged to iterate and tune the model further.

Next, we'll package our result and see how we can draft a story for the use case.

# Packaging the solution

We now have a model in place that gives us relatively good accuracy. As a ballpark figure, we can say that we achieved an overall 75% accuracy with a TPR of 70% and TNR of 75% (scope exists to improve this further).

How does it add up to the use case's revenue story? With our model in place, we can say that we will correctly predict a power outage 7 out of 10 times. So we have saved the losses that happen because of power outages by 70%. Now, we also incorrectly predicted a power outage when it wasn't, that is, approximately 2.5 out of 10 times. Let's say that there was a cost associated with stocking diesel when it was predicted that the next day will be having power outages; this cost will tax the losses saved from the correct prediction (penalty).

The overall FPR is low and also the cost associated with stocking diesel for power outages is generally much lower than the losses due to unplanned power outages. Therefore, we are still in a good position to add value to the solution. Let's assume that the cost of stocking diesel for the next day is $100 and the losses due to unplanned power outages is $300. Then, for every 100 cases, there are approximately 35 cases that will have unplanned power outages.

Therefore, total loss = 35 * 300 = $10500.

With the predictive model, we correctly predict 7 of 10 cases, that is, 24.5 of 35 cases.

Therefore, losses reduced = 24.5 * 300 = $7350.

With every incorrect prediction, we lose $100 for unnecessarily stocking diesel, that is, 2.5 of 10 time is 25 of 100 times = 25 * 100 = $2500.

Therefore, net losses reduced = 7350 – 2500 =$4850.

Now, comparing the net losses reduced ($4850) with the original losses ($10500), we have reduced the losses by ~50% (46%).

This number is clearly tangible for a solar infrastructure use case.

Therefore, we can summarize that we have solved the problem of uncertainty in power outages by reducing the losses by 50% (with assumptions) for the end customer.

# Summary

In this chapter, we reinforced our decision science learnings by solving an altogether new use case for the solar energy industry. We started on the same roots of problem solving by defining the problem and designing the approach and blueprint for the problem. We studied that the problem statement in our use case is much more specific and narrowed-down compared to the previous use case. We solved the problem of *uncertainty in power outages* from the solar tech. After having a clear definition of the problem statement, we explored the sensor data from solar panels and infrastructure to find patterns and associated signals. After gathering the ground context of the data and domain (through research and an SME), we engineered features to solve our problem better.

We then leveraged these features and the machine learning algorithms that you learned in the previous chapter to build predictive models that could predict the chances of power outage from the solar panel infrastructure a day in advance. With basic business assumptions, we packaged and validated the potential of our solution for the customer. By predicting the chances of power outages from the solar tech in advance, we are able to reduce the losses by 50%.

We have therefore traversed through the entire journey of problem solving in a fast-track mode and reinforced our learnings on decision science for IoT. In the next chapter, we will touch base on the next level of problem solving-**prescriptive** science. We will use a hypothetical example and overlay real-life examples to understand how to outlive business disasters.

# 7
# Prescriptive Science and Decision Making

Predictive analytics scales the power of analytics and decision making to a paramount level. We can consider our daily life as an example. If we have an answer to the 'when' question, it can help us take better decisions to secure our future. Visibility into the future makes life easy for everyone. The same holds true for problem solving in decision science. The nature of the problem can be descriptive, inquisitive, predictive, or prescriptive. Prescriptive science or **Prescriptive Analytics** answers the question '**So what, now what?**' and aims at improving the outcome of the problem. We often ask this question after we see an issue in the routine operations.

Prescriptive analytics is a **fuzzy transition** from the combination of descriptive, inquisitive, and predictive analytics. The problem reaches a point where we continuously iterate through different questions either to recover from a disaster or further improve the solution. In this chapter, you will learn the nuances of prescriptive analytics using a hypothetical example. You'll learn what actions can be taken to recover from a disaster or further improve the solution using our learnings from the descriptive + inquisitive + predictive stack. We will connect the dots and study the interconnected nature of a problem in decision science in more detail as we complete the end-to-end problem stack.

The following topics will be covered in this chapter:

- Using a layered approach and test control methods to outlive business disasters
- Tying back results to data-driven and heuristic-driven hypotheses
- Connecting the dots in the problem universe
- Storyboarding and making sense of the interconnected problems in the problem universe
- Implementing the solution

# Using a layered approach and test control methods to outlive business disasters

Prescriptive science results from the convergence of descriptive, inquisitive, and predictive analytics. It is used as a layered approach and iterated till the time we reach a promising solution. To understand the concept lucidly, let's simplify it by reconstructing the abstract and ambiguous words in a layman's way.

## What is prescriptive analytics?

Prescriptive analytics helps us answer the question 'So what, now what' in the problem solving exercise, that is, **it helps us improve the outcome**. It is the final layer in the problem solving stack that results from the convergence of the previous three types: descriptive + inquisitive + predictive.

We'll consider a very simple example to study this in more detail. Consider a telecom giant (say AT&T, Verizon, and so on) who provides multiple services such as broadband connections, IPTV, mobile telephone connections, and so on The director of the **Customer Experience Team**, say Mark, wants to solve a problem. The problem initially starts from the first layer, that is, *Descriptive Analytics* where we try to answer.

## What happened?

The team under him studied various reports and analyzed the data to find out that the overall operational cost for the contact center (call center) has increased by 20%. This was mainly due to heavy traffic in incoming calls from customers in the past few weeks from a certain geographic area.

# Why and how did it happen?

There was congestion in the network for some areas of operation that resulted in slow Internet speed, call drops, and so on. Irate customers have been continuously reaching out to customer care executives with complaints and bill/refund issues.

# When will it happen (again)?

The team explored the data and built various predictive models to predict when a customer would make his next call (say after eight days) and forecasting models to predict the call volumes expected in the upcoming weeks. The numbers show an alarming increase in the number of calls to be handled by the customer care agents.

# So what, now what?

The director of customer experience, Mark, is now under pressure. To solve the problem, he needs his team to quickly fix the issues to mitigate a business disaster. The heavy call volume will choke the bandwidth of the agents, increase call wait times for the customers, registered complaints will be unresolved, and eventually pinch customer experience. Some irate customers may even discontinue using the services and opt for a competitor's services/products. This would result in huge business losses and also hamper the company's brand value. Mark needs to take immediate actions to resolve the issues and alleviate the impact of the disaster.

Now that we have an overall idea of the example, let's try to understand the answer to the question 'So what, now what' in brief. The team has completed the initial set of analyses and traversed through the descriptive, inquisitive, and predictive nature of the problem. Therefore, we have answers to the 'What', 'Why', and 'When' questions. We now reach the point when we ask 'so what...' (The heavy increase in call volume to customer service agents will ultimately cause huge business losses.) and '**Now what...**'. (The team needs to take quick countermeasures to solve the problem and thereby alleviate the disaster.) As a remedy, we will start small with a couple of small fixes, but by the time we solve them, many new problems would be discovered. To solve these problems, we iterate through the problem stack until we have a solution for the entire problem.

Prescriptive analytics is therefore a result of the convergence of insights and answers gathered from the entire problem stack. The entire process can be summarized using the following image:

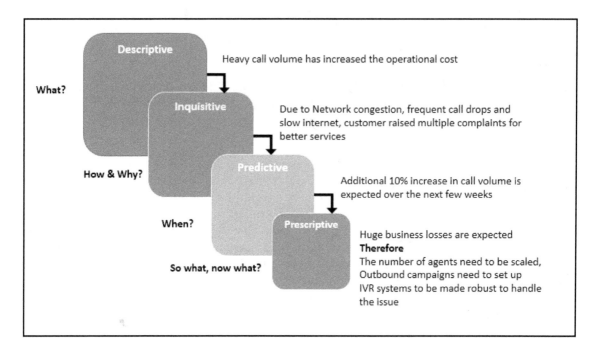

In a nutshell, prescriptive analytics can be defined as finding the best course of action for a given situation.

Now that we have a sound understanding of prescriptive analytics, let's study a couple of measures to see how the best recommended actions for a given situation can be derived.

# Solving a prescriptive analytics use case

Let's consider a hypothetical use case to closely understand the different approaches that can be leveraged to outlive a business disaster. We will be using the layered approach to solve the problem; that is, we will start from descriptive and then move on to inquisitive and predictive solutions. Converging all the learnings from the three layers, we will approach prescriptive analytics. In most cases, while solving problems using prescriptive analytics, we touch base on newer problems. The layered approach iterates through each problem in the entire stack and eventually solves the entire set of interconnected problems in the problem universe. We studied about the interconnected nature of problems in Chapter 1, *IoT and Decision Science* and Chapter 2, *Studying the IoT Problem Universe and Designing a Use Case*.

We'll consider a use case from the telecom industry (hypothetical) on similar lines to the example we studied earlier, but a bit more detailed and slightly different.

## Context for the use case

A leading telecom giant with multinational presence provides mobile telephone services, IPTV, and broadband services for consumers as well as corporates. The customer experience team for the telecom giant operates a contact center with support for chat, incoming voice calls, IVR, outbound campaigns, and e-mails to resolve customer complaints. The director of the customer experience team, Mark, is responsible for smooth operations with minimum operational cost without a compromise on customer satisfaction.

Let's frame the use case using the same set of questions as we did previously.

## Descriptive analytics – what happened?

Mark recently studied that the operational cost for the call center has been surging due to increasing call volumes. Let's take a closer look at this. What if the number of calls have increased because the number of customers have also increased, or is it a seasonal pattern where we observe a generally higher call volume during the year?

To conclude the finding, we need to slice and dice the data and confirm affirmatively whether there is indeed an increase in the operational cost due to increased call volume. If the call volume is due to the increasing customer base, then we can't justify increasing operational costs due to increased call volume. As mentioned earlier, Mark's responsibilities include maintaining smooth operations at minimum operational cost **without** compromising on customer experience.

The following visualizations showcase the results from the slice and dice operations on the data (hypothetical data).

We'll first take a look at the annual call volume and the YoY (year on year) % increase in call volume:

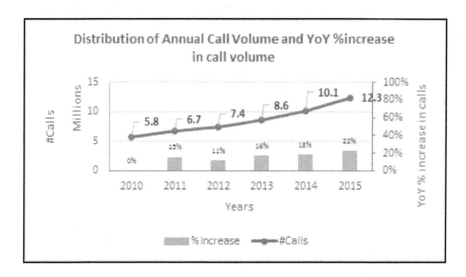

We can clearly see that there is a consistent increasing trend in the annual call volume when considered for the past five years. The bars indicate the YoY% increase in the call volume and it shows almost consistent increase. The least % increase was observed in the year 2012, that is, 11%; in most cases, it shows a steady increase.

Can the increase in calls be due to increasing customers?

Yes, definitely. As the number of customers increase, the number of calls received in the contact center will also increase. However, we need to check whether the increase in call volume is proportional to the increase in customers or not. How can we check this?

To get an approximation of whether the increase in call volume was in proportion to the increasing customer base, we need to define a **normalized dimension** or **vector**; basically, a **Key Performance Indicator (KPI)** that is normalized with respect to the calls or customers. We can define a KPI such as **calls per customer**-the total number of calls by the total number of active customers.

Let's plot the distribution of calls per customer across the years:

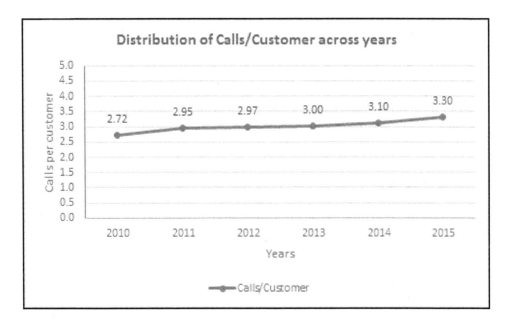

As we can see, even though the number of calls have increased as the customer base increased, the number of calls per customer has definitely increased by a good percentage from 2014 to 2015. This can help us confirm that overall there has been a significant increase in the annual call volume for the contact center.

Next, we need answers for why has there been an increase in the overall annual call volume? This means that we need to touch base with inquisitive analytics.

# Inquisitive analytics – why and how did it happen?

To understand why the overall call volume increased, we need to follow the same vanilla procedure. We will define the problem, brainstorm and hypothesize over a variety of factors, and design the blueprint for the solution (problem solving framework). In the exploratory data analysis phase, we will deep-dive into the data to find out the reasons for the increase in call volume.

Among all the hypotheses that we will collect, one of the factors will be '**repeat calls**', that is, customers calling in again and again for the same issue. A simple business rule that helps us define a repeat call would be another call from the same customer within 48 hours. Our hypothesis would be framed as, the calls per customer has increased that eventually increased the annual call volume and this was mainly due to repeat calls from customers. Customers called back again to get more clarity on the issue as it was not mentioned in the first call.

This seems like a valid hypotheses. Let's deep-dive into the data to see how the distribution of data looks:

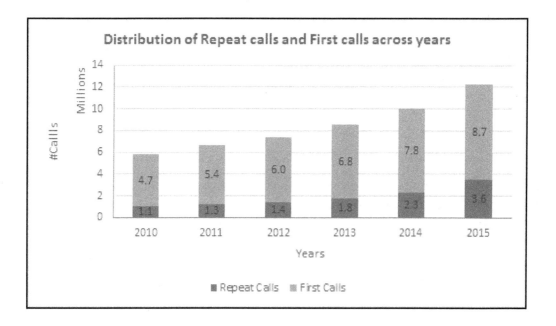

We can see that repeat calls contribute to ~20% of the overall call volume for each year. However, is this still relevant? It could be in sync with the increasing call volume each year. To validate our hypothesis, we will need one more view to study whether there was indeed an increase in the repeat call rate. The following image showcases a plot of stacked bar charts with the percentage of Repeat calls and First calls for the respective year:

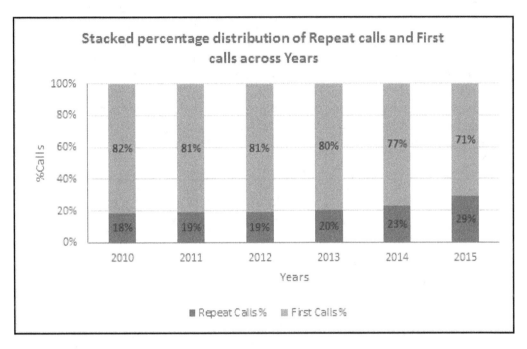

Yes, we can now conclude that our hypothesis is true; that is, there is indeed an increase in the repeat call rate year on year. This could be one of the potential reasons for the increase of calls per customer in the current year.

However, if the customers are repeating a call, how are they repeating it? Is it for the same reason or a different reason?

Usually, an incoming call is assigned a call type by the IVR or agent who is handling the issue. A call type could be anything such as 'Internet not working', 'Slow Internet', 'Billing Issue', 'Do not disturb activation', 'top-up plans', and so on. Now, the question is if a customer calls for Internet Troubleshooting and calls again within 48 hours for a billing issue, is it really a repeat call or just coincidence?

Even though our hypothesis seems valid, we still need to check for more validity. If 20 out of 100 calls are repeating (based on our business rule) and if 15-18 of them are repeating for a different reason, then we can't really attribute repeat calls as one of the factors for the increasing call volume. It could be a generic issue coincidentally being tagged as a repeat call.

Let's take a look at the distribution of data for repeat calls with a more granular view on the reason code, that is, **same reason repeat calls** and **different reason repeat calls**. We can define a 'same reason repeat call' as an additional call from the same customer within 48 hours for the same reason and a 'different reason repeat call' for a different reason. So, if a customer calls once for 'Slow Internet issue' and again within 48 hours for the same reason, it would be 'same reason repeat call'; otherwise, if the same customer makes another call within 48 hours for some other reason, say 'Billing Issue' or 'Top up plans', it would be classified as a 'different reason repeat call'. The following chart shows the distribution of repeat calls as same reason and different reason across the years:

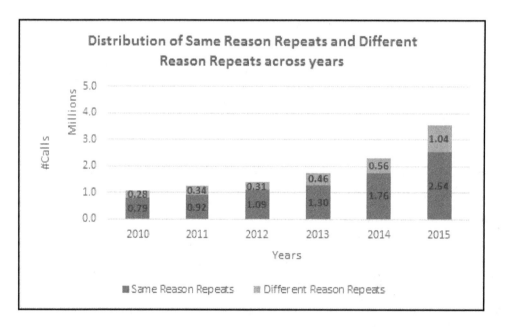

We can note that majority of the repeat calls are for the same reason. Approximately 1/4th of the calls repeat for a different reason that may be a genuine repeat or could be just a coincidence. The following graph plots the stacked percentage distribution of same and different reason repeat percentage calls across years and we can see that a different reason repeat ranges between 20-30 in most cases:

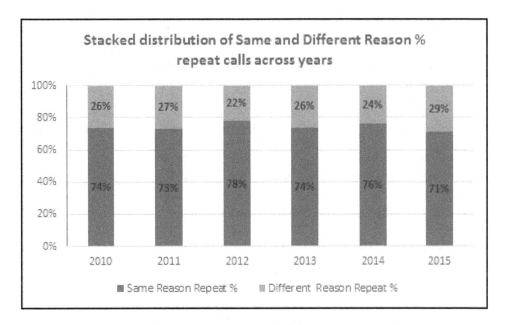

So we can affirmatively conclude that high repeat call rate is one of the factors that have contributed to the increase in the overall call volume.

What next? We now have answers to 'What', 'Why, and How' for the problem. How can predictive analytics help us?

# Predictive analytics – when will it happen?

Mark now has a very fair understanding about the problem. His team has studied the root causes for the problem and would now like to enhance the results using predictive analytics. In a generic scenario, with the power of prediction, we can develop various powerful and robust machine learning algorithms that will help in predicting the following:

- Total number of monthly calls expected for the next six months: This will help the team work toward optimizing staffing to handle a high volume of calls more efficiently
- Predicting the volume of monthly repeat call rate for the next six months:This will give the team the visibility to act on reducing the repeat calls by studying the patterns causing repeats

- Predicting the number of repeat calls that will be received in the immediate next day: This will prepare the team with the skills required to learn the reasons for repeats and take action on avoiding further repeats
- Predicting in real time whether the customer will repeat call in the next 48 hours: This will help in taking live action during the call to mitigate the chances for a repeat call

For simplicity, let's assume the following results for the first three techniques in the preceding list:

- 8-10% MoM (Month on Month) increase in the call volume for the next six months
- Around 10% MoM increase in the volume of repeat call rate for the next six months
- Approximately 10% increase in the number of repeat calls expected for the immediate next day

# The inception of prescriptive analytics

With this visibility into the future, Mark's team will have a concrete understanding for the immediate next steps they would need to execute in order to improve business. This is where prescriptive analytics starts surfacing in the problem solving journey.

Prescriptive activity starts once you have an understanding about what has happened or you know what is probably going to happen. Consider an example in our day-to-day life. Let's say that you are a third-year student in computer engineering. Your semester exams are approaching in a month's time and you need to start preparing for the exam. Based on your performance in the previous semesters, you have an understanding about your skills in programming. Say, you ace at programming but struggle with computer networks. You would then prepare accordingly by dedicating more time to study a computer networking course. Similarly, let's assume that you got to know from your professor about a very easy math exam and you already excel in mathematics. You will definitely spend less energy preparing for the math exam. This is how prescriptive analytics works.

At a high level, you are trying to solve a problem and you have insights into the root cause for the problem or you know probably what is going to happen next. You would then tweak your solution accordingly to improve the outcome. Prescriptive analytics is an iterative process and requires a lot of trial and error to optimize the outcome.

In the preceding use case, we have an understanding about the nature of events that have happened and insights about the events that are about to happen. As a part of the solution, Mark would now work toward fixing things to mitigate the perils of a disaster. Let's see what sort of damage will occur assuming that the predictions are 100% correct (though predictions are not always 100% correct).

The incoming call volume from customers has seen a surge in recent times (past few months) and, based on the predictions, it seems that there would be approximately 8-10% month on month increase in the call volume. This cues for a huge resource crunch in the customer service agents in the coming months. Currently, we have approximately 1.2 MN calls a month from the entire customer base. If a consistent 8-10% MoM increase in the call volume is expected for the next six months, we would receive on an average two MN monthly calls post six months. If we do simple math, we'll understand that we need to double the number of agents to accommodate the surplus calls. This is definitely not an ideal situation. We can definitely increase the number of agents to solve the problem, but this needs to be done cautiously without incurring huge operational expenses. The **best way** would be to slightly increase the staffing capacity and simultaneously work toward countermeasures to reduce the incoming calls.

So technically, we have two high-level solutions to solve the problem:

- Increase the staffing capacity to accommodate more number of calls
- Implement countermeasures to reduce the incoming calls

Countermeasures to reduce the incoming calls is a very broad topic; this would cover multiple points as follows:

- Making the IVR more robust to complete the call within the IVR
- Setting outbound campaigns through e-mails and automated IVRs with solutions for common issues
- Resolving the technical issues immediately for which customers are frequently calling
- Educating the customers about the next steps on the call to avoid a repeat call
- Releasing self-help guides over the Internet for customers to resolve trivial issues on their own and so on

We can see that a single problem has now been broken down into multiple smaller problems. Each of these problems need to be solved individually and would probably require an end-to-end problem solving method for each of them. Moreover, all of these smaller problems are actually interconnected; we can't solve the main problem without each individual problem being solved. You learned about the problem universe in Chapter 1, *IoT and Decision Science* that detailed the nature of interconnected problems. The problem universe can be studied in more detail when we reach the prescriptive analytics layer. The following image depicts the interconnected problem universe for our problem:

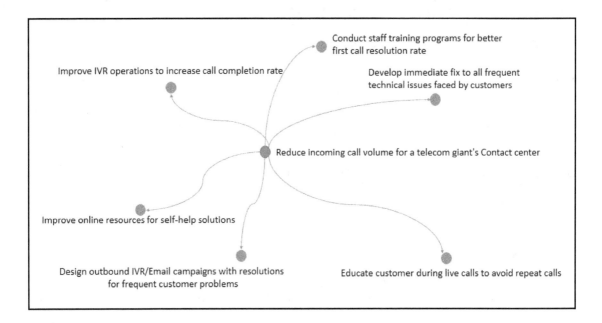

## Getting deeper with prescriptive analytics

To improve the outcome based on the results of the inquisitive and predictive analysis phase, there are a variety of different methods. In business disasters, the team will be usually running low on time as a resource and therefore the luxury of extensive trial and error exercises will not be available. In order to keep the process agile and resilient, most businesses use the A-B testing or quick test and control techniques to assess the effectiveness of their solutions without impacting the entire business. Let's study a few examples of implementing these strategies for our use case.

# Solving the use case the prescriptive way

As a part of the prescriptive analytics solution, businesses often need to validate how effective the current prescription is. Will it cause huge damage, will the customer dislike it, or will it actually improve the business? To find answers to all these questions, we implement a very simple strategy called the 'Test and Control Analysis'.

# Test and control analysis

In test and control analysis, we choose two sample tests randomly from the entire population for the experiment. The only rule being that the two samples should be identical in behavior; that is, if we choose samples of customers for the experiment, both the groups should have a similar behavior, say, demographically or based on the customer type for business. We will design a simple experiment: targeting customers using e-mails with lucrative offers for a festive season. From the two sample groups that we have identified, the experiment is conducted only on one of them; we call it the '**test**' group. The other group with no experiments conducted is called the '**control**' group. We can study the impact of our experiment by comparing the differences in the results from the test and control group.

Let's say that you want to test the effectiveness of an e-mail campaign on discount offers for a retail outlet. You identify a test and control group for the experiment and send out e-mails/mailers only to the test group. We will then see how differently the test group behaved when compared to the control group. If the response from the test group was much better than the control group, we can conclude that the effectiveness of the e-mail campaign is **positive**, that is, people are enthusiastic about the offer. If there is no major difference, we can conclude that the effect is **neutral**, that is, no major impact was seen from the campaign. In some cases, an e-mail campaign may also have a **negative** impact where the control group had a better response than the test group.

Using the test and control method, we can easily study the impact of different experiments designed on smaller samples without rolling it to the entire population. Such experiments help businesses take better decisions to improve the outcome for a problem that they are solving with reduced risk. We can witness similar experiments quite often in real-life scenarios. Facebook's recent 'Live Video' feature was initially rolled out to only a small community and, based on the results and feedback, more and more users groups and eventually everyone was given access to the feature.

# Implementing Test & Control Analysis in Prescriptive Analytics

In our use case, we have reached a point where we have various insights from the predictive analyses and a sound understanding about the root cause from the inquisitive analysis. We have also designed a **miniature problem universe** that reflects the interconnected nature of problems for the problem that we are solving. To keep moving, we need to design a few experiments to improve the outcome, that is, reduce incoming calls.

Let's see what kind of experiments we can conduct to improve the outcome based on our learnings in the inquisitive and predictive analytics phase. We'll touch base on a few of the smaller problems identified in the problem universe.

# Improving IVR operations to increase the call completion rate

All incoming calls first pass through the IVR before reaching an agent. If we improve the IVR operations, we can reduce the incoming call volume. To increase the IVR call containment rate or completion rate, we need to identify the loopholes where customers are transferring the call to an agent. A few broad areas can be identified where we can take action by analyzing the IVR data:

- Identifying frequent paths traversed by a customer
- Studying frequent options for which a call was transferred to an agent
- Nodes where the customer was confused to select an option (for example, the language/verbiage was too complicated and so on)

Based on the findings, we can implement a few fixes that may help customers to finish the call within the IVR. For example, adding the Spanish language as an option may reduce the call transfers or adding a new application to the IVR, say, an option to automatically raise a complaint for billing issues (which was previously not available) may reduce the incoming call volume. However, in most cases, the stakeholders can't be cent per cent sure whether these are the best techniques to solve the problem and improve the outcome. Therefore, as a safe option, we can choose the **test and control** analysis option. We can test the new feature with a small sample (test group) and compare the results with a control group. If the results are favorable, that is, we see a higher call completion rate in the test group than the control group, we can roll out the feature to larger samples.

# Reducing the repeat calls

In most cases, due to insufficient knowledge provided during the call, the chances of a customer repeating the call is high. However, it would be difficult for an agent to reiterate information again and again to all customers. Moreover, it will also increase the call duration and therefore the operational costs. In a more optimized way, we can leverage the machine learning model built in the predictive analytics phase to aid the agent better.

If the machine learning model can predict in real time, say within 15 minutes in a 20 minutes call, the agent handling the call can selectively take a better chance to educate the customer about the next steps to avoid a repeat call. Targeting only the potential customers will not cause a burden on the agent and will increase the overall call duration.

Similarly, if we can predict whether the customer will be repeating the call for a different reason, the agent can take a better shot at pointing to a few e-resources for the customers' self-help based on the nature of a call. Let's say if the call is identified for a slow Internet connection issue and in most cases, a slow Internet issue call is followed up by a billing issue call, then the agent can educate the customer about self-help resources to get additional billing assistance. These measures can further help reduce a repeat call.

The same vanilla test and control methods can be used to assess the effectiveness of the machine learning models and the agent's performance to reduce the repeat calls from customers. The process can be implemented by selecting an appropriate test and control group of customers and later studying the effectiveness of the experiment using a comparative study.

# Staff training for increasing first call resolution rate

Improving the agent's skillsets to handle the call better within the same call will also help reduce repeat calls. Staff training is an expensive deal and therefore it can also be experimented on using a test and control analysis method.

Prescriptive analytics is an iterative and exhaustive step with numerous experiments to improve the outcome. In the cases of business disasters, the luxury of test and control will not always be an option. In such cases, historic patterns and heuristics are used to conclude the chances of the experiment to succeed and the experiment is rolled out to all the affected operations at once.

# Tying back results to data-driven and heuristic-driven hypotheses

In decision science, the problem solving exercise is a continuous process. This can be evident from the problem universe diagram that we saw in the previous section. Each of those smaller problems can again be broken into multiple smaller problems and connected to a plethora of another set of problems. At every step, we become more aware about the nature of the problem; that is, it gradually moves from the **muddy** phase to the **fuzzy** phase. The more aware we are about the problem, the more means we have to solve the problem. At this point, if we revisit the data-driven hypotheses (DDH) matrix and heuristic-driven hypotheses (HDH) matrix, we will see the scope of a small improvement in all dimensions. We can probably articulate better hypotheses, and we can see more granular ways to slice and dice the data. Studying the results again from the data-driven hypotheses test, we can interpret the results better and all in all we would feel that if we would now solve the problem, we can solve it better. Many times, we will tangibly see the benefits of iterating through the problem solving exercise and therefore iterate in a quick-fashioned way through the entire problem solving journey. With the iteration, the solution for the problem definitely witnesses an incremental improvement.

The trigger for the iteration in this journey to eventually improve the outcome and solving the problem happens when we tie back our results and learn while revisiting the HDH and DDH. The convergence of HDH and DDH and revisiting the matrix is a crucial point in the decision science life cycle. All major innovations and breakthroughs have been observed while revisiting the solution journey; in our case, we have a structure and a simplified journey path articulated in a well-versed problem solving framework, that is, the HDH and DDH matrix.

Let's assume that we have the problem solving framework for the current use case designed similar to the ones that we designed in the use cases we solved in the previous chapters. When we reach the prescriptive analytics phase, we will have touched base on many new hypotheses and smaller problems than we would have in the beginning. Tying back these results to the framework helps the problem evolve better. This is true for every problem solved in the industry. The following image depicts the flow of the problem through different phases:

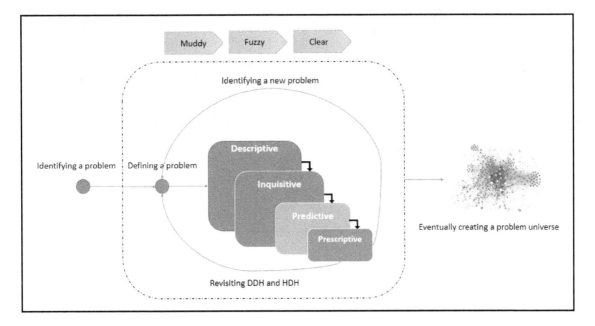

We can see that, as we progress through prescriptive analytics after an iteration of problem solving, we will either revisit the DDH and HDH (defining a problem) or even identify a new problem. Iterating through this cycle using the problem solving framework helps us solve our problem faster and in a structured and more matured fashion.

When a new problem is identified in this process, it often has an association with the root problem. It could be either a small problem derived from the current problem or a completely different problem but still associated with the current problem. Designing the problem universe, that is, an interconnected network of problems, is again a new problem. We need to identify and assess the association of the newly identified problem with the current problem by understanding the impact and its priority. In some cases, it may make sense to pause solving the current problem and move on to the newly associated problem because, without solving that, the current problem would hit a roadblock. Let's study in brief the interconnected nature of the problems in the problem universe.

# Connecting the dots in the problem universe

If we take a look at the problem universe that we designed for our telecom giant's use case, we can see that we have identified multiple problems. A few are basically the hypotheses that we might have missed while brainstorming for HDH; additionally, due to limited visibility of the domain, we might have missed out during the creation of DDH. After reaching prescriptive analytics, we would have ideally finished one complete iteration of the problem. At this point, we will have reinforced our understanding about the problem and domain better. We can leverage this to improve the problem further with another round of iteration, but in some cases, we might find out a few new problems that are completely different from the current problem we are trying to solve. For our use case, refer to the following problem universe:

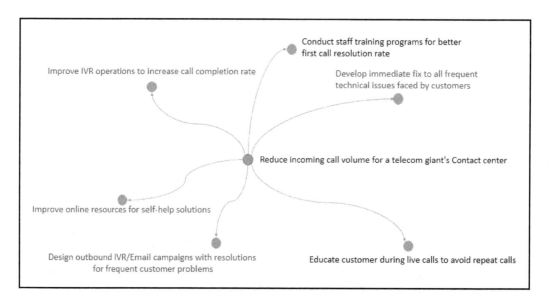

The problems highlighted in red are actually new problems. Staff training and customer education are smaller problems that can be categorized as enhancements to the current problem for which we can revisit the DDH and HDH. However, the other four are new problems that have some association with the current problem. For instance, improving online resources for self-help is a completely different problem where we would deal with the website, the Android and iPhone app, the user experience and design, and understand customer navigation journey and website aesthetics. It requires the intersection of new disciplines such as design thinking and behavioral science to study the user's behavior on the website and so on. Solving this problem eventually has an impact on reducing the incoming call volume but in itself is a completely different problem.

Similarly, the other nodes, that is, 'Fixing technical issues' is more of a networking and hardware problem, designing outbound IVR and e-mail campaigns is a marketing problem, and so on. The true fact that all problems are interconnected in nature can be clearly studied from the preceding example. The biggest hurdle that we face in such a scenario is understanding what to prioritize. We are in a position where we can see the scope to improve the current problem further as well as solve multiple new connected problems. In such a situation, teams take a pause and prioritize on the available options. Here, solving all of them is important but it may not be possible to solve all of them simultaneously, so where do we start from?

A significant amount of domain knowledge and business sense will be required to take a call in such situations. Teams work out on the immediate benefits and opportunity in each new problem after each step. A small focus is spent on enhancing the current problem, and a major focus is invested on solving a new problem that has the biggest impact. With reference to our use case, we have identified four new problems:

- Fixing the technical issues frequently faced by customers
- Improving the IVR operations to increase the call completion rate
- Improving online resources to aid in self-help solutions
- Designing outbound IVR and e-mail campaigns with resolutions to the frequent customer complaints

The list is not exhaustive but covers the high-level areas that can be touched base on right after one iteration in the problem. With the limited business and domain knowledge we have, we can assess and prioritize the preceding four new problems. Let's say that Mark's team has 10 decision scientists on board and at a time at least 4-5 members are available for a project, that is, solving one problem; we can say that Mark's team has the bandwidth to solve two problems simultaneously. We now need to prioritize the problems in such a way that they do not cause a deadlock. Let's say that we choose Improving IVR operations with the highest priority, but midway realize that this problem has a huge dependency on another problem we identified earlier, then we reach a deadlock where one team or the other would need to halt operations till the dependency is over.

Assigning priority is a mammoth task and is generally done after thorough discussions and analysis. For the preceding use case, we can say that the highest priority is to fix the ground fundamental issues, that is, the issues casing network outages, slow Internet speed, and call drop-offs. Once we have the fundamental problem solved, we can work toward improving the IVR operations, then improve online resources for self-help, and finally design a robust outbound campaign to resolve the issues in an automated way. The priority assigned is based on the limited context provided for the use case. Real-life complications are gargantuan. The problem universe will never be like the simplified version that we have drafted.

Connecting the dots in the problem universe is the art of prioritizing the problems and enhancements to be solved first. It will be a rare scenario where the business will have the bandwidth to solve all problems simultaneously. Designing a problem universe in such a way that the associations and priority can be sensed in a glance makes solving the problem easier. The following image depicts a simplified problem universe where one can interpret the priority and level of association between interconnected problems:

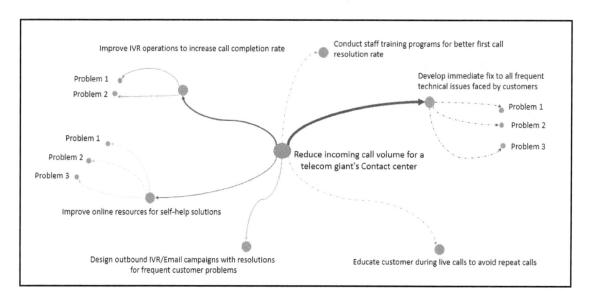

As we can see, it is visually intuitive to make sense while connecting the dots. The association strength can be visualized using the weight of the edge, and the color of the edge can be used to denote the priority of the problem-red with the maximum priority and blue with the least. Dashed edges are used to indicate enhancements where we need to revisit the DDH and HDH whereas a solid line identifies new problems. Using this simplistic visualization, an intuitive view of the problem universe can be depicted to aid in easy consumption while connecting the dots.

# Story boarding – Making sense of the interconnected problems in the problem universe

The problem solving journey is very long and iterative in nature. Once we have designed a version of the problem universe, we will have a fair understanding that solving the problem will definitely take much longer than we anticipated. The process being iterative in nature doesn't mean that seeing tangible results should take time. It becomes increasingly important to evaluate the value from results derived so far and the results expected in the roadmap designed.

In decision science, storyboarding (the art of conveying the results in the most lucid way) is of paramount importance. In fact, it is in any problem, but here when we have a holistic view of the problem, we know that the problem keeps evolving. At every step, it becomes increasingly important to realize the value delivered and the value that will be delivered by solving the connected problems. Storyboarding requires drafting the results in a sequence such that it is simple yet intuitive and can be consumed by any stakeholder involved in the project.

Adding **dollar value** to each milestone and showcasing the impact in pure numbers will add an altogether different taste to the story.

Let's consider our telecom use case to understand this. We are currently at a point where we have completed one iteration of the problem solving exercise and traversed through the length and breadth of the problem solving stack in decision science; that is, we traversed through the descriptive + inquisitive + predictive + prescriptive phase of decision science. We have drafted a version of the problem universe and designed a minimalistic version of the problem universe. We have connected the dots and have a fair understanding of the next steps. We now need to represent our findings and results in a way that it captures the value and provides enough meat for the next phase to be executed. Mark would need to provide answers to the leadership team and his company to take the solution ahead.

 Fixing technical issues such as network congestion and call drops has been ignored in the following story as these actions are beyond the scope of the customer experience team.

We'll try to formulate the dollar value and opportunity in our use case and the roadmap based on a few assumptions. Let's assume that the cost of handling one call for an average duration by an average paid agent is $7. We have approximately one MN calls a month at present and around 12 MN calls annually. Therefore, the annual expenses would be around $84 MN.

With the current scenario-8-10% MoM increase in calls-we will see the monthly call volume reach 1.5 MN by the end of the sixth month and a net increase of >two MN calls; that is, if there were one MN calls per month in the next six months, the total call volume would be around six MN. However, with an average 8-10% increase in calls every month, we would have a total of ~8.2 MN instead of six MN. Therefore, the additional 2.2 MN calls will result in an increased operational cost of $15 MN (assuming that the cost of each call is $7). Our immediate objective is to reduce the losses that will be incurred due to the increased call volume and improve operational expenses.

We have identified a few areas for improvement and identified the next steps for the roadmap. We now need to draft the dollar opportunity that we can seize with the current results and how we can do so with our roadmap. Consider the total call volume for the next six months, that is, 8.2 MN calls (worst case). A major call volume is building up due to the increasing repeat call rate. We see around 25% of the total call volume as repeat calls from a customer that translates to 25% of 8.2 MN, that is, ~2 MN calls costing more than $14 MN operational expenses. Therefore, our immediate opportunity is to reduce the $14 MN expenses from the repeat calls.

# Step 1 – Immediate

We have built a machine learning technique that can predict in real time whether the customer will repeat call in the next 48 hours. Furthermore, we will be able to predict whether he will repeat for the same reason or a different reason. With such a model in place, the agent who is answering live calls will be able to take a better attempt at avoiding a repeat call. Let's say that we will be able to reduce around 60% of the repeat calls with this method in place. This translates to 60% of two MN calls, that is, 1.2 MN calls, that is, $8.6 MN.

# Step 2 – Future

In an attempt to further reduce the incoming calls received, we plan to improve the IVR call completion rate. This will result in more and more number of calls getting resolved within the IVR without the agent needed to answer the call. With new improvements to the IVR, we can expect around 25% reduction in the overall call volume. So instead of seven MN calls for the next six months (7 MN = 8.2 MN – 1.2 MN:= the repeat calls reduced from step 1), we can expect a reduction of ~1.75 MN calls (25%).

Similarly, with even more long-term plans-improving online resources and setting up outbound campaigns-we can expect an additional 15% reduction in the calls, that is, 15% of 5.2 MN (7 MN – 1.75 MN = 5.2 MN), which translates to ~0.8 MN calls.

All in all, we have an immediate opportunity to reduce the call volume from 8.2 MN to 7 MN calls with the repeat propensity prediction for a customer in real time, that is, 1.2 MN calls = $8.6 MN.

With our future plans in place and expecting a moderate outcome, we can seize an opportunity to reduce minimum 1.75 MN +0.8 MN calls in the incoming traffic by improving the IVR operations and online resources for the customer's self-help. Therefore, we have an opportunity to save 1.75 MN +0.8 MN = 2.5 MN calls x $7 = ~$18 MN. With our business benefits drafted neatly, we can now pitch the story. Mark can use this strong use case and benefits to convince the leadership team and CEO about the problem solution and next steps.

The entire use case can be simplified in a simple story as follows:

The customer experience team has studied increasing call traffic from customers in the past few months that has increased the operational expenses and also affected the consumer experience. The team analyzed the various causes for the problem and understood that the core reason for high call volume is mainly the increasing repeat call rate. The team leveraged various forecasting and predictive techniques and studied that the call volumes are expected to increase by 8-10% every month for the next six months. With such a heavy surge in call volumes, the business expects to see additional 2.2 MN calls costing more than a $15 MN increase in operational expenses.

The team has proactively developed immediate measures to reduce the repeat call rate by ~60% in the next months, which reduces the operational expenses by $8.6 MN, and has laid down concrete plans to further reduce operational expenses by $18.6 using a variety of strategies to reduce call volumes by improving IVR operations and online resources for a customer's self-help. The roadmap to solve the issue will not only help reduce the expected increase in operational expenses, but will further reduce the cost than the current call volume without compromising on consumer experience.

The story can be visually interpreted using the following simple flow diagram:

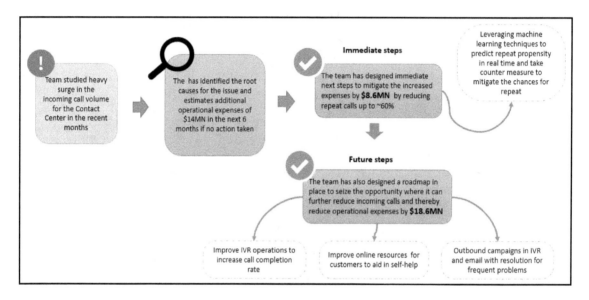

This storyboarding exercise will help Mark win his leadership team approval for his strategy. Here, we have kept all the details very simple yet intuitive for the business stakeholders to consume. The storyboarding exercise needs execution after every milestone in the problem solving journey. A milestone can be considered the end of an iteration in the solution stack, as we finished for our use case. Based on the storyboard, we can further contemplate whether the benefits of the roadmap designed will be valuable for execution or require modifications.

# Implementing the solution

The final step in our problem solving journey is to implement the solution. We discussed about the implementation that would roll out immediately as per our plan; that is, developing a solution where the agent will be notified in real time whether a customer will repeat the call in the next 48 hours. To make the solution more actionable, we can design an association rule table that will calculate the association between different call reasons (categories). This will come in handy when the agent is notified that the customer will repeat in the next 48 hours for a different call reason. The association rule table can then be leveraged by the agent to understand the most probable reason for the repeat call and then take additional steps to mitigate the chances of a repeat.

Once we have all the previous steps in place, implementing the solution is just following the steps we designed as a part of our journey, that is, solving a business use case end-to-end. When we finish one end-to-end iteration, we traverse through all the stages of the decision science life cycle, once. At the end of the iteration, we define the roadmap for the next journey; that is, we implement the current solution and get ready to evolve the solution with the problem.

Reflecting on the entire process in the journey, we can be confident about the clarity of thought that we have in order to move ahead. We know exactly what are we solving, why we are solving it, and how we are solving it. With the storyboarding exercise that we have, the entire journey formulated into the most concise format that can be consumed by every business stakeholder in the most lucid way. With this, Mark would get a green signal from his company to go ahead and so the process finishes part one and moves on to part two and so on.

# Summary

In this chapter, we touched base on the final stage of the problem solving journey-prescriptive analytics. We borrowed a hypothetical use case from the customer experience team of a telecom industry. To solve the problem, we leveraged the layered approach in problem solving and quickly traversed through the descriptive, inquisitive, and predictive path. You then learned about prescriptive analytics and saw how it can be leveraged to enhance the outcome and answer the questions: So what, now what?

To learn the decision making process in decision science, we studied how the problems iterate in reality and how we can solve them better by revisiting the DDH and HDH matrix in our problem solving framework. We further studied how problems are interconnected in nature and how the evolution of a problem can be studied, captured, and proactively solved in a structured way by designing the problem universe and connecting the dots to make more sense of the problem. Finally, we studied how to confidently draft an intuitive yet lucid story to represent our findings and next steps designed as a part of the roadmap to solve the ever-evolving interconnected problem.

Therefore, so far we have explored all the phases of decision science and learned how to solve problems for the Internet of Things industry using multiple use cases. In each use case, we touched base with different types of analytical techniques used in decision science- Descriptive, Inquisitive, Predictive, and finally Prescriptive. You also learned how to tackle the problem while it progresses through its own life cycle-muddy to fuzzy to a clear state.

In the next chapter, we will learn about the disruptions in the industry with Internet of Things. We will discuss in brief how IoT has instrumented a revolution in fog computing, cognitive computing, and a few other areas.

# 8
# Disruptions in IoT

With the Internet of Things paradigm sensing increasing penetration in every industrial vertical, we have witnessed phenomenal disruptions in the IoT fraternity. Success stories are shooting up in every industrial vertical by demonstrating the value and potential of IoT. Artificial intelligence, machine learning, deep learning, robotics, genomics, cognitive computing, fog computing, edge computing, smart factory, and a plethora of other disruptions have emerged with IoT. We have directly or indirectly benefited from these disruptions while leveraging the innovations in technology used in our daily chores. As time progresses, we can affirmatively expect to scale this even better.

Connected assets and connected operations have now become a reality, and we will see disruptions in IoT with the convergence of innovation from multiple disciplines. To name a few, the increasing volume of data has fostered the growth of deep learning in IoT, edge computing or fog computing has boosted the development of state-of-art smart assets, and human thinking and machine intelligence together have disrupted new areas in industrial and healthcare IoT. We have witnessed all the sci-fi fantasies we saw in the movies a decade back now becoming a reality. In this chapter, you will learn in brief about a few of the disruptions in IoT due to the convergence of innovations from other disciplines.

You'll learn the following topics in brief:

- Edge/fog computing – exploring the fog computing model
- Cognitive computing – disruptive intelligence from unstructured data
- Next-generation robotics and genomics
- Autonomous cars
- Privacy and security in the IoT ecosystem

# Edge/fog computing

The topic of fog computing has been getting a lot of traction in recent years. The concept has been in the research and experimental phase for quite some time, but with the recent growth of IoT, edge computing has starting evolving from the "Innovation Trigger" phase to the "Peak of inflated expectation" phase (referring to Gartner's Hype cycle). The edge computing concept got such phenomenal traction that Cisco coined the term fog computing as an inspiration from the legacy architecture of cloud computing.

Let's understand the **fog computing** concept in layman terms**.**

Edge computing/fog computing is an architecture where the computing of data, applications, and services is pushed away from the centralized cloud to the logical extremes of the network, that is, the **edge**. This approach requires leveraging resources that may not be continuously connected to a network such as laptops, smartphones, tablets, home appliances, manufacturing industrial machines, sensors, and so on. There are a variety of other names for the edge computing architecture such as mesh computing, peer-to-peer computing, grid computing, and so on.

In the cloud computing architecture, the centralized server takes care of the entire computing required for the application or device. However, with the IoT ecosystem, following the same principle becomes increasingly cumbersome. Try to recollect the logical stack of IoT that we studied in Chapter 1, *IoT and Decision Science* which is the IoT ecosystem can be logically decomposed into four components-Data, Things, People, and Processes. In the data dimension, we are aware that, even though gargantuan volumes of data is being generated from the connected devices, most of this data is transient in nature; that is, the value of the data is lost within a couple of minutes after generation. Therefore, the art of processing this data to extract value from the data as soon as it is produced and storing it for various analytical needs is altogether a different discipline.

Processing the data and extracting intelligent signals from it requires computing to be pushed to the local nodes-devices. These devices are equipped with the minimum required computing power and data storage facility to aid in the process. After computing, only the rich and condensed yet reusable data is transmitted back to the cloud. If we would have continued leveraging cloud computing in the IoT ecosystem, scaling the solutions and infrastructure would have become an immediate bottleneck while keeping it a viable process. Moreover, with the cloud computing architecture in place, transmitting such a huge volume of data from the devices to the cloud and then processing and extracting data for all devices would choke the network and require mammoth storage and computing resources. Additionally, the data volumes are expected to double in a very short while. Cloud computing would clearly not be a viable option for the IoT ecosystem, and that's where a more viable and innovative solution was conceptualized that favors immensely for the IoT architecture.

With fog computing in place, the computing power is pushed toward the extreme logical ends, thereby making the devices self-sustained to a certain extent in taking smart decisions. The storage and computing load on the centralized server can be reduced to a fraction and results can be achieved faster as communication is also blazing fast, as only rich and condensed data is sent to the server. With the disruption of fog computing in IoT, we have witnessed a variety of new threads that have triggered innovation.

The following image demonstrates the fog computing architecture:

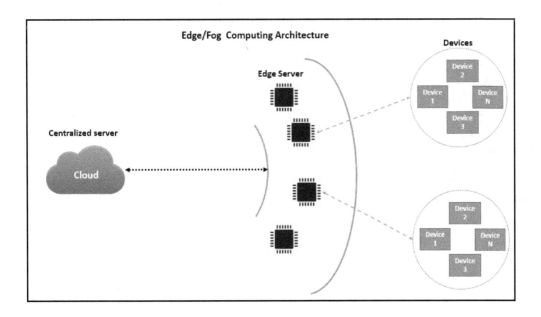

As we can see, multiple devices are clustered together to form a smaller network that is connected to a single computing node. In some cases, a single device is allotted to a single computing node rather than a cluster. We'll explore the fog computing model in detail with a hypothetical use case and learn how IoT has embraced fog computing to deliver the state-of-art smart connected devices, but first, let's cement our foundations of fog computing using a very lucid example.

Let's assume that your mobile phone has a fitness application that keeps track of the number of calories you burn in a day and gives you a daily report about how many calories were burnt along with some statistics compared to your goal and historic performance. It does so by calculating the number of steps you walk in a day. Your phone is equipped with a variety of sensors such as a pedometer, accelerometer, and so on. These sensors can capture data for every granular movement of the phone; that is, at a microsecond level, the x and y coordinates of the phone can be captured.

Finding how many steps you walked in a day can be studied by capturing a pattern in the sequence of the x and y coordinates. Let's say that the phone is in your pocket while you walk; there is a slight uplift in the y coordinate while the x axis moves ahead. The plot of the coordinate data from the sensors in the phone will form a pattern to detect a complete cycle of walk. Using these patterns, we can count the number of steps walked by the user. The following diagram illustrates this idea:

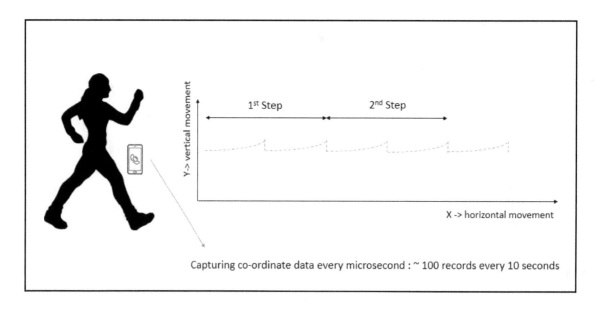

Now, if we try to think from a simple cloud computing perspective, the process would have been to collect the entire log of data from the pedometer-~50 MB for one day and send it across to the cloud server. The server then analyzes the data, detects the number of steps walked, converts it to the number of calories burnt using some business rule, and sends the results back to the mobile phone. If there are approximately 500 MN users, the volume of data required to be sent to the cloud through the network and processed on the cloud can take the network and computing and storage resources for a toss. However, if we use the fog computing architecture, the mobile phone's internal computing power and storage resources can be used to count the number of steps every 30 minutes of activity and discard the granular log data. At the end of the day, the application on the smartphone can send the aggregated sum of the number of steps walked by the user that would be around <<1 KB in size.

Therefore, we can not only reduce the load on the centralized server, but also efficiently use the existing resources to make a smarter and viable solution. The name fog computing was used to get a sense of cloud computing extended to the edge like actual fog on Earth.

# Exploring the fog computing model

Now that we have a fair understanding about fog computing, let's study a hypothetical use case to understand how it works in a real-life scenario and what benefits it adds to the IoT ecosystem. Fog computing, apart from making the cloud architecture scalable, adds a plethora of benefits such as making the device connected to the network smarter in a revolutionary way. We have been loosely defining the term 'smart devices'. In a simplified way, we can define a smart device as a device that can take decisions on its own to improve a particular outcome. For example, a smart AC that adjusts the room's temperature based on the number of people present and the ambient conditions. It may also power off the operations on its own to save energy consumption. These are basically decisions taken by the device on its own by learning a couple of events and leveraging historic data. We refer to these devices as **smart devices.**

Let's consider a use case from the manufacturing industry similar to the one we studied earlier. Let's say that a large manufacturing firm has a plant setup in India to manufacture detergent. The manufacturing process can be assumed to be similar to the use case considered in Chapter 3, *The What and Why – Using Exploratory Decision Science for IoT* which was a five-stage process where raw materials are added and processed at each stage and the final output is collected from the last stage-stage 5. In each stage, there are different machines that are used for the processing of raw materials, say a large industrial mixer that will mix all the added raw materials together or a heater that will heat all the ingredients together.

Consider one such machine from the entire process, say a mixer (vertical or horizontal mixer), a machine that ingests different raw materials and mixes them to produce a resultant mixture for the manufacturing process. The operation of the mixer would be that it mixes the different raw materials ingested by spinning the drum at a predefined velocity for a definite time. This machine consumes a finite amount of energy for its operations.

What if we make this device a '**smart mixer**' leveraging the IoT ecosystem?

If we recollect the manufacturing use case studied earlier, we can understand that the use case is already an IoT use case. A plethora of sensors are deployed to capture data for a variety of parameters that are then sent to the server (cloud) for further analysis. We studied earlier how we can leverage decision science and IoT to solve the problem of improving the quality of the detergent produced. Let's take a small part of the use case a little further by making the machines used for the process 'smarter'.

The mixer that we have considered for the use case consumes high power for its operations. How do we improve the efficiency of power consumption?

This is where we touch base with **fog computing.**

Previously, the IoT architecture that we considered was leveraging the cloud to store and analyze the data for decisions, but to make the asset/machine a 'smart machine', we need to embrace the fog computing architecture; that is, adding the ability to compute the real-time data streams locally and learn from historical signals to aid the machines in taking decisions to improve an outcome. So what would be this outcome? Consider the scenario where we are building a fog computing network by leveraging machine learning to optimize the power consumption of the machine. Therefore, the machine will have the understanding to take actions based on the current set of events to improve the outcome, power consumption. The following image helps in visualizing the operations of the mixer:

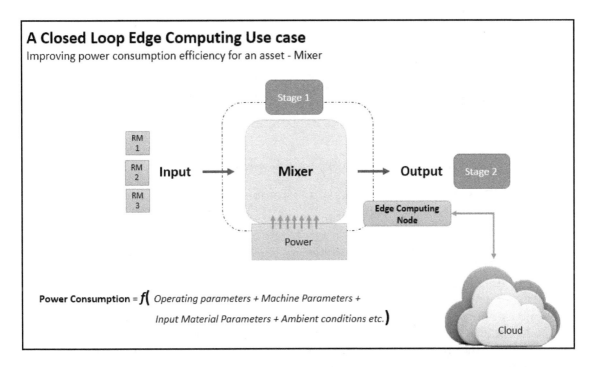

## A Closed Loop Edge Computing Use case
Improving power consumption efficiency for an asset - Mixer

**Power Consumption** = $f($ *Operating parameters + Machine Parameters +*
*Input Material Parameters + Ambient conditions etc.* $)$

As we can see, the mixer receives an input of different raw materials (RM1, RM2, and RM3) used for the manufacturing process. The mixer then mixes the raw materials to form a consolidated mixture by spinning the drub for a finite time at a predefined velocity. The power consumption generally increases with the increased quantity of the input, time of operation, speed at which the machine is operating, and so on. The interesting part here is that we can improve power consumption of the machine as a function of a variety of parameters than we can imagine. In a nutshell, we can develop a machine learning model that can **predict the consumption of power** as a function of the *operational parameters* such as torque, vibrations, rpm of the drum, temperature of the machine, pressure, and so on, machine parameters, *input raw material parameters* such as quality parameters and quantity parameters, and finally ambient conditions. It is certain that the power consumption patterns will be seen differently under a different set of values for the considered parameters.

We can build the algorithm as follows:

Power consumption = function (Operational parameters + Machine parameters + ambient conditions + raw material parameters)

The algorithm can be developed by learning from the historic data stored in the cloud. Once the algorithm is built, it can be deployed to the edge network where it can run in real time to take decisions based on the learnings. The algorithm will be used to create a set of self-learning equations that can then be leveraged to take self-decisions.

This self-learning would be something like the following (an oversimplified representation):

- Temperature between x1 and x2 and Torque > x3 and ..., then power consumption = y1 := optimum
- Temperature > x4 and ..., then power consumption = y2 := 30% above optimum
- Reduce temperature to x1 and x2

Based on these self-learning rules, the machine can adjust the operating parameters by increasing or decreasing the settings to stay in the optimum power consumption mode. The rules and learnings can be updated once in a while when the data is sent to the cloud and the cloud updates the machine learning model using the new datasets. Once updated, it is pushed back to the edge, and the edge nodes then leverage the updated model to update the rules and further improve the outcome.

Today, we can witness fog computing on a more realistic scale in most personal computing devices such as laptops, smartphones, smartwatches, and tablets. The most common example would be the Windows 10 restart scheduler. After the updates are automatically downloaded, the system studies the user's usage pattern to understand the most appropriate time to restart the system and install the updates. The time when the user usually has his laptop on but has the least activity is studied and the intelligent decision to restart and install the updates is initiated. In the manufacturing and engineering industries, fog computing in IoT is slowly picking up.

Therefore, leveraging the edge computing architecture, computing is pushed to the edge nodes (logical extremes of the network) and this gives the machine the ability to sense real-time data and take instant actions to mitigate business losses. In the preceding use case, improving power consumption is just one of the possible outcomes to improve. Edge computing can be used to do a variety of enhancements in real time such as mitigating asset failure or improving output quality. Say, a rule has been learned that if the temperature increases beyond x1, vibrations increase beyond x2, and the machine operates in this state for over 10 continuous minutes, then the chances that the machine will break down will be 80% or a rule that states the optimum operational setting to get the best quality output from the raw materials. Based on the rule, the machine will automatically take a decision to change the operational settings to outlive the disaster or improve the quality of the outcome. In a nutshell, by pushing computing to the edge, we push intelligence also to the edge, thereby making devices or assets able to take self-decisions to improve an outcome and become smart devices.

# Cognitive Computing – Disrupting intelligence from unstructured data

As we see evolution in connectivity, computing, and technologies, we see disruptions continuing in the industry. IoT has been a blessed recipient of many disruptions due to its charm. We have lately seen the evolution of cognitive computing in the IoT ecosystem.

Cognitive computing can be defined as the third era of computing where it solves problems that have increased complexity and uncertainty, that is, the human kind of a problem. To solve such problems, the systems have been designed to mimic the way the humans solve a problem.

So on a general note, how do we learn? Humans learn from experiences. At any point of time, there is a flow of information that we consume from the world. We learn how to react to new situations based on our historic learnings; we teach ourselves how to learn. The simplest evidence for this can be, say you are asked to solve a puzzle that you have never heard before. How do you solve it? You think and recollect your understanding about the situation, analyze the different paths you can take, and then finally choose the best one based on some factor, say the confidence that the solution is the best. In such scenarios, your brain continues to learn based on the new problems it has been exposed to. The more and more diverse problems you have faced, the more you learn. Such problems are called human problems as there is an extremely high amount of complexity, ambiguity, and uncertainty to solve them.

Machines have never been designed to solve such problems. Every machine designed will be solving a specific problem that will have complete clarity in its nature. For example,, a car can only be used to drive from one point to another by a driver. It can never decide the route to be taken on its own (ignore autonomous cars for the time being).

However, today we can take the same human approach for computers, that is, design computers to learn on their own without explicit programming. Cognitive computing is therefore called the **third era of computing**. The first era was made of tabulating machines like the calculator, then came the second era where we could program the computer to do a specific task. Finally, now we have the third era of computing where we can design computers to solve problems by self-learning.

# So how does cognitive computing work?

Designing cognitive computing requires massive computing power. The legacy systems, where we leverage machine learning and deep learning techniques to predict a regression line or classify an object was a very specific problem. To a certain extent, we need to define the scope of the problem and substantiate enough data for the machine to learn to predict. Moreover, this prediction is limited to the nature of the problem defined. An algorithm designed to predict the sales for an organization will not be able to predict whether a cancer patient will survive or not.

In cognitive computing, the system is designed in a way to learn how a human brain works by mimicking how a brain works. The brain receives tons of information through its five senses and learns how to react to different situations. Say, you accidentally touch the vessel while making tea and burn your hands; the next time you would automatically be more cautious as you have learned the implications. The event may be completely new, but has now registered in your mind and will probably help you react in an improved way even in a different scenario. Similarly, the computer also receives a vast pool of structured and unstructured data and a continuous stream of events. It tries to find insights and learnings by starting with a simple hypothesis and then validating the hypothesis using the data it has access to. In process of validating the hypothesis, it may come across a counterintuitive result; it will learn from these results and create a self-learning repository. Such systems become increasingly beneficial for our daily activities. The overall process of cognitive computing can be simplified with the following image:

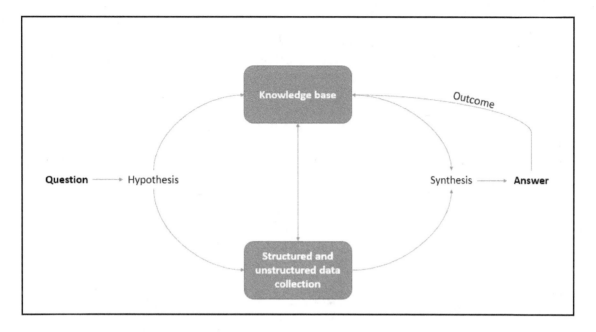

It starts with a simple question that might be triggered with an event, that is, sensing something new. The question is decomposed into a simplified hypothesis and if it is already learned, the actions are synthesized and articulated for the scenarios leveraging the knowledge base, and the result is drafted. The result can be a set of actions or an information showcase. However, if the hypotheis has never been learned or validated in history, the system reaches out to the vast pool of structured and unstructured data to validate the hypothesis and find the best results. The learnings are then stored in the knowledge base so as to help in future. The results are syntehsized and an actioable outcome is drafted. The outcome, if not in sync with the expectation, is passed back to the knowledge base.

To cement our understanding even further, the entire concept of cognitive computing can be juxtaposed with a daily life use case. Refer to the preceding digram and juxtapose the following components to the working of a cognitive computing example.

Let's assume that one day you develop a minor health issue, say an upset stomach (**Question**). You are now trying to understand how to ease your pain. You try and recollect in the past that you encountered a similar pain and the doctor prescribed medicine A, which is readily available in the pharmacy store (**KnowledgeBase**). You quickly reach to the store to purchase it. After consuming a tablet, you take a nap for your stomach to get better (**Synthesis** to **Action**). An hour passes by, but you still don't feel good. You try to recollect what you had for dinner yesterday, but you don't remember anything unusual. By now, you have also starting feeling vomiting sensations and a headache (**Outcome**). You reach out to the Internet to understand more about the situation and study that the symptoms are indicating a viral fever spreading quickly in the vicinity (**collection of unstructured and structure data**). You now know that the fever is due to the sudden climactic change and many friends in your neighborhood are also experiencing the same. You now reach out to a doctor for proper medications. You take the prescribed medications and get well in a while. Now you know that there is a chance of your body having a headache and upset stomach whenever there is a sudden climactic change (**Knowledge base**).

# Where do we see the use of cognitive computing?

The uses of cognitive computing are expected to see a wide adoption in the IoT ecosystem across industry verticals such as consumer products, healthcare, manufacturing, and so on. To understand the uses, we'll consider a very simple example. Let's assume that you are a working professional who uses a variety of smart connected devices in the IoT ecosystem. Let's get a little more sci-fi; assume that your phone has an app like Google Now or Apple Siri and can talk to you based on events. Let me walk you through a story where you can experience phenomenal value from cognitive computing in IoT and later, we'll try to understand in brief how it worked.

# The story

You wake up early morning to go to your office. Your smartwatch notifies you that your **deep sleep** time has increased by 20% due to the exercises you did during the week. You feel fresh and go through your normal chores and leave for office on time. While you step out of your house, the electricity goes into **power saver mode**. When you board your car, the screen on the car dashboard notifies you that the usual route you take to office has heavy traffic congestion and suggests an alternative route. You don't like traffic and therefore opt for the alternative but longer route. When you are in your car, it knows it's you. It sets the AC to your preferred setting, reads out the local news for the day from your preferred news channels, automatically adjusts the seat as you like, and plays songs from your favorite music station. You are still driving and your smartwatch has detected that you missed having your breakfast today. The phone locates your coordinates and suggests the best breakfast places on your way. As you always prefer South Indian food for breakfast, the suggestion has listed all popular South Indian hotels for you. You park your car and enter the hotel to order your regular choice; instantly your phone reminds you about the 'Power Tuesday offer' available at the restaurant on new varieties. You give the new dishes a shot and thoroughly enjoy them. While billing, you don't use cash; the application in your phone automatically selects the best credit card you have with the best offers for the deal and completes the transaction. You reach office and start working on your assignment and head back home for lunch as it is half-day at office. While heading back, you take another new route based on the suggestions to avoid traffic. Midway, you get notified about the happening places you can explore. You are a photography enthusiast and therefore your phone notifies you about a very famous and beautiful church on the way. It collects the reviews online and also tells you about your friends who had been there and their opinions. You find it interesting and so you stop by. You are amazed by the beauty of the place and use your phone to capture memories. When you finally reach home, you see that the lights and AC had been powered off in your absence to save electricity. As you enter, all the settings are initiated to make you feel comfortable. You switch on the TV and enjoy a football match with some noodles for lunch.

What a comfortable life, isn't it?

# The bigger question is, how does all of this happen?

The answer is simple-it learns on its own. We have already witnessed many of these innovations in our daily life. If you use an Android phone, you would have noticed that it understands your daily route to the office and the time at which you travel. Triangulating traffic and GPS data, it notifies you about better alternatives you can take. The flight tickets in your mail are automatically read and it notifies you about the time when you should leave your place to reach the airport on time. It also triangulates a multitude of information from the web and other sources to find out whether your flight is delayed and so on. When you land at your destination, it recommends the best hotels nearby, weather forecast, and important places to visit.

Let's take a pause and try to understand how different things we saw in our sci-fi story can actually happen. Today, we are living in a connected world. Directly or indirectly, we are connected to so many things that we don't realize it. Our attachments to the smartphone alone is enough to identify the kind of person we are and predict what we do on a daily basis. Our attachment to the digital world is so deep that our behavior can be easily studied with the data that is captured through our interaction with the digital world. Let's take a step-by-step approach to understand how cognitive computing decodes the different innovations on its own.

Your smartphone/smartwatch is aware about how you sleep. When you are in deep sleep, your eye movements, the motion of the body, pulse of the body, and tons of other parameters behave very differently when compared to you simply lying on the bed. Tracking your behavior throughout the day, the smartwatch understands whether you are in **deep sleep** or lying on the bed. The sensors installed in every room of your house is able to understand the presence of a person, and triangulating this information with your smartphone/smartwatch's presence, it understands it's you. Your periodic movements and routine tasks show a pattern. Your house is now pretty much aware about when it can expect you to step out of your house. You take the same route to office, say a 10 Km drive on the highway. Your smartphone understands that you travel on the same route to your destination on a daily basis. It automatically understands the time when you travel and the time taken to travel. When it finds heavy traffic on your daily route, it proactively searches for alternative routes that will take you to your destination. Your car can also understand your presence and has studied the kind of adjustments you usually set for the AC, music system, seat, and so on. It automatically sets it up for you and shows the latest news from the collections that you usually browse on your phone or tablet. Your phone studies the kind of places and restaurants you visit for breakfast, lunch, and dinner. It also understands that you like South Indian restaurants than other cuisines as you often visit them more. As you travel, whenever popular restaurants are located nearby, it notifies you about the choices.

The process is simple; cognitive computing tries to learn on its own like any human would do. You go to church every Sunday in the evening; it finds a pattern that around 4 P.M., you leave from your place and travel to a particular location on every Sunday. The next time the time of the day matches, it will notify you about the best time to leave from your place to reach on time. It has learned that there is a pattern that it finds interesting. It tries to validate the hypothesis using historic data and learns about the result. The next time it finds a suitable scenario to utilize these learnings, it will use them. Cognitive computing is now deeply integrated with the voice assistive applications you use on your smartphone like Siri and Google Now. The more you use them, the more they are adapted to help you.

# Next generation robotics and genomics

With increasing innovations in the industry due to IoT and other fields, every field senses a new growth dimension in some way or other. With IoT booming, we saw edge computing picking up in the industry. Edge computing played a pivotal role in industrial IoT, enhancing a machine's operational efficiency and adding various other benefits. Edge computing not only fostered the innovations in industrial IoT, but also cemented the foundations for cognitive computing. Cognitive computing solutions boosted with the simplified architecture of edge, providing a scale as an easier and hassle-free dimension aided in phenomenal improvements to the robotics industry.

# Robotics – A bright future with IoT, Machine Learning, Edge & Cognitive Computing

Today, with cognitive computing, machine learning, edge computing, and IoT, we have the robotics industry shaping up into a state-of-the-art technology. Robotics have been in place and been used extensively in the manufacturing, automobile, and other industries. We have already seen the benefits of robotics and automation in industries and today it is more widespread. However, with the convergence of multiple domains, we see technological innovations catapulting with cross-pollination among innovations from different industries. The advancements in robotics have seen phenomenal growth by leveraging IoT, machine learning, edge computing, and many other fields. The smart factory concept is now becoming a reality. Robotics strengthened with context-aware and connected systems are now doing wonders in the fourth industrial revolution.

Let's study in brief about how IoT plays a game-changing role in robotics.

The third industrial revolution brought in place automation at the core. We could program machines and design them to work with four-decimal precision accuracy. The reduction in operational time, efficiency in utilizing resources, and many other benefits have been manifested with robotics and automation. With IoT, we are now in the connected world. The machines today are aware about what's happening with other machines and are 'smart' to take decisions on their own to improve an outcome. Robotics automation can take the 'smart' feature one level ahead by leveraging the disruptions in the industry.

Let's assume that you are responsible for the operation of a manufacturing plant that produces soft drinks for consumers, say Coke. You have engineers in the plant who are experts in automating the entire process using computer programs specifically designed and coded for specific machines. Now assume that you have a new drink coming in the market, say Diet Coke. Setting up the diet coke manufacturing line is done by modifying the program for the regular coke. A few changes have to be incorporated that can change the process to intake the new ingredients along with newly defined quantities and changes in the operating process by a small percentage. Even though these changes are minimal, the efforts required to set up the end-to-end automated plant will be mammoth. All the machine/robots are interconnected and have a dependency on each other. Changing small things here and there will require modification of the entire process by a substantial fraction. Basically, the computer engineer would need to code in order to accommodate every new change, even if it's a small one. As an improved way, what if we have robotics that can learn how to react to small incremental changes on its own? Leveraging machine learning, the gargantuan volumes of data from the industrial IoT ecosystem coupled with cognitive and edge computing ushers in a whole new level of smartness in these robots.

Robotics can now be made smarter to learn to adapt to small changes instantly without an engineer codifying the instructions. It understands how to tune the process to improve operational and manufacturing efficiency. It knows how to change the routine operations to accommodate new events. The necessity for human intervention to manually code every bit of intelligence is no more required. The robots are smart enough to learn on their own. The impact of robotics in business can also be witnessed when it is leveraged in areas such as agriculture, mining, and so on. Innovations in the industry have made the availability of robotics cost-effective and very affordable.

By far, the biggest advancement can be witnessed in the consumer's personal assistant robots in IoT. We have watched it in many sci-fi movies and have loved it. Remember the robot in the movie, Interstellar, who keeps assisting Cooper during the space travel? Everyone wishes to have one for their personal use. It will be great if we had a personal robot who could help us in our personal errands, daily activities, and also be a friend if required. The biggest difficulty in bringing such things to reality was the challenge in adding contextual information to a machine. Using a robot as a personal assistant becomes increasingly tiresome if you need to elucidate the entire context for every activity in your daily chores.

Let's assume that you have a robot who can assist you in your personal activities and is capable of understanding and responding to human speech; we'll call him 'Tim'. You have organized a party at home for your friends in the evening and you are busy making arrangements for this. You have Tim to help you out. Think about this scenario: you need Tim's help to order some food and beverages for the evening online. To get Tim working on this task, you would need to command, "Tim, please order x, y, z and drinks from abc.com and ask him to deliver to the address 'House number 543, 24th Main road, 5th cross, ABC area, State, Country' on the name 'xxxx xxxx' and use my credit card 'xxxx-xxxx-xxxx-xxxx' with the credentials 'xxxxx' and so on." Think about adding such detailed information for each task. Things are okay for once or twice but then it becomes increasingly frustrating to take help. What if you miss out briefing some minor details? You may end up in a jeopardy. Also try to imagine a scenario where you have to seek Tim's help in cooking; it is again a mammoth task to get this done.

On the contrary, assume if the task was as simple as telling Tim to order pizza and coke for the evening. Tim finds out the best deal available for your preferred pizza choices and uses your credit card that has the best offer for the deal. Similarly, if you need Tim's help in cooking, you can tell him to cook pasta for five people and Tim would do the rest. If there isn't enough pasta or any ingredient is missing, Tim takes care of ordering the required ingredients and materials for the cooking. Once the ingredients are available, Tim cooks the pasta referring to the guidelines from your preferred website and customizations that you usually prefer.

Such phenomenal automation and intelligence in robotics is only possible when it learns on its own to understand contextual information. We can make it happen by leveraging multiple disruptions in the tech industry such as IoT to capture data from every connected device you use, machine learning and deep learning with semi-supervised algorithms to learn from history and predict the future, and edge computing and cognitive computing to leverage local decision-making power and contextual information to build smarter robotics.

The growth of intelligence and smartness in robotics have opened new horizons for their uses:

- Doctors are now leveraging smart robotics to assist in medical operations
- Manufacturing industries have become agile to accommodate incremental changes and enhancements to products in real time
- Restaurants have started embracing robotics via drones for home delivery and other services in restaurants

- Heavy engineering and life-threatening tasks in mining and other industries are smoothly completed using robotics
- Personal assistant robots (like Tim in our example) are on the verge of becoming a reality
- Energy, oil and gas, and similar industries have increased the adoption of robotics and IoT to foresee a day when fully automated rigs roll onto a job site using satellite coordinates, erect 14-story-tall steel reinforcements on their own, drill a well, then pack up, and move to the next site
- Fishing industries in Tundra regions now embrace robotics to work in adverse climates at ease

# Genomics

The genomics discipline is not a direct recipient of the IoT industry, but the cross-pollination of technologies has propelled advancements in the process by leveraging genomics in the healthcare IoT. Genomics is a vast discipline that requires a sound background in biology to study in-depth. We'll surface the topic at a 1,000 ft. view and understand how IoT can foster genomics for a bright and healthy future.

Genomics is an area within genetics that concerns the sequencing and analysis of an organism's genome. The genome is the entire DNA content that is present within one cell of an organism. Experts in genomics strive to determine complete DNA sequences and perform genetic mapping to help understand diseases. Studying the genome data-DNA-is an extremely vast area. Virtually every human ailment has a significant relationship with our genes. For a prolonged period, doctors were able to leverage genetics to study only birth defects and a few other diseases. This was because studying these patterns was fairly straightforward and studying anything more than this was unimaginable. However, today with phenomenal computing and processing capabilities, the mammoth data collections about human DNA can be leveraged by scientists and clinicians with powerful tools to study the role that genetic factors and the environment play in much more complex diseases.

# So how does genomics relate to IoT?

IoT has a lot to offer in the healthcare industry, but the penetration of the digital dimension in healthcare has not been at par with the technology industry. Most researchers and doctors believe that if the healthcare industry overcomes the legacy technologies and embraces the digital world, a plethora of opportunities would open up under a radically new term "Internet of Bio Things". Today, we barely have a fraction of the medical history of the patient in digital form. However, had everything been digital in a way that physicians could have accessed it using secure and private search engines, it would have added tremendous value to the healthcare industry. There are processes streamlined to digitalize future medical records and past hard copies, but this has its own challenges and bottlenecks.

It is here that genomics can be leveraged. The Human Genome Project, which was led at the National Institutes of Health (NIH) by the National Human Genome Research Institute, produced a very high-quality version of the human genome sequence that is freely available in public databases. Moreover, the data is completely anonymized. There are countless such research databases of genomic information available today. Most are not connected to each other, but would deliver more meaningful results if they were. A massive consortium of scientists are trying to build tools that will make such repositories interoperable, which is in itself a challenging deal. If these databases are connected not only to each other, but also to other anonymized information curated from smartphones and smartwatches, each element in that system would have infinitely more value than it does on its own.

The healthcare industry would then witness radical changes with these innovations. A physician would understand more accurately the reasons for a particular illness that you suffer from. The genome data coupled with other medical records can be leveraged to study what diseases you are genetically prone to. Further analysis can be used to develop the best-suited medicines for the disease you are suffering by virtually experimenting with the wide array of medicines for the specific genetic structure.

Furthermore, this rich information, if utilized with proper security and regulations, can be studied to help mankind benefit from world-class healthcare. Developing medicines can be more customized for a set of population based on their genetic characteristics and so on. However, this comes with its own challenges with security and privacy as the biggest roadblock. We'll discuss more about privacy and security toward the end of this chapter.

# Autonomous cars

The final topic that we will discuss in this chapter for disruptions in IoT is autonomous cars. Autonomous cars have been surfacing the technology innovations for quite some time but are yet to hit mainstream production. Most cars that have some sort of autonomous feature are still limited only to the flagship vehicles from the premium carmakers. Google's self-driving cars have been making news for a while and have seen quite a hefty progress in the accuracy of self-driving. Autonomous cars are defined at the cusp of innovation in the industry. It combines learnings from IoT, artificial intelligence, machine learning, cognitive computing, and edge computing and delivers a world-class solution that has been fancied for a really long time. We'll understand a few important aspects about autonomous cars in order to understand the concept. We'll first touch base on the vision and inspiration for which autonomous cars had been developed. We'll study about the miniscule forms of self-driving car features already present in a couple of cars today. You'll then learn about how an autonomous car works and how the IoT ecosystem and other technology disruptions have been leveraged. Finally, we'll understand about how autonomous cars are going to change the future of driving.

# Vision and inspiration

Most people believe that autonomous cars were first developed to bring more ease and comfort to human life; sure they do but this was still secondary. The true vision that triggered an attempt to build self-driving cars came from the care for human life. Approximately, 1.2 mn people die everyday and a significant portion from this number is reported due to human errors, primarily car accidents. If you look at the biggest reason for deaths among people aged 25 to 35, we can see accidents as the biggest contributor. To err is human, so we can't really do anything beyond a point. Negligence and adrenaline rush is bound to happen while driving no matter how strict the laws are. Self-driving cars as a project, if successful, can help us reduce the deaths due to road accidents and therefore save more lives. This was the inspiration that triggered many engineering companies and even tech companies such as Google to develop a self-driving car. Today, we have seen success stories from many companies. Google has been using self-driving cars to capture visual imagery for Google Maps. Audi, Volvo, and recently Tesla have demonstrated their abilities in developing self-driving cars. Even though we have seen substantial success in the area, it will still take some time for mass production and industry-wide adoption. As of now, it is a luxury feature available with the premium flagship cars. Now that we have a fair understanding about autonomous cars, or self-driving cars, we'll move on to study how they work.

# So how does an autonomous car work?

The simplest assumption would be that it uses a variety of sensors. Yes, this is true, but how many and how? To understand this in the most lucid way, just consider the case of you driving the car and try to think about the things that you would need to be aware of. Technically, the first and most important part would be the need to see the road, the second, the surroundings, and finally the route. These three simple things can be achieved quite easily using technology. Of course, the way the human brain perceives and understands things while you drive is quite different, but still we can definitely achieve most of it.

A usual autonomous car will be having a few sensors or sonar systems, GPS, and a laser imaging sensor, that is, LIDAR (Light illuminating detecting and ranging) on the roof. The following diagram showcases a bare-bone version of the self-driving car:

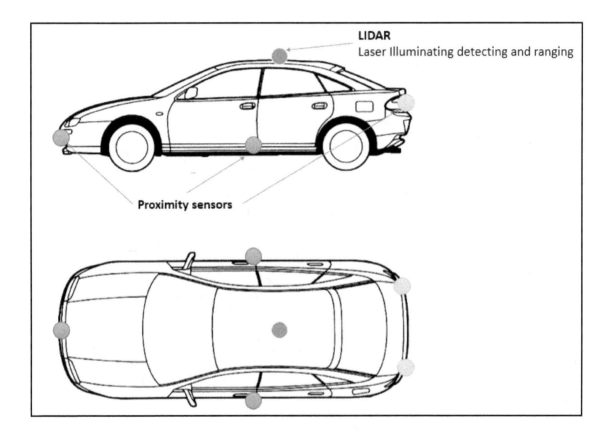

The proximity sensors sense what objects are there nearby and the distance from them; this can also be sensed using powerful SONAR systems and the LIDAR sensor, that is, the sensor that measures distance by illuminating a target with a `laser` light and builds a 3D map for the car to understand its immediate surroundings and understand the speed of the moving objects in real time. Finally, the GPS helps the car understand where it is currently located and where it needs to go (the route). Using a combination of the proximity sensors to identify nearby objects, say within 100 m (the road), LIDAR sensor to create a 3D map and understand the real-time speed of nearby objects (the environment), and finally, GPS to navigate (route), the car can be made into a self-driving car. The following image shows a sample image for a car sensing the surroundings using LIDAR:

# Wait, what are we missing?

Things are definitely not as simple as they have been elucidated. There are numerous challenges in executing this. Firstly, there are at least 8-10 proximity sensors that continuously record data about their immediate surroundings. Triangulating information from all of these sensors and studying the position of objects around the car requires deep analysis and sophisticated algorithms. Controlling the speed of the car, braking system, and steering based on the results from the sensor and imagery data is not a plain set of conditional rules. It requires state-of-the-art algorithms that take a human-like call to make decisions. Some cars leverage high-vision cameras to sense the ambient surroundings. Sophisticated deep learning techniques are leveraged to extract features from the real-time vision for the car and create a parallax vision. To aid its operations in quick turn-around time, there are three different types of communication that helps in fostering the intelligence for the self-driving car.

# Vehicle – to – environment

It uses the sensors and laser imaging tools to understand the immediate surroundings and therefore take decisions in self-driving.

# Vehicle – to – vehicle

This type of communication would be possible once we have all self-driving cars or at least smart cars on the road. The cars can emit signals about their understanding of the ambient surrounding to other cars, say to the cars running immediately behind. These signals are vital to self-driving cars as in some cases, the front vision and sensing capabilities are limited or blocked due to the presence of another car in the vicinity. In such cases, signals from the car in front can be leveraged to learn the surroundings more accurately.

# Vehicle – to – infrastructure

This type of communication is also possible only in the future, say by the time we have smart cities in place. Information about traffic signals, road congestion, and live traffic updates can be passed on to cars in real time by the infrastructure to take more accurate decisions while self-driving.

Today, some forms of self-driving cars are already established in the market. Mercedes Benz, BMW, and other premium carmakers have added features such as auto-parking, emergency braking, lane correction, and so on, which are smaller forms of self-driving cars. These features with more intelligence and decision making power are leveraged to design fully autonomous cars.

# The future of autonomous cars

Google has been the pioneer to demonstrate fully autonomous cars; today many more are up in the line. However, it is still quite far from viability. On another note, the future does definitely look promising. We have already seen tangible results from the experiments in self-driving cars. Today with the increasing adoption from other players and support from the government and regulatory bodies to design standard communication channels and protocols for cars to talk to each other, the infrastructure, mass production, and widespread market penetration will become a reality very soon.

When we try to look at the future of autonomous cars, we find it a very hard game to guess. All the fantasies we saw in sci-fi movies like iRobot have already become a reality. We have seen state-of-the-art self-driving cars from multiple carmakers, so what can we expect in the future?

The answer can be completed in one simple sentence: better integration with your connected devices. As time passes, we will witness phenomenal changes in self-driving cars as they deeply integrate in a more cognitive way to your digital world. You'll see the car responding to your emotional changes, say playing music based on your mood, optimizing the route to save fuel and time, reducing the chances of accidents to 0%, deep integration with the smart city infrastructure, faster speeds while travelling, smart and collaborative movements in congested roads, and many more.

# Privacy and security in IoT

We have studied in brief about the disruptions in IoT and have explored how IoT has opened up various new areas for innovation. We saw how edge computing, cognitive computing, machine learning, artificial intelligence, and other disruptions have fostered new areas like autonomous cars, next-generation robotics, and genomics, but we have missed studying one vital dimension in IoT-privacy and security of the data. With great detail about the data that can help us do wonders come great threats of security and privacy. In IoT, the security and privacy requirements are paramount. There cannot be any compromise in the IoT ecosystem to leverage the benefits to mankind. A small loophole is enough to cause a disaster to large organizations, governments, and individual citizens.

Exposing the data in an IoT system will make the system vulnerable to cause disasters to mankind. A user's medical data and digital data is extremely sensitive and confidential and cannot be leveraged by anyone else without his consent. The risks associated with the leakage of such confidential data can cause huge disasters to the individual and the whole mankind. The following are some of the key challenges that need to be addressed in IoT right away.

# Vulnerability

With millions and millions of devices connected to the network in IoT, we have billions of vulnerabilities exposed. The device that equips various sensors sends the data through gateways into the infrastructure. Each of these data streams are vulnerable to confidentiality. Exposing such granular-level data can raise tremendous security concerns to different organizations. In a couple of industries, such information leaks can jeopardize the entire organization.

The risks of leaking extremely confidential data such as fingerprint data used to authenticate, passwords used for all online websites, net banking credentials, and so on can cause massive financial losses to consumers. Even small loopholes like access to the motion data of a phone can be tapped by hackers to detect what people type, which can be then leveraged to study passwords and credit card details entered by users.

# Integrity

The IoT infrastructure will continuously ingest high-velocity live streams of data from different sensors installed in a plethora of devices. How sure can the system be about the integrity of the data? What are the chances that the data has been compromised to mislead the results inferred? Let's say that the solar panels data and consumption patterns from the use case that we studied in Chapter 6 have been compromised. The end customer will get zero visibility into what is happening at the site and misleading insights about the energy sustainability till the next sunrise. Moreover, the consumer can also be falsely charged with an unrealistic bill for the amount of solar energy generated. Such compromises will shatter the business rather than providing additional revenues.

For the consumer electronic devices that are a part of the IoT ecosystem, hackers can access messages and tamper them before sending them. There have been a few cases in large organizations where hackers have barged the security layer and sent fraudulent e-mails from the leadership team to multiple stakeholders to jeopardize business.

# Privacy

Protecting consumer and organizational privacy becomes challenging with the increasing adoption of IoT in the consumer and industrial domains. With increased connectivity and smooth data transmission across devices, it becomes increasingly difficult to secure private and confidential information from falling into the wrong hands. An illegitimate access to your smartphone risks unwanted and undesired access to your private information such as e-mails, photographs, text messages, and call logs. The kind of feeling we would have when our personal and private texts and photographs are leaked is similar to the kind of feeling an organization feels when private and confidential information is illegitimately accessed by any unauthorized persons.

To address the challenges, we need to design systems that are robust and secure to mitigate the risks associated with security and privacy in the IoT ecosystem. Here are a few, yet not exhaustive, areas that need to be looked into to address the issues. There are three main areas to add security as a dimension.

# Software infrastructure

Software infrastructure includes the cloud network, edge network, and operating system on the IoT device. A part of the software infrastructure has already scaled high in terms of maturity in security, but edge and IoT's operating system are fairly new. It will require a fair amount of time before we peak the security awareness and practices in the new members of the software infrastructure. Key improvements are focused on device authentication, stringent access and resource control systems for improved security, data encryption, and so on.

# Hardware infrastructure

Hardware infrastructure includes the sensors and devices that connect to a network. Trusted computing plays a pivotal role in addressing challenges in hardware devices. In trusted computing, the computer will consistently behave in expected ways, and the behavior will be enforced by computer hardware and software. The scrutinized and enforced behavior is rendered by designing the devices with a unique encryption key inaccessible to the rest of the system.

# The protocol infrastructure

The final dimension in the ecosystem that needs to be addressed for security and privacy concerns is the protocol infrastructure. The communication and data transmission among the connected devices is regulated and controlled via a protocol. Any loopholes or backdoors in this layer can expose a billion means for hackers to exploit. Numerous organizations today are opening up their ideas to build a more secure communication protocol for IoT.

# Summary

In this chapter, we studied the disruptions in IoT. We studied how the growth of IoT has emerged innovations in different fields and how other fields have leveraged IoT directly or indirectly to trigger disruptions in the market. We explored the fog or edge computing model and saw how the IoT infrastructure can be scaled efficiently while still keeping it a viable solution. To study **the fog computing** model in detail, we explored a hypothetical use case similar to the manufacturing use case studied in earlier. We saw how connected devices or assets can be designed to become state-of-the-art smart devices where intelligence is pushed to the logical extremes of the network, promoting quick and intelligent self-decisions to improve an outcome.

We explored **cognitive computing,** a fairly new but very promising and interesting area emerged from the convergence of artificial intelligence, IoT, and edge computing. We saw how machines can be designed to learn on their own and solve a human-like problem that is uncertain, ambiguous, and complex. We hypothesized a simple sci-fi story (which is almost reality now) and studied how cognitive computing has been leveraged to make human life comfortable and also productive.

We then moved one step deeper into the disruptions from IoT; we studied how IoT, artificial intelligence, fog computing, and cognitive computing together can be leveraged to develop next-generation robotics. We understood in brief how the competencies in **robotics** have evolved over the years and how IoT fostered the maturity of robotics in the industry to innovate. We studied a small example using the Coke manufacturing plant to see how robotics can be leveraged to reap the benefits of IoT and provide smart solutions. We also took a brief look at **genomics** and studied at a high level how IoT and genomics together can bring wonders to the healthcare industry.

Lastly, we explored in depth the autonomous car concept and delved deeper into its conceptualization and studied how an **autonomous car** was designed. We explored how the different pillars of the industry coupled with IoT and new disruptions were converged to evolve even new disruptions in such a short while. We also studied how self-driving cars leveraged the power of IoT, the beauty of the automobile industry, and the intelligence of AI and cognitive computing coupled with the horsepower of fog computing to aid the mind-boggling autonomous cars become reality. Finally, we studied, apart from the phenomenal benefits, how **privacy and security** have opened up even more options for hackers to vandalize the innovation by exploiting the system loopholes. We understood the importance of building a robust and secure ecosystem to help IoT flourish, innovate, and create newer disruptions in the industry to make human life secure, comfortable, and productive.

In the next chapter, we will discuss how IoT has innovated and disrupted the industry to lay the foundations for a promising future. We'll study the new business models that IoT has opened up and how our routine life will witness revolutionary transformations.

# 9
# A Promising Future with IoT

We have studied the length and breadth of IoT and decision science and also solved multiple use cases to cement our thoughts foundationally. In the previous chapter, we explored the disruptions in the industry due to IoT and studied how they fostered many more disruptions where IoT played a pivotal role. In this final chapter, we will study how IoT would deliver a promising future for mankind. This chapter will focus on emphasizing the importance and impact of smarter decisions in IoT by showcasing a glimpse into the promising future that has been triggered by IoT. We will start by studying an extremely important business model that emerged in the industry with the inception of IoT, that is, the **Asset as a Service** or **Device as a Service** model. Combined together, the asset and device models cover the consumer as well as the industrial sectors to offer cost-effective solutions for customers and higher revenues for business.

We will also understand in brief how IoT is going to meticulously render a promising future for us by exploring in detail about the smartwatch and the evolution of smart healthcare and smart cars. We will explore in brief how the smartwatch will play a game-changing role in the healthcare industry and study the evolution of connected cars to smarts cars and connected humans to smart humans. By the end of the chapter and the book, we will have successfully completed our first steps with IoT and decision science and get ready for the astounding journey with smarter decisions.

Overall, to orchestrate our journey in smarter decisions, we have studied in detail about IoT, learned the art of defining, designing, and solving an IoT problem, and also explored the disruptions in IoT. Finally, we will now focus on the future of IoT.

In this chapter, we will cover the following topics:

- The IoT business model – asset/device as a service
- Smartwatch – a booster to healthcare IoT
- Smart healthcare – connected humans to smart humans'
- Evolving from connected cars to smart cars

# The IoT Business model – Asset or Device as a Service

The Internet of Things started with the simple concept of Connected Devices and Connected Assets. A small network of connected devices made a lot of tasks easier and intuitive that were not feasible earlier. Gradually, connected devices/assets opened up new opportunities with smart devices/assets. In no time, the evolution paced up, and we had a tangible implementation of smart devices in every dimension of consumer electronics, home appliances as well as industrial assets. As the technology matured, the concept of smart factory evolved, that is, **Industry 4.0** or the fourth industrial revolution, and eventually smart connected operations became a reality that was complemented with success stories from different parts of the globe.

The **Asset as a Service model** has its roots in the vanilla 'lease model' widely adopted in the world. You can lease your house, vehicle, or some appliance for a while and earn money for the time period it was utilized, say a week or month. The idea of leasing out your house was fairly straightforward, but when it comes to leasing out your car or a machine in the factory, the model has its own challenges. You would probably take very good care of your car, but when you lease it, the chances that the person would be equally careful is not guaranteed. Let's say that he drives your car with excessive luggage and drives recklessly. Overspeeding, drifting, acceleration while braking, and many other driving habits can cause serious damage to your car and can go completely unnoticed in the near future. The lease amount will never make up for the latent damages to your car and therefore makes it a non-viable solution. The same story is valid for industrial assets. There are only a few dimensions that can be used to measure the true quantified usage for the lease amount, such as time, the distance travelled, or some industrial measures like manufacturing quantity to calculate the usage for the assets and so on. There is a lack of clear and concrete means to capture most of the dimensions that could help in defining the true usage during the lease period.

IoT has seen widespread adoption. Installing a wide variety of sensors along with the ability to connect to a network and communicate to other devices makes the entire idea of capturing the true usage and damages to the asset or device a reality. A plethora of sensors installed that capture data at the most granular level required, say every microsecond, can be leveraged in newer avenues that were not initially contemplated. This is usually called **disruption due to convergence**, that is, innovation in one area triggers innovations and disruptions in associated and non-associated fields. The best example to understand this would be the invention of the radio. The radio was actually invented 20 years after radio waves were discovered. The discovery of radio waves were never aimed to invent the radio, but disruption spread its waves across the industry over time. Let's understand in brief about the Asset as a Service model in IoT with a practical example and how it will change the dynamics of the industry in no time.

# The motivation

In this fast changing world, change is the only constant. This is definitely a cliché, but holds perfectly valid for the model. The modes and means for business used by various industries have seen phenomenal changes in a very short stint. Business processes had to evolve to meet the ever-increasing and dynamic requirements from the consumers. In such a constantly evolving world, it becomes increasingly difficult for businesses to make huge investments for the required infrastructure. For example, consider the taxi aggregator company, Uber, who has made availing cab services easier than ever. Let's assume that the company owns all the vehicles as a part of the business strategy. With increasing business, they would have to purchase more and more number of cars to meet business requirements. Finally, a day would come when the company would own around 10 MN cars for its services and, say the world would have no more petrol/diesel reserves. The automobile industry would then see a radical change with the development of electric or solar powered cars. At this point, for Uber to replace the existing 10 MN cars with new electric cars would be a mammoth cost and make it completely unviable. However, what if the company had leased out the cars rather than owning them? It would be extremely convenient for them to replace the fossil fuel cars with the new electric cars.

Business requirements evolve and result in radical changes with disruption. With the advent of technology, the evolution of changes have become faster. In such a dynamic world, for any business, it would not be a great option to heavily invest in the infrastructure. It would make economic sense to have an agile strategy to accommodate newer and improved assets in the business services as the requirements evolve. The industry therefore expects to see a huge shift in the trend from owning assets to leasing assets, that is, leveraging the **asset as a service** business model. The advent of IoT has made designing an economic and strategically viable business model a reality by leveraging the asset as a service model.

The new business model helps consumers keep their costs low and evolve faster with new requirements with a manifold increase in revenue per asset in the longer run. Say a company sells a device (like a laptop) for $800. It can instead lease it on a quarterly subscription for $100 for the first two years and then $60 for the next three years, thereby making > $1500 in five years. Consumers who require a laptop for only six months would always leverage the 'Laptop as a Service' model rather than purchasing it and then selling it after use.

# Real life use case for Asset as a Service model

Let's take a simple use case relating to our everyday life and understand in detail how beneficial the asset as a service model can be for consumers as well as business stakeholders. Consider that you are the CEO of a multimillion dollar company and you crave for luxury cars. You love to drive the latest luxury model from premium carmakers and therefore you end up selling your old car and buying a new car almost every year. Over a period of time, you realize that the resale value gets tarnished as it is a used car and you bear significant losses due to frequent car change plans. You are rich and you can definitely afford these losses for your passion, but still it would be great if you could find a better and cost-effective alternative. You then get to know about ABC Company (hypothetical) that provides 'Luxury Cars as a Service'. The company offers a program where you can use a car as long as you want and only pay for the usage. Let's say that you use a 7 Series BMW for one year, you would pay a premium only for the services you used in the time period. The company has designed an algorithm that takes into account the time for which you used the car + the number of miles you drove + the impact on the car quality (like damages) to calculate the total amount. You do a simple math and understand that this amount is significantly lower when compared to the losses incurred while selling the car. You find it awesome!

This model can immensely help you in reducing the losses incurred while getting a new car and also relieves you of the effort required in reselling your car and its necessary paperwork. You can change your car every year and opt for the latest and best model available in the industry. Say you are a big fan of BMW; every year in the month of January, you will see a new model that you would like to use. 'Luxury Car as a Service' is your best companion. The consumer can opt for a more cost-effective plan whereas the car company can earn more money in the longer run and also be safe from latent damages to the car. With a wide range of sensors installed, the company can understand whether you have overspeeded or caused any damages to the car internally or externally. All damages caused can be accounted and you need to pay for it. Overall, this business model proves a boon for consumers as well as business.

Consider a parallel scenario for an asset that is not as expensive like a luxury car; the model still holds a viable solution. The asset/device as a service model can be extended to any device or machine in any price range.

# How does it help business?

We have already studied how leveraging 'Asset as a Service' has helped consumers as well as businesses in the longer run. Let's explore in brief how it will really work. Today, most businesses are agile. They are always in a state where there exists a need for quick experimentation at scale. New businesses can be set up at an alarming speed if the environment is conducive for the business to grow. Earlier for a big multinational company to start their business in a new country, it was a fairly difficult process to complete the operational overheads. Once the initial process is completed, we need to set up an office space and source logistics for our operations. Here starts our mammoth investment.

The biggest hurdle in setting up, expanding, or even experimenting a new form of business is the time and capital investment that it consumes. Let's say that we are a U.S.-based large brewery chain, and as a part of our expansion program, we are focusing on new markets for additional business. The team has found a lot of potential in Bangalore, India for the brewery. We are not really sure about whether starting a new brewery outlet in Bangalore would be successful, but it is definitely worth giving a try.

To start the operations, we need a huge capital investment. Investment would cover the cost for the purchasing of the logistics required to brew beer, such as containers and machines for the malting, preparing the mash, brewing the wort, fermenting, pasteurizing, and finally packaging. Say we can purchase these machines locally and integrate them easily to build the automated brewing machine. The cost for the entire setup, that is, only machinery, would be around $5 Mn. Finally, renting a 5,000 sq. ft. place and purchasing assets such as computers, air conditioners, music systems, LED monitors, kitchen equipment, dish washers, and almost everything else required to start operations would cost another $5 MN. So, investing $10 Mn in a new business and risking everything without certainty about the success of the brewery would be a big reason to worry. Not taking a risk is a bigger risk as we may miss out on lucrative business opportunities. Let's assume the worst case scenario; we start business operations and realize within six months that the business can no longer sustain the competition from local players and it would be ideal to close operations. Selling back all the acquired logistics and reverting to previous operations would render a substantial loss. There is a very high chance that we may only fetch $3.5-4 MN after the resale of all the assets purchased for the operations within six months. Overall, we can understand that time and capital investment cause a big hurdle for many existing business to experiment with new avenues.

What if we could get rid of most of these pain points and alleviate the risks by a huge chunk? Yes, this could be possible if we leverage the **Asset as a Service** model. For this use case, assume that there is a business partner who can provide us with everything required for our brewery operations as a service by leveraging the powerful IoT ecosystem. We probably need to provide a security deposit of $2 Mn and only pay for the services we use. Every asset provided by the company will be installed with a plethora of sensors to monitor and measure the usage at the most granular levels. The means to detect any damage to the machine or inappropriate usage that may reduce its efficiency, in fact everything required to quantify the usage of the machine/asset at the most granular level, is set up at the location. The 'Asset as a Service' model can now be leveraged to build a business model that will contract to charge you on the total pitchers of beer brewed keeping aside the damage cost (example). Therefore, we have nothing to worry about the infrastructure setup and only pay for the services we have used. The operational cost would now be a nominal fee that would increase as we scale your operations.

After a considerable time period in business, say six months, based on the business conditions, there are basically three outcomes that we would have. Let's contemplate how each of them can be catered to.

# Best case scenario

Operations are doing really well and we see a lot of traction from customers. We are now confident about continuing and expanding our business further. We can either continue to use the Asset as a Service model and scale rapidly, or, to increase the profit margin, we can now confidently invest money in the business and grab more profits.

# Worst case scenario

We understand that there is huge competition from other players and it is becoming increasingly difficult to survive operations while making a profit. It seems like closing down operations in Bangalore for the time being makes more sense. We can then end the contract with the company for their assets used. They would charge us around $2 MN for the usage and a small portion for the overall depreciation of the assets and return 90% of our security deposit. We have now lost altogether only ($2 MN + $1 MN from your deposit), that is, $3 MN. It is definitely a loss, but still much better than the other way round. Had we purchased all the required assets and sold them back, we would have probably lost around $6-7 MN.

# Neutral case

Our business has fared pretty decently but we may still need some more time before we can confidently take a call to quit or scale operations. We can now continue using the same model for another six months, which would cost another $2 Mn.

# Conclusion

All in all, the Asset as a Service model mainly helps businesses quickly experiment, start, or scale business with minimized investment and reduced risks. On the other hand, the party providing the services has a lucrative deal to reap three-fold profits from each asset in due course of time.

The same holds true for consumers. The Device as a Service model can be implemented in consumer electronics and home appliances. There are a variety of devices that we use only for a short while but still we end up purchasing them. Say, we purchase a DSLR and only use it for 30 days in all, including our travel and vacations during a year. Won't it be great if we could use DSLR as a service and only pay a fraction of the price for our actual use? Also, we would have the ability to use the latest DSLR available in the market every time we take a vacation. Cost effectiveness becomes the de facto objective in the Asset as a Service model.

# Leveraging Decision Science to empower the Asset as a Service model

Decision science becomes indispensable when we touch base with IoT. The Asset as a Service model has received phenomenal traction in the industry due to the visibility it provides in usage patterns of the asset and device. However, the decision making process is still hazy and requires advanced analytics with decision science to deliver what would be required for the success of the business model.

Understanding damages, measuring the usage of the asset, studying the impact on efficiency, and depreciation of the asset holistically is a mammoth task. The industry uses the **grey box model**, that is, the combination of the physics/thermodynamics of machine processes and math together to define and understand the machine usage as a new fundamental unit. The grey box model combines the learning from math and couples it with the universal learnings leveraged in thermodynamics, physics, and other related fields of the industry to study an event. To make it simple, let's consider the case of driving a car. We all know that reckless driving, overspeeding, and acceleration during braking hampers the efficiency of the engine. However, it is an extremely difficult task to determine whether any of these events have actually caused damage to the engine or car using a data-driven strategy. Identifying these events is fairly easy, but quantifying the impact of these events on the engine is an extremely difficult task. We just cannot devise a rule like acceleration while braking for more than 10 seconds causes 0.5% damage to the overall car. It requires combining the learnings from deep industrial processes, physics, thermodynamics, automobile engineering along with decision science to design a process that can quantify the effects of the events on the asset.

'Asset as a Service' and 'Device as a Service' business models are soon set to change the business dynamics radically. The widespread adoption of these business models in consumer electronic devices as well as industrial machinery has already starting gathering success stories. Very soon, we will witness widespread adoption for the same.

# Smartwatch – A booster to Healthcare IoT

The healthcare industry is experiencing a serious technology boom with the inception of IoT. Connected devices are continuously being leveraged in healthcare to innovate solutions and reduce costs. Smart hospitals and other innovations have been conceptualized where doctors and patients have a digital connection that can aid faster access to health records and other details that can be used to study the current and historic conditions of the patient precisely. Also, as we studied in `Chapter 8`, *Disruptions in IoT* with the growth of IoT and the emerging disruptions, the use of genomics for better healthcare solutions is already being practiced.

At the same time, we can see the **smartwatch** industry gathering a lot of traction. The smartwatch is basically a watch that can connect to different devices such as your smartphone, other smartwatches, and other smart devices. It is generally equipped with a wide variety of sensors and does much more than showing time. Sensors such as an accelerometer, gyroscope, pedometer, heart rate monitor, ambient temperature, barometric sensor, magnetometer, oximetry sensor, skin conductance and temperature sensor, and also GPS have been installed in smartwatches to collect and process data at the most granular level (almost every microsecond). All these sensors combined together reveal many unseen dimensions about human behavior that can be beneficial for the healthcare industry. The smartwatch is more prominent today among athletes and sports enthusiasts, but this will soon change. Mainstream consumers are expected to embrace the adoption of smartwatches for an enhanced lifestyle.

The smartwatch can keep track of the number of steps you walk and understand the amount of calories you burn, it can tell you whether you are undertaking too much physical stress or not, and it can also study the amount of sleep your body needs. Mostly, we have an abstract understanding about all these events, but these details can be very specific for different individuals. There are new advancements in the sensor technologies that can analyze your heart rate, sweat, and body temperature and leverage the data for a variety of medical diagnostics that can help you stay healthy. The following diagram shows a high-level picture of what kind of data is captured and how physicians and healthcare research professionals leverage the data:

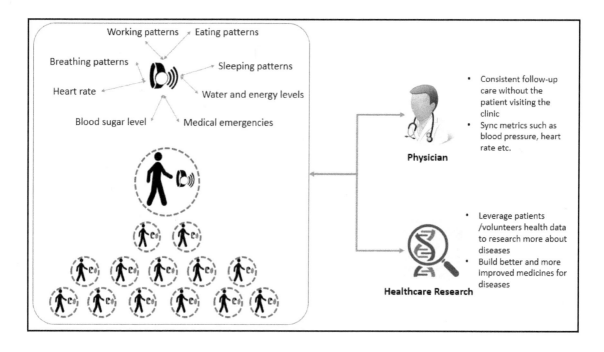

The preceding figure explains the futuristic view of smartwatches. The market is positive about significant improvements in the smartwatch technology that will be able to sense your daily habits such as eating, working, and sleeping habits and analyze human behavior with more precise details. You can expect to get real-time recommendations from your smartwatch for the best-eating habits to boost your energy levels and stay fit. It can study and analyze the sweat on your body and recommend the appropriate quantity and the time when you should consume water or energy drinks to stay energetic. It can study your heart rate and walking speed and recommend you to slow down or speed up. It can study your sleeping patterns and recommend that you sleep more if you are falling short. To a certain extent, the eating habits and nutritional quality of the food can also be studied using advanced sensors. There are sensors that can understand how stressed you are by studying your breathing patterns. These details can then be sent across to your personal doctor who can leverage your complete medical history and current lifestyle with high precision to recommend medicines for your illness.

Next, we can also expect smartwatches to predict in advance the chances of you falling prey to fatal diseases and thereby reducing the chances of death. We can also expect critical alerts to your dear ones when you are in medical emergencies. All in all, we can see a revolutionary change in the healthcare industry primarily because of the smartwatch. The story doesn't end here. This rich and informative data from consumers can be leveraged by research professionals to study more about diseases. The medical research organizations have always faced the scarcity of volunteers in medical assessments for the research study. Tech leaders like Apple have stepped ahead to devise infrastructure where people can volunteer and contribute to medical researches using the smartwatch and smartphone.

# Decision science in health data

Leveraging sensors to capture data from the smartwatch and communicating it to other devices is only one part of the story. The exciting part is finding signals from data to aid decision making. The smartphone sends you recommendations to improve your health, for which it needs to sense, process, and analyze data using a plethora of algorithms from machine learning, artificial intelligence, and edge and cognitive computing. It again requires a decision scientist to leverage additional skills from multiple disciplines such as healthcare and behavioral science along with others. The art of converting digital impressions to user behavior, extracting meaning from the behavior, and finally providing recommendations require a decision scientist to don multiple hats. Results captured from the heart rate monitor and analyzing sweat can be leveraged to recommend periodic consumption of water or energy drinks to keep the body energy and fluid levels maintained. The study of breathing patterns can help us understand whether the person is frustrated, stressed, or experiencing a medical emergency. Establishing the trigger points for such events is again not based on simple conditional rules derived from aggregated study of data. The overall process can be summarized in the following figure:

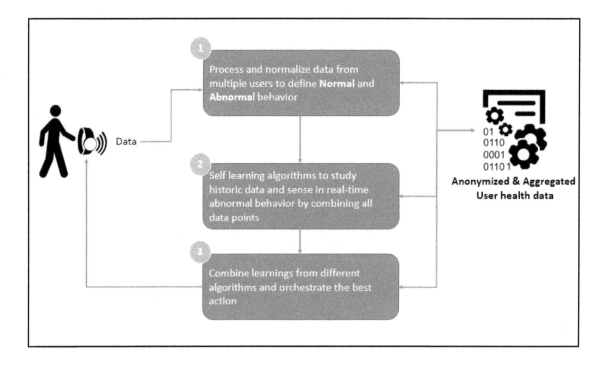

The data captured from the smartwatch is anonymized and stored in a central repository. It is further studied and analyzed using a variety of artificial intelligence self-learning algorithms to define the normal and abnormal behavior for people. The algorithms sense the presence of these patterns in the user's health data and respond in real time by combining the learnings to orchestrate the best course of actions and recommendations. A combination of neuroscience, biology, healthcare, and various other disciplines is leveraged to design self-learning algorithms that can aid humans in living a healthy life.

## Conclusion

Smartwatches have revolutionized the healthcare industry with IoT and the disruptions that emerged from it. The benefits have already been validated by the industry and continue to evolve phenomenally. In the coming days, we will see widespread adoption of the smartwatch in the community, which will then help mankind benefit from better health and a secured and improved lifestyle.

# Smart healthcare – Connected Humans to Smart Humans

The title may sound weird, but it definitely doesn't mean that we are not smart. Yes, we are already smart individuals, but the 'smart' in this context refers to the smartwatch that identifies an individual. We have already studied how the smartwatch has added phenomenal value to the healthcare industry. Most of us have already used the smartwatch or fitness trackers like Nike's Fitbit, Apple's Watch, and many more from other brands. We have always used these devices to track our health and exercise plan or study the calories burnt and so on. We call the smartwatch an integral part of the IoT fraternity, but we still missed out on emphasizing an extremely vital mode of communication in the smartwatch, that is, **smartwatch-to-smartwatch communication**.

Yes, the communication between different smartwatches can help us take the smartness in it to the next level. When smartphones can talk to each other and take decisions based on the data signals, it can pretty much change our lifestyle. With the widespread adoption of smartphones, it became increasingly easy for us to reach out to our near and dear ones. We no more need to worry whether our children have reached home safely after the journey or panic when they are late in arriving. We can simply call up and understand where they have reached and what took them such a long time. With smartphones, the communication became closer and the impact was pretty much visible on our lifestyle. The smartwatch too can be leveraged for the same story, though the communication would be more for health reasons.

Let's say that you are a family of six, like husband, wife, two children, and grandparents. Each member owns a smartwatch. You are the husband and you would love to keep track of your family's health. The smartwatch can provide you with real-time feed on the health alerts of your near and dear ones. At the end of the day, you get an update informing you whether your children had enough exposure to sunlight during the day, whether everyone had sufficient nutrients consumed for the day, and so on. You can also be informed whether your parents (grandparents) had their medicines on time. With these rich and informative real-time updates about your family, you can take the best measures with the least efforts to ensure that everyone in your family stays fit.

Your lifestyle would be completely different with such an environment. Consider the following scenario to understand the impact of the 'smart human' evolution in healthcare. You start adding more leafy vegetables to your family's diet based on the recommendations from the smartwatch that studied the need for more nutrients in your children's diet. You have a complete idea about your parents' (grandparents) blood sugar level who are suffering from diabetes. The watch gives you updates about when you need to arrange for insulin injections for them. Your wife is very busy with her work in office and therefore she barely found time to work out in the gym for the past 10 days. You are now aware about your wife's lagging fitness goals and you lend a helping hand in her work to ensure that she gets back to the workout routine and stays healthy. Your parents are old; the watch can do the best in worst case scenarios. It will send out quick alerts to you and your wife when your parents need medical attention. All in all, you have the best knowledge with the least efforts. Every informative signal that needs your attention is provided right away in the most concise format and you can be confident about doing the best to keep your near and dear ones fit.

Doesn't this sound great? Imagine how convenient and wonderful it would have been if all of us had such an amazing childhood. Things would have been really easy for our parents to take care of us. With time, we will see the smartwatch connections spread more like a social network. Your friends can also be sent alerts if required for an emergency. Just like Facebook gives you a heads-up when one of your close friend is in your nearby vicinity, the smartwatch can be leveraged to give a heads-up to your best friends in case you are in need for a medical emergency. The GPS data can be triangulated and the nearest friends who can quickly reach your physical location can be of great help. Simultaneously, signaling your personal doctor and the nearby hospital to quickly make arrangements for your emergency can be automated.

Life gets easier and more comfortable to live with such technologies being widely used. The higher the number of smartwatch users in the market, the better the connection between users. Unlike just a connection, we share our health/life with others to take a better decision, and therefore the name 'Smarter Humans' where you take data-driven smart decisions to stay healthy.

# Evolving from connected cars to smart cars

We touched base on the healthcare industry in more detail by understanding how the smartwatch can be a game changer. Leveraging the increased adoption of the smartwatch helps in evolving from connected humans to smart humans. The same success story holds true for multiple industries. We have witnessed the transformation of dumb assets into connected assets and its evolution to smart assets. We will explore the last topic of the book to understand how IoT has laid foundations for a promising future. We'll study the evolution of connected cars to smart cars.

Today, this topic is more of a concept and has seen only a fraction of the possibilities adopted in reality. The autonomous car is also a part of this evolution, but there are many more things that are possible. In the previous chapter, we studied how the autonomous car was born from the disruptions in the industry due to IoT. We studied in brief about the improved integration of the autonomous cars with our daily use connected gadgets. If we recall the definition of smart devices that we studied in Chapter 1, *IoT and Decision Science* we defined a smart device as any device that is connected to multiple other devices and can take self-decisions to improve an outcome. Here, the outcome could be one or many. In the evolution of connected cars to smart cars, the number of outcomes the car tries to improve by taking self-decisions increases by a scale. The smart car will be more than just a car that takes you from A to B. It will be a luxury, which is meticulously crafted for you. The following figure illustrates how different features that improve an outcome have emerged during the evolution of connected cars to smart cars:

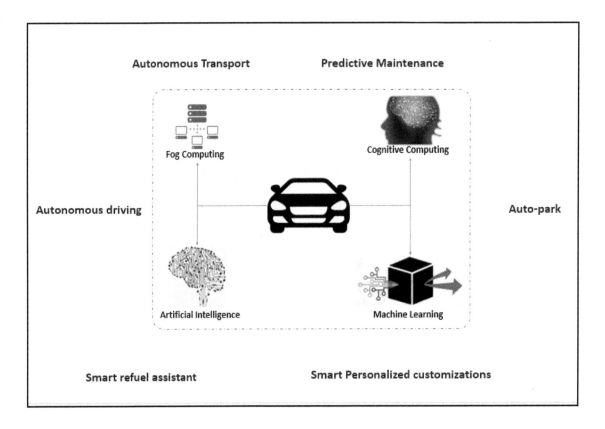

Let's try to imagine the different possible outcomes that the smart car would improve. A few points that would cross our thoughts right away would be autonomous driving, auto-engine tuning for improved life and performance, auto-parking, and so on. In `Chapter 8`, *Disruptions in IoT* we studied a hypothetical example to understand how cognitive computing disrupts the IoT industry to learn like humans and integrate with other services to provide better services. Taking parallels to the use case, we can understand that the smart car will basically be able to add context as a dimension to learn and improve outcomes that will make human life easy. Here are a few features that can be expected to be a smart car feature very soon.

# Smart refuel assistant

While driving long distances, we often miscalculate the refueling interval. We may either end up halting multiple times or fall short of fuel while driving. The smart car can study the mileage of the car and understand how far the car will travel without refueling. Triangulating this information with the GPS data, it can find out the best and nearest fuel station to refuel. It can work as simple as alerting the driver to refuel at the fuel station located in the next five miles; otherwise, the car may run out of fuel as there are no fuel stations for the next 50 miles.

# Predictive maintenance

It can understand the performance of the car using a variety of metrics such as engine efficiency, emission, vibration and oil levels, heating levels, torque, and many more. Usually, we take a ballpark estimate and service our cars roughly every 1,000 miles, but in reality it can be much less or more. Smart cars can leverage a grey box model combining machine learning, artificial intelligence, and various disciplines in automobile engineering to discover the best time for maintenance considering the end objective to optimize performance and yet be cost-effective.

# Autonomous transport

The next big thing after autonomous driving is autonomous transport. You can ask your car to drop your children to school and come back, or you can ask your car to pick you up from the airport and drop you home. Automated transport will be a revolutionary move but would need the maturity curve of cognitive computing and artificial intelligence to be more robust. A combination of these technologies can be used by the smart car to understand human requests like 'drop me to the airport'. It can understand your home location and your parking. It can autonomously take decisions to reach the airport on time to pick you up based on your flight timings and the traffic data. If you take the train everyday to travel to your office, it can learn the appropriate time to pick and drop you to the station on time.

Many more innovations are bound to surface the smart car technology. Our life is going to be merrier than we imagined and dreamed through the sci-fi movies that we watched a decade ago. The smart car and autonomous transport is an ambitious project and will definitely take some time to mature and become available for consumers, but when it comes, the impact and adoption will be mammoth.

# Concluding thoughts

Looking at the future to study how promising the world is going to be, we have only affirmative answers. The thought-provoking fact that we often ponder would be where did the trigger happen and how did so many things bloom that every industry and every nook and corner embraced technology to build the foundation of a smart and promising future. The answer is just one word-IoT. To understand why IoT is the core reason for every upcoming innovation, just contemplate over the triggers in human history that helped mankind evolve.

In the ancient days, the invention of fire and wheel was the revolutionary breakthrough that throttled inventions and discoveries in the human race. In the past few centuries, the invention of industrial machines, printing press, and computer was the revolutionary breakthrough that catapulted growth and transformation in every corner. In recent years, it was the birth of the Internet that revolutionized the world and today it is the 'Internet of Things'. The disruptions and breakthroughs with IoT that we discussed in Chapter 8, *Disruptions in IoT* that render a promising future to the world are only a small collection of examples. The exhaustive list would be gargantuan and beyond the scope of any book to cover. The whole idea to draft the last two chapters was to emphasize the importance and scale of the impact that decision science would deliver via IoT. The use cases that we tried to solve in earlier chapters are the building blocks for the revolution in IoT.

# Summary

In this chapter and this book, we have navigated through a beautiful journey of building smarter decisions from IoT when it intersects with decision science. We started our humble journey by understanding the fundamentals of decision science, the Internet of Things, and industry-standard frameworks to solve a problem. We spent quality time to understand the problem more concretely by studying the different dimensions that can be used to define a problem. In the second chapter, we touched base with two important areas of the IoT problem universe-Connected Assets and Connected Operations. You learned to design the approach and draft the blueprint for a problem using the problem solving framework. We leveraged a real IoT use case from the manufacturing industry where we tried to solve the problem of improving the quality of the manufactured product.

In Chapter 3, using the R software, we practically attempted to solve the business use case we defined and designed in Chapter 2. You learned the nuances of descriptive and inquisitive analytics. By performing a variety of exploratory data analyses to test our previously defined hypotheses and validating them with various statistical techniques, we articulated the required answers for the 'what' and 'why' questions.

In Chapter 4, we entered the world of predictive analytics and learned to build statistical models such as linear regression, logistic regression, and decision trees. You learned how the problem evolves from a descriptive to inquisitive and predictive phase and developed solutions that could help us see the future and answer the 'when' question. In Chapter 5, we further explored the predictive analytics area by leveraging machine learning and deep learning to improve our results. By the end of the chapter, we completed one iteration of the problem solving journey while it evolved through the descriptive to inquisitive to predictive phases.

In Chapter 6, we cemented our foundations in decision science by leveraging another iteration of problem solving. We attempted to solve another IoT use case from the renewable energy industry. We quickly designed and developed the business problem with our learnings of the problem solving framework and practically solved it leveraging predictive analytics. In Chapter 7, we touched base on the final phase of a problem in the decision science stack, that is, prescriptive analytics. We studied the phenomena of prescriptive analytics by exploring a hypothetical use case from the telecom industry. We studied how the business leverages the answers to 'why' and 'when' questions to outlive a disaster, that is, take prescriptions. We understood the entire journey of the problem in decision science and explored in brief how business connects the dots in the problem universe. We also studied the art of storyboarding to validate and showcase our results in the most consumable and lucid format.

Finally, in Chapter 8, we explored the disruptions in industry with the inception of IoT. We explored a handful of examples to study how IoT has accelerated disruptions in various disciplines and how they contribute their innovations to the world. We studied about fog computing, cognitive computing, next-generation robotics and genomics, and the concept of autonomous cars. We understood in brief how one disruption triggers another disruption and eventually how the benefits of all new disruptions are converged to the ecosystem. In Chapter 9, we studied how the disruptions in IoT are going to build the foundation of a smart and promising future for mankind. We explored the nuances of the 'Asset as a Service' and 'Device as a Service' business models and also understood more about IoT healthcare and studied the evolution of connected humans to smart humans and connected cars to smart cars.

In a nutshell, we studied the intersection of IoT and decision science and the importance and impact of smarter decisions by taking a sneak peek into the future of the connected world.

# Index